Sources and Resources of
Feminist Theologies

Quellen feministischer
Theologien

Sources et resources des
théologies féministes

Yearbook of the European Society of Women in Theological Research

Jahrbuch der Europäischen Gesellschaft für die theologische Forschung von Frauen

Annuaire de l'Association Européenne des femmes pour la recherche théologique

Volume 5

Sources and Resources of Feminist Theologies

Quellen feministischer Theologien

Sources et resources des théologies féministes

Editors:
Elisabeth Hartlieb
Charlotte Methuen

Kok Pharos Publishing House - Kampen
Matthias-Grünewald Verlag - Mainz

YEARBOOK OF THE EUROPEAN SOCIETY OF WOMEN
IN THEOLOGICAL RESEARCH, 5

ISBN Kok Pharos 90 390 0215 0
ISBN Grünewald 3-7867-2061-4
Typesetting Veronika Schlöder
Cover design by Margret Omlin-Küchler/adapted by Dik Hendriks

Contents

Theme

Forum

Dialogue

From the Countries

Women's Traditions in Europe

Bookmarket

Actualtities

Editorial

The theme of this Yearbook could be interpreted in many ways, for feminist theologies, by their very nature, draw upon and make use of a wide range of sources and resources. As feminist theologians we are informed by, struggle with and seek sustenance from what have typically been regarded as Christian sources and resources (biblical, theological and spiritual), but we seek also to integrate insights from other disciplines and from our own lives. It seemed to us impossible and unsatisfactory to try to encompass this enormous range of different sources and resources. Instead, we have taken a hermeneutical approach, asking how feminist theologies engage with and use the traditional 'four pillars of theology'—scripture—tradition—experience—reason.

The task, posed by systematic theology, of reflecting upon these sources, their function and their role as norms, is one which is not only necessary for feminist theologies. Nevertheless, given their radical criticism of traditional theological, historical and exegetical interpretations, this task is of particular importance for feminist theologies and theologians. Using arguments drawn from the history of theology and the sociology and psychology of religion they have uncovered the patriarchal origins of not only traditional interpretations but of the biblical texts themselves. It has thus been recognised that text and tradition are characterised by a common sexism and androcentrism and in this way the distinction between them has been blurred. The consequent challenge to the canon and to the authority of scripture has grown to include the question of the sense in which authority and meaning can be attributed to them at all. This question can be complemented by others: What role does the past play in our definition of ourselves, and do we need to seek a 'historical ideal'? What importance have texts and traditions outwith the canon and those of other religious traditions? To what extent is western feminist theology aware of its own limitations?

Parallel to this development is the central role held by experience in feminist theologies. Themes such as corporeality, sexuality, violence and violent relationships, previously dismissed as of little or no importance, have been identified as theologically relevant and considered from the perspective of women. Thus the experience of women has gained significance and become the material from which theology is constructed. However, little consideration has been given to the questions of the ways in which this experience can remain the direct expression of one individual while at the same time becoming a collective, normative criterion. What qualifies the experiences of one woman as religious or as feminist? If biological determinism is rejected, can specifically female religious experience still be identified? How can the sensual, corporeal dimension of experience be located between biological determinism and the rejection of the body? And what are we to make of the identification of the themes of corporeality and sexuality as specifically female in feminist theology? These questions are made still more pointed by the post-modern critique of the subject, which pluralises the subject 'woman' and questions the possibility of calling upon one common experience. Which experiences of which women are relevant for feminist theology?

The question of reason as a 'source' has scarcely been addressed from the perspective of feminist theology, although the argument that women's perspective is privileged by their status as a marginalised group is drawn largely from feminist epistemology. Feminist critique of rationality and feminist epistemology both need to be developed further and their indebtedness to and implications for contemporary sociology and the wider critique of science need to be better investigated. Above all, a reflection upon the relationship between power and knowledge, recognised by feminist theology of liberation at an early stage, needs to take place in this context and not only in that of the critique of church and theology.

This range of questions is diffuse but also vital. They are addressed in this volume by the essays contained in the sections theme and forum. These are complemented by three substantial historical essays, and by reports from Spain, the Netherlands, and Germany which highlight the differences in the contexts and opportunities of European women in the past and today. Two women theological students in Zaire offer their response to feminist theology. Finally, we offer a reflection on the European Women's Synod in 1996 and a bibliographical section.

This volume would have been impossible without the help of Jutta Bletz, Christel Colberg, Marit Johannsen, Hélène Loetz and Rosemary Selle who variously typed the bibliography and checked the final proofs.

Elisabeth Hartlieb and Charlotte Methuen
Frankfurt/Heidelberg April 1997

KWOK Pui-Lan

The Sources and Resources of Feminist Theologies: A Post-Colonial Perspective

Introduction

1997 marks the end of 155 years of British rule over Hong Kong. The return of Hong Kong to China signifies the end of the British colonial era and the decline of European influences over the destiny of formerly colonized peoples. In 1800 the British Empire consisted of 1.5 million square miles and 20 million people. By 1900 the Victorian empire was made up of 11 million square miles and about 390 million people. In the 1920s the West controlled almost half the world's territories and total world population. Today, most of the colonies have regained political independence and Hong Kong is one of a few remnants of the colonial past.

About 500 years ago, African, Asian, and Latin American peoples were forced to join the emerging world order with Europe as its center as a result of the discovery of sea routes, flourishing trade, the colonization process, the genocide of indigenous peoples, the imposition of slavery and the systemic rape and sexual oppression of subjugated women. Since the Second World War, most of the colonies have become independent political entities, but they have been subjected to the continued control of the West through the mass media, economic domination of the world market, political influences, and military intervention. The Cold War era divided the world according to different ideologies. Since the late 1980s the rapid transformation of the world has led to the redrawing of the world map, the re-examining of the legacy of the Cold War, and the revisioning of the world order. A leading political scientist in the United States predicts the "new world order" to be a clash of civilizations.[1] Another suggests it will be a struggle between the "Jihad" and the "McWorld".[2] What will be the

---

1 Samuel P. Huntington, *The Clash of Civilizations and the Remaking of World Order* (New York: Simon & Schuster 1996), 51, 91.

2 Benjamin R. Barber, *Jihad vs. McWorld: How Globalism and Tribalism are Re-*

prospects of the formerly subjugated and colonized peoples in this "new world order"?

In the summer of 1997, a group of European women theologians will meet on the beautiful Mediterranean island of Crete to discuss the sources and resources of feminist theology. How will they envisage the future of the European Community and their roles as European feminist theologians in the post-colonial era? What will they see as the major social and political forces that are shaping the world in the 1990s? How will they reclaim the rich traditions of theology inherited from the past, while they simultaneously critique their patriarchal and colonial impulses? How will they explore the images, metaphors, and languages of feminist theology from their own cultural contexts? What will they offer as hope for people struggling for survival in many parts of the world?

This paper contributes to the dialogue by raising questions regarding the sources and resources of feminist theology from a post-colonial perspective. Both the terms "post-colonial" and "feminist theology" have been interpreted very differently. In this article "post-colonial" refers to the cultural practices and reading strategies emerging in societies that have experienced colonization. "Post-" refers not only to the period after the colonies have regained their political independence. Rather, it refers to the period since the onset of colonialism and continues to the present, because colonialist strategies persist in new forms.[3] Feminist theology is used here to refer to the global theological current emerging from many diverse contexts that affirms the dignity of women and their struggle for justice. Given the heterogenous understanding of the terms and the relatively recent introduction of post-colonial discourse to theological studies, what I am presenting must be seen as a provisional attempt to promote conversation and dialogue, rather than a finished product providing definitive answers.

Women's Experience

Women's experience has been the most contested source and resource of feminist theology. Feminist theologians have different opinions on what

shaping the World (New York: Ballantine Books 1996). "Jihad" refers to religious and tribal fundamentalism and "McWorld" means global consumerist capitalism.

3 Bill Ashcroft, Gareth Griffiths, and Helen Tiffin (eds.), *The Post-Colonial Studies Reader* (London and New York: Routledge 1995), xv.

constitutes women's experience and how experience, given its diverse and changing nature, can be normative in theology. I would like to analyze four issues that have emerged in the discussion of the use of women's experience in feminist theology: the truth claim of theology based on women's experience, the universalizing tendency in feminist discourse, the postmodern challenge to the notion of "subject," and the politics of difference and solidarity among women.

Since feminist theologians cannot rely on Scripture and tradition for truth claims because of their androcentric perspective, they have appealed to women's experience as a source and criterion of truth. Women's experience is invoked to challenge the orthodox notions of revelation and dogma by exposing their historical and constructed character. Furthermore, women's experience is also invoked to demystify the androcentric bias of humanism in liberal theology.[4] As Rosemary Radford Ruether has said: "The uniqueness of feminist theology lies not in its use of the criterion of experience but rather in its use of *women's* experience, which has been almost entirely shut out of theological reflection in the past."[5]

Feminist epistemological frameworks based on women's experience have been subject to serious scrutiny.[6] Rebecca Chopp distinguishes two alternative epistemological approaches: standpoint theory and social constructionism. She argues: "There can be a variety of forms of standpoint theory, from the position of Mary Daly, who argues that women's knowing is ontologically different from men's, to the position of more romantic feminist theologians, who will suggest that women essentially know more about loving, living, or even God."[7] People who have suffered under colonialism will not readily embrace this standpoint theory for they have

4 Mary McClintock Fulkerson, *Changing the Subject: Women's Discourses and Feminist Theology* (Minneapolis: Fortress 1994), 51-52.

5 Rosemary Radford Ruether, *Sexism and God-Talk: Toward a Feminist Theology* (Boston: Beacon 1983), 13, emphasis hers.

6 Sheila Greeve Davaney, "Problems in Feminist Theory: Historicity and the Search for Sure Foundations" in: Paula M. Cooey, Sharon A. Farmer, and Mary Ellen Ross (eds.), *Embodied Love: Sensuality and Relationship as Feminist Values* (San Francisco: Harper & Row 1987), 79-85.

7 Rebecca Chopp, "Eve's Knowing: Feminist Theology's Resistance to Malestream Epistemological Frameworks" in: Elisabeth Schüssler Fiorenza and Mary Shawn Copeland (eds.), *Concilium* 1996/1: *Feminist Theologies in Different Contexts*, 116-23, here 119.

seen that their colonizers have been both men and women. Female colonizers, either through their overt support of the colonial regimes or through their silent complicity because of their own internalized oppression, have not demonstrated themselves to know more about loving and God.

The other approach, Chopp says, is the social constructionist approach which posits that "knowledge itself is always historical, always related to power and interests, and is open to change and transformation."[8] Feminist theologians who support this position refute the essentializing of women's experience and stress the diversity of experiences. Since women's experiences are always shaped by the complex interaction of factors such as class, race, colonialism, and sexual orientation, women's viewpoints will always be situated and perspectival. The emphasis on the historical character of knowledge and experience has opened more room in feminist discourse for dialogue and conversation, and for multiply oppressed women to articulate diverse theological voices based on racial, cultural, class, religious, and linguistic differences.

Many Third World feminist theologians and minority scholars in the United States have challenged the universalizing tendency of middle-class, white feminists in projecting their own experience as representative for all women. Delores S. Williams, an African American theologian, has pointed out that there are substantial differences in white women's and black women's experience of patriarchy in the United States. While white women are oppressed by patriarchy, they at the same time benefit from the protection and privilege bestowed by the patriarchical white-controlled American institutions. Such protection is not offered to black women.[9] Williams further observes that while white feminists give priority to issues such as rape, domestic violence, women's work, inclusive language, the gender of God, black women have accented women's liberation and black families' liberation from domination of white males and females and give priority to issues such as physical survival, economic justice, educational opportunities, political participation, and encountering God as family.[10]

---

8 Ibid., 120.

9 Delores S. Williams, "The Color of Feminism: Or Speaking the Black Women's Tongue" in: *Journal of Religious Thought* 43:1 (1986), 42-58, here 48-49.

10 Ibid., 54.

Given the fact that women live in different socially constructed worlds, what are the complex reasons giving rise to a universalized way of thinking about women's experience? In *Inessential Woman*, Elizabeth Spelman traces the philosophical roots of this problem in the western tradition.[11] Plato and Aristotle, she points out, used the argument that human natures are different to justify the unequal position of different groups in society. To counteract such claims, feminist thinkers such as Simone de Beauvoir and Nancy Chodorow choose not to highlight the differences among women to avoid a hierarchical ranking, and to posit that sexism affects all women alike. Spelman shows that "the notion of a generic 'woman' functions in feminist thought much the way the notion of generic 'man' has functioned in Western philosophy: it obscures the heterogeneity of women."[12]

Universalizing, however, is more than a philosophical trap as Spelman suggests. It is also rooted in the complex social and material contexts of the expansion of the West and the superimposition of western cultures onto other peoples. Samuel P. Huntington has rightly pointed out: "Universalism is the ideology of the West for confrontation with non-Western cultures. . .The non-Wests see as Western what the West sees as universal."[13] The assumption that human experience of western people is the norm for everybody is not just an intellectual blind spot, but is heavily influenced by the colonial experience. The appeal to universal human experience and the inability to respect diverse cultures are expressions of a colonizing motive: the incorporation of the other into one's own culture or perspective.

Just as white women in North America have to investigate how their gendered selves are also racialized, European women have to ask how their construction of gender is affected by their experience of colonizing others. Historian Evelyn Brooks Higginbotham has pointed out the cult of true womanhood that taught women to be gentle, domestic, and ladylike in nineteenth-century America was not applicable for black women such as Sojourner Truth, who had to plough, plant and gather the harvest into

---

11 Elizabeth V. Spelman, *Inessential Woman: Problems of Exclusion in Feminist Thought* (Boston: Beacon 1988).

12 Ibid., ix.

13 Huntington, *The Clash of Civilizations* (as note 1), 66.

the barn. Furthermore, the cult of white womanhood was made possible only with the exploitation of the labor of black women.[14] Borrowing Higginbotham's insights, we have to ask in what ways the accumulation of wealth and the exploitation of women in the colonies affected Victorian conceptions of womanhood. How did the experiences of colonialism influence the literary imagination of British women? What kind of subjectivity did Charlotte Brontë construct for Jane Eyre and Bertha Mason, the white Jamaican madwoman in the attic?[15] In the rush to reclaim Jane Eyre as the heroine of a "feminist" novel, why have so many feminists forgotten the imperialist impulse that set the stage for the story?[16]

At a time when women are claiming their historical and theological subjectivity, postmodern and poststructuralist theories challenge the very notion of the "subject." These theoreticians point out that there is no autonomous and transcendent "I" that is not marked by social coding and discursively constituted. The ensuing debate among feminists focuses on whether we can speak of "women," of "subjectivity" and of "agency" and what are the implications for the struggle against injustice. Feminist theologians who work within a poststructuralist framework emphasize the subject as constructed by discourse. Others who are suspicious this will lead to "no reality outside the text" argue for women's subjectivity and agency for social change. While these are important debates, there is another aspect that has not received sufficient attention, that is, the constitution of Third World women as subjects in feminist discourse.

Tracing western feminist scholarship on Third World women, Chandra Talpade Mohanty points out western feminists have the tendency to represent "Third World woman" as a singular, ahistorical, and monolithic subject. The images used in western feminist scholarship to describe Third World women include women as victims of male violence, universal dependents of men, victims of the colonial process, targets of religious ideologies, and prey of development policies. These images are offered as sharp contrasts to those of western women who are portrayed as

---

14 Evelyn Brooks Higginbotham, "African-American Women's History and the Metalanguage of Race" in: *Signs* 17 (1992), 251-74, here 256-57.

15 Charlotte Brontë, *Jane Eyre* (New York: Puffin Books 1991, first published in 1847).

16 This insight is from Gayatri Chakavorty Spivak, "Three Women's Texts and a Critique of Imperialism" in: *Critical Inquiry* 12 (1985), 243-61, here 244-47.

secular, liberated, and able to control their own lives.[17] Not only secular western feminists, but also religious feminists display condescension when talking about their Third World "sisters." In her global study of the sado-rituals done against women, Mary Daly can only imagine Indian women as burned-alive immolated subjects, Chinese women as eroticized feet-bounded subjects, and African women as genitally mutilated subjects.[18]

Since Third World women are either completely invisible or are continuously mis-represented in western feminist scholarship, how can we speak of solidarity across differences? This question has become urgent in feminist theology because the past two decades saw the emergence of a plurality of voices, some with new names for their theological projects: womanist theology (African-American), mujerista (Hispanic/Latina), Asian, African, and Latin American feminist theologies. As there is an increasing number of minority people living in Europe, there will be feminist theologies coming from these minority communities in the future.

Two dominant metaphors have been offered to denote the solidarity of women in feminist theological discourse: "sisterhood" and "women-church." In *Beyond God the Father*, Mary Daly suggests that women who left the patriarchal church can form the "sisterhood of cosmic covenant."[19] The use of "sisterhood" has been criticized because of its familial ideology, its bourgeois individualism, its assumption of the nurturant and reproductive roles of women within the family, and its confining to women with common roots.[20] But few have noticed how the space metaphor is used in "global sisterhood" or "cosmic sisterhood." Daly says that the new sisterhood occupies a new space. At times she refers to this

17 Chandra Talpade Mohanty, "Under Western Eyes: Feminist Scholarship and Colonial Discourses" in: Chandra Talpade Mohanty, Ann Russo, and Lourdes Torres (eds.), *Third World Women and the Politics of Feminism* (Bloomington: Indiana University Press 1991), 51-80.

18 Mary Daly, *Gyn/Ecology: The Metaethics of Radical Feminism* (Boston: Beacon 1978).

19 Mary Daly, *Beyond God the Father: Toward a Philosophy of Women's Liberation* (Boston: Beacon 1973), 155.

20 See Elizabeth Fox-Genovese, "The Personal Is Not Political Enough" in: *Marxist Perspectives* 2 (1979-80), 94-113, and Elisabetta Donini, "Women and a Politics of Diversity: A Perspective of Radical Immanence" in: *Yearbook of the European Society of Women in Theological Research* 2 (1994), 59-68, here 65.

space as abstract and mental, "a province of the mind."[21] At other times, she describes such space in concrete spatial terms: "our space set apart," "it is not static space but constantly moving space," and "its center is on the boundaries of patriarchy's spaces."[22] Daly's spatial imagery suggests there is a common space we can call "ours" and there is a "transparent space" in which we can find ourselves and each other because everything is visible under our gaze.[23] A post-colonial perspective must insist that not all women are included in the pronoun "our," the boundaries of patriarchy's space are not the same, and the transparent space is constructed because of the power difference implicit in the white gaze.

Elisabeth Schüssler Fiorenza has proposed the controversial image of women-church. Her explanation of "women-church" has been constantly refined in response to her critics[24] and she currently prefers to render it as "*ekklesia* of wo/men."[25] *Ekklesia* is a political term denoting the assembly of free citizens to decide their own affairs. Schüssler Fiorenza admits that the translation of the term into church does not hold together the double meanings of democratic assembly and church.[26] In response to postmodern challenges, she introduces the term "wo/men" to indicate that "women are not a unitary social group but rather are fragmented and fractured by structures of race, class, religion, heterosexuality, colonialism, age, and health."[27]

In a post-colonial setting, "ekklesia of wo/men" can only be understood by a few academic elites. "Wo/men" is hardly translatable because other languages may not have similar devices to indicate the "fracture" and "fragmentation." Except in Korea, the notion of women-church is a

---

21 Daly, *Beyond God the Father* (as note 19),156.

22 Ibid., 157.

23 Alison Blunt and Gillian Rose, "Introduction: Women's Colonial and Postcolonial Geographies" in: Alison Blunt and Gillian Rose (eds.), *Writing Women and Space: Colonial and Postcolonial Geographies* (New York: Guilford Press 1994), 1-25, here 6.

24 See Elisabeth Schüssler Fiorenza, *But She Said: Feminist Practices of Biblical Interpretation* (Boston: Beacon 1992), 5-7.

25 Elisabeth Schüssler Fiorenza, *Jesus: Miriam's Child, Sophia's Prophet: Critical Issues in Feminist Christology* (New York: Continuum 1994), 24-27.

26 Schüssler Fiorenza, *But She Said* (as note 24), 128.

27 Schüssler Fiorenza, *Jesus* (as note 25), 24.

non-starter in Asia because the church is associated not only with patriarchal authority but also with colonial power. Whether as the assembly of self-identified women and supportive men, or as a feminist space or public sphere to articulate a counterhegemonic discourse against kyriarchical power, the concept of women-church has not made explicit the material conditions in which women of such diversity can gather and work together. Why do the formerly colonized subjects want to gather with their oppressors or to occupy the same space? How can we guarantee that such women-church is not a false inclusion, a democracy dictated by the interests of the powerful, and a space marked by the interests of the few?

I agree with womanist theologian Shawn Copeland when she urges us to go beyond the clichéd rhetoric of solidarity and raise the question of the moral obligation of speech in relation to action.[28] She elaborates:

> Solidarity is a wrenching task: to stand up for justice in the midst of injustice and domination; to take up simplicity in the midst of affluence and comfort; to embrace integrity in the midst of collusion and co-optation; to contest the gravitational pull of domination.[29]

She does not see difference as a problem for solidarity, because she insists "not difference, but indifference, ignorance, egoism, and selfishness are obstacles to [it]."[30] The plurality of feminist theological discourse will be a threat and a fragmentation if the politics of identity leads to competition and isolation. This happens when identity is seen as a possession or treated like a commodity to be exchanged and competed in the market. On the other hand, the multiplicity of theological voices will provide mutual critique and enrichment if we understand that identity is always constructed in relation to others. We cannot understand ourselves without listening to others, especially to those we have oppressed or have the potential to do so. Such critical engagement is the beginning for solidarity.

Scripture

For women who choose to remain within the Christian tradition, the Bible is still an important source and resource for theology. Using the critical

---

[28] M. Shawn Copeland, "Toward a Critical Christian Feminist Theology of Solidarity" in: Mary Ann Hinsdale and Phyllis H. Kaminski (eds.), *Women & Theology* (Maryknoll: Orbis Books 1995), 3-38, here 18.

[29] Ibid., 29-30.

[30] Ibid., 24.

lens of a hermeneutics of suspicion, feminist scholarship has critiqued many traditional claims regarding the Bible. Feminist theologians have challenged the authority of the Bible, the boundary of the canon, and the androcentric bias of the text and the history of interpretation. Seeking to construct feminist models of interpretation, they have scrutinized the master's tools, created feminist frames of meaning, and developed different norms of interpretation. Reconstructing women's early Christian history, they examined the everyday lives of women, women's religious leadership in church and synagogue, and the marginization of women in the patriarchalization of the church. Reclaiming the Bible as bread and not stone for women, they proposed new liturgical usage of the Bible, alternative methods of feminist Bible study, and liberating paradigms for teaching biblical studies.[31]

These issues are significant for women in diverse contexts. In the past decade, feminist scholars from the Third World and from minority communities in the United States have increasingly contributed to the emerging feminist biblical scholarship.[32] From a post-colonial situation, we need to discuss a few issues before the Bible can be used as a resource for feminist theology: the use of the Bible in colonial discourse, the influence of colonialism in the academic study of the Bible, and the possibilities of developing post-colonial readings of the Bible. The Bible is an integral part of the colonial discourse. The introduction of the Bible and Christian faith to foreign lands was used to justify the political and military aggression of the West. For example, Hong Kong was ceded to the British in the same unequal treaty in 1842, which granted permission for missionaries to preach in the seaports of China. To teach the Bible and to spread the Gospel was seen as the "civilizing mission" of the West, or the "white men's burden." Selective passages from the Bible were emphasized to justify this cause: the Great Commission of Jesus to go and

---

31 For a helpful guide to the breadth of feminist scholarship on the Bible, see Elisabeth Schüssler Fiorenza (ed.), *Searching the Scriptures* (New York: Crossroad 1993) vol. 1: *A Feminist Introduction*.

32 See e.g. Renita J. Weems, *Battered Love: Marriage, Sex, and Violence in the Hebrew Prophets* (Minneapolis: Fortress 1995), Elsa Tamez, *The Amnesty of Grace: Justification by Faith from a Latin American Perspective* (Nashville: Abingdon 1993), and Kwok Pui-lan, *Discovering the Bible in the Non-Biblical World* (Maryknoll: Orbis books 1995). [German edition: *Interpretation als Dialog* (Luzern: Edition Exodus 1996)]

make disciples of all nations (Matt. 28:19) was given unprecedented attention during the time of colonization of India.[33] Revered as the revealed Word of God, the Bible was seen as a prized possession of the West. The Bible thus served as a "signifier" that functioned to support western beliefs in the inferiority and deficiency of "heathen" cultures. Furthermore, revelation through the Bible was regarded as special revelation. Insights and wisdom offered by other religions and traditions could at best be classified as general revelation. This biased view reinforced the superiority of Christianity in the evolutionary scheme of religion. Even the "great" theologians of the twentieth century were not immune from seeing the world through this superiority complex. Although Karl Barth insisted that God judges all religions, including Christianity, he upheld the centrality of the Bible as God's special revelation. Karl Rahner, in his generosity, labelled people of other faiths as "anonymous Christians."[34]

The introduction of the Bible to other cultures was a mixed blessing for women. In order to teach women to read the Bible, Christian missions established girls' schools, catechism classes, and women's Bible study classes. However, the curriculum of these mission girls' schools were meant to instill the cult of true womanhood and to reinforce domesticity of women.[35] Because of sexual propriety, women missionaries were sent to the mission field to work among women. These women missionaries wrote voluminous amounts of materials about their lives in foreign lands in mission pamphlets, local religious news, and memoirs to generate support for mission. Such religious literature popularized the idea that "heathen" women were miserable, groping in the dark, waiting for the light to be brought to them. Before the advent of the mass media, this widespread literature shaped the opinion of European and American women on Third World women, a legacy that has far-reaching effect to the present. While the enthnocentrism of missionaries working "in the frontiers" has been criticized, the academics studying the Bible in the metropolitan centers of Europe were seen as immune from cultural

---

33 R. S. Sugirtharajah's presentation at the annual meeting of the Society of Biblical Literature, 24 November 1996.

34 Karl Rahner, "Observations on the Problem of the 'Anonymous Christian'" in: *Theological Investigations* (New York: Seabury 1976), 14:280-94.

35 See Kwok Pui-lan, *Chinese Women and Christianity, 1860-1927* (Atlanta:: Scholars Press 1992), 104-6.

imperialism. Little reflection has been done on the relationship between the emergence of the historical critical method and the ascendency of power of Europe. There are two reasons for this oversight. First, the historical critical method was seen as a progressive tool to challenge church dogma and the authority of the church in the West. Second, the method was considered by its practitioners as scientific, objective, and value-neutral. Focusing on the bygone era of the Greco-Roman world, historical critical research was not supposed to be clouded by the political interests of the time. However, if we examine historical criticism from an international frame, a different picture begins to emerge. We can cite as an example the first quest for the historical Jesus, a paramount concern of historical criticism.[36] Some of the key spokespersons of the first quest were not disinterested scholars. D. F. Strauss (1808-1874) was a supporter of a strong and united Germany under the hegemony of Prussia and defended Germany's position in the Prusso-Austrian war.[37] Ernest Renan (1823-1892), who was passionate about French high culture, went to Phoenicia and Syria under the auspices of Napoleon III.[38] An interpreter of Bach's organ music, Albert Schweitzer (1875-1965) left us not only a *summa* of the first quest, but also an autobiography detailing his life as a "jungle doctor."[39] Labeling African people as "primitive creatures" without much progress, his autobiography displayed deep-seated cultural superiority. The expansion of Europe into other parts of the world affected these scholars' conceptualization of both western civilization and Christianity. The comparative study of myths and religions in the same period showed that "primitive" people were mythical, superstitious, and idolatrous. To prove that Christianity was infinitely superior to other religions, all the "nonsense" of virgin birth, miracles, and supernatural happenings surrounding Jesus had to be discarded. This could only be

---

36 For details, see my forthcoming article "Jesus/the Native: Biblical Studies from a Postcolonial Perspective" in: Fernando F. Segovia and Mary Ann Tolbert (eds.), *Reading from this Place*, 3.

37 Albert Schweitzer, *The Quest of the Historical Jesus* (New York: Macmillan 1968, first published in 1906).

38 Ibid., 180.

39 Albert Schweitzer, *Out of My Life and Thought: An Autobiography* (New York: Henry Holt 1949).

done by a "critical" and "scientific" study of the Bible which would lead to a historical Jesus free from mythological trappings.

The quest of the historical Jesus was far from being value-neutral. The political interests of Europe determined the questions to be asked, the gathering of data, the framework of interpretation, and the final outcome. The historical critical method must be situated within the cultural space and political configurations of its time. We must begin to question its assumptions about historical consciousness, historicity, and historiography from a post-colonial perspective. The historical questions raised by this method may be too limiting for people in other contexts. As Renita Weems has said, the negative result of historical criticism has been "to undermine marginalized reading communities by insisting that their questions and experiences are superfluous to Scripture and their interpretation illegitimate, because of their failure to remain objective."[40] In fact, other cultures have other assumptions about history and their own historical method. A *western* historical criticism should not be taken as universally valid because *western* notions of historical process are not universally held. We have to learn from insights from other cultures to broaden our historical imagination.[41]

The discussion of post-colonial interpretation of the Bible has gained momentum among Third World scholars and intellectuals within the indigenous and diasporic communities.[42] R. S. Sugurtharajah has said that the post-colonial perspective will have to go beyond a mimicry of western critical method and an Orientalist valorization of ancient pre-colonial cultures.[43] It has to negotiate a different past, which was not

40 Renita J. Weems, "Reading Her Way through the Struggle: African American Women and the Bible" in: Cain Hope Felder (ed.), *Stony the Road We Trod: African American Biblical Interpretation* (Minneapolis: Fortress 1991), 57-77, here 66.

41 See e.g. Brian K. Blout, *Cultural Interpretation: Reorienting New Testament Criticism* (Minneapolis: Fortress 1995).

42 A new series on post-colonial criticism of the Bible will be published by Sheffield Academic Press.

43 The following discussion is taken largely from Sugirtharajah's essays. See "From Orientalist to Post-Colonial: Notes on Reading Practices" in: *Asia Journal of Theology* 10 (1996), 20-27, and "Orientalism, Ethnonationalism and Transnationalism: Shifting Identities and Biblical Interpretation" in: Mark G. Brett (ed.), *Ethnicity and the Bible* (Leiden: E. J. Brill 1996), 419-29.

reified, glorified, and unitary. Employing tools from critical theory and cultural studies, post-colonial criticism exposes the relationship between power and knowledge, challenges both imperialist and nationalist claims, and maintains the posture of a "fighting literature." There are several characteristics of post-colonial criticism: (1) it challenges the totalizing forms of western interpretation, exposing its co-optation by imperial interests and destabilizing its frames of meaning; (2) it is a counter-hegemonic discourse, paying special attention to the hidden and neglected voices in the Bible; (3) it places the Bible within the multifaith context of many Third World situations; (4) it encourages and welcomes contributions from marginalized groups that have not been fully heard: the dalits, the indigenous peoples, the migrants, people in diaspora and in borderland, and especially women in these communities; and (5) it learns from and debates with other hermeneutical frameworks, such as post-modernism. Post-colonial feminist criticism looks at the Bible from the vantage point of women multiply oppressed because of race, class, and colonialism. It examines how marginalized women in the Bible are rendered invisible, consigned to signify the other, and denied of speech. At the same time, it reconstructs the lives of these women and plots a counterhegemonic feminist discourse based on fragments and traces that are still left in the biblical tradition. I have found the social-historical construction of women in early Christianity by Luise Schottroff very helpful.[44] Instead of focusing on the activities of female leaders of the church as other feminist scholars have done, she illuminates the everyday lives of ordinary women. As a result she offers many valuable insights into the lives and work of poor women and slave women from which post-colonial critics can learn.

Tradition

Tradition is an important source of theology for Catholic theologians. Although its influences may not be so pervasive in Protestantism, most Protestant theologians acknowledge it has bearings in their theological reflection. Discussion of tradition is critical in feminist theology because tradition defines the memory of the Christian community. Women have

44 Luise Schottroff, *Lydia's Impatient Sisters: A Feminist Social History of Early Christianity* (Louisville: Westminster/John Knox 1995).

been shut off from shaping the collective memory of the church: they have been excluded from discussions of biblical canon, the debates of the creeds, the deliberation of church pronouncements, and the formulation of church doctrines. Furthermore, women who are not of European and Euro-American descent often feel that the western theological tradition has been taken for granted as the universal tradition for churches around the world. From a post-colonial perspective, the notion of tradition and its boundaries must be reconceptualized and radically expanded. Three issues need to be addressed: multicultural investigations of Christian tradition, the use of resources from cultures historically not shaped by Christianity, and future visions of tradition informed by feminist insights and struggles from the global context. In recent decades, western feminist theologians have exposed the androcentric bias of western Christian tradition. Those with a more positive evaluation of tradition tried to delineate a liberating tradition within the tradition, or to correlate the radical prophetic tradition with women's experiences.[45] Others who are more critical argue that all tradition must be scrutinized through the critical feminist lens and women have the freedom to choose and reject traditions.[46] Feminist theologians have also delved into alterative sources and resurrected stories and experiences of marginalized women's communities. They have given us new information regarding early women martyrs, medieval women mystics, witches, Beguines, slave women, and women in colonialism. Others have offered new interpretations of church doctrines and teachings, and re-examined theological debates and controversy. Building on these foundations, we can now move to the new phase of subjecting Christian tradition to an international and multicultural critique.

Christianity has always defined itself through its contacts with other cultures: Judaism and Hellenistic traditions, the so-called "barbarian" attack, the threat of the Muslim world, and the encountering of cultures and peoples of the Third World. Since the conversion of Constantine,

---

45 Letty Russell, *Human Liberation in a Feminist Perspective* (Philadelphia: Westminster 1974), 87-88, and Rosemary Radford Ruether, "Feminist Interpretation: A Method of Correlation" in: Letty M. Russell (ed.), *Feminist Interpretation of the Bible* (Philadelphia: Westminster 1985), 111-24.

46 Elisabeth Schüssler Fiorenza, "The Will to Choose or to Reject: Continuing Our Critical Work" in: Russell, *Feminist Interpretation* (as note 45), 125-36.

Christianity has had complex relationships with imperial powers. The rise and fall of empires affected theologians' outlook on the world and their views about morality and social order. For example, Augustine's formulation of original sin would not have gained acceptance without the changing political situation in the late fourth and early fifth centuries.[47] A multicultural and post-colonial evaluation will help us see in sharp relief how the Christian tradition has been shaped through interactions with other cultures throughout the ages. The work of Jewish feminist theologians such as Judith Plaskow has pointed to the troubling anti-Semitic trends in Christian thought, including the work of western feminists.[48]

Feminist theologians from many parts of the world can participate in this new phase by posing new questions, revealing western cultural bias, and constructing new discourse. Elsa Tamez has critically evaluated the central notion of justification by faith from the vantage point of Latin Amcrican situations.[49] Womanist theologian Delores S. Williams has exposed the limitations of traditional theories of atonement, especially the surrogacy of Jesus who was believed to have died for our sin.[50] Korean theologian Chung Hyun Kyung has argued for a life-affirming, survival-centered form of spirituality.[51] These insightful discussions have radically transformed our way of looking at traditional doctrines and enlarged our collective memory. Besides critiquing western Christian tradition, feminist theologians from diverse cultures are exploring the use of myths, legends, and other literary resources for theology. In many Third World countries, the white male Christian tradition has been treated as the normative text, while indigenous traditions become the context of processes of inculturalization or contextualization. But from a post-colonial perspective, the primacy of the whole western tradition is contested and indi-

---

47 Elaine Pagels, *Adam, Eve, and the Serpent* (New York: Vintage Books 1989), 98-126.

48 Judith Plaskow, "Anti-Judaism in Feminist Christian Interpretation" in: Schüssler Fiorenza, *Searching the Scriptures* (as note 31), 117-29.

49 Tamez, *The Amnesty of Grace* (as note 32).

50 Delores S, Williams, *Sisters in the Wilderness: The Challenge of Womanist God-Talk* (Maryknoll: Orbis Books 1993), 161-67.

51 See her controversial address at the World Council of Churches, "Come, Holy Spirit—Renew the Whole Creation" in: Michael Kinnamon (ed.), *Signs of the Spirit: Official Report, Seventh Assembly* (Geneva: WCC 1991), 37-47.

genous resources should be used on an equal footing and interpreted intertextually with western sources. Mercy Amba Oduyoye of Ghana uses the rich depository of popular wisdom in what she calls "folktalk" in her articulation of God's saving power,[52] while some Asian feminist theologians have begun to draw insights from their multi-scriptural traditions and from the wisdom of women passed from generation to generation.

The use of these indigenous sources has been derogatorily condemned as sycretistic by some western male theologians.[53] They look at the new theological landscape with alarm and suspicion because the terrain is so unfamiliar to them, but have completely forgotten that Rudolf Bultmann called Christianity syncretistic without any negative connotations.[54] It was the success of Christianity in adapting to its cultural context and its ability to change as circumstances required that made it a viable tradition. In the history of western Christianity, many cultural elements of the West have been adopted, including philosophy, art, symbols, and music. Nobody raises an eyebrow or condemns such practices as syncretist. But when feminist theologians around the world explore new expressions of faith, they are labeled as heretical or syncretist! Third World feminists are aware that there are both liberating and oppressive components in indigenous traditions.

Kenyan theologian Musimbi Kanyoro has called for a "cultural hermeneutics" to unpack the layers of cultural interpretations women have inherited.[55] Citing the example of Africa, she says missionaries and westerners tended to see African cultures as "totally barbaric" or "undeveloped." In response to such biased views, some male African theologians in the 1960s and 1970s initiated the process of "inculturation" which attempted to Africanize Christianity. But they overlooked the

---

52 Mercy Amba Oduyoye, *Daughters of Anowa: African Women & Patriarchy* (Maryknoll: Orbis Books 1995).

53 See the discussion in Jeffrey Gros, "Christian Confession in a Pluralistic World" in: *Christian Century* (26 June-3 July 1991), 644-46.

54 Rudolf Bultmann, *Primitive Christianity in Its Contemporary Setting* (London: Thames and Hudson 1956), 177-79. Bultmann was influenced by the work of Herman Gunkel.

55 Musimbi Kanyoro, "Cultural Hermeneutics: An African Contribution" in Ofelia Ortega (ed.), *Women's Visions: Theological Reflection, Celebration, Action* (Geneva: WCC 1995), 18-28.

question of women and culture and ignored women's suffering in the name of preserving cultural heritage.

The need to look at indigenous tradition with critical eyes is recognized by feminist theologians from other continents. Elsa Tamez, for example, also challenges cultural violence against women and begins to explore the ways some of the myths in Latin America are used to legitimize unequal relationships.[56] Such cultural hermeneutics will need to be developed in conversation with feminist movements that are gathering momentum in different parts of the world and in the discussion of feminist theories appropriate to specific contexts. In the twenty-first century, I anticipate an increasing demand from formerly colonized and enslaved peoples to participate in shaping and expanding the Christian tradition. The post-colonial era offers unique opportunities for Christianity to interact with diverse cultures in the world not as a missionizing force or a conquering ideology. Christianity is on the threshold of becoming more multilingual and multicultural than before and is opening itself to learn from other traditions. Just as it has interacted in the past with Greek philosophy, scholastic thought, the Enlightenment, and the scientific revolution, Christianity will be brought into dialogue with other cultures in a more substantial way in the future. Christianity may not look the same as before, but it will learn to speak many peoples' tongues. Feminist theologians, together with other liberation theologians committed to justice and peace, are at the forefront of this emerging process. Just as we should not universalize "women's experience," we should also guard against an essentialized understanding of "Asia," "Africa," "Latin America," or the "Third World." Feminist theologians from these contexts are challenging monolithic and stereotypical views of Asian women, African women, or Latin American women. They are aware that because of the lack of educational opportunities and access to the media, only a small number of Third World women's voices have been heard. In the near future, they hope that creative ways can be found so that minority women in the Third World, indigenous women, migrant women workers, and younger women can contribute to the articulation of global feminist theologies.

---

56 Elsa Tamez, "Cultural Violence against Women in Latin America" in: Mary John Mananzan et al. (eds.), *Women against Violence: Spirituality for Life* (Maryknoll: Orbis Books 1996), 11-19.

Abstracts

Der Artikel diskutiert den Gebrauch von Frauen-Erfahrung, Schrift und Tradition als Quelle feministischer Theologien aus postkolonialer Perspektive. Die Autorin argumentiert, daß die Neigung, Frauen-Erfahrung zu universalisieren, nicht nur ein philosophisches Thema ist, sondern mit dem Vorgang der Kolonisierung verbunden ist. Sie behandelt die Frage, in welcher Weise sich der Kolonialismus auf die akademische biblische Forschung auswirkt und erkundet Strategien postkolonialer Leseweisen. Sie plädiert für eine multikulturelle Kritik christlicher Tradition und zeigt beispielhaft, wie feministische Theologinnen in einem Kontext der Dritten Welt die Grenzen der Tradition erweitern.

Se plaçant dans une optique post-coloniale, cet article analyse l'utilisation de l'expérience féminine, des Ecritures et de la tradition en tant que sources pour les théologies féministes. L'auteure démontre que la tendance à universaliser l'expérience des femmes n'est pas seulement un enjeu philosophique, mais qu'elle se rattache aussi au processus dela colonialisation. Elle explique comment l'expansion coloniale a affecté l'étude académique de la Bible et elle examine des stratégies pour passer à une lecture post-coloniale. Préconisant une critique multiculturelle de la tradition chrétienne, elle donne des exemples de la manière dont les théologiennes plongées dans les réalités du Tiers Monde élargissent le cadre de la tradition.

KWOK Pui-lan was born and grew up in Hong Kong. She received her doctoral degree from Harvard Divinity School and is Associate Professor of Theology at Episcopal Divinity School, Cambridge, USA. Active in the ecumenical movement, she is the author of *Chinese Women and Christianity, 1860-1927* and *Discovering the Bible in the Non-Biblical World* (*Interpretation als Dialog* in German).

Jonneke BEKKENKAMP

Vom Lesen und Leben*
Zur Neudefinition des Kanons in der feministischen Theologie

Einleitung

Die Frage nach dem Wert der Bibel als geistiger Autorität wird zur Zeit sowohl unter dem Gesichtspunkt des Feminismus als auch des Pluralismus gestellt. Dabei wird auf den androzentrischen Charakter vieler Bibelgeschichten und die Notwendigkeit eines interreligiösen Dialogs hingewiesen. Einerseits wird für die Suche nach alternativen Texten und Traditionen plädiert, andererseits für eine Relativierung der eigenen Texttradition. In meiner Arbeit als Dozentin für Frauenstudien, Theologie und Literatur versuche ich beiden Zielsetzungen gerecht zu werden.

Mein Ausgangspunkt ist, daß, was dem einen heilig ist, für einen anderen noch lange nicht heilig zu sein braucht. Um ein sinnvolles Zusammenleben, eine Ökumene, möglich zu machen, ist es jedoch wichtig, daß wir uns Rechenschaft über unsere Gründe für die Auswahl der Texte, die wir lesen, und die Art, wie wir sie lesen, geben.

Die Unzufriedenheit feministischer Theologinnen mit dem biblischen (und theologischen) Kanon hat zu verschiedenen alternativen Vorschlägen geführt, die ich nachfolgend in einer Übersicht über vier Lesemodelle schematisch darstellen werde. Die ersten drei Modelle sind als Basismodelle zu verstehen, da die Art und Weise, in der feministische Theologinnen moderne Literatur lesen, häufig als eine Kombination dieser

---

* Das Material für diesen Artikel entstammt meinem Buch *Canon en Keuze. Het bijbelse Hooglied en de Twenty-One Love Poems van Adrienne Rich als bronnen van theologie* (Kampen: Kok Agora, 1993) [Kanon und Auswahl. Das biblische Hohelied und die Twenty-One Love Poems von Adrienne Rich als Quellen von Theologie], und zwar hauptsächlich dem letzten Kapitel. Der Kürze wegen habe ich die meisten Verweise auf das Hohelied und die Twenty-One Love Poems allen lassen. Was daher verloren gegangen ist, ist die Weise, in der die Deutung moderner Poesie die Deutung der biblischen Poesie beeinflußt und umgekehrt, und damit eine Aufklärung der Kanon-Frage als einer hermeneutischen Frage.

Modelle analysiert werden kann.[1] Auf der Grundlage der sehr kurzgefaßten Skizze dieser Modelle entwickle ich dann ein viertes Modell. Mit diesem vierten Modell werde ich mich etwas ausführlicher beschäftige

Lesen als Theologin und Feministin: Vier Modelle

Die verschiedenen Möglichkeiten, als Theologin und Feministin Texte auszuwählen und zu interpretieren, lassen sich meines Erachtens mit vier Modellen charakterisieren. Was haben diese gemein, worin unterscheiden sie sich?

Was sie gemein haben, kann ich am besten anhand einer Abbildung darstellen, die meiner Übersicht über die verschiedenen Modelle zugrunde liegt:

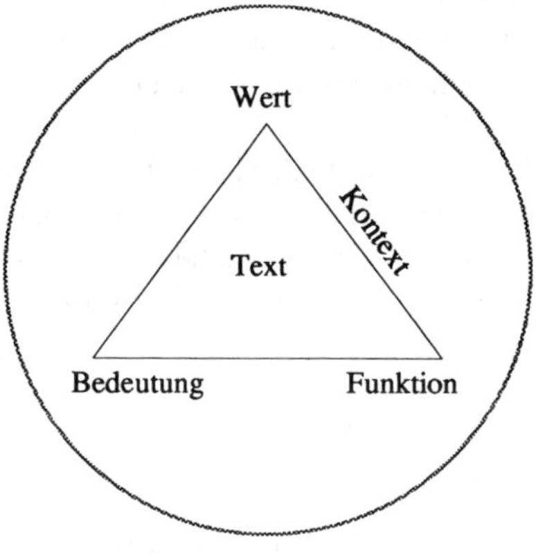

Diese Abbildung ist ein Versuch, die Beziehungen zwischen der Funktion, der Bedeutung und dem Wert eines Texts darzustellen. Die Funktion eines Quellentextes der Theologie könnte man global damit beschreiben, daß er dem Leben Form, Wert und Richtung gibt. Hinsichtlich dieser Funktionsbestimmung besteht weitgehend Einigkeit. Die Frage, die sich daher stellt,

1 Bei meiner Beschreibung dieser Modelle habe ich nacheinander die folgenden Texte verwendet: Rosemary Radford Ruether, *Womanguides. Readings toward a Feminist Theology* (Boston: Beacon Press 1985) von Judith Plaskow, *Sex, Sin and Grace: Woman's Experience and the Theology of Reinhold Niebuhr and Paul Tillich* (Lanham, Md: University Press of America 1980) und von Carol P. Christ, *Diving Deep and Surfacing: Women Writers on Spiritual Quest* (Boston: Beacon Press 1980).

ist, ob man den Wert von Texten, die traditionell als Quelle von Theologie fungiert haben, neu zur Diskussion stellt oder versucht ihre Bedeutung neu zu bestimmen. Es besteht ein weitverbreitetes Bedürfnis, an dem Wert kanonischer Texte, wie Bibeltexten, nicht zu rütteln. Wenn man jedoch nicht nur die Funktion, sondern auch den Wert eines Textes festlegt, führt dies, bei sich ändernden Umständen, zu enormen Verschiebungen in der Interpretation. Der revolutionäre, aber zugleich sehr naheliegende Ausgangspunkt aller Lesemodelle ist der Gedanke, daß es bei der Interpretation Grenzen gibt und es hin und wieder möglich sein muß, den Wert eines Textes, selbst eines Bibeltextes, neu zur Diskussion zu stellen.

Das ist es, was die vier Modelle gemein haben. Unter Berufung auf die Funktion, die die Theologie zu erfüllen beansprucht, werden Kriterien entwickelt, um den Wert von Texten neu zu thematisieren. Die Modelle unterscheiden sich darin, ob sie die Identität der Leserin als Feministin bzw. als Theologin problematisieren oder nicht. So komme ich zu vier Modellen.

Man kann sowohl als Feministin als auch als Theologin Texte so lesen, als ob 'Feministin sein' oder 'Theologin sein' mehr oder weniger feststehende Identitäten wären, und versuchen die daraus resultierenden Identitätskonflikte so recht und schlecht es geht zu lösen. Das ist das erste Modell.

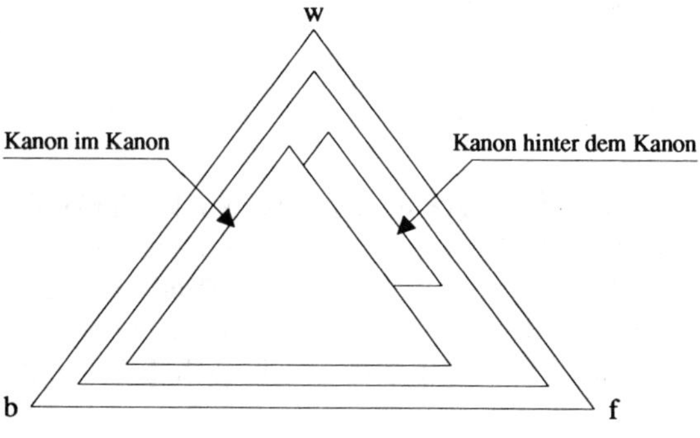

Modell 1

Wie in der vorigen Abbildung steht f für Funktion, b für Bedeutung und w für Wert. Theologie ist in diesem Modell eine Hermeneutik des Daseins mit Hilfe einer bestimmten—in unserem Fall christlichen—Tradition. Diese Tradition wird jedoch als unvollständig und unfertig aufgefaßt. In der Auswahl der Texte ist dieses Modell daher ein Wachstumsmodell.

Der alte Kanon wird in diesem Modell auf drei Arten durchbrochen. Zum ersten, indem ein "Kanon innerhalb des Kanons" gebildet wird, eine Sammlung von Texten, die die Prüfung der feministischen Kritik durchstanden haben. Zum zweiten, indem ein "Kanon hinter dem Kanon" postuliert wird: die überlieferten Geschichten werden als nur eine Hälfte der Geschichten gesehen, die hätten überliefert werden können, wenn das aufgeschrieben und bewahrt worden wäre, was aus der Sicht von Frauen von Bedeutung war. Zum dritten, indem die moderne Literatur als Aktualisierung einer auf diese Weise stets angepaßten Tradition annektiert wird.

Die *Twenty-One Love Poems* von Adrienne Rich[2] können im ersten Modell als eine produktive Rezeption der biblischen Liebespoesie gesehen werden, der wir im Hohelied begegnen.[3] In bezug auf einen solchen neuen Text wagt die Modell-1-LeserIn sich bis an die Grenze der Aneignung und des Sich-eigen-Machens eines Textes. In bezug auf einen bereits kanonisierten Text (wie das Hohelied) begibt sie sich an die Grenze des Hineinlesens und Einlebens. Mit zunehmendem Abstand zwischen kanonischem Text und "neuem" Text nimmt die Gefahr des Hineinlesens zu. Aber jede Auslegung ist in mehr oder weniger starkem Maße eine Form des Hineinlesens. Jede LeserIn wendet bestimmte positions- und personengebundene interpretatorische Codes an, ohne die eine Bedeutungsbestimmung undenkbar ist. Die Hinzufügung "neuer" Texte zur Bereicherung des Kanons von Kirche und Theologie ließe sich in diesem Licht als eine Art explizitere Darstellung des eigenen Literaturhintergrundes auffassen. Wenn wir das so bewerten, ist ein erster Schritt zu einem zweiten Lesemodell gemacht, in dem "neue" Texte (im untenstehenden Schema das kleine Dreieck links) explizit in der Funktion eines "bedeutungsbestimmenden Kontexts" aufgeführt werden.

---

2 Adrienne Rich, *Twenty-One Love Poems* (California: Effies Press 1976), auch enthalten in Adrienne Rich, *The Dream of a Common Language: Poems 1974-1977* (New York: Norton 1978).

3 Siehe *Canon en Keuze*, S.139-146. Der Term "produktive Rezeption" bezieht sich auf einen Unterschied, der bei Sekundärtexten zwischen produktiver und hermeneutischer Rezeption gemacht werden kann: "Produktive Rezeption" hat zum Zweck, eine Geschichte neu zu schaffen, die hermeneutische hingegen soll eine Geschichte, so wie sie ist, zugänglich machen (Bal et al., *En Sara in haar tent lachte... Patriarchat en verzet in bybelverhalten* (Utrecht: Hes 1984:24).

Das kleine Dreieck rechts stellt den biblischen Kanon dar, die größeren Dreiecke aktuelle Manifestationen der christlichen Tradition. Das äußerste Dreieck im Schema des ersten Lesemodells könnte eine dieser Manifestationen sein. Die Theologieauffassung, die dem zweiten Lesemodell zugrunde liegt, ist unverändert die einer Hermeneutik des Daseins mit Hilfe einer bestimmten—in unserem Fall der christlichen—Glaubenstradition. Im Gegensatz zum ersten Modell wird diese Tradition hier jedoch nicht als eine nicht-abgeschlossene Vergangenheit, sondern als ein dominanter Teil der Gegenwart behandelt. Das zweite Modell ist ein Konfrontationsmodell. Der Kanon wird von außen her durchbrochen. Die Modell-2-Leserin nimmt für sich die Rolle einer externen Expertin in Anspruch, die beurteilt, ob bestimmte Bibeltexte als theologische Entwürfe für bestimmte heute lebende Frauen ihre Funktion erfüllen, nämlich dem Leben dieser Frauen Form, Wert und Richtung zu geben.

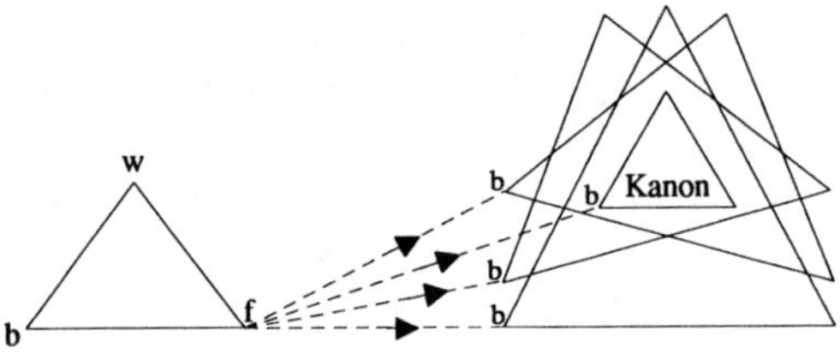

Modell 2

Die Identität der Leserin als Frau und Feministin wird in dem Sinne problematisiert, daß weder unterstellt wird, daß diese Identität von vornherein bekannt ist, noch daß sie für alle Frauen gleich ist. Die Funktion neuer Texte wie den *Twenty-One Love Poems* (das linke kleine Dreieck) ist die *Konstruktion* eines weiblichen Lesers, einer Leserin, die den Texten auf der rechten Seite eine Bedeutung geben kann, wobei man ihnen weiter die Funktion zuerkennt, dem menschlichen Leben Form, Wert und Richtung zu geben.

Der Vorteil des zweiten Lesemodells gegenüber dem ersten ist, daß die Leserin sich der Möglichkeit anderer Auslegungen bewußter ist und sie die Entscheidung für ihre Auslegung nicht nur mit einem Verweis auf ihr Frau-Sein begründet, sondern mit einem Verweis auf die Frau, die sie sein will. Die sie ansprechende Frauenliteratur, die sie dabei einsetzt, bildet im dritten Lesemodell den primären Text. Die Funktion dieser Literatur verlagert sich von der eines Skripts zum Lesen kanonischer Quellen zu der einer authentischen und autonomen neuen Quelle von Theologie. Schematisch läßt das dritte Lesemodell sich wie folgt beschreiben:

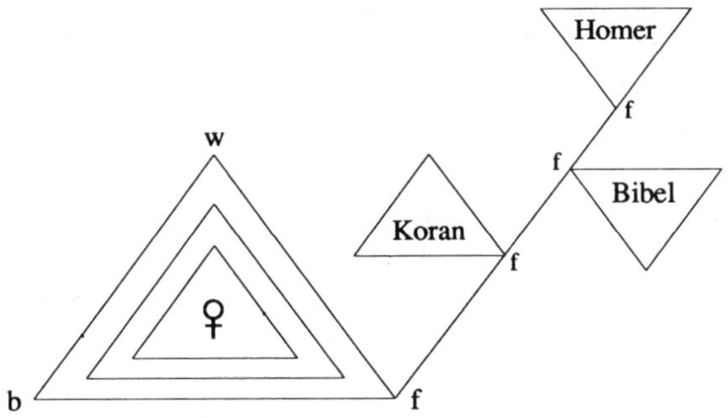

Modell 3

Das große Dreieck läßt sich als vergrößerter Ausschnitt des linken Dreiecks in Schema 2 auffassen. Es repräsentiert eine bewußt getroffene Auswahl von Frauentexten. Ich nenne dieses Modell das Modell des weiblichen Kanons. Es wird angestrebt, eine autonome Sammlung von Texten zu bestimmen, in deren Zentrum Texte stehen, die innerhalb der Frauenbewegung als verbindender und inspirierender Faktor fungieren. Dieser neue Kanon müßte für Frauen dieselbe Funktion erfüllen wie der Koran für Moslems, die Bibel für Christen und Homer für die antiken Griechen. Der Religionsbegriff—und daher die Auffassung von Theologie–wird radikal funktionalisiert: Religion wird über ihre Funktion (dem Leben von Menschen Form, Wert und Richtung zu geben) definiert, für die es verschiedene Realisierungen geben kann. Theologie wird als Hermeneutik des Daseins anhand einer zu (re-)konstruierenden Tradition von Frauenkultur aufgefaßt. Tradition ist in diesem Modell keine nicht-abgeschlossene Vergangenheit, wie in Modell 1, auch keine abgeschlossene Gegenwart, wie in Modell 2, sondern ein Auftrag: das, was (noch) zu überliefern ist. Mit der (Re-)Konstruktion einer Frauentradition wird eine "Erfahrungsgeschichte" geschrieben, auf die auch die Leserin, die die kanonischen Texte von Kirche und Theologie als Frau lesen will, sich berufen kann.[4] In diesem Sinne sind die beiden ersten Lesemodelle vom dritten abhängig, und ist die Bildung eines weiblichen Kanons eine neue Art und Weise, Literatur zu interpretieren.

Wenn wir die ersten drei Leseweisen als eine fortlaufende Geschichte lesen, so sehen wir, wie die Leserin sich in Bewegung setzt, von einem theologischen Diskurs her, hin zu einem neuen Gebiet von Wahlmöglichkeiten. Bei der ersten Leseweise steht sie noch mitten im theologischen Diskurs. Indem sie den Blick auf die in diesem Diskurs ins Abseits gedrängten Elemente richtet, versucht sie in dem Bild, das hierin von der christlichen Glaubenstradition gezeichnet wird, eine Verlagerung der Schärfenebene zu erreichen und als logische Fortsetzung dieser Verlagerung ein "Wachstum" dieser Tradition zu stimulieren. Bei der zweiten Leseweise geht sie mit einem Bein über den theologischen Diskurs hinaus, um von außen her eine klarere Sicht auf das zu erhalten, was sich drinnen abspielt. Wenn sie bei der dritten Leseweise auch das zweite Bein nachzieht, entwickelt sich eine Bewegung, die jedoch dadurch zu stagnieren droht, daß das Lesen als Frau nicht problematisiert wird. Im vierten Lesemodell wird angestrebt, diese Bewegung in Gang zu halten.

Das vierte Lesemodell: multiperspektivisches Lesen.

Es ist nicht einfach, das vierte Lesemodell schematisch darzustellen. Die Schwierigkeit ist, eine Bewegung und damit das Verlassen eines monoperspektivischen Standpunkts, bildlich darzustellen. Eine Darstellung dieses Modells als Abfolge der in den vorigen Kapiteln geschilderten

---

4 Ich verweise hier auf die Problematik einer Inanspruchnahme der Erfahrung der LeserIn, so wie diese zusammenfassend in Jonathan Culler, *On Deconstruction*, besprochen wird. *Theory and Criticism after Structuralism* (London: Melbourne and Henley 1983) 43-64. Wie auch Maaike Meijer in *De Lust tot Lezen. Nederlandse dichteressen en het literaire systeem* (Amsterdam: Van Gennep 1988) 232 [Die Lust zum Lesen. Niederländische Dichterinnen und das literarische System] erklärt, steht diese Erfahrung nicht von vornherein zur Verfügung: "Sie ist nicht schon vor dem Text da, sondern ist selbst eine von früheren Texten gebildete, von einer gesellschaftlichen Gruppe konstruierte *Geschichte*".

Modelle geht in die richtige Richtung. Der in Modell 3 vorgelegte neue Kanon wird seinerseits kritisch betrachtet. Vor dem Hintergrund anderer Kontexte von (Frauen-)Literatur wird der Anspruch angefochten, daß die darin gesammelte (Frauen-)Literatur den Erfahrungen von Frauen im allgemeinen (Modell 2) Form, Wert und Richtung gebe. Dies kann dann entweder zu einer Verlagerung innerhalb dieses Kanons (Modell 1) oder zu einer ganz neuen Auswahl (Modell 3) führen, die dann wiederum kritisch betrachtet wird, usw. Ein Problem bei dieser Darstellung des vierten Modells als einer Reihe aufeinanderfolgender Modelle ist jedoch, daß sie monoperspektivisch bleibt. Wie in einem Film ziehen die Bilder eins nach dem anderen vorbei. Dies erzeugt eine Illusion von Bewegung. Die einzelnen Bilder werden jedoch als Standardfotos von einem festen Punkt aus aufgenommen. Diese Darstellung kann daher dem Aspekt nicht gerecht werden, daß der Leser in Bewegung ist, soweit diese Bewegungen nicht nur linear sind, sondern auch zirkulär, und soweit sie in der Zeit nicht nur aufeinanderfolgen, sondern auch, in der Form von Erinnerungen, ein bestimmtes Maß an Gleichzeitigkeit aufweisen.

In den Fotocollagen des englischen bildenden Künstlers David Hockney sehe ich dagegen eine perfekte Visualisierung des vierten Lesemodells. Ich reproduziere ein Foto eines der sogenannten "joiners", dem im französischen *Vogue* vom Dezember 1985 erschienenen "Place Furstenberg", um anschließend anhand der Philosophie, die dieser Art des Fotografierens zugrunde liegt, zu versuchen, die Theorie des vierten Lesemodells präziser zu formulieren.[5] Das Original von Hockneys "Place Furstenberg" läßt sich, obwohl es aus Fotos zusammengestellt ist, schwer in einem Foto einfangen. Der aus dem Übereinanderkleben von Fotos resultierende geschichtete Aufbau der Darstellung geht verloren.[6] Die

5 Ich stütze mich dabei auf das 1988 erschienene Buch *Hockney on Photography. Conversations with Paul Joyce* (London: Jonathan Cape Ltd. 1988), in dem die Gespräche, die Joyce im Laufe eines Zeitraums von fünf Jahren mit Hockney führte, niedergelegt sind.

6 "The later pictures, like the "Place Furstenberg", would be very, very hard to make copies of. That one is thickly layered with photographs, sometimes one on top of another because I changed it so much. In a way, even that physicality gives it something which you feel. Before there might have been simple overlaps, now they are much more complex. We've decided not to let anyone else reproduce it, but to make big Cibachrome copies so that it's clearly a photograph of a photograph. So there's only one now, and I'll keep it, that's the solution" (Joyce, *Hockney on Photography*, 119).

Place Furstenberg, Paris, August 7,8 and 9, 1985
(photographic collage, © David Hockney, reproduced with permission)

Aufnahmen für diesen Joiner dauerten beinahe vier Tage, und alle in diesem Zeitraum aufgenommenen Fotos wurden darin verarbeitet, aufgrund des Gedankens, daß durch das Weglassen eines Fotos der zeitliche Ablauf gestört und damit die Wirklichkeit manipuliert würde. Die Collage würde zu einer Montage und die Darstellung unscharf:

> To me cutting only leads to *un*clarity. What did you cut out? Why did you cut it out? Something you didn't like was there, you wanted a sharp edge. There are ways to do it without cutting which would keep the flow of time, keep it moving around and, therefore, the eye moving around. If you cut it the eye will stop or at least have to pause.[7]

7 Joyce, *Hockney on Photography* (as note 5), 94.

Hockneys erste Joiner entstanden mehr oder weniger zufällig, aus Unzufriedenheit über die Ergebnisse der Weitwinkel-Fotografie. Im Grunde verwendet er die Kamera in diesem fotografischen Werk als ein Zeicheninstrument. Innerhalb einer allgemeinen Perspektive sind die Joiner multiperspektivisch. Das heißt, solange der Betrachter stillsitzt, hat er das Gefühl einer einzigen Perspektive, aber sobald er sich bewegt, gibt es deren viele; und man muß sich bewegen, um sie sich ansehen zu können. Die Augenmuskeln lassen es einfach nicht zu, sie in einem Blick zu erfassen: "In fact, the closer things are to us, the more our eyes have to move. With the joiners the effect is a very strong one of putting you into the place. It gives you a much greater feeling of being there."[8] Man sieht sich nicht schnell an ihnen satt: "the longer you look, actually, the more you create space in your head because you're converting time to space."[9] Sie brechen die Gesetze der Perspektive, die wir kennen, und sind stark vom Kubismus der Malerei und insbesondere dem Werk Pablo Picassos inspiriert. Joyce erkennt im fotografischem Werk Hockneys einen revolutionären Kern, "a moving consciousness at war with established notions of photographic 'realism'."[10]

Steht die Fotografie im Ruf, realistisch zu sein, und wird der Kubismus als Anfang der abstrakten Malerei gesehen, so kehrt Hockney dieses Verhältnis um: Der Kubismus ist ein Versuch, die Welt so, wie sie wirklich ist, abzubilden, und die Fotografie ist eine Abstraktion der Wirklichkeit. In der westlichen Kunst hat die Kamera mehr als 350 Jahre lang unsere Art des Sehens beherrscht. Die Camera obscura wurde ca. 1580 entdeckt, und viele Renaissance-Maler verwendeten sie. Hockney vergleicht die von der Kamera beeinflußte Art des Sehens damit, mit einem Auge durch ein Fenster zu blicken, oder mit einem Sehen im Korsett. Der Vorteil liegt in der Tiefenwirkung (Perspektive), aber das Zeiterlebnis geht verloren:

> Perspective is a theoretical abstraction that was worked out in the fifteenth century. It suddenly altered pictures: it gave a strong illusion of depth; it lost something and gained something. At first the gain was thrilling, but slowly, very slowly, we became aware of what had been lost. That loss was the depiction of the passing of time. We thought this way of looking was so true that

8 *Ibid.*, 82-83.

9 *Ibid.*, 113.

10 *Ibid.*, 9.

> when the photograph came along it seemed to confirm perspective. Of course, it was going to confirm perspective because it was exactly the same way of looking, from one central point with one eye fixed in time.[11]

Perspektive ist von einem festen, aber zugleich fiktiven Punkt abhängig: "if you try to walk up that point you'd never get there, it's like the end of the rainbow!"[12] Die Umkehrung dieser alten "one point perspective" hat in Hockneys Sicht auch theologische Konsequenzen:

> In the old perspective you are totally rigid. The furthest point from you is theoretically infinity, which means that if the infinite is God, it's always a long way away. You never get there. One hundred per cent of our images in the world are like that. When you reverse the perspective, that point is movement, you're moving. Infinity then is everywhere, including in you, which is far more interesting theologically, isn't it? God is then within us, and actually we are a part of God.[13]

Es geht nicht darum, daß wir nicht alles perspektivisch sehen. Wir sehen alles perspektivisch, aber nicht mit nur einem Auge und in einem Augenaufschlag. Hockney kritisiert an einer monoperspektivischen Art des Sehens sowohl, daß sie primitive Bilder ergibt, als auch, daß sie für uns schädlich ist. Primitiv ist zum Beispiel, die Begrenztheit der Schärfenebene in Fotos; die Unmöglichkeit, verschiedene Objekte in unterschiedlichem Abstand zum Objektiv scharf abzubilden. Schädlich ist, daß mit der Vorspiegelung eines neutralen Standpunkts und eines objektiven Zuschauers die Rolle des Betrachters vollständig verdrängt wird: "In order to give the feeling of objects in space, they take away your body, and you become a theoretical point. It must be doing damage to us."[14] Was die Joiners interessant macht, ist, daß sie das Thema behandeln, wie wir etwas sehen, und nicht einen Punkt in der Kamera, der etwas sieht. In diesem Sinne kommen sie näher an die Wirklichkeit unserer Erfahrungen heran. Wie kubistische Malereien sind sie bestrebt, unseren Bewegungen in Raum und Zeit gerecht zu werden und damit unserem Lebendigsein. Wenn Picasso zum Beispiel ein Gesicht malt und dabei zugleich verschiedene Seiten des Gesichts zeigt, so berücksichtigt er die Bewegungen dieses Gesichts und die des Betrachters zu diesem Gesicht. Zu keinem Zeit-

---

11 *Ibid.*, 34

12 *Ibid.*, 101.

13 *Ibid.*, 109.

14 (Joyce, *Hockney on Photography* (as note 5), 123.

punkt sieht ein Gesicht, wenn die Bewegung angehalten wird, so aus, aber dennoch muß, so Hockney, das Gesicht in unserem Kopf so aussehen, besonders im nachhinein. Mit seinen Erinnerungsbildern bezieht Picasso den Betrachter und sich selbst als Betrachter mit in das Bild ein. Wenn man von etwas zugleich Vorder- und Rückseite sehen kann, bedeutet dies, daß man als Betrachter im Bild enthalten ist. Man ist kein Voyeur, der aus einem Abstand zusieht, sondern ein Teilnehmer.

In *Canon en Keuze* habe ich durch eine paraphrasierende Erläuterung von Richs *Twenty-One Love Poems* ein bestimmtes Lesemodell vorgestellt. Das war möglich, weil dieser Zyklus multiperspektivisch ist. Die eine Erkenntnis über die Gedichte kompliziert die andere, aber wischt sie nicht weg. Die ersten drei Lesemodelle sind jedoch jedes für sich monoperspektivisch, in dem Sinne, daß der Leser von einem einmal eingenommenen Standpunkt aus bestimmten Texten Autorität und Bedeutung beimißt. Insoweit diese Standpunkte von den in der Theologiegeschichte eingenommenen Standpunkten abweichen, können von dort aus neue Texte und Bedeutungen ans Licht gebracht werden. Indem sie dies tun und indem sie den eigenen Standpunkt reflektierend begründen, schaffen sie mehr Klarheit über die gängigen Standpunkte und zeigen, daß diese genauso monoperspektivisch und keineswegs neutral sind. Auch das vierte Modell des Lesens als Frau und als Theologin erhebt weder einen Anspruch auf Neutralität, noch strebt es Neutralität an. Im Gegensatz zu den ersten drei Modellen berücksichtigt das vierte Modell jedoch, daß die Leserin in Bewegung ist. Die Leserin steht nicht im Mittelpunkt einer interpretierenden Gemeinschaft, sondern bewegt sich, ihre eigenen Kreise ziehend, in verschiedenen Umfeldern. Sie kollidiert dabei mit Texten, die darin als heilige Bücher gehandelt werden. Diese Bücher verändern sie oder lassen sie kalt. Sie ist Frau, aber dauerhaft auf der Suche nach der Frau, die sie sein will; sie ist Theologin, im theologischen Diskurs geschult, aber nicht auf ihn beschränkt. Theologie bleibt in dem vierten Modell eine Hermeneutik des Daseins, und genausowenig wie in den vorangehenden Modellen spielt diese Hermeneutik sich in einem luftleeren Raum ab. Der Traditionsbegriff erhält jedoch wieder eine andere Besetzung. In den ersten beiden Modellen ist Tradition das, was von einer bestimmten Gemeinschaft als glaubwürdig überliefert wurde und von den Erben dieser Tradition angepaßt und ausgebaut werden muß. Im dritten Modell ist Tradition das, was eine bestimmte Gemeinschaft in der Gegenwart als verbindend und inspirierend erlebt und daher in einer oft schon vergessenen Vergangenheit aufspürt. Im vierten Modell ist es beides, und mehr als nur das. Die Erkenntnis, daß es nebeneinander und gegenüber einander verschiedene Traditionen gibt, führt hier nicht nur zu einer pflichtgemäßen Relativierung der "eigenen" Tradition, sondern auch zu einer Suche nach Berührungspunkten und neuen, komplexeren Wahrheiten. Einerseits führt dieses Modell zu Auflösungserscheinungen: Die Beweglichkeit der Leserin greift die Grenzen der interpretierenden Gemeinschaften an. Andererseits birgt dieses Modell, indem es für Berührung und Begegnung offensteht, das Versprechen eines universelleren—da pluralistischen—Kanons in sich.

Kriterien der Textauswahl

Alle feministischen Textsammlungen und Leseansätze sind bestrebt, eine Änderung im theologischen Diskurs zu bewirken, und in der Begründung dieser Änderungen spielt eine Berufung auf die Funktion, die Theologie zu erfüllen beansprucht, eine herausragende Rolle. In den ersten beiden Modellen liegt das Schwergewicht auf der funktionalen Komponente in einer Definition der Theologie als "einer Hermeneutik des Daseins mit Hilfe einer bestimmten—in unserem Fall christlichen—Tradition". Im dritten Modell werden Funktionen auf einem höheren Abstraktionsniveau bestimmt, nicht im Rahmen einer bestimmten religiösen Tradition.

Wer gemäß dem zweiten Lesemodell liest, nimmt für sich die Rolle einer externen Expertin in Anspruch: Sind theologische Entwürfe (für bestimmte Frauen) geeignet, ihre Aufgabe zu erfüllen, nämlich dem Leben von Menschen Form, Wert und Richtung zu geben? Dieser funktionale Ansatz, ermöglicht es, Kriterien zu entwickeln, um Texte auf ihre theologische (Ir-)Relevanz hin zu untersuchen. Funktionen etablieren Kriterien.

In meiner Formulierung der Kriterien für eine Textauswahl benutze ich die von Jan van Luxemburg, Mieke Bal und Willem Weststeijn dargestellte Einteilung.[15] Diese Einteilung beruht auf den verschiedenen Kontexten, in denen man einen Text betrachten kann: 1) in Beziehung zur LeserIn (Emotivitätskriterien); 2) in Beziehung zur Wirklichkeit (Realismuskriterium und kognitive Kriterien); 3) in Beziehung zu den persönlichen Auffassungen der LeserIn (Meinungskriterien); 4) in Bezie-

15 Jan van Luxemburg, Mieke Bal und Willem Weststeijn, *Inleiding in de Literatuurwetenschap* [Einführung in die Literaturwissenschaft] (Muiderberg: Coutinho 1982) in einem Absatz über Kriterien bei Werturteilen.

hung zu sich selbst (textinhärente Kriterien) ; 5) in Beziehung zu anderen Texten (Traditionskriterien) und 6) in Beziehung zur AutorIn.

Funktionen etablieren Kriterien: "Verschiedene Funktionen ergeben andere Kriterien oder eine andere Hierarchie der verwendeten Kriterien."[16] Die Funktion, die Texte in einer Hermeneutik des Daseins erfüllen sollen, habe ich damit umschrieben, daß sie dem Leben von Menschen Form, Wert und Richtung geben. Die Forderung, daß ein Text menschlichen Erfahrungen Form gibt, macht das Realismuskriterium relevant: "ein Werk ist gut, wenn es die Wirklichkeit richtig, vollständig oder typisch abbildet."[17] Die Forderung, daß ein Text menschlichen Erfahrungen Wert gibt, führt auf Emotivitätskriterien. Die Forderung, daß ein Text menschlichen Erfahrungen Richtung gibt, führt auf politische, religiöse und moralische Kriterien (Meinungskriterien).[18]

Um eine Begegnung dieser verschiedenen Traditionen zu fördern, überwiegen im vierten Lesemodell diese funktionalen Kriterien und textinhärente Kriterien. Kriterien, die sich mit der Beziehung Text-Autor und Text-Texte (Traditionskriterien) beschäftigen, werden dadurch nicht als irrelevant beiseite geschoben. Die Begründung einer Textauswahl auf der Grundlage dieser Kriterien ist hier jedoch vor allem als Erklärung des Kontexts zu sehen, in dem die erstgenannten Kriterien zur Geltung kommen.

Ganz vorläufig möchte ich im folgenden einige Kriterien vorstellen. Einerseits sind sie eine Begründung meiner Auswahl der Twenty-One Love Poems in *Canon en Keuze*. Umgekehrt ist meine Wahl von Kriterien zur Textauswahl auch das Ergebnis meiner Deutung dieser (und anderer) Poesie. Um mit Annette Kolodny zu sprechen:

---

16 *Ibid.*, 82.

17 *Ibid.*, 182.

18 Die Art und Weise, in der in der genannten *Inleiding in de Literatuurwetenschap* [Einleitung in die Literaturwissenschaft] diese unter einen gemeinsamen Nenner gebrachten Kriterien beschrieben werden, unterstellt eine Auffassung von Politik, Moral und Religion als System mehr oder weniger fester Überzeugungen: "Ein Werk ist gut, wenn es gemäß den Wünschen des Kritikers Stellung bezieht oder wenn es, eventuell ohne daß der der Autor dies wollte, eine vom Kritiker für wichtig gehaltene Situation belegt" (Luxemburg, *Inleiding* 83). Wenn man von Literatur erwartet, daß sie Richtungen aufzeigt, kann man es jedoch auch als bedeutsam ansehen, daß eine neue Perspektive geboten wird. Dies ist nur dann möglich, wenn es ein gewisses Maß an Diskontinuität zwischen Text undLeserIn gibt.

> (...) we read well, and with pleasure, what we already know how to read; and what we know how to read is to a large extent dependent upon what we have already read (works from which we developed our expectations and learned our interpretative strategies). What we then choose to read—and by extension, teach and thereby "canonize"—usually follows upon our previous reading.[19]

Emotivitätskriterium: Intensität.

Bei Emotivitätskriterien geht es um die Beziehung Text-LeserIn. Sie beschreiben die erwünschte Wirkung eines Texts auf die LeserIn. Bei der Beurteilung eines Texts kommt die LeserIn an zwei Momenten mit ins Spiel. Zuallererst ist die Auswählende selbst LeserIn. Ihre Subjektivität bestimmt die Bewertung, auch die Bewertung aufgrund anderer Kriterien als Emotivitätskriterien.[20] Zum zweiten hat die Auswählende bei der Textauswahl eine bestimmte (fiktive oder wirkliche) Gruppe von LeserInnen im Auge.

Es ist schwierig, die LeserInnengruppe zu umschreiben, auf die man sich im vierten Lesemodell richtet. Die Auswählende folgt den eigenen Vorlieben, in der Hoffnung, daß diese von vielen geteilt werden. Da und insoweit sie jedoch kein vollkommen einmaliges Individuum ist, sondern, prosaisch gesagt, ein "Ort, an dem sozial-kulturelle Konstruktionen des Subjekts zusammenkommen"[21] werden diese Vorlieben in der Praxis vor allem von verwandten LeserInnen geteilt werden. Indem sie die Position oder Positionen, von denen aus sie liest, so ehrlich wie möglich explizit macht, gibt sie sowohl die Beschränkungen ihrer Auslegung zu erkennen als auch die Bereitschaft, diese Beschränkungen im Verlauf des Lesens zu überschreiten. Die Wirkung, die angestrebt wird und von der die Auswählende in der Rolle als LeserIn zeugt, ist ein Gefühl zu leben. Der Text

---

19 Annette Kolodny, "Dancing through the Minefield: Some Observations on the Theory, Practice and Politics of a Feminist Literary Criticism" in: Elaine Showalter, *The New Feminist Criticism. Essays on Women, Literature and Theory* (London: Virago 1985), 154.

20 Ein interessantes Beispiel ist die Beurteilung des biblischen Hohenlieds anhand der Strukturkriterien. Strukturkriterien behandeln den gewünschten Aufbau, den Zusammenhang und die Einheit (oder gerade den fragmentarischen Aufbau) eines Texts. Das Verständnis der tatsächlichen Struktur des Texts, unabhängig also von der damit verbundenen Beurteilung, variiert jedoch von Kritiker zu Kritiker (Francis Landy, *Paradoxes of Paradise. Identity and Difference in the Song of Songs*, Sheffield: Almond Press 1983, 36.

21 Meijer, *De Lust tot Lezen* (as note 4), 166.

vermittelt den Hauch der Verzückung, der Bewunderung und des Erstaunens, den wir hin und wieder erleben;[22] er bringt durcheinander, entführt und zerrüttet und de-automatisiert so die LeserIn;[23] er ermöglicht uns, "to *see* more, to *hear* more, to *feel* more."[24] Ich fasse diese angestrebte Wirkung unter dem Nenner "Intensität" zusammen.

Text-Wirklichkeits-Kriterium: die andere Wirklichkeit und die Wirklichkeit des anderen.

Die Worte "die andere Wirklichkeit und die Wirklichkeit des anderen" sind theologisch und ethisch mit Konnotationen aller denkbaren höheren und tieferen, besseren und gerechteren Wirklichkeiten beladen. Ich habe sie hier gewählt, um eine Sicht der Wirklichkeit zu beschreiben, die dem Verlassen eines monoperspektivischen Standpunkts inhärent ist. Ich gehe dabei davon aus, daß Texte eine Sicht der Wirklichkeit bieten. Texte geben der Wirklichkeit Bedeutung, die schon lange eine Bedeutung hat. Ebensowenig wie Fotos oder Malereien sind Texte - wissenschaftliche oder literarische - mehr oder weniger gelungene Abspiegelungen der Welt. Hockney nennt den Gedanken, daß man die Welt neu schaffen könne, naiv: "Where would you put it? Next to the whole world?"[25] Damit stellt er sich jedoch keineswegs auf einen "antirealistischen" Standpunkt. Den Gedanken, daß wir aus einem enttäuschen Glauben daran, die Wirklichkeit neu schaffen zu können, die Schlußfolgerung ziehen sollten, daß wir unsere Aufmerksamkeit am besten ganz vom Sehen der Wirklichkeit ab- und zur Analyse von Sehprozessen hinwenden sollten, bezeichnet er selbst als intellektuelle Korruption.[26]

---

22 Salman Rushdie, *Imaginary Homelands. Essays and criticism 1981-1991* (London: Granta Books, 1991), 63.

23 Meijer, *De Lust tot Lezen* (as note 4), 63.

24 Susan Sontag, *Against Interpretation* (London: André Deutsch, 1987), 14.

25 Joyce, *Hockney on Photography* (as note 5), 49.

26 "The intellectual corruption is a complicated issue, but generally there was a belief that an art that was representational was inferior. Somehow people believed there had been a progress which meant we'd moved on from mere representation to a truer definition of art. The idea seemed naive to me. Their theory suggested we had no more to learn from looking at nature than simply seeing what the process of looking was like. It *couldn't* be true" *Ibid.*, 74.

Sprache und andere Zeichen sind lebensnotwendig, da sie es uns ermöglichen, in eine Beziehung zu einer anderen Wirklichkeit und der Wirklichkeit des anderen zu treten. Daraus ergibt sich die Verantwortung, die Hockney und Rich als Maler bzw. als Dichterin empfinden: "If we are to change our world view, images have to change;"[27] "The necessity of poetry has to be stated over and over, but only to those who have reason to fear its power, or those who still believe that language is 'only words' and that an old language is good enough for our descriptions of the world we are trying to transform."[28]

Konventionelle Vorstellungen der Wirklichkeit erweisen sich oft als weniger realistisch und eher typisch. Wenn man jedoch *weiter* hinsieht, so tritt das Problem auf, das Rich in "Split at the Root" formuliert:

> Sometimes I feel I have seen too long from too many disconnected angles: white, Jewish, anti-Semite, racist, anti-racist, once married, lesbian, middle class, feminist, exmatriate southerner, *split at the root*—that I will never bring them whole. (...) I feel the tension as I think, make notes: *If you really look at the one reality, the other will waver and disperse*.[29]

Lesetheoretisch kann dieses Problem, daß eine Wirklichkeit verschwimmt, wenn man eine andere genau betrachtet, erhellt, aber nicht gelöst werden, indem wir den Leser "aufteilen" (der Leser als Weiße, als Jüdin usw.). Wir können einer Lösung der Aufgabe, für neue Unterschiede, sowohl innerhalb als außerhalb des Lesers, Raum zu schaffen und "vorhandene" Unterschiede zu berücksichtigen, nur näherkommen, indem wir monoperspektivische Standpunkte verlassen, ohne sie zu vergessen. Die eigenen Identitäten als LeserInnen aufs Spiel zu setzen macht das Lesen nicht nur spannender und entspannend, sondern auch "echter", d.h. eindringlich und bedrohlich:

> PJ: (...) once you had a fixed perspective and a lens the world seemed to be ordered, it must have seemed they made order out of chaos, and that's why we keep returning to that notion. We don't like chaos, we prefer order. DH: Yes, that's it, but the perspective that gave order to them will not give order to us. We have to make another order.[30]

---

27 *Ibid.*, 157.

28 Adrienne Rich, *On Lies, Secrets and Silences: Selected Prose 1966-1978* (New York: Norton 1979), 247.

29 Adrienne Rich, *Blood, Bread and Poetry. Selected Prose 1979-1985* (London: Virago 1987), 122.

30 Joyce, *Hockney on Photography* (as note 5), 108.

Die Ordnung einer anderen Ordnung, auf die Hockney abzielt, ist nicht übersichtlich. Das Sehen dieser Ordnung ist von einer bestimmten Art des Sehens abhängig, die mit innerer Beteiligung und Bewegung zu tun hat. Wie Rich in ihren "Notes toward a Politics of Location" schreibt: "I need to move outward from the base and center of my feelings, but with a corrective sense that my feelings are not *the* center of feminism."[31] Der Kontext dieses Zitats ist eine Beschreibung der weißen Rezeption schwarzer Frauenliteratur. Rich nimmt bei weißen Feministinnen eine Tendenz wahr, diese Literatur in eine gewisse Ecke zu drängen, indem sie sie lediglich als Kritik an weißem feministischem Rassismus oder als eine mögliche Bereicherung des weißen Feminismus lesen. Damit, so fährt sie fort, isolieren wir uns; was sie wiederum auf die Frage bringt, die sie beschäftigt: "Who is *we*?"[32] Das Verlassen monoperspektivischer Standpunkte bedeutet sowohl von der Komplexität unser eigenen Gefühle auszugehen als auch die Illusion aufzugeben, daß alles, was uns berührt, auch besonders an uns gerichtet sei. Die neue Ordnung, die wir so schaffen, die Ordnung, die aus uns "wir" macht, wird niemals stabil sein. Sie kommt und geht dort, wo in Begegnungen mit einer anderen Wirklichkeit und der Wirklichkeit des anderen die sich ändernde Wirklichkeit verständlich wird.

Meinungskriterien: Verbundenheit und Kraft

Bei Meinungskriterien geht es um die Beziehung zwischen einem Text und den Meinungen der LeserIn. Die Kriterien dieser Art, die ich vorstellen möchte, zielen nicht so sehr darauf ab, ob ein Text auf eine von der Kritikerin gewünschte Weise Stellung bezieht, und auch nicht darauf, ob er Patentrezepte anbietet, um unser Leben zu gestalten, sondern darauf, daß er die Wirklichkeit so beschreibt, daß wir uns davon berührt fühlen. Der Text muß sich auf unsere eigene Fähigkeit stützen, abzuwägen und Entscheidungen zu treffen. Negativ formuliert beinhaltet dieses Kriterium etwa die Ablehnung sexistischer oder rassistischer Texte, in denen Menschen eine bestimmte Identität aufgedrängt wird, die oft auch noch als minderwertig dargestellt wird.

---

31 Rich, *Blood, Bread and Poetry* (as note 29), 231.

32 *Ibid.*

Die Formulierung Verbundenheit und Kraft habe ich den Fragen entnommen, die Rich im dritten Gedicht ihres Bündels *Sources* stellt:

Whith whom do you believe your lot is cast?
From where does your strength come?

I think somehow, somewhere
every poem of mine must repeat those questions

which are not the same. There is a whom, a where
that is not chosen that is given and sometimes falsely given

in the beginning we grasp whatever we can
to survive[33]

Die Frage "With whom do you believe your lot is cast?" fragt sowohl nach dem Schicksal und dem Zufall als auch nach empfundenen und gewählten Parteinahmen. Die Frage "From where does your strength come, you Southern Jew?/ Split at the root, raised in a castle of air?" drängt sich in Sources III auf, nachdem sie in Sources II schon beantwortet ist:

I refuse to become a seeker for cures
Everything that has ever
helped me has come through what already
lay stored in me. Old things, diffuse, unnamed, lie strong
across my heart.
This is from where
my strength comes, even when I miss my strength
even when it turns on me
like a violent master.

Die Kraft von *Sources* liegt darin, daß es sich die interne Dynamik dieser Fragen zunutze macht. In der Frage "*With whom do you believe your lot is cast*" liegt die Antwort auf die Frage "*From where does your strength come*". Die Frage "*From where does your strength come*" macht den Unterschied in der Frage "*With whom do you believe your lot is cast*" produktiv. Dieser Unterschied, erklärt mit den Worten "There is a *whom*, a *where*/ that is not chosen that is given", bleibt in Bewegung. Was Rich als "falsely given" ablehnt, ist sowohl eine Trennung als auch ein heiliger Verbund dessen, was gegeben und was gewählt ist.

In ihrem Versuch, das gespaltene Bewußtsein, in dem sie aufgewachsen ist, zu heilen, wirft Rich ihr Schicksal nicht ab, sondern sie untersucht es auf verborgene Möglichkeiten hin. Indem sie verschiedene Formen der

33 Adrienne Rich, *Sources* (California: Heyeck Press 1983) 12.

Schicksalsverbundenheit erkennt und untersucht, schafft sie eine empfindsame und intelligente Form der emotionalen Bindung, die ich, wenn ich Rich paraphrasiere, als "faithful without a faith" umschreiben würde.[34]

Textinhärente Kriterien: Bewegung und Klarheit.

Diese Besetzung textinhärenter Kriterien drückt eine Bevorzugung von Texten aus, die Bewegung ausdrücken, ohne daß dies auf Kosten der Klarheit geht. Hierzu kann ich wiederum Hockney zitieren, der über seine fotografischen Arbeiten bemerkt: "There's no way you can see the joiners all at once. It's impossible. Your eyes won't let you. The muscles won't let you. So you get a feeling of life looking at them (...) You start moving around, you are forced to look at every piece of it: you couldn't do that if the pictures weren't clear. (...) Finally, the joiners are about clarity, which is a quality I'm always striving for. It's something you do have to strive for. Shapes do change when you move: they are fluid really, even though they seem solid."[35]

So wie in dem, was Hockney als Erinnerungsbild bezeichnet, bleibt in Texten, die die Kriterien "Klarheit" und "Bewegung" erfüllen, das Vorangehende weiter anwesend. Je konkreter Adrienne Rich wird, so bemerkt Gelpi, desto visueller wird ihre Poesie: "Poetry functions as the vehicle for seeing and for fixing what one comes to see. It is the camera with lens and focus, and poems are snapshots."[36] Allmählich wandelt sich jedoch ihre Sicht der Poesie als einer Kamera und von Gedichten als "Schnappschüssen", ohne daß sie dabei aber in einen abstrakten Formalismus zurückfällt. Ein Gedicht muß mehr sein als eine Momentaufnahme: "The poem as a snapshot is no longer enough: stasis is death."[37] Gelpi nimmt eine Tendenz zu längeren Sequenzen wahr; "a juxtaposition of images, spaced out on the page so that the sensibility can react and make connections". Als Beispiel dieser neuen Technik nennt er die erste Sequenz von "Shooting Script": "The effect is not a static list of images but a flow of interacting and mutually clarifying images: at once linear

---

34 "Because without a faith/ you are faithful (...)" (Rich, *Sources* XXIII).

35 Joyce, *Hockney on Photography* (as note 5), 61.

36 Barbara Gelpi-Charlesworth and Albert Gelpi, *Adrienne Rich's Poetry. Texts of the Poems, the Poet on her Work, Reviews and Criticism* (New York/ London: W.W. Norton & Co., 1975), 135.

37 *Ibid.*, 143.

and encircling."[38] Ihre Gedichte wandeln sich von Momentaufnahmen in "Momente der Veränderung": "the moment of change is the only poem."[39] Rich beschreibt diese Verschiebung wie folgt:

> Without for one moment turning my back on conscious choice and selection, I have been increasingly willing to let the unconscious offer its materials, to listen to more than the one voice of a single idea. Perhaps a simple way of putting it would be to say that instead of poems *about* experiences I am getting poems that *are* experiences, that contribute to my knowledge and my emotional life even while they reflect and assimilate it. In my earlier poems I told you, as precisely and eloquently as I knew how, about something; in the more recent poems something is happening, something has happened to me and, if I have been a good parent to the poem, something will happen to you when you read it.[40]

Traditionskriterien: Re-vision.

Der Begriff Re-vision entstammt Richs Essay "When We Dead Awaken: Writing as Re-Vision": "Re-vision—the act of looking back, of seeing with fresh eyes, of entering an old text from a new critical direction—is for women more than a chapter in cultural history: it is an act of survival."[41] Re-vision als Kriterium für Textauswahl bedeutet, daß ein Text nicht danach beurteilt wird, in welcher bestimmten Texttradition er steht, sondern danach, in welchem Maße es der AutorIn gelingt, ein eigenes Verhältnis zu dieser Tradition zu entwickeln. Kraft zur Erneuerung oder gerade Treue zu einer bestimmten Tradition sind dabei weniger von Bedeutung als Kenntnis dieser Tradition und vor allem Freiheit gegenüber dieser Tradition. So schreibt Rich über die dominante literarische Tradition, die im akzeptierten literarischen Kanon verkörpert wird: "We need to know the writing of the past, and know it differently than we have ever known it; not to pass on a tradition but to break its hold over us."[42]

In dem Gedanken vom Schreiben als Revision liegt eine wichtige Revision des Begriffs Revision. Die Wörterbuchbedeutung von "revision" verschiebt sich von "überarbeitete Fassung (eines Buches)", "Änderung"

---

38 Gelpi, *Adrienne Rich's Poetry* (as note 36), 144. "Shooting Script" in Adrienne Rich, *The Will to Change: Poems 1968-1970* (New York: Norton, 1971), 51-67.

39 Rich, *The Will to Change* (as note 38), 49.

40 Gelpi, *Adrienne Rich's Poetry* (as note 36), 89.

41 Rich, *On Lies, Secrets and Silences* (as note 28), 35.

42 *Ibid.*

oder gar "Wiederholung" zum Schreiben als Neu-Betrachten, Neu-Benennen und dadurch Neu-Leben. In zunehmendem Maße wird Rich sich jedoch bewußt, wie unfrei sie in ihrem Schreiben ist. Sie entdeckt, daß ihre persönlichen Auffassungen weniger einmalig sind, als sie dachte: "My personal world view, which like so many young people I carried as a conviction of my own uniqueness, was not original with me, but was, rather, my untutored and half-conscious rendering of the facts of blood and bread, the social and political forces of my time and place."[43] Ihre Begegnung mit schwarzen Frauen und deren Literatur lehrt sie, daß "even our 'women's cultures' are rooted in some Western tradition."[44] Ihre konkreten Erfahrungen mit Unfreiheit bringen sie jedoch nicht dazu, das Verlangen nach Freiheit aufzugeben. Das nennt sie das Schlimmste, was sein könne: "the failure to want our freedom passionately enough".[45] Diese Erfahrungen bringen sie allerdings zu Zeiten und Orten zurück, zu Büchern und Bewegungen, Organisationen und Traditionen, die die verschiedenen Identitäten, die sie mit sich mitträgt, bestimmt haben.

Rich beschreibt diesen Schritt, der im dritten Lesemodell noch nicht berücksichtigt ist, als "moving into accountability, enlarging the range of accountability."[46] Während sie sich anfänglich noch als "Split at the root, neither Gentile nor Jew,/ Yankee nor Rebel" sieht,[47] tritt an die Stelle dieses "weder - noch" allmählich ein "sowohl - als auch". Als Schriftsteller fühlt sie die Verantwortung "to keep searching for teachers who can help me widen and deepen the sources and examine the ego that speaks in my poems—not for 'political correctness', but for ignorance, solipsism, laziness, dishonesty, automatic writing."[48] Man beachte, daß das Erweitern in diesem Zitat vor dem Vertiefen kommt. Sie gräbt nicht dort, wo auf alten Landkarten Quellen eingezeichnet sind, sondern dort, wo das Ego, das aus ihren Gedichten spricht, an die Grenzen stößt, die es überschreiten will.

---

43 Rich, *Blood, Bread and Poetry* (as note 29), 171.

44 *Ibid.*, 219.

45 Rich, *Twenty-One Love Poems,* (as note 2), poem VII.

46 Rich, *Blood, Bread and Poetry* (as note 29), 123.

47 Rich, *Sources* (as note 33), 39.

48 Rich, *Blood, Bread and Poetry* (as note 29), 187.

Kriterium über die AutorIn: Liebe

Das, was wir über das Geschlecht des Autors eines Texts wissen, über ihre Homo- oder Heterosexualität, ihre religiösen und politischen Überzeugungen, ihr Alter und ihre Kultur, ihre Farbe und Nationalität, bestimmt unvermeidlich unsere Auswahl bestimmter Texte mit, wie auch die Art und Weise, in der wir diese Texte lesen. Mit der Einführung von "Liebe" als Kriterium will ich ausdrücken, daß die dadurch gesetzten Beschränkungen real sind—auch Liebe hat einen stark konventionellen Aspekt—aber nicht alles bestimmend. Liebe ermöglicht manchmal, Grenzen zu überschreiten, und wenn wir unsere Liebe ernst nehmen, verpflichtet sie uns, unsere eigenen Wahrheiten anhand der Wahrheiten des anderen neu zu definieren.

Zum Schluß:

Gegen die Hinzufügung alternativer Texte und Traditionen als autonomer Quellen von Theologie wird der Einwand vorgebracht, daß dies zu Willkür führen würde. Wenn sich im Laufe der Zeit auch eine gewisse Gewöhnung an eine Pluralität an Interpretationen eingestellt hat, so stoßen die damit direkt zusammenhängenden Vorschläge zur Veränderung des Kanons unvermindert auf heftigen Protest. Der Schein von Einheit, den eine Vielzahl von Interpretationen derselben Texte noch bietet, wird radikal durchbrochen, wenn sich zeigt, daß andere Texte als heilige Texte gelesen werden können und die Bibel als Mickey Mouse. Für klassisch ausgebildete Theologen bedeutet dies nichts weniger als eine Identitätskrise. Dennoch bin ich der Ansicht, daß jeder Text, der innerhalb bestimmter Gruppierungen oder Bewegungen dem Leben von Menschen Form, Wert und Richtung gibt, theologisches Interesse verdient. Das erfordert eine Neudefinition von Theologie als einer Disziplin von Fragen und den Abschied von der Vorstellung einer privilegierten Sprache.

Mein in diesem Artikel präsentierter Vorschlag eines vierten Lesemodells ist ein Schritt in diese Richtung. Ich messe Projekten eines weiblichen Kanons (Modell 3) und Neuinterpretierungen der etablierten Kanons (die ersten beiden Modelle) weiter große Bedeutung bei. Ein weiblicher Kanon kann, indem er als Gegenmonopol von Texten fungiert, als Instrument zur Durchbrechung androzentrischer Kanons dienen. Zum zweiten ist ein Kanon bzw. die Herausbildung eines Kanons aus Kommunikationsgründen wichtig. Ohne Kanon, ohne gemeinsame Geschichten, keine Gemeinschaft.[49] Ich sehe einen Kanon als einen Rastplatz, an dem wir verschnaufen können, ein verführerischer Ort, aber ein "unmöglicher" Ort, um daran festzuhalten. Sobald die Suche nach einer eigenen Identität in eine Flucht in die Geborgenheit der eigenen Identität umschlägt, beschneiden wir die Möglichkeiten von Leben und Liebe unter uns. Die eigene emotionale Bindung an bestimmte Texte, ob dies nun Bibeltexte sind oder dieses Projekt eines weiblichen Kanons gesammelter Texte, führt bei denjenigen, die diese Texte als eine ein für allemal festgesetzte Vorgabe und für alle gültige Offenbarung beanspruchen, zu Stillstand und Isolation.

Von den im etablierten Kanon enthaltenen Texten wird häufig behauptet, daß wir um diese nicht herumkämen. Meine These ist, daß wir nicht darum herumkommen, einen Kanon zu bilden, daß wir aber sehr wohl wählen können, welche Texte wir darin aufnehmen wollen und welche nicht. Die Frage ist lediglich, wer wählt und aufgrund welcher Kriterien. In diesem Artikel habe ich—hinsichtlich der Quellen von Theologie—ansatzweise einige Kriterien zur Textauswahl formuliert. Es geht mir nicht darum, hierzu unter feministischen Theologen Übereinstimmung zu erreichen. An dem Gespräch über den Wert von Texten als Quelltexten von Theologie ist mir mehr gelegen als an dem Ergebnis. Meine Formulierungen provozieren hoffentlich neue und andere Formulierungen. Die Rubrizierung möglicher Kriterien zur Textauswahl in sechs Kategorien—die darauf hinweisen soll, daß jeder Text auf mehreren Niveaus beurteilt werden kann—kann hoffentlich dafür sorgen, daß das Gespräch nicht darin versandet, daß unvergleichbare Kriterien, etwa ästhetische und moralische, gegeneinander ausgespielt werden. Das Gespräch muß in Gang bleiben. Über Geschmack läßt sich streiten. Der Zweck dabei ist das, was Maaike Meijer in *De Lust tot Lezen* [Die Lust zum Lesen] (als Reaktion auf *The Resisting Reader* von Judith Fetterly) die Kultivierung der Lust zum Lesen nennt: "(...) die Kultivierung der Lust zum Lesen stärkt daher genauso die Verteidungsfähigkeit gegen Versuche kultureller Vergewaltigung wie eine sich widersetzende Lesehaltung. Geschmack, Qualitätsbewußtsein und Genuß führen zur

49 In einem Essay, in dem sie sich kritisch zu der Rolle äußert, die Kanons in Kirche und Theologie gespielt haben, weist Carol Christ auf diesen Aspekt von Kanons hin ("Heretics and Outsiders: The Struggle over Female Power in Western Religion" in *Soundings* 61 (1978) 3, 278).

Ablehnung dessen, was einem nicht gefällt. Sexueller Mißbrauch von Frauen wird von einem Klima erleichtert, in dem Frauen das Recht zur eigenen Lust abgesprochen wird. Das gilt auch für die Lust zum Lesen."[50]

Aus dem Niederländischen von Detlev Hauschildt

Abstracts

Jonneke BEKKENKAMP esquisse trois modèles permettant aux théologiennes féministes de choisir et d'interpréter les textes; elle y joint une description détaillée d'un quatrième modèle basé sur la philosophie de l'artiste britannique David Hockney. Les modèles se distinguent par le fait qu'ils s'adressent oui ou non à des lectrices spécifiquement féministes et théologiennes. Ce faisant, elle explore de nouveaux moyens pour évaluer la valeur des sources de la théologie et élabore des critères de sélection pour ces textes, critères basés sur la fonction qu'ils sont destinés à remplir.

Jonneke BEKKENKAMP sketches three models by which the feminist theologian may select and interpret texts and offers a detailed description of a fourth model based upon the philosophy of the British artist David Hockney. The models are differentiated in the extent to which they characterise the reader as feminist and theologian. She thereby seeks new ways of assessing the value of the source texts of theology and develops criteria for the selection of such source texts based upon the function which they are meant to fulfil.

Jonneke BEKKENKAMP ist Dozentin im Bereich Women´s Studies für Theologie und Literatur an der Universität von Amsterdam. Sie ist einer der Direktorinnen (Leiterinnen) des niederländischen Forschungsprogramms zu Körperlichkeit, Religion und Gender, das im Fachbereich für Theologie und Religionswissenschaft der Universität von Groningen angesiedelt ist.

50 Meijer, *De Lust tot Lezen* (as note 4), 14.

Elizabeth STUART

Experience and Tradition: Just Good Friends

Feminist theology, at least in the west, appears to be in some sort of crisis over the place of experience in its methodology. This is a serious situation because the defining characteristic of feminist theology has always been the centralising and privileging of women's experience. Charles Winquist has noted, 'the framing of a discourse is the enfranchisement of a voice. ... Liberation and revolution are often about voice, about being allowed to speak. The diverse politics of liberation are not just about politics. They are also about epistemology and, conversely, epistemology is always also about politics.'[1] In framing their theological discourse Christian feminists have endeavoured to enfranchise the voices of Christian women and have proclaimed the beginning of a theological revolution which will eventually result in the liberation of all. As always, this revolution is predicated upon the twin tasks of deconstruction and reconstruction. Feminist theology deconstructs patriarchal theology at least partly by exposing the lie of its objectivity. Indeed, it has been part of the general task of feminism to expose the fact that 'objectivity' is the name men give to their subjectivity. Men have placed their own experience at the heart of all their epistemology, including their theology, but concealed it under the mask of eternal, universal and divine truth.

The article which is widely regarded as having launched the modern feminist theology movement, Valerie Saiving's "The Human Situation," is a perfect example of this deconstruction/reconstruction approach which centralised women's experience.[2] Saiving drew attention to the way in which dominant Christian understandings of sin as self-centredness and pride did not actually reflect women's practice. On the contrary, she

---

1 Charles E. Winquist, *Desiring Theology* (Chicago: University of Chicago Press 1995), 50.

2 Valerie Saiving, 'The Human Situation: A Feminine View' in: Carol Christ and Judith Plaskow (eds.), *Womanspirit Rising: A Feminist Reader in Religion* (San Francisco: Harper and Row 1979), 25-42.

argued that under patriarchy women are largely deprived of any sense of self and if they sinned it was in a tendency to sacrifice one's self for others to the point of self-negation and in allowing oneself to be wrapped in a fog of triviality. Ever since, feminist theology has been engaged in the double task of unravelling patriarchal theology and weaving new theologies from the strands of women's experience. It has formed part of the new feminist epistemology, which has sought to transcend the dualities of patriarchal epistemology that pitted reason against emotion, objectivity against subjectivity, reality against fantasy and 'hard data' against 'soft data'.[3] Feminist theologians, like all feminist scholars, know that scholarship is 'passionate' and 'interested' and that this does not invalidate it but simply means that there are limits to the claims that can be made on the basis of it. Feminism has replaced the scientific model of epistemology, which places truth 'out there' as something to be discovered, with a creation epistemology. We create knowledge out of our experience, which is not simply to collapse the divine completely into our internal experience but to say that knowledge is created in the midst of human relationship—in betweenness, which is where, according to Scripture, God resides (I Samuel 20,23; Song of Songs 8,6). The divine is not trapped in the subjectivity of the individual but is always beyond and bigger than us and yet in the midst of the mess, muddle and pain of human relating. We create our knowledge of her out of our encounters with her and our creation is a constant, fluid movement for she is a God of surprises, a teasing, weaving, spiralling, dancing God or as R.S. Thomas has put it, 'such a fast God, always before us and leaving as we arrive.'[4]

We need to attempt to clarify exactly what is meant by 'women's experience' in this context, for feminist theologians have not always taken the trouble to explain this central tool. We are not talking about raw personal experience. Feminist theology is not simply a modified version of the Protestant principle of the truth and revelation of personal experience, although it has undoubtedly been influenced by this concept. Such a principle propels matters of faith and praxis into the purely private realm from which women have fought so hard and long to expel themselves; it rests on the myth of an autonomous selfhood which feminism has been con-

3 Liz Stanley and Sue Wise, *Breaking Out Again: Feminist Ontology and Epistemology* (London and New York: Routledge 1993), 60.

4 R.S. Thomas, 'Pilgrimages' in *Frequencies* (London: Macmillan 1978).

cerned to undermine. Also, as Linda Hogan has pointed out, 'Women's experience is a central resource certainly, but since it is basically fractured it requires interpretation, evaluation and critique. Feminists must be able to acknowledge and arbitrate among competing subjectivities, since women do not share a uniform experience or material reality. Thus some theoretical input is essential.'[5] This theory derives from women's personal experience and is itself constantly open to being challenged and reshaped by it. But when we talk about placing women's experience at the centre of feminist theology we are talking about experience which has already been reflected upon and therefore taken into the public realm of knowledge. It is women themselves who have reflected upon their experience and, to use imagery I adopted in my book *Just Good Friends*,[6] woven their threads of individual experience into a larger tapestry. When this is completed and we stand back from it there may have formed a pattern, a trail, a map which we can recognise as the shadow of the divine. Women's experience, even their individual personal experience is multifaceted, as Ellen Leonard has noted, 'By experience I include all that contributes to our situation, both our political and personal contexts and our near and distant histories.'[7] Pamela Dickey Young has divided women's experience into five categories: bodily experience, socialised experience (the experience of being made into a 'woman' by society with its particular construction of femininity), feminist experience, which is a response to and radical questioning of socialised experience, historical experience, i.e. the recovery of women's history, and individual experience.[8] Each of these has proved to be a rich seam for theological reflection and for a while the category of women's experience was unproblematic.

There was some early debate about the origins of women's experience as a distinctive reality—did it reside in an essential difference from men or was it the product of social construction? Most feminist theolo-

5 Linda Hogan, *From Women's Experience to Feminist Theology* (Sheffield: Sheffield Academic Press 1995), 17.

6 Elizabeth Stuart, *Just Good Friends: Towards A Lesbian and Gay Theology of Relationships* (London: Mowbray 1995).

7 Ellen Leonard, 'Experience as a Source for Theology: A Canadian and Feminist Perspective' in: *SR* 19.2 (1990), 143.

8 Pamela Dickey Young, *Feminist Theology/Christian Theology: In Search of Method* (Minneapolis: Fortress Press 1990), 53-69.

gians eventually opted for the latter explanation and the shift is particularly perceptible if we compare Saiving's article with Judith Plaskow's reflections upon the subject of sin published twenty years later.[9] Interestingly the pendulum has since begun to swing back a little, with the realisation that feminism may have unconsciously bought into the nature/culture and body/mind dualisms and, by embracing the social constructionist view as a way of avoiding the pitfalls of a 'biology is destiny' approach, in the process downplayed the importance of the body which is a source of knowledge which feminists have been keen to reclaim. Women's difference from men is now coming to be understood to reside in a much more complex dialectical relationship between body and society.[10] From the beginning, feminist theologians also differed widely over the relative normativity/authority of women's experience in theology. Some, perhaps most prominent among them Elisabeth Schüssler Fiorenza, affirm the absolute normativity of women's experience. Only texts, theologies and practices which contribute towards the liberation of women can be regarded as revelatory and only women-church—the global movement of feminist women and men who seek to realise in Church and society a discipleship of equals—has the authority to determine whether this is the case. Others seek to bring the norm of women's experience into creative partnership with other Christian norms, believing that a distinctively Christian feminist theology must appeal to more that just women's experience and recognise the normativity of some aspects of the tradition.[11] We will return to this question later because it has become caught up in a much more fundamental issue—the issue of difference. When Judith Plaskow set out to take Saiving's reflections further she was careful to identify Saiving's descriptions of women's 'sin' as a lack of sense of self and passivity with the experience of white, middle-class women in the west.[12] An awareness of the social construction of gender difference necessarily makes one aware that, because different societies construct and interpret gender differently,

---

9 Judith Plaskow, *Sex, Sin and Grace: Women's Experience in the Theologies of Reinhold Niebuhr and Paul Tillich* (Landham: University of America Press 1980).

10 Elaine Graham, *Making the Difference: Gender, Personhood and Theology* (London: Mowbray 1995), 123-46.

11 Young, *Feminist Theology/Christian Theology*, 71-114.

12 Plaskow, *Sex, Sin and Grace*.

women are going to have different experiences. However, despite this scrupulous attempt to acknowledge the situatedness of all experience and the reflection upon it that leads to knowledge, feminist theologians continued to believe that there was enough commonality in women's experience to continue to be able to speak out of it and weave theologies with it confident of its ability to 'ring true' and reflect and incarnate liberatory praxis of at least a sizeable number of women. It is this assumption that is now questionable and which might be seen to threaten the feminist theological project.

In the last twenty-five years we have witnessed and taken part in a rising cacophony of women's theological voices. This is beyond doubt an extraordinary grace, akin, as Rebecca Chapp has suggested, to the breaking out of tongues described in Acts 2.[13] Black, Asian, Hispanic, lesbian, and disabled women are among those who have claimed a theological voice, largely in reaction against the universalising tendencies of white, middle-class western women's theology in which they could not see their own reflection. Their strong, different voices have cracked the smooth wall of feminist theology. Ironically their voices have drawn our attention to their silence, to the extent and manner of the exclusion of various types of women's experience from feminist theology. It is a grace which also exposes a wound, 'a wound that does not bleed until it is made visible and marked as a silence.'[14] And in that silence a question forms itself: does this diversity and difference make 'women's experience' an ultimately meaningless category?

Postmodernism, which has provided feminism with the intellectual tools to challenge the subjectivity and historicism of patriarchal theology, also turns its spotlight on feminism itself. The postmodern insistence on the radical localisation of experience and knowledge may also render the whole concept of women's experience meaningless, even when it is precisely and scrupulously defined. As the autonomous self dies, our own individual experience may be all we are able to reflect upon with any integrity. As a white British woman whose family played a part in spreading and protecting British imperialism I do not want to be implicated in what Linda Hogan has identified as the theological

13 Rebecca Chopp, *The Power to Speak: Feminism, Language, God* (New York: Crossroad 1995).

14 Winquist, *Desiring Theology*, 53.

imperialism of universalising tendencies, assuming the normativity of my own experience.[15] Nor do I want to engage in the imperialist practice of appropriating other women's materials simply to legitimate my own work[16] -- a practice into which white feminists too easily fell with regards to womanist theology. I recently read two statements from competing candidates for a position of high office in a theological association. One was a male liberal scholar, the other a female feminist theologian. They both included only one quotation in their addresses. Each cited a (different) womanist theologian. Both candidates sought to legitimate themselves by nodding in the direction of difference and diversity. They both sought positions of power by standing on the back of a black woman, and failed to reflect on the absence of a black candidate for the position. We fall too easily into the trap of using another's work to pretend that we acknowledge diversity, whilst simply seeking to incorporate their view into ours.

But nor do I want to be silenced by the radical relativism of postmodernism, for whilst talking to oneself is undoubtedly in many circumstances a strategy of resistance and survival there is little point in wasting the earth's resources in talking to oneself out loud and in public through books, articles, media and teaching, if that is all one can do. If all we can do with our newfound voices is shout our own personal experience at one another we will simply render each other deaf and exhausted. The strategy of privileging the experience and reflection of particular groups of women is one response to these problems.

> The appeal, then, is to the experiences of particular women whose very existence is constantly thwarted and endangered. These women, conscious of their oppression and committed to liberation, have the most to contribute to the elaboration of strategies for radical social change. Their experiences are privileged at the theoretical as well as the practical level, in the elaboration of liberative discourses and of effective political action, precisely because they are

---

15 Hogan, *From Women's Experience to Feminist Theology*, 166.

16 Toinette M. Eugene, Ada Maria Isasi-Diaz, Kwok Pui-Lan, Judith Plaskow, Mary E. Hunt, Emilie Townes and Ellen M. Umansky, 'Appropriation and Reciprocity in Womanist/Mujerista/Feminist Work' in: *Journal of Feminist Studies in Religion* 8.2 (1992), 91-122.

> better able to envision a future radically different from the oppressive present from which they benefit the least, if at all.[17]

Privileging the experience of those who have had least voice would at first sight indeed be a noble theo-ethical response to the crisis of experience. There are two reasons for being suspicious of it. In what I think to be one of the most important books on and of feminist theology to be published in recent years (although I find it impossible to concur with some of the analysis) Angela West exposes and questions the assumption that seems to lie behind the epistemological privileging of the experience of certain women. This is that suffering purifies us and our knowledge and therefore it is possible to create a hierarchy of oppression in which white, middle-class, able-bodied, heterosexual women find themselves at the bottom (for a change) able only to offer knowledge severely tainted by relative privilege and power but able somehow to be saved by those whose terrible oppression has given them a place at the top of the hierarchy—a sort of reworking of the atonement story.[18] What West calls 'salvation by sisterhood' is really a further exploitation of our 'sisters', it is a plundering of the treasury of grace which they have laid up for us because of their excessive suffering. This is partly why white, middle-class, heterosexual women frantically search for women of difference to sit on committees or speak at conferences. But because we need their suffering we are paralysed in our attempt to relieve it. As West points out, few of us in the west would be willing to pay the real price of freedom and flourishing for women of the third world—dearer food, clothes and mortgages—and thus we are implicated in the system that produces their suffering. And I know from personal experience that even though feminist theology longs to hear the voice of lesbian women (at least in theory) very few feminist theologians who are not lesbians themselves are prepared to stand in public political solidarity with lesbian women. Whatever this is about it is not about mutuality.

West also questions whether suffering does produce purified experience, knowledge and behaviour. Her experience of the painful split among the community of women at Greenham Common makes her

17 Ada Maria Isasi-Diaz, 'Experience' in: Letty M. Russell and J. Shannon Clarkson (eds.), *Dictionary of Feminist Theologies* (London: Mowbray 1996), 94.

18 Angela West, *Deadly Innocence: Feminism and the Mythology of Sin* (London: Mowbray 1995), 162-9.

doubtful. My own experience of working among groups of lesbian and gay Christians makes me extremely sceptical, because whilst some superb work is done and some wonderful reflection woven, there is always a great deal of internal confusion, pain and self-destructive behaviour. We are all locked in the structures of sin. Epistemological privileging also does not generally work because privileging can be a way of ignoring. Linda Bellos, the British black, lesbian socialist, made an impassioned plea at a recent conference for an equal voice, not a privileged voice, because she felt that to be privileged was more often than not to be put on a pedestal too high for anyone to really hear and see. What is needed, she argued, is real mutual, reciprocal engagement. Whilst at times, therefore, it might be vitally important that some shut up in order that the voices of others might be heard (something that is also pricey—how many of us would be prepared to return our publishing contracts, give up our teaching posts, refuse invitations in order that the voices of women different from us would have a chance to be heard?) claiming epistemological privilege for certain voices is fraught with difficulties.

But is mutual, reciprocal engagement possible or does the recognition of historicism and subjectivity render us incapable of speaking at all? Are we paralysed by the possibility of the 'ah but' that waits to pounce on every sentence we speak or write? Are we to be trapped forever in the epistemological foyer that Charles Winquist identifies, 'Every definition of thinking becomes problematic because its privilege will always be contested. There is the knot. We are always in the foyer . . .'[19]

On a purely academic level theological aphasia could easily be induced in a womanist, mujerista, Asian, lesbian or disabled feminist theologian acutely conscious of difference. For it is not only privileged women who have to contend with this challenge: how dare I as a lesbian speak on behalf of other lesbians, even those like me in terms of race and class? But there is something profoundly incongruous about a silent feminist, and in particular a silent Christian feminist. The finding of voice is central to both traditions. Whereas patriarchal western tradition has viewed difference as a problem and sought to deal with it by encasing it in hierarchy, it need not be problematised to the point of inducing paralysis. Sara Ruddick has argued that, as feminists seek to demolish the notion of

19 Winquist, *Desiring Theology*, 92.

universal truth, difference becomes less problematic.[20] She proposes an alternative epistemological model which takes full account of difference and of the situatedness of all knowledge. This is the notion of cumulative knowledge and it has some connections with the quilting metaphor beloved of many feminist theologians. We do theology out of our own situatedness, within the context of the wider feminist theological project. We add our panel of reflection to that of others and in the process the whole quilt is changed and our own panel is invested with new meaning by being part of a bigger project. We are creating a body of knowledge which will only ever be partially accessible to us because it is an ongoing project. Pieces which appear to us not to fit, which clash with the dominant patterns, may in fact be the first pieces in a new direction of the pattern. This epistemology of accumulation seems to me to be almost embarrassingly 'orthodox' in terms of Christian theology. There is at the heart of the Christian tradition a belief that although there has been a unique revelation of the divine in the person of Jesus of Nazareth there is and there always will be more to come, as the same Spirit which was incarnate in Jesus continues the process of unfolding the rich tapestry of the being of God (John 16:12-13). The Church's claim to be the guardian of truth therefore can never be absolute, for somewhere the awkward, impish, Spirit is still doing her work.

Feminist theology has centralised this foundational Christian belief but of course it also needs to apply it to itself. All theological reflection, including that by feminists, needs to be grounded in humility or what Carter Heyward has called a theology of 'not knowing for sure',[21] which involves acknowledging one's non-neutrality and situatedness and therefore the possibility of being wrong. This in turn serves to create a space for genuine mutual encounter, dialogue and friendship and perhaps revelation. Humility properly understood should not induce paralysis because humility involves self-confidence, a daring willingness to take a calculated risk, whilst at all times acknowledging it to be a risk. Difference reminds us to be humble. Angela West has put it well, 'difference is dangerous; like a dropped stitch.'[22] One of the reasons we

20 Hogan, *From Women's Experience to Feminist Theology*, 61.

21 Carter Heyward, *Staying Power: Reflections on Gender, Justice and Compassion* (Cleveland: Pilgrim Press 1995), 7.

22 West, *Deadly Innocence*, 46.

fear difference is that it will unravel our designs. But perhaps it is there, in that danger of unravelling, that the presence of the divine is most obvious. The Native American Goddess Spiderwoman from the Hopi legend is depicted as a weaver-creator. She wove men and women. She was the first to create any design and then taught her people how to weave them. Every design contains her spirit, but every design also contains a flaw so that her spirit can escape from it and be free. When we force ourselves to confront difference, we are made aware of the dropped stitches in our own designs and the need to adjust our weaving not by simply coarsely adding the silver strands of other women's experience to our own design, for that would have the same effect as sewing new patches on old wine skins, but by engaging in mutual, reciprocal exchange within the context of mutual humility and attempted solidarity.

An epistemology of accumulated knowledge is also orthodox in the sense that it is eschatological—it recognises that truth is not presently available to us in its entirety but lies in the future. Feminist theology has tended to adopt a rather ambiguous attitude to eschatology, rightly rejecting the 'dualistic, deterministic, and other worldly'[23] nature of it as it has been fashioned in the Christian tradition, and which has served to distract attention from justice in the present. Yet, as Catherine Keller has pointed out, feminist theology stands firmly within the tradition of dissident millennialism, 'Indeed, whether or not they use the term eschatological, feminist theologians return persistently to the prophetic themes of collective hope for the disenfranchised, for bodily, social and cosmic renewal.'[24] Whilst we seek to realise right-relationship in our own time, we recognise the constraints placed upon us and look forward to a time when those constraints will be removed. In attempting to live the dream we become aware of the suction of sin, of how difficult it is to resist the forces of wrong-relation, of how enmeshed we are in socio-political webs of injustice. The recovery of the Sophia myth has been one of the most important and positive developments in recent feminist theology providing an epistemology which makes sense of our experience of the divine in uncontrollable immanence, but Angela West is surely right to remind us that 'in our justifiable excitement about Sophia, and our

23 Catherine Keller, 'Eschatology' in: Russell and Clarkson (eds.), *Dictionary of Feminist Theologies* (London: Mowbray 1996), 87.

24 Ibid., 87.

desire to reclaim her, we seemed to have forgotten to reclaim her opposite number—Dame Folly' (Proverbs 9, 13-18).[25] This passage reminds us that it is sometimes extremely hard to tell the difference between wisdom and folly and femaleness is no natural guarantor of such discernment, nor are women immune to the deceptive inducements of Dame Folly. Indeed, fallibility, foolishness, the experience of the suction of sin is an experience which all women do share—it is a commonality that binds us together not in despair but in creative humility. It sharpens our eyes and fingers as we weave and it makes room for the Spirit who refreshes and reinvigorates us to join in her dance. Part of our experience is the painful challenge of difference and the awareness of our own folly which it brings. The need to unpick and reweave our own designs becomes part of our experience.

Reflection upon liberating action within community is also part of the feminist and Christian traditions. I want to suggest that it is also the rooting of feminist theologians in communities of liberating action that prevents theological aphasia, because it is in these communities that we learn that in the midst of difference it is still possible to experience commonality (which, as Hogan has pointed out, is not sameness[26]) and it is in the midst of such communities of action that feminist theologians find that commonality and participate in reflection upon it. I would want to argue that it is involvement in communities of action that authorises feminist theologians to speak and we should be highly distrustful of the theology of those who might wish to maintain the academic/activist dualism. A feminist isolated from a community of resistance, uninvolved in the struggle for voice, justice and empowerment, may just as well be speaking for and to herself. Charles Winquist has reminded us that, in the person of the 'father of modern theology' Schleiermacher, we see the dangers of isolating ourselves from theological communities, for Schleiermacher constructed a theory and theology of religion out of an experience most of us have not had, the experience of absolute dependence.[27] A theologian rooted in a community or communities of action and reflection is not only able to perceive and live the twin realities

25 West, *Deadly Innocence*, 194.

26 Hogan, *From Women's Experience to Feminist Theology*, 61.

27 Winquist, *Desiring Theology*, 4.

of commonality and difference (perhaps better put as commonality in difference) but is able constantly to 'check out' her theological articulation and reflection with those communities, so that it becomes part of their work of liberating praxis and also a gift to others. Of course here the theologian joins the feminist sociologist, as defined by Liz Stanley and Sue Wise, who does not seek to hide her self in her research but recognises that 'the kind of person that we are, and how we experience the research, all have a critical impact on what we see, what we do and how we interpret and construct what is going on.'[28] Whilst to some extent the theology of a feminist theologian will always remain hers alone, her participation in communities of action and resistance will widen and texture her voice. None of us are deposits of pure personal experience. We are, as the authors of Genesis 2,7 noted, like pieces of clay never hardened but continually being moulded and remoulded, not only by our personal encounters but by the experiences of others as they are carried to us and into us through personal encounters. A feminist theologian in creating her theology keeps it wet and malleable and when those with whom she stands throw mud at it she does not brush it off but seeks to incorporate it into the texture of the clay. And so, of course, feminist theology is never stable or fixed but constantly in process. Unfortunately this reality can be hidden behind our cultural tendency to treat the written word as immutable so that there is a danger of a feminist orthodoxy and doctrinal 'package' emerging which nobody actually wants. Perhaps the advances in information technology, which some predict will herald the end of the book, will rescue us from this fate.

As I have previously mentioned, the question of the normativity of the tradition has been much debated in feminist theological circles. That debate must take on a new dimension in the shadow of postmodernism, for with the erosion of all the Enlightenment certainties upon which secular feminism was based we might well see the unstitching of all we have woven. Here Christian feminists are ironically in a stronger position than their secular sisters (perhaps for the first time in the history of modern feminism) for we have a pre-Enlightenment tradition on which to draw, which affirms the equality of all before God and the divine affirmation of justice, mutuality and compassion. Perhaps then it is the Christian tradition that carries feminist discourse through the foyer of

---

28 Stanley and Wise, *Breaking Out Again*, 60.

epistemology. Perhaps with impish irony Spirit/Sophia presents us with an erstwhile if not enemy then unfriendly relative as our saviour from the postmodernist soup of competing subjectivities. One of the follies of some feminist theology has been the tendency to lock experience and tradition into some sort of dualistic relationship. In fact, as Rosemary Radford Ruether pointed out long ago, what constitutes the Church's tradition is itself simply the reflected-upon experience of our ancestors in faith:

> Human experience is the starting point and the ending point of the hermeneutical circle. Codified tradition both reaches back to roots in experience and is constantly renewed or discarded through the test of experience. 'Experience' includes experience of the divine, experience of oneself, and experience of the community and the world, in an interacting dialectic.[29]

The radicalness of feminist theology lies simply in its cheek in pointing this out, in its insistence that women's experience be included in the hermeneutical circle, and recognising the rhetorical nature of the tradition as it has been handed on to us, taking seriously the voices that lie beneath its dominant discourse. We seek to resurrect these and weave them into the tradition. We make these claims on the basis of central beliefs and symbols of the tradition itself. Tradition is not something alien and apart from women's experience. In seeking to do theology from the basis of our own experience we become part of the tradition, the quilt of feminist theology becomes joined to a much larger quilt. It is from the tradition that we learn how to weave the cloth that becomes our patch of the quilt and some of its golden threads are evident in our own stitching for they have formed and inspired us and are an intrinsic part of us. But the addition of our quilt also casts the designs of the tradition in a new light. Much of it emerges as flawed but the tradition also casts its own light upon our own weaving and quilting, asking some pointed questions of it. And perhaps it is the part of the tradition that has been woven by women that particularly disturbs us and asks us to re-examine our analysis of our own experience.

It was our ancestors' devotion to their dead which prompted me, as someone who had previously subscribed to the apparently standard Christian feminist view that life after death was an untenable belief in a

---

29 Rosemary Radford Ruether, *Sexism and God-Talk: Towards a Feminist Theology* (London: SCM 1983), 12.

religion stripped of dualisms and that the whole concept of sainthood equally was unredeemable, to do a bit of unpicking and reweaving. Not only had our sister ancestors found support and encouragement in dialogue with the dead, but I also discovered that many of my Christian feminist contemporaries found similar strength in women who had lived long ago, strength that was mediated not just through example but through genuine relationship. And so I set about exploring whether it was possible to develop a feminist theology of sainthood and came to the conclusion that it was.[30] This is but one example of the tradition rescuing feminist theology from descending into mere ideology (difference serves a similar purpose) and feminist theology returns the favour by rescuing the tradition from the suction of patriarchy. The relationship between experience and tradition is dialectical and immensely complex because they are part of each other. Angela West has called tradition 'the jury of time', like a 'court in permanent session'.[31] It is important to realise that this is not just a case of the past judging the present, for as I have indicated no theology rooted in the gospels could authentically affirm that revelation has been confined to the past. It is the means by which Christianity continues to authenticate itself by constant self-interrogation. An affirmation of the eschatological dimension of Christianity does not imply that the recent is necessarily closer to the truth than the past but it does assert that tradition is not yet complete. The lesbian theologian Nancy Wilson, drawing upon her experience of living in an area often affected by earthquakes, has begun to construct a tentative 'seismic theology'. We tend to operate on the assumption that the earth is solid and that the maps drawn for us by our forebears will remain accurate apart from one or two human-made diversions. However, earthquakes remind us that the earth is in fact fluid and that at any time forces can erupt, necessitating a redrawing of our maps.[32] Similarly we cannot rely completely on the theological maps drawn up by our ancestors in faith because we might be in the midst of an eruption of the spirit which necessitates the redrawing of the maps of revelation. Our ancestors also include our feminist foresisters and those

---

30 Elizabeth Stuart, *Spitting at Dragons: Towards a Feminist Theology of Sainthood* (London: Mowbray 1995).

31 West, *Deadly Innocence*, 92.

32 Nancy Wilson, *Our Tribe: Queer Folks, God, Jesus and the Bible* (San Francisco: Harper 1995), 183.

whose reflections have influenced feminist theology profoundly even though they may not be dead. Even yesterday's map-maker is open to scrutiny in a seismic world.

Tradition provides feminist theology with a means of communicating and constructing theology amid the reality of difference, for it provides us with a common language and system of symbols. It is the translation of our experience into the grammar of Christianity that enables us to speak to others whose experiences may be very different from our own. It is the use of a common language and central symbols and the commitment to divinity and truth which their use communicates that forces us to wrestle with each other even when we disagree. The use of common language summons us to hear one another. It is the means by which we can begin to make sense to one another and engage in mutual, reciprocal exchange. Without the language of a tradition we do tend to end up literally talking to ourselves or buying into the language of another system, which, like the grammar of Enlightenment, may prove incapable of withstanding much analysis. The language and symbolism of the Christian tradition may be extremely problematic; it may well need constant reform in order to express the experience of the divine as clearly as possible; but it is a language that still 'speaks' to people, that still has the capacity to speak liberation and hope, and that still has the capacity to act as a powerful counter-speak to the propaganda of injustice. It is a dangerous, subversive language of dissent. It is a language which up to now has stood the test of the 'jury of time' (partly because it is able to reform itself). If Christian feminists do not want to end up talking to themselves or finding themselves pining or wallowing in 'epistemological solitude'[33] then they have no choice but to engage with the tradition, dialogue with the dead, weave with the ancestors and translate their experience into the language of the community of tradition.

In my own work I have sought to do theology out of the experience of lesbian (and gay) people. The lesbian voice still goes largely unheard in British feminist theology. I recently attended a conference on feminist theology where no distinctive i.e. identified lesbian voice was heard. Yet a hastily arranged meeting on lesbian spirituality during a lunch break attracted nearly half of the attendants. Informal discussion among those who were now identifiable to each other as lesbians revealed a deep

33 West, *Deadly Innocence*, 81.

discomfort with some of the dominant assumptions that had emerged at the conference, most importantly the assumption of the centrality of motherhood and its idealisation. Of course some of the lesbians were also mothers but it was the essentialising of woman that seemed to lie behind much of what was being said that disturbed and decentred us to such an extent that none of us felt able to challenge the speakers from a lesbian standpoint. We were made as unsafe and silent by the assumption of sameness among fellow feminists as we are in the Churches and in society at large.

It was to shatter this false mirror of sameness and to attempt to make something of the lesbian voice heard in the midst of endless Church debates on 'homosexuality', largely conducted by heterosexuals with a smattering of non-identified gay men and mostly focused around whether it is theologically possible to incorporate lesbians and gay men into the institution of marriage, i.e. to what extent it is possible to spread the mantle of heterosexuality to others, that I set about attempting to articulate and reflect upon some of the insights that had emerged in the lesbian and gay groupings to which I belong. I then repeatedly tested my reflections out on those same groups and on others, including non-lesbian and gay Christian groups. Although the resulting book, *Just Good Friends,* was in the end my sole responsibility, it was the product of many people. It does not represent the views of all lesbian and gay Christians (probably not even the majority) but it does represent the theological reflection of a significant number and therefore justifies its existence and voice.

My central contention was that the apparent tendency among a significant proportion of lesbian and gay people to define their most important and intimate relationships in terms of friendship might well constitute a movement of the Spirit in our times, and specifically in western culture which seems to be engulfed in a social and theological crisis over matters of sexuality and relationship. My argument was that lesbian and gay people may well be prophets in our times, living according to a relational paradigm which not only manifests the Christian virtues of mutuality, justice and equality better than the dominant relational paradigm (i.e. marriage) but may also recall the whole Christian community to a model of God and human living which has run like a silver thread through the Christian tradition from the first.

Sociological research has confirmed what I found out for myself, working in the lesbian and gay liberation movements, namely that friendship is unusually important to lesbian and gay people and often their primary relational category. The most important research in this field was undertaken by sociologist Kath Weston, who engaged in an in-depth study of the lesbian and gay community in the San Francisco Bay area of the United States of America, focusing on their understanding of kinship.[34] What Weston found in this community were extremely strong kinship networks but they were based not upon blood-ties but upon friendship. Rejected by their blood families or isolated from them for fear of rejection lesbian and gay people had been forced to create new patterns of relating and living which were not regarded as an alternative to friendship, as heterosexual relating often is, but as an extension to friendship. These units operated with extremely fluid boundaries akin to the African-American model of family. In another study Peter Nardi and Drury Sherrod found that lesbians, in particular, were extremely uncomfortable with any attempt to draw some sort of relational line between the categories of lover and friend.[35] Of course Mary Hunt, in her superb study of female friendship, had already demonstrated the compatibility of the relational model of friendship (as it is understood by women) with a feminist theo-ethical praxis.[36] Whereas under the patriarchal gaze friendship has either been idealised as an inherently rare and exclusively male relationship, or become an idealised folly for demonised sexuality, or as in our day and culture dismissed to the private realm and trivialised, among women of many ages friendship especially with other women has been life-sustaining and vital. The qualities of women's friendships have been and are that they are based upon equality, mutuality and justice and they are inclusive. It is possible and usual to have more than one friend. Friendship also has a social and political dimension because people are motivated to work for social change by their love for their friends. Friendship is an inclusive relationship in that it is technically available to all no matter what class, gender, sexual orientation or race. All can be united in the common project of friendship.

---

34 Kath Weston, *Families We Choose: Lesbians, Gays, Kinship* (New York: Columbia University Press 1991).

35 Peter Nardi and Drury Sherrod, 'Friendship in the Lives of Gay Men and Lesbians' in: *Journal of Social and Personal Relationships* 11 (1994), 185-99.

36 Mary Hunt, *Fierce Tenderness: A Feminist Theology of Friendship* (New York: Crossroad 1991).

My concern was slightly different from Hunt's in that I wanted to concentrate on friendship as a paradigm for sexual relationships and also because I wanted to ground the paradigm much more solidly in the Christian tradition. It seemed to me that not only was it possible for lesbian and gay Christians to receive from the tradition a theological language in which to articulate their intimacy and therefore gain a voice, but that tradition might offer some very interesting and liberatory challenges to our current notions of sexuality. Reading the scriptures through a lesbian and gay hermeneutic, it is possible to detect a silver thread of sexual subversion running through the Hebrew and Christian scriptures. It is the sexually different and therefore undesirable who act as agents of divine will, thus ensuring the progress of the history of salvation. Nancy Wilson has drawn attention to the part played by eunuchs in this regard.[37] But perhaps more important is the fact that when we look in the scriptures for models of intimate relationships which exhibit the qualities of justice, equality and mutuality, we will be sorely disappointed if we look to biblical marriages, all of which seem to be constructed on the model of slavery. Indeed, the only male/female relationship that demonstrates any of these qualities is that described in the Song of Songs, which is itself an illicit relationship—as Heather Walton has put it, 'The love is certainly heterosexual, there is no question of this, but not straight in a straightforward way.'[38] The only other relationships in the scriptures that demonstrate any of the qualities we would expect in right-relationships are same-sex friendships. In the passionate friendship between David and Jonathan two men of different social standing manage to transcend to some extent at least the barriers to their relating and reach a level of equality. We find a mutual rejoicing in each other which they choose to express in the form of a covenant which affected all their other relationships. We find a relationship that was socially subversive and threatened the throne of Israel.

In the love between Ruth and Naomi we find two women prepared to defy religious and social convention in order to be together. Ruth clings to Naomi, in a deliberate echo of Genesis 2, 24 where a man clings to his wife. Indeed as Wilson notes 'Ruth takes the role of husband and of son

37 Wilson, *Our Tribe*, 281-85.

38 Heather Walton, 'Theology of Desire' in: *Theology and Sexuality* 1 (1994), 33-4.

to Naomi, by giving her a son.'[39] Indeed, Ruth and Naomi use men to get what they want, in order that their friendship might survive and flourish. This is not to suggest that David and Jonathan were 'gay' or that Ruth and Naomi were 'lesbian' but it is to suggest that there is a 'family resemblance' between the love which they incarnate between them, which is bodily, passionate, socially subversive and religiously dubious, and the experience of many lesbian and gay people. For centuries lesbian and gay people have read the Scriptures and felt a sense of kinship with these characters and others, a kinship which they do not feel with people, whoever they were, who are condemned in passages which have been used as 'texts of terror' by the Church to justify our oppression and marginalisation.

Similarly, in the life and teaching of Jesus we encounter a man whose life was lived in the context of passionate friendship and who called people out of the patriarchal construction of the family and marriage into a new type of kinship based upon friendship—a 'kindom', to use Ada Maria Isasi-Diaz's phrase, a new type of relating in which the twin gates of exclusion, property and purity, would have no part. Could it be possible that some lesbian and gay people in the west are currently picking up a pattern that was first woven in biblical times, perhaps even by Jesus himself, and which to varying degrees of visibility has been kept alive in the Christian tradition, in the work of people like St Aelred and Aquinas? Could it be that the kindom of God is currently incarnate in its fullest form amongst those who are often identified either explicitly or implicitly as anti-Christ? These were my questions not only to the wider Christian community but also to the lesbian and gay communities themselves, for whom practising theological humility might involve accepting this prophetic mantle which is often harder to bear than walking away from Christianity altogether or playing the role of beggar seeking a place at the table.

But the tradition also asks some hard questions of us. In particular, of course, it reminds us of the fact that it is modern western medicine that has constructed the categories of homosexual and heterosexual into which we categorise ourselves. We are challenged to analyse to what extent this has been a good and bad thing. It has undoubtedly been positive in the sense that it has provided the tools for some people to build a distinctive sense of self and political identity. It has provided a means by which

39 Wilson, *Our Tribe*, 155.

those who so choose can avoid marriage. But we also have to ask to what extent has this categorisation also led to a restricting and policing of desire, which has resulted in the privatisation of sexual desire, thus placing it in arenas where it is largely free from scrutiny and judgement according to the criteria of justice, equality and mutuality. Sexuality, our desire for connection with the world around us in right-relationship, has been reduced and confined to sexual desire and cleverly policed so that any acknowledgement of the multi-dimensional nature of desire meets with accusations of advocating promiscuity. In the writings of women (and men) down the ages we are confronted by those who enjoyed passionate friendships with people of both sexes or managed to enjoy same-sex passion whilst also enjoying happy marriages. They challenge our categorisations of ourselves and suggest the possibility that these categorisations may actually be one of the things preventing a wider realisation of kinship.

I would agree with Hunt that placing friendship at the heart of our theo-ethical praxis would yank the Churches out of the sticky morass into which they find themselves sinking as they endlessly debate matters of sexuality. Relationships would be judged on the quality of friendship which they displayed or had the potential to display and not on gender. It would also have the advantage of uniting lesbian, gay, bisexual, heterosexual, celibate and single in a common project of building up friendship in the world through various different types of relationship. The centralisation of friendship would also involve the recognition of the importance of relationships with non-human creatures. But the tradition warns us against idealising friendship. David and Jonathan's friendship was finally thwarted by the social system in which they lived. Ruth and Naomi could not escape the expectations and demands of the patriarchal structures in which they were enmeshed. Friendship did not save Jesus from the cross, indeed it partly took him to it. Endeavouring to base one's relationships upon friendship does not automatically transport you into a magical forest of equality, mutuality and justice, as lesbian and gay people know only too well. We live in and are formed by structures of sin. We are not taught how to be friends, we are taught how to exploit one another. It is extremely hard to break out of these patterns of wrong-relating and, in fact, it is impossible. We might be deeply impressed by Kath Weston's account of the kinship networks formed in the San Francisco Bay area. We might say that there lesbian and gay people incarnate the ideals of the kindom to an impressive degree, but we simply cannot ignore the fact that the community there exists at the expense of the previous population—largely poor and members of the ethnic minorities who were driven out of the area by rising house prices as relatively affluent gay people moved in and gentrified the place. In order that one type of friendship might flourish another other had to be displaced. This is the awful, miserable tragedy of human existence which feminist theology has not been terribly good at acknowledging. There are also some people with whom we cannot be friends and to call them friends would be to do further violence to them: those people whom we in western Europe ruthlessly exploit for the sake of cheap living. Whether we are aware of this and are endeavouring to change the economic system or not, we are nevertheless caught in its trap and involved in its machinations. We cannot claim to be friends with someone whilst standing on their neck. All we can hope to be in this sort of situation is *friendly*, i.e. endeavouring to work towards the day when real friendship will be possible, and the absence of friendship motivates that work. All this serves to remind us of our need to be redeemed, to be saved, to be somehow lifted above the terrible forces (which are internalised in our selves) that work against friendship in our world. In other words it reminds us of our need for God who, as Trinity, is a community of persons in mutual relation (in other words, friends), in whom is incorporated both the joy and pain of friendship, in whom relationship has failed and been redeemed. Thus God storms out of the dropped stitches of our lives and theology to take us up in her dance of passionate friendship, wheeling us around to make us face situations anew.

The gay theologian Gary David Comstock has developed a hermeneutic of friendship:

> Instead of making the Bible into a parental authority, I have begun to engage with it as I would a friend—as one to whom I have made a commitment and in whom I have invested dearly, but with whom I insist on a mutual exchange of critique. ... Although its homophobic statements sting and condemn me, I counter that those statements are themselves condemned by its own Exodus and Jesus events.[40]

Friendship necessarily involves mutual honesty, challenge and argument and such exchanges only matter and bring about transformation and the deepening of relationships within the context of an ongoing committed relationship. Engaging with the tradition as with a friend is vital because

40 Gary David Comstock, *Gay Theology without Apology* (Cleveland: The Pilgrim Press 1993), 11-12.

it is only in the context of this ongoing relationship that Christian feminist theology makes any sense. From it we get the language, imagery and symbolism to make sense of our experience and to communicate with those who are different, searching for our commonality in difference. To place oneself within the Christian feminist tradition is to assert that it is from this particular tradition that one chooses to get one's primary maps for locating the presence of the divine in our world. These maps may prove to be flawed and need to be rewritten, other maps may prove helpful in this task, but it is nevertheless to centre oneself in a cartographic tradition which enables us to travel, which gives us some confidence to set out on the journey.

In both the primary tools of theology—experience and tradition—we experience something of the nature of grace. In a very real sense we are 'given' our experience, it is what we end up with and although we have undoubtedly had a hand in arriving at that place, by the choices we have made, we could not really predict where those choices would lead us. There is, therefore, no point feeling guilty about the particular life experience one has ended up with, but one does have choices about how one reflects upon it and what conclusions, including actions, are drawn from it. Tradition is something one has even less control of, it is given to us and we are not responsible for it, but since it is nevertheless part of us we are responsible for its development. Postmodernism has demonstrated that we cannot abandon our tradition, or shove it into a metaphorical nursing home, for it contains the only rock on which we can base our claims. We need our tradition; we need her wisdom; we need her maps, even though we may find ourselves needing to take and map out different paths. In reflecting upon some lesbian and gay experiences of defining relationships I realised how it might be possible to move from specific experience through the tradition towards something approaching a universal norm, which because friendship is such a broad and multi-layered concept could yet honour diversity and difference. Much more work needs to be done in developing a theology of friendship to see if this is a real possibility. But it was in the process of this reflection that I became aware how vital a friend tradition is to experience (even if it is at times an exasperating, offensive friend). Indeed, the only way out of the present crisis that feminist theology is experiencing around the centralising of experience lies in befriending the tradition.

Abstracts

Der Artikel fragt nach dem Platz der Erfahrung in der gegenwärtigen Krise feministischer Theologie. Historisch gesehen war Erfahrung eine zentrale Kategorie feministischer Theologie, doch die wachsende Anerkennung der Verschiedenenheit der Erfahrung von Frauen stellt den Erfahrungsbegriff epistemologisch in Frage. Die Verfasserin argumentiert, daß Erfahrung von Frauen in all ihrer Verschiedenheit für feministische Theologie zentral bleiben muß. Sie könne indes nur befreiend und transformierend wirken, wenn sie in ständigen kreativen Austausch mit der christlichen Tradition gebracht wird. Als Beispiel dafür wird der Dialog zwischen lesbischen feministischen Christinnen und der Tradition angeführt.

Cet essai analyse la crise actuelle de la théologie féministe concernant la place de l'expérience dans le processus théologique. Historiquement parlant, l'expérience a été un concept crucial pour le projet féministe, mais la reconnaissance croissante de la diversité des expériences féminines a soulevé certaines questions quant à l'utilité de ce concept d'expérience en tant qu'outil épistémologique. L'auteure soutient que l'expérience féminine dans toute sa diversité doit rester un élément central de la théologie féministe et qu'elle peut servir d'instrument de libération et de transformation, à condition cependant que ce soit dans le cadre d'un dialogue constant et créatif avec la tradition chrétienne. Ce type d'échange est illustré par le dialogue créatif que certaines chrétiennes féministes lesbiennes entretiennent avec la tradition.

Dr Elizabeth STUART is Senior Lecturer in Theology at the University of Glamorgan, Pontypridd, Wales. She is also executive editor of the academic journal *Theology and Sexuality*. She has had six books published including *Just Good Friends: Towards a Lesbian and Gay Theology of Relationships* (Mowbray) and *Spitting at Dragons: Towards a Feminist Theology of Sainthood* (Mowbray).

Elisabeth GÖSSMANN

Frauentraditionen im Christentum in ihrer Relevanz für heutige Feministische Theologie und in ihrer kirchlichen Einschätzung

Wenn in diesem Beitrag von der Tradition der Glaubensauslegung bei schreibenden Frauen, insbesondere seit dem Mittelalter, die Rede sein soll, so gilt es vor allem, uns deren vergessene Inhalte bewußt zu machen, die in ihrer Kontinuität bisher kaum wahrgenommen sind. Selbst bei denjenigen christlichen Schriftstellerinnen, zu denen es eine weitläufige Forschung gibt, wurde zumeist nach ihren literarischen Abhängigkeiten von Kirchenvätern, philosophischen Autoritäten etc. geforscht, aber nicht nach einem roten Faden, der sich möglicherweise von früheren zu späteren Frauenschriften zieht und auf ein gemeinsames Interesse oder gar auf nahezu gleichbleibende Erfahrungen von Frauen im Rahmen ihrer jeweiligen Kirchlichkeit schließen ließe. Wenn wir aber mit einer "Hermeneutik des Verdachts" die alten Frauentexte lesen, entdecken wir Kontinuitäten, die uns heute weiterhelfen und die wir nicht übersehen dürfen, wenn wir uns nicht selbst jener Geschichtsvergessenheit schuldig machen wollen, die wir Männern in Bezug auf weibliches Schreiben vorwerfen.

Da Frauen mit ihren Schriften in ihrem von der männlichen Haupttradition abweichenden Sondergut gegen diese reagierten, wird für uns Heutige erkennbar, daß sie bestimmte Grundzüge androzentrischer Tradition nicht akzeptierten und sich andere Fundamente ihres Glaubensverständnisses in Bezug auf die eigene Kreatürlichkeit und Handlungsbefugnis sowie auf ihr Gottes- und Menschenbild zu schaffen wußten.

Im ökumenischen Bewußtsein Feministischer Theologie können wir uns alle mit diesen unseren Vorschwestern verbunden und zu unserer Wegbahnung in die Zukunft ermutigt fühlen, aber uns sollte auch klar werden, welche androzentrischen Konstrukte von unseren Vorschwestern schon abgebaut worden sind, so daß wir sie eigentlich nur zu zitieren brauchten, ohne uns weitere Mühe der Widerlegung machen zu müssen. Ob wir selbst in katholischer oder aus der Reformation hervorgegangener

Kirchlichkeit beheimatet sind, die Linie der Frauentradition führt zu uns und mahnt uns, mehr als dies bisher geschehen ist, mit ihrem Gedankengut weiterzuarbeiten.

Dies wirft aber gerade für die Frauen, die sich weiter im Rahmen katholischer Kirchlichkeit bewegen wollen, die Frage auf, welche Relevanz denn im katholischen Verständnis "Tradition" hat, wenn sie von Frauen stammt, und welche Forderungen wir gegebenenfalls zu stellen haben. Es geht also hier nicht nur, wie in anderen Bereichen auch, darum, daß Frauen sich ihre Geschichte und besonders die ihres Denkens mühsam rekonstruieren müssen, sondern in der Theologie wie in der Kirche geht es um die offizielle Anerkennung der Frauentradition als Glaubenstradition.

Methodisch kann eine erst in ihren Anfängen steckende theologie- und philosophiegeschichtliche Frauenforschung nur so vorgehen, daß sie weibliche Glaubensauslegung und -übermittlung komparativ zu männlichen Entwürfen verschiedenster Provenienz in den Blick nimmt. Wenn wir synchron und diachron die Pluralität der theologischen Schulen und die jeweiligen Abweichungen der Frauentradition analysieren, sind wir auf dem Weg zu einer Ganzheit, die uns erst erahnen läßt, was christliche Tradition in ihrem Prozeß von Bewegung und Gegenbewegung bis in unsere Zeit ausmacht.

I Der Ort der Frauentradition im katholischen Traditionsverständnis

Wenn hier von katholischem Traditionsverständnis die Rede ist, so soll dabei das neue Interesse für die Tradition der Glaubensübermittlung in der evangelischen Theologie nicht unerwähnt bleiben. Nur ist dieses Thema wegen seiner dogmatischen Verbindlichkeit im katholischen Bereich problematischer, was schon allein an der kirchlichen (und späteren theologischen) Sozialisation meiner Generation deutlich wird.

Als Kind im Grundschulalter lernte ich im Katechismus-Unterricht von zwei Glaubensquellen, der Heiligen Schrift und der "mündlichen Überlieferung". Als Gymnasiastin fragte ich meinen Religionslehrer, was denn unter der letzteren zu verstehen sei, und erhielt die Antwort, es handele sich dabei um das, was in der Bibel nicht oder nicht ausdrücklich stehe, aber von den Kirchenvätern als christliche Lehre angesehen und im Laufe der Zeit schriftlich niedergelegt worden sei.

Als Theologiestudentin im 1. Semester (Münster 1947) bei der Bibliotheksführung mit der Kirchenväter-Ausgabe von Migne vertraut gemacht, wunderte ich mich, empfand auch leichten Unwillen, als ich auf dem Rücken des Bandes 197 oben "Patres Latini" und darunter "Hildegardis Abbatissa" las. Kann oder muß denn eine Frau wie Hildegard von Bingen unter die lateinischen Kirchen-"väter" gerechnet werden?, fragte ich mich damals. Aber immerhin war sie vom Herausgeber nicht übergangen, und man konnte sie lesen. In meiner späteren mediaevistischen Ausbildung tat ich es auch, als wir uns in unserm Institut mit dem 12. Jahrhundert beschäftigten, aber in den Lehrveranstaltungen kam sie ebenso wenig wie andere Frauen vor. Das mag daran gelegen haben, daß "Mystik und Frömmigkeitsgeschichte", wo schreibende Frauen, wenn überhaupt wahrgenommen, eingeordnet wurden, als Fach in theologischen Universitätsfakultäten meist ausgespart blieb, zuweilen aber in der Ausbildung im Priesterseminar vorkam. Daran zeigt sich schon, daß die Theologie mit Frauen als Traditionszeuginnen nicht rechnete. Die meisten schreibenden Frauen lernte ich ohnehin im Germanistikstudium oder durch romanistische und anglistische Forschungsarbeiten kennen, die aber nicht an den theologischen Implikationen der jeweiligen Frauentexte interessiert waren und vom Bekannten abweichende Bibelauslegungen von Frauen oft genug aus Unverständnis abwerteten.

Während meines Studiums in München lernte ich die neuere Entwicklung des katholischen Traditionsbegriffs seit der Romantik und bis zur Zeit der Dogmatisierung der leiblichen Aufnahme Marias in den eschatologischen Zustand (1950) näher kennen.[1] Die Ansicht, daß das kirchliche Lehramt, also Papst und Bischöfe, die authentischen Träger der Überlieferung seien, was den totalen Frauenausschluß mit sich bringt, zieht sich zwar durch die Schriften der Theologen des 19. bis zur Mitte des 20. Jahrhunderts, wird aber allmählich in bestimmter Hinsicht modifiziert.

In Anknüpfung an Johann Adam Möhler, der die Tradition als das "fortwährend in den Herzen der Gläubigen lebende Wort" umschrieben hatte, vollzog sich über die katholische Tübinger Schule hinaus eine—selbst wenn sie noch lange ungenannt blieben—auch für Frauen günstige Auflockerung des Traditionsbegriffs. Tradition wurde nun nicht mehr als eine Art Materialbörse für in der Bibel nicht vorfindliche Lehren, sondern

---

1 Das Folgende ist in ausführlicher Form nachzulesen bei Michael Schmaus, *Katholische Dogmatik* III,1, *Die Lehre von der Kirche* (München: Max Hueber 1958), 758-777.

als etwas Lebendiges, stets Gegenwärtiges gesehen. Kardinal Newman, der "das Zeugnis der Laien in Fragen des Glaubens" in seiner gleichnamigen Schrift von 1853 ernst zu nehmen versucht, indem er den alten Begriff vom Glaubenssinn oder instinctus fidei im Hinblick auf die Wirksamkeit des Heiligen Geistes in allen interpretiert, behält zwar die strikte Unterscheidung zwischen Lehramt und den übrigen Gläubigen bei, jedoch hält er, im Zusammenhang mit der Frage der Definierbarkeit der Immaculata conceptio Marias (1854), es für ratsam, daß das Lehramt sich nach dem Glauben der Kirchenmitglieder erkundigt. Abhängig davon ist das Lehramt für Newman jedoch nicht.

Bei Johann Baptist Franzelin gewinnt 1870 die Gesamtgemeinschaft der Gläubigen (wobei auch die Frauen "mitgemeint" sein müssen) weiter an Bedeutung, weil sie für Glaubensbewußtsein und Glaubensbekenntnis zuständig ist. Aber nur das authentische Lehramt kann sie vor Irrtümern in Glaubensdingen bewahren. Franzelins Schüler Matthias Joseph Scheeben arbeitete aufgrund eines organischeren Kirchenkonzepts mit den Begriffen "Lehrkörper" und "Glaubenskörper" und betonte, daß der Lehrkörper zugleich auch dem Glaubenskörper angehöre. Die in der Überlieferung weitergegebene Offenbarung authentisch zu bezeugen und autoritativ vorzuschreiben, bleibt jedoch auch für ihn Sache des Lehrkörpers. Nur aufgrund der Integration des Lehrkörpers in den Glaubenskörper hat nach Scheeben die gesamte kirchliche Gemeinschaft am "Charisma der Unfehlbarkeit" teil.

Der in der Mitte dieses ausgehenden Jahrhunderts einflußreiche Mannes Dominicus Koster (OP) geht gegenüber früheren Integrationsversuchen einen Schritt weiter. Die aktive Überlieferung scheint auch bei ihm noch Sache des Lehramtes zu sein, aber er stuft den Glaubenssinn der einfachen Gläubigen so hoch ein, daß nach seiner Ansicht die Bischöfe vor einer Dogmatisierung diese nicht nur nach ihrem Glauben befragen können, sondern dies auch müssen, was wiederum im Umkreis der Fragen zur Definierbarkeit des letzten Mariendogmas (1950) zum Problem wurde. Das waren Diskussionen, die ich als Theologiestudentin miterlebte.

Koster kennt noch ein vermittelndes Glied zwischen einfachen Gläubigen und Mitgliedern des Hirtenamtes: die Kirchenväter und Kirchenlehrer. Damit wird respektiert, daß es auch solche gab, die nicht Bischöfe wurden, denen aber eine eigene Lehrkompetenz und Trägerschaft von Überlieferung zukommt. Natürlich ist auch diese Zwischengruppe, deren Autorität immer schon feststand, ursprünglich männlich konzipiert. Aber es stellt sich doch die spannende Frage, was es bedeutet, wenn Rom, wie es zu unserer Zeit geschieht, zwei oder drei Frauen zu Kirchenlehrerinnen erklärt.

Um mit meiner Meinung nicht hinterm Berg zu halten: Es ist nicht einmal ein Kurieren am Phänomen, sondern nur eine nachträgliche Befreiung dieser wenigen Frauen der Vergangenheit von den Bedingungen und Beschränkungen der Weiblichkeit, die durch die kirchenrechtliche Fixierung unechter Paulusstellen wie Schweigegebot und Lehrverbot, zustande gekommen sind. Dies geschieht zu Ungunsten aller anderen schreibenden Frauen in der langen Geschichte christlicher Tradition, die damit weiter unter diesen Beschränkungen gehalten werden. Die sich daraus ergebende Forderung werde ich am Schluß formulieren.

Tradition ist auch in christlich-kirchlicher Verwendung ein Sammelbegriff für eine Vielfalt von Traditionen, die sich zwar in einzelnen Elementen, aber nicht grundsätzlich gegenseitig ausschließen können. Das sieht man am Unterschied der Lehre und Spiritualität etwa der Franziskaner und der Dominikaner im Mittelalter mit ihren jeweiligen Schulen, gerade auch in Bezug auf ihr Frauenbild. Selbstverständlich waren auch die schreibenden Frauen, deren Werke uns in reicher Fülle erhalten blieben, selbst wenn wir mit großen Verlusten rechnen müssen, von der Lehre und Spiritualität ihres oder des sie "betreuenden" Ordens (meist war die Seelsorge gegenseitig) beeinflußt. Aufgrund von Weiterführung vorhandener Traditionen, aber auch in Abweichungen von diesen, kam es zu einer eigenständigen Frauentradition im Christentum. Es kann kontinuierlich festgestellt werden, daß Frauen an bestimmten theologischen Themen besonders interessiert sind, eigene Gedanken entwickeln und anderes meiden. Ihnen geht es um die Schaffung einer eigenen Lebenswelt aus dem Glauben, auch über die Grenze zwischen im Kloster und in der Ehe lebenden Frauen hinweg.

Was hat nun das II. Vaticanum im Hinblick auf das Thema "Frau und Tradition" gebracht? Mit meinen eigenen Worten von 1967 gesagt: "Es gibt nach den Konzilstexten keinerlei Zurücksetzung der Frau gegenüber dem Mann, sei es in ihrem geistlichen Leben, sei es in den neu entdeckten Funktionen des Laienstandes, sei es in der Anerkennung ihrer Wirksamkeit in der modernen Gesellschaft und Öffentlichkeit."—"Wenn die Kirchenkonstitution von den einzelnen im Volke Gottes spricht, gleich welchen Standes oder Geschlechts, verwendet sie das Wort discipuli, Jünger."—"Das Dekret über das Laienapostolat zieht ausdrücklich eine

Parallele zwischen Gesellschaft und Kirche, ja, scheint sogar den gesellschaftlichen Entwicklungen einen Hinweischarakter für die erweiterten Funktionen der Frau in der Kirche zuzubilligen."—"Der Laienstand soll also keineswegs mit der neu entdeckten 'Weltoffenheit' gleichsam auf die Welt abgedrängt werden, es ist vielmehr so, daß die Erfahrungen aus der Welt von Mann und Frau in die Theologie eingebracht werden müssen."—"Man denke nur an die immer mehr heraufziehenden Probleme der Manipulation des menschlichen Lebens in der Massengesellschaft, wo entschieden werden muß, ob bestimmte Zukunftsplanungen noch mit dem Menschenbild der christlichen Offenbarung vereinbar sind oder nicht. Solche Entscheidungen lassen sich nicht fällen ohne Theologie und auch nicht ohne eine Mitarbeit der Frau in der Theologie. Dies alles wird vom Konzil ausdrücklich genannt und befürwortet."—"Freilich ist mit dem, was das Konzil theoretisch fordert, noch nicht die Möglichkeit zur praktischen Verwirklichung ergriffen, und freilich wird es noch viel 'innerkirchlichen Widerstand' geben, wenn die Frauen darauf drängen, die ihnen vom Konzil zugebilligten Funktionen zu erfüllen."[2] Obwohl hier implizit Frauen als Trägerinnen von christlicher Überlieferung angesprochen sind, blieben die Enttäuschungen der nachkonziliaren Zeit bekanntlich nicht aus.

Einen weiteren Wandel in der Interpretation des katholischen Traditionsbegriffs zeigt der vom jungen Ratzinger verfaßte Artikel "Tradition" im *Lexikon für Theologie und Kirche*, der während des Konzils und noch vor der Verabschiedung der Konstitution über die Offenbarung verfaßt wurde. Er ist gekennzeichnet durch die Überwindung der Zwei-Quellen-Theorie. Die Bibel wird nun nicht mehr "als Gegenüber zur Tradition, sondern als ein Element in ihr" bestimmt. (Bd. 10, Sp. 293) Nicht "sola scriptura", sondern Tradition wird also der umfassende Begriff, wobei es nicht auf die "archivarische Bewahrung" der Jesusüberlieferung ankomme, sondern auf "Gegenwart vom Geist her", ohne daß der "geschichtliche Grund" preisgegeben werden dürfe. Vom Traditionszeugen heißt es, er dürfe zwar nichts hinzufügen, habe aber "umso mehr zu verkündigen und auszulegen." Letztlich bleibt dieser Begriff an den der successio apostolica, also doch wieder an das Lehramt gekoppelt, und an

2 Vgl. Elisabeth Gössmann, *Das Bild der Frau heute* (Düsseldorf: Haus der Katholischen Frauen 1967, 2. Aufl.), 41-50.

Frauen als Traditionszeuginnen scheint trotz dieser zunächst so vielversprechenden Einbettung der Schrift in die Tradition nicht gedacht zu sein.

Nach dem Konzil hat Michael Schmaus das Verhältnis von Schrift und Tradition folgendermaßen zusammengefaßt: "Die Schrift ist Ausdruck der mündlichen Überlieferung, die mündliche Überlieferung aber ist Voraussetzung und nachfolgende Auslegung der Heiligen Schrift". Als "Träger der Überlieferung" nennt er "das ganze Gottesvolk", das aber die ihm zukommende Überlieferungstätigkeit "nur in Einordnung und in Unterordnung unter das kirchliche Lehramt" vollziehen könne.[3] Das Konzil hat immer den Akzent auf die Übereinstimmung aller im Glauben gelegt und auch das Lehramt dazu aufgerufen, wegbereitend für den innerkirchlichen Konsens zu wirken und nicht ohne Not Menschen auszugrenzen.

All dies gibt der Frage nach weiblicher Überlieferungsträgerschaft neue Brisanz. Wir wollen heraus aus dieser Ambivalenz: einerseits aktive Überlieferungsträgerinnen zu sein, andererseits doch dem Lehramt untergeordnet, in dem wir nicht vertreten sind. Es gibt Überlieferung, bevor es ein Lehramt gab, und es gibt zunehmend Fälle, in denen Übereinkunft mit dem Lehramt nicht erreichbar ist. Was ist mit den Frauen in der Überlieferung vor der Abfassung der Evangelien, die Jesus als Jüngerinnen folgten, die ihn im Gespräch zu veränderter Konzeption seiner messianischen Aufgabe brachten? Was ist mit den von Paulus als seine Mitarbeiterinnen gewürdigten Frauen, die z. T. schon vor ihm in ihrem Dienstamt standen, die von ihm als "diakonos" oder "apostolos" bezeichnet wurden?—den Frauen, die später in ihren mystisch-theologischen Werken die Bibel anders auslegten und "viel zu verkündigen" hatten? Sind sie etwa nur im privaten Bereich ihrer häuslichen Umwelt tätige Glaubensvermittlerinnen, wie die Scholastik meinte? Ihrem Selbstverständnis entspricht das jedenfalls nicht.

Um noch härter zu fragen: Können wir nach dem Papstbrief "Ordinatio sacerdotalis", der uns ausgerechnet zu Pfingsten 1994 "beglückte" und den die Glaubenskongregation Ende 1995 für "unfehlbar" zu erklären versuchte, als Katholikinnen noch bestehen, wenn wir uns im offensichtlichen Widerspruch zu diesen römischen Äußerungen befinden? Soll denn

---

3 Michael Schmaus, *Der Glaube der Kirche* I 1 (Sankt Ottilien: Eos 1979, 2. Aufl.), 215. 229. Vgl. auch Achim Buchenmaier, *Schrift und Tradition seit dem Vaticanum II* (Paderborn: Bonifatius 1996).

durch den mit dem Amtsausschluß gegebenen Ausschluß der Frauen vom kirchlichen Lehramt und dessen Interpretations- und Definitionsmacht, ethischer Normenbildungs- und Entscheidungsbefugnis das hierarchische Geschlechterverhältnis, trotz entgegenstehender Lippenbekenntnisse, de facto immer noch aufrecht erhalten werden? Soll der Alleinvertretungsanspruch des Männlichen für das Allgemeinmenschliche weiter konserviert werden?—ein Denken, das vor dem Christentum da war und durch die Rezeption antiker Philosopheme das Evangelium verfälscht hat?

Wohl nicht von ungefähr erschienen nach den römischen Äußerungen von 1994/95 und den in Wechselwirkung damit stehenden verschiedenen Kirchenvolksbegehren in den *Stimmen der Zeit* von 1996 Beiträge, die den Begriff der Tradition auch unter kommunikations- und rezeptionstheoretischen Aspekten samt Konfliktsituationen in den Blick nehmen und feministische Hermeneutik nicht aussparen. Betont wird die "Beteiligung aller" an Tradition, ihr Prozeßcharakter als ein Zeiten übergreifendes Kontinuum, als durch Vermittlung gegenwärtig gewordene Erinnerung, als Kritik einschließende Auslegung, als gruppenstiftend und zugleich subjektbildend. Bei Bertram Stubenrauch (478-486) ist weiter davon die Rede, daß möglicherweise "der Tradierungsprozeß ins Stocken gerät", daß "Tradition gegen Tradition abgewogen werden muß", daß "gute Traditionen verschüttet, ungute aber wohl etabliert und fest im Kollektiv verankert sein" können—alles für unser Unternehmen hochaktuelle Beobachtungen. Der vorkonziliare Überlieferungsbegriff, nach welchem dem kirchlichen Lehramt ein "Traditions- und Auslegungsmonopol" zukomme, wird ausdrücklich abgelehnt zugunsten eines Glaubens, "der von jedem Christen und jeder Christin innerhalb der Kirche, aber je auf seine oder ihre Weise gelebt, verinnerlicht und verlebendigt" werde, wogegen das Lehramt nur "eine Ausformung eines gemeinschaftlichen Bewußtseins" darstelle. Traditionsgeschehen sei auch das Aufgreifen neuer Problemfelder wie der Bedeutung der Frau oder des interreligiösen Dialogs. Kritisiert wird, daß "die Möglichkeit einer Äußerung des Glaubenssinnes, wie das Lehramt sie besitzt", den übrigen Kirchenmitgliedern bis heute fehle, "ein schmerzliches Vakuum der innerkirchlichen Kommunikationsstruktur".

Christoph Böttigheimer (547-554), der aufgrund der Konzilstexte alle Getauften als "Subjekt des innerkirchlichen Wortgeschehens" bezeichnet, sieht im Hinblick auf apostolisches Wirken "eine Differenzierung zwischen Laien und Klerikern" als "grundsätzlich unzutreffend" oder "obsolet" an und führt den Begriff einer gewissen Volkssouveränität in der Kirche ein, ohne jedoch das kirchliche Lehramt grundsätzlich zu relativieren. Mit Dietrich Wiederkehr versteht er "Konsens in der Wahrheit" als "Konvergenz auf Wahrheit hin" und beklagt den Mangel an Organisationsformen, "die es den Gläubigen ermöglichen würden, (...) in Glaubensfragen an der kirchlichen Entscheidungsfindung so mitzuwirken, wie es der apostolischen Sendung aller (...) entsprechen würde".

Demgegenüber beleuchtet Wolfgang Beinert (381-392) am Rezeptionsgeschehen in der Kirche den Begriff des Gehorsams, der nur auf Gott gerichtet sein kann. "Annahme und Übernahme eines Gutes, auch einer Weisungsvorgabe, aus freier Einsicht bezeichnen wir aber nicht mehr als Gehorsam, sondern als Rezeption." Tragödien der katholischen Kirche wie die Modernismuskrise werden darauf zurückgeführt, daß der geschichtliche Charakter lebensweltlicher Gegebenheiten übersehen, der Glaube also nicht mit den jeweiligen Lebenskontexten versöhnt worden sei. Das Lehramt wird mit Nachdruck dazu aufgefordert, die anderen Bezeugungsinstanzen des Glaubens zu rezipieren. Beinert versucht sich in einer Eingliederung der Frauentradition, indem er auf den Einfluß der Mystikerin Juliana von Lüttich bei der Einführung des Fronleichnamsfestes verweist. Der heutigen feministischen Bewegung in der Kirche und der Feministischen Theologie schreibt er Impulse zur "Subjektwerdung der Laienchristen" zu. Rezeptionsgeschehen bedeutet für ihn Gegenseitigkeit.

Beinert plädiert zwar für eine relative Unabhängigkeit der einzelnen Glaubensinstanzen voneinander, da es im Unterschied zur weltlichen Demokratie in der Glaubensgemeinschaft keine Setzungen der "Basis" gebe, hält aber fest, daß "im Fall der Nichtzustimmung einer Vorgabe von Lehramt oder Theologie die Lebenskraft, die geistliche Fruchtbarkeit, die Wirksamkeit" fehle, "tatsächlich bleibt sie tot". Mit Beispielen aus der Geschichte stellt er zur Debatte, daß es sich in einem solchen Fall "um gar keine Definition handelt, selbst wenn sie alle Kennzeichen einer solchen trägt", und empfiehlt dem Lehramt, eine Rezeptionsverweigerung durch die Gläubigen äußerst ernst zu nehmen.

Diese in der "Männertheologie" geführte Diskussion ist für die Frauentradition wichtig: Sie ist eine zu Unrecht verdrängte, verschüttete, in vielen Aspekten eine "gute", die gegen "etablierte, fest im Kollektiv verankerte" nicht nur "abgewogen", sondern als kontrastiv dazu bewußt gemacht werden muß. Sie bricht seit Jahrhunderten ein angemaßtes männliches Auslegungsmonopol und war als Traditionsgeschehen präsent, auch wenn Frauen von der zeitgenössischen Theologie keine Lehrautorität, sondern "nur" prophetisches Wirken zugestanden wurde. Frauen waren seit je "Subjekte des innerkirchlichen Wortgeschehens", und deshalb kann man auch nur unter Einschluß ihrer gegensätzlichen Konzeptionen, nicht mit der männlichen Lehrautorität allein, geschichtlich gesehen, von "Konvergenz auf Wahrheit hin" sprechen. Wie auch die heutige Frauenkritik am interreligiösen Dialog bestätigt, haben Männer sich bisher kaum mit der gleichen Intensität, wie sie etwa einen core-to-core-Dialog mit dem Buddhismus zu führen bemüht sind, in eine weibliche Lebenswelt hineinzuversetzen gesucht, obwohl das Umgekehrte durchaus behauptet werden kann.[4]

II Tradition und Gegentradition

Vorbemerkung: Das Genre des Schreibens ist selbstverständlich verschieden bei den Geschlechtern. Die als wissenschaftlich geltende Summen- und Traktatliteratur sowie Bibelkommentare zu verfassen, ist Frauen wegen des Lehrverbots im allgemeinen bis zum 19. Jahrhundert nicht möglich, abgesehen etwa von Passagen ihrer Briefliteratur, wo sie auf gestellte Fragen antworten können, oder von besonderer männlicher Förderung durch Herausgabe ihrer Werke. Da ihnen prophetisches Schreiben zugebilligt wird, sind Visionsbeschreibungen, Auditionen und deren Auslegung das ihnen adäquate Medium theologischer Aussage. Es geht hier nicht um die "Echtheitsfrage" solcher Erlebnisse, sondern um die damit erzielte Zustimmung zu oder Abweichung von Inhalten der männlichen Tradition. Im Mittelalter, als in den theologischen Schulen für das katholische Frauenbild bis in die Mitte des 20. Jahrhunderts die Weichen gestellt werden, ist die Nicht-Zustimmung von Frauen an theologischen Brennpunkten geradezu revolutionär. Freilich war dies bis zur Hochrenaissance, als Frauen deutlicher zu reden beginnen, nur in vorsichtiger Form möglich, indem männliche Auffassungen zunächst einmal quasi-zitierend wiederholt und in einem zweiten Ansatz dann umgewertet, abgewandelt, unterwandert bis auf den Kopf gestellt wurden. Die Literaturwissenschaft fand den hilfreichen Begriff "double-voiced discourse" für solches

---

4 Vgl. Elisabeth Gössmann, "Feministische Kritik an universalen Wahrheitsansprüchen" in: *Neue Zeitschrift für Missionswissenschaft* Sonderband (1996), 312-350.

Verfahren, wo gleichsam mit einer Stimme die Tradition der dominanten Gruppe aufgegriffen und mit einer anderen wieder in Frage gestellt wird.[5]

Abgesehen von einigen Schriftstellerinnen der Renaissance, gebrauchen die meisten Frauen bis zum 18./19. Jahrhundert eine auf das weibliche Geschlecht bezogene, doppelpolige Bescheidenheitstopik, in der ihr Ungelehrtsein und ihre Armseligkeit, also die Grundzüge des männlichen Frauenbildes, geschickt untergebracht werden, um andererseits ihre Unabhängigkeit von irdischen, "fleischlichen" Lehrern zu betonen und sich auf unmittelbare göttliche Erleuchtung zu prophetischem Künden zu berufen. Mittelalterliche und frühneuzeitliche Schriftstellerinnen fordern in nicht durch den Mann vermittelter Gott-Unmittelbarkeit, daß ihre Schriften von allen beherzigt werden, ob sie selbst als Kritikerinnen gegen die Korruption des Klerus kämpfen oder sich als vertraut mit den Mysterien des Glaubens bezeichnen. Deshalb werden Ausdrücke wie "Privatoffenbarung" weder ihrem Selbstverständnis, noch ihren Werken gerecht.

1 Gottebenbildlichkeit und Gottesrepräsentanz

a. bei männlichen Autoren:

Daß Frauen als Traditionszeuginnen nicht einkalkuliert sind, beruht auf einer patristisch-scholastischen Geschlechter-Anthropologie, die sich auch in der Neuzeit noch, oft genug über die Konfessionsgrenzen hinweg, gehalten hat. Zwar gilt für den gnadenhaften Bereich und die Berufung zum Heil Gleichheit der Geschlechter, aber für alles Innerweltliche, und dazu gehört auch die kirchliche Ordnung, gilt die Unterordnung der Frau.[6] Es wird sich zeigen, daß diese Unterscheidung nicht immer eingehalten ist. Durch die Rezeption antiker philosophischer Systeme verstärkt sich seit den "klassischen" Kirchenvätern und insbesondere im 13. Jahrhundert der Zirkelschluß zwischen androzentrischer Bibellesung und Rezeption antiker Philosopheme, die sich gegenseitig zu bestätigen scheinen. Das Kirchenrecht, wie es im 12. Jahrhundert im Dekret des Gratian zusam-

---

5 Vgl. Gisela Brinker-Gabler, "Frauen schreiben. Überlegungen zu einer ausgewählten Exploration literarischer Praxis" in: Dieselbe (Hg.), *Deutsche Literatur von Frauen* I (München: Beck 1988) 11-36.

6 Dies ist die These von Kari Elisabeth Børresen, *Subordination and Equivalence. The Nature and Role of Woman in Augustine and Thomas Aquinas* (reprint, Kampen: Kok Pharos Publishing House 1995).

mengestellt wurde, geht davon aus, die Frau sei nicht Bild Gottes.[7] Bis zu Beginn des 20. Jahrhunderts wird unter Vernachlässigung von Gen 1,26 aus 1 Kor 11,7 geschlossen, die Frau sei nur durch den Mann vermittelt, in schwächerer Weise gottebenbildlich.[8]

Theologisch liegt die folgenschwerste Diskriminierung der Frau in der Behauptung ihrer Unfähigkeit zur Gottes- bzw. Christusrepräsentanz, die Zielpunkt der männlichen Lehre von der verminderten Gottebenbildlichkeit der Frau ist. Wie viele vor und nach ihm, hat Thomas von Aquin neben der Anerkennung eines geschlechtsneutralen, auf das Heil zielenden Sinnes von Gottebenbildlichkeit den Ausschluß des weiblichen Geschlechts von der Fähigkeit, Gott zu repräsentieren, formuliert und damit eine große Wirkungsgeschichte hervorgerufen: "Aber in Bezug auf etwas Sekundäres findet sich das Gottesbild im Mann, und in Bezug auf dieses findet es sich nicht in der Frau. Denn der Mann ist Ursprung und Ziel der Frau, so wie Gott Ursprung und Ziel der gesamten Schöpfung ist."[9] In diesem "Sekundären" aber liegt die Ermächtigung des Mannes und die Entmächtigung der Frau, zumal die Frau hier zur Repräsentantin der Schöpfung degradiert wird und keinen eigenen Daseinssinn hat. Dieser Thomas-Satz findet sich, selbstverständlich ohne Nennung seines Namens, auch in frühprotestantischen Handbüchern. Er wirkte also konfessionsübergreifend als "Ökumene im Negativen".

Daß die Scholastik den Mann als das innerweltliche Prinzip der Gottesrepräsentanz sieht, hat auch mit der Abwehr manichäisch-gnostischer Strömungen zu tun, die in verschiedenen Varianten neben den "guten" Gott als Schöpfer alles Geistigen (und wegen der Identifizierung von "männlich" mit "geistig" zuweilen auch des Männlichen!) dualistisch den Demiurgen als Schöpfer alles Materiellen (und wegen dessen Identifizierung mit "Fleisch" zuweilen auch des Weiblichen!) stellten. Gegen die-

7 Vgl. Ida Raming, *Der Ausschluß der Frau vom priesterlichen Amt. Gottgewollte Tradition oder Diskriminierung?* (Köln/Wien: Böhlau 1973) 7-77.

8 Vgl. Helen Schüngel-Straumann, Elisabeth Gössmann, "Gottebenbildlichkeit" im *Wörterbuch der Feministischen Theologie* (Gütersloh: Gerd Mohn 1991) 173-181.

9 "Sed quantum ad aliquid secundarium imago Dei invenitur in viro, secundum quod non invenitur in muliere. Nam vir est principium mulieris et finis, sicut Deus est principium et finis totius creaturae." Summa theol. I q.93 a.4 ad 1. Für das Folgende vgl. Daniela Müller, *Frauen vor der Inquisition* (Mainz: Philipp v. Zabern 1996).

sen Dualismus berief sich die Scholastik auf den *einen* Schöpfergott, von dem Geistiges und Materielles stammt, und wollte diesen auch innerweltlich in dem *Einprinzip Mann* gespiegelt sehen. Als Entsprechung zur Schöpfungskraft Gottes diente dabei die männliche Zeugungskraft.

Verminderte weibliche Gottebenbildlichkeit wie Verweigerung von Gottesrepräsentanz bringt Beschränkung weiblicher Gottessymbolik mit sich. In Schriften von Mystikern kommt sie zwar zuweilen vor, aber von der "strengen Wissenschaft" wird sie ausgespart. Anselm von Canterbury begründet dies in seinem "Monologion" mit der männlichen Superiorität und der Kraft des männlichen Samens. Aber in seiner Gebetsliteratur gebraucht er dennoch die Muttersymbolik für Jesus.[10]

b. in der Frauentradition:

Auf sämtliche Herabminderungen weiblicher Gottebenbildlichkeit reagiert die Frauentradition mit ihrem beredten Schweigen. Derartiges wird nicht erwähnt. Stattdessen wird eine uneingeschränkte weibliche Gottebenbildlichkeit nuancenreich beschrieben, die auf ein Gottesbild mit sowohl weiblichen wie männlichen Zügen bezogen ist.

Wenn die göttliche Gerechtigkeit sich im Menschen spiegelt, so ist das für Hildegard von Bingen (12. Jh.) "gleichsam etwas Männliches" (quasi virile), und wenn sich die göttliche Barmherzigkeit im Menschen spiegelt, so ist das "gleichsam etwas Weibliches" (quasi femineum).[11] Deutlich korrigiert sie auch das scholastische Modell von der Spiegelung des Schöpfergottes durch das innerweltliche Einprinzip des Mannes mit seiner Zeugungskraft. Sie ruft in ihrer Interpretation von Gen 1,26f. das "phallokratische" Bewußtsein auf den Boden der Tatsachen zurück, indem sie das menschliche *Paar* als das innerweltliche *Einprinzip* darstellt und so die Frau auf die gleiche Stufe der Gottebenbildlichkeit und Gottesrepräsentanz mit dem Mann erhebt.

10 Vgl. dazu Caroline Walker Bynum, *Jesus as Mother. Studies in the Spirituality of the High Middle Ages* (Berkeley/Los Angeles/London: University of California Press 1982) 113-115.

11 Für das Folgende in seinem weiteren Kontext und für die Stellenangaben vgl. Elisabeth Gössmann, *Hildegard von Bingen. Versuche einer Annäherung*, Sonderband in: Dieselbe (Hg.), Archiv für philosophie- und theologiegeschichtliche Frauenforschung (München: iudicium 1995).

"So werden durch Mann und Frau die vielen hervorgebracht, die dennoch aus dem einen Schöpfer hervorgehen. Denn wäre der Mann allein oder die Frau allein, so würde kein Mensch geboren werden. Daher sind auch Mann und Frau eines."[12] Nicht allein das "dennoch" in diesem Zitat, sondern auch Hildegards Warnung der Frauen vor den Katharern zeigt, daß sie mit der antignostischen Argumentation vertraut ist und die Einheit des menschlichen Paares als Spiegelung göttlicher Schöpfungskraft sieht, die nur vollständig sein kann durch die Einheit von Weiblich und Männlich. Zwar hatte dieses Denken zunächst noch keinerlei Rückwirkung auf die scholastische Tradition, aber diese eigenständige Absetzung vom männlichen Denkmodell ist nichts weniger als die Abkehr von Androzentrik und als Frauentradition sicher höher zu bewerten als der Einfluß der Juliana von Lüttich auf die Einführung eines Festes. Unter den zahlreichen Symbolisierungen des Göttlichen wie des Menschlichen in weiblicher Form—Töchter Sion können bei Hildegard sowohl männlich wie weiblich sein—ist ihr Gleichnis von der Mutter und der Tochter Sion (Scivias I, 4) wohl am eindrucksvollsten.[13]

Ähnlich wie Hildegard hat Gertrud von Helfta (13. Jh.) im 2. Buch ihres "Legatus divinae pietatis" (Gesandter der göttlichen Liebe) ein meditatives Gespräch mit Christus (Audition) beschrieben, wo sie ihn zu sich sagen hört: "Wie ich das Ebenbild Gottes des Vaters in der Gottheit bin, so wirst du für die Menschheit das Bild meines Wesens sein."[14] Aus dieser Zusicherung zieht sie weitgehende Konsequenzen für ihre Kompetenz zum Handeln.

Selbstverständlich vergißt auch Christine de Pizan nicht zu erwähnen, daß Gott die Frau "in der Würde der Ähnlichkeit zu ihm"[15] erschaffen hat, die bei ihr wie schon bei Hildegard besonders in Erkenntniskraft

---

12 "Ita per masculum et feminam multi procreantur, qui tamen ab uno creatore procedunt. Nam si masculus solus, vel si femina sola esset, nullus homo generaretur. Unde etiam vir et femina unum sunt." (Liber divinorum operum II,5,43.)

13 Da dieser und andere Texte von Hildegard oft nicht adäquat übersetzt sind, kann man nur am lateinischen Urtext erkennen, was Hildegard wirklich gemeint hat.

14 Gertrud die Große von Helfta, *Gesandter der göttlichen Liebe,* ungekürzte Übersetzung von Johanna Lanczkowski (Heidelberg: Verlag Lambert Schneider 1989) 25.

15 Übersetzung von Andrea Echtermann in: Elisabeth Gössmann (Hg.), *Kennt der Geist kein Geschlecht?* Archiv (wie Anm. 11) Bd. 6 (München: iudicium 1994) 21.

und Weisheit, ratio und sapientia, gesehen wird. Diesen und anderen Frauen geht es bei der Deutung von Gen 1,26f. vor allem um die unbeschränkte Teilhabe des weiblichen Geschlechts an der *einen* menschlichen ratio, die die göttliche Erkenntniskraft abbildet. Damit werden männliche Unterstellungen von weiblicher Vernunftschwäche zurückgewiesen.

Aus der frühneuzeitlichen Frauentradition sei Marie de Jars de Gournay erwähnt, die 1622 eine Schrift zur Egalité von Männern und Frauen verfaßte. Darin verspottet sie in ironischer Weise die Männer, die infolge ihres einseitig männlichen Gottesbildes "ihren Bart mit der image de Dieu verwechseln" und deshalb auch diejenigen von der Gottebenbildlichkeit aussperren, die ihnen im Bartbesitz nicht gleichen.[16] Von den Folgen dieser Korrektur an männlicher Arroganz wird noch die Rede sein.

Insgesamt sehen die Frauen in der für ihr Geschlecht von ihnen reklamierten Gottebenbildlichkeit, modern gesagt, so etwas wie Menschenrechte für die Frau. Sie lassen nicht zu, daß man ihnen gleiche Würde und gleiche Fähigkeiten wie dem männlichen Geschlecht streitig machen will.

2 Schöpfung, Sündenfall und die Folgen

a. bei männlichen Autoren:

Hier geht es um allgemein Bekanntes. Schon innerbiblisch setzt die androzentrische und frauenfeindliche Sicht ein, und zwar mit der Betonung der (positiv gewerteten) Ersterschaffung des Mannes, der bei der Frau die negative Priorität der Erstverführung durch die Schlange entspricht, sowie den Folgerungen an Entmächtigung der Frauen, die in 1 Tim 2,9ff. daraus gezogen werden. Ähnlich war schon in Sir 25,24 der Eintritt von Sünde und Tod in die Welt auf die Frau projiziert worden. In der Väterzeit wird daraus ganz allgemein "Eva, die Verführerin" des Mannes, bei Tertullian die Frau als "Tor des Teufels" (ianua diaboli), bei Augustinus die stolze Eva, die sein wollte wie Gott, während der kluge Mann, der erkannte, daß dies nicht möglich ist, sozusagen nur mitsündigte, um Eva nicht allein verloren gehen zu lassen. Sein Beitrag zur Ursünde wird also zum "Kavaliersdelikt" herabgemindert. Der "starke" Mann und die "schwache" Frau werden hier schon deutlich hervorgekehrt. Petrus Lombardus (12. Jh.), dessen Sentenzenwerk alle späteren Theologen bis

---

16 Marie de Jars de Gournay ist vorgestellt in Archiv (vgl. Anm. 11) Bd. 1 Kap. 1 (München: iudicium 1984).

zur frühen Neuzeit, den jungen Luther eingeschlossen, kommentieren mußten, spricht vom "tumor" des Stolzes in der Evasbrust.[17]

Anläßlich der weiblichen "Gehorsamsverpflichtung" gegenüber dem Mann vertreten die meisten Theologen der Scholastik sogar eine doppelte Unterordnung der Frau, eine sanfte bereits im Urstand, eine harte als Sündenfolge. (Daß der Mann dabei auch zum Gewinner jener "Erbsünde" genannten Krise wird, fällt erst spät einem Theologen auf.) Erstere wird bei Thomas von Aquin begründet mit dem "Gut der Ordnung" (bonum ordinis), wonach die Weiseren die weniger Weisen, also die Frauen, leiten müssen; letztere mit dem sogenannten Strafwort Gottes an Eva. Die Begründung der ersteren muß auf Latein zitiert werden, denn sie birgt mehrere Deutungsmöglichkeiten und zudem Übersetzungsschwierigkeiten: "...naturaliter femina subiecta est viro, quia naturaliter in homine magis abundat discretio rationis." (Summa theol. Teil 1, q.92 a.1 ad 2) Man kann den Satz bösartig so lesen, daß er besagt, die Frau sei kein Mensch. Aber das hat Thomas, wie sein Gesamtwerk erweist, nicht gemeint.[18] Also lesen wir ihn im Sinne der viel beklagten Gleichsetzung von "Mann" (vir) mit "Mensch" (homo) als klassisches Beispiel dafür und übersetzen: "Von Natur ist die Frau dem Mann untergeben, weil von Natur im Menschen (=Mann) die Unterscheidungskraft der Vernunft überwiegt."

Mit der Autorität des Aristoteles werden auch in der mittelalterlichen Naturphilosophie Begründungen für die weibliche Intellektschwäche versucht. Die "höheren" der kosmischen Elemente, nämlich Feuer und Luft, werden primär als männlich identifiziert, die "niederen" dagegen, Wasser und Erde, als weiblich. Auf diese Weise wird die Mann-Frau-Hierarchie kosmisch legitimiert, und die weiblichen Begabungen werden herabgesetzt, da aus den "niederen" Elementen auch die ungünstige Temperamentenmischung beim weiblichen Geschlecht folge ("kalt und feucht" im Gegensatz zu "heiß und trocken" beim Mann.) Noch bis ins 18. Jahrhundert haben Frauen ihre Energie darauf richten müssen, diese für sie so negative Lehre zu widerlegen.

---

17 Zu Tertullian, Augustinus und Petrus Lombardus, aber auch zur Frauentradition, vgl. Monika Leisch-Kiesl, *Eva als Andere. Eine exemplarische Untersuchung zu Frühchristentum und Mittelalter* (Köln/Weimar/Wien: Böhlau 1992).

18 Diese Auffassung gab es aber lange genug. Vgl. Archiv (wie Anm. 11) Bd. 4, *Ob die Weiber Menschen seyn, oder nicht?* 2. erweiterte Aufl. 1996, besonders die Einleitung.

b. in der Frauentradition:

Wenn es um die Auslegung von Gen 2 geht, beweisen die Frauen des Mittelalters ihre Fähigkeit zur Umwertung auf erstaunliche Weise, und die Frauen der frühen Neuzeit kommen einer Vorform von historisch-kritischer Bibellesung schon recht nahe; beides wohl aufgrund ihrer Einbeziehung von Erfahrungen, die sie der männlichen Sicht von weiblicher Minderbemitteltheit als Geschöpf widersprechen lassen. Die männliche Rede von der Stärke des eigenen und der Schwäche des anderen Geschlechts wird umgewertet in die von der weicheren Stärke der Frau. So schreibt Hildegard, daß Gott den Menschen männlichen Geschlechts mit größerer Stärke geschaffen habe, die Frau aber von weicherer Kraft.[19] Zu 1 Kor 11,9, wonach die Frau um des Mannes willen geschaffen ist und nicht umgekehrt, erlaubt sie sich eine prophetische Korrektur: "und der Mann um der Frau willen."[20] Die eben geschaffene Eva bezeichnet sie als Abglanz göttlicher Schönheit, eine neuplatonische Deutung weiblicher Gottebenbildlichkeit.

Da der Literalsinn der Schrift in der vorkritischen Exegese als historisch genommen wird, betonen die Frauen bis in die Neuzeit die Erst-erschaffung des Mannes, aber nur, um eine Umwertung herbeizuführen, die zunächst im Sinne der Gleichheit, später auch im Sinne der Überbewertung des weiblichen Geschlechts ausfällt. Hildegard führt die physische Stärke des Mannes auf seine Erschaffung aus der Ackererde zurück, die größere Agilität, Grazilität und Geschicklichkeit der Frau aber auf ihre Erschaffung aus schon beseelter menschlicher Leiblichkeit. Daraus leitet sie her, daß der Mann mit seiner Feldarbeit die Frau ernährt, er aber ohne die Textilienarbeit ihrer geschickteren Hände "nackt bleiben" würde. Beide Geschlechter haben also ein "Privileg" vor dem andern, das jeweils sowohl das Physische, als auch das Soziale betrifft. Die scholastische Naturphilosophie verändert Hildegard, indem sie die beiden mittleren Elemente, Luft und Wasser, vornehmlich weiblich, und die beiden extremen, Feuer und Erde, stärker männlich identifiziert. Damit hat sie die

19 "Deus creavit hominem, masculum scilicet majoris fortitudinis, feminam vero mollioris roboris." (De operatione Dei II, 5, 43).

20 "Mulier propter virum creata est, et vir propter mulierem factus est." (Scivias I, 2).

kosmische Legitimierung der Mann-Frau-Hierarchie und ihre negativen Konsequenzen für die weiblichen Temperamente aufgelöst.

Die Evasschuld wird von Hildegard herabgemildert zum Betrogenwerden durch die Schlange, das Gottes Erbarmen und seinen Erlösungsratschluß hervorruft. Wie Mechthild von Magdeburg und viele andere Frauen betont sie die Gleichheit der Sünde beider Stammeltern. Den tumor des Stolzes läßt Hildegard nicht in der Evasbrust sitzen, sondern sie gibt ihrer allegorischen Gestalt der superbia eine männliche Brust, weil sie den tumor eitler Überheblichkeit eher beim männlichen Geschlecht ansiedeln will. Die Unterordnung der Frau hat Hildegard biologisch verfremdet und entschärft: Die Frau sei "viro subjecta", dem Mann untergeben, heißt es in ihrer Zeit. Das bezieht sie auf den Zeugungsakt und versteht es wörtlich als "daruntergelegt", damit der Mann in sie seinen Samen ergieße und sie in ihrem Leib daraus ein Kind bilde.

Bei Christine de Pizan wird neben der geistigen Gleichheit der Geschlechter die leibliche Vorzüglichkeit der Frau betont. Sie ist das zuletzt im Paradies aus edlerer Materie als der Mann erschaffene Meisterwerk Gottes, das vollkommene Geschöpf, aber daß sie Adam betrogen hat, wird bestritten. Denn nach Christine fehlte der Frau die Absicht zum Betrug. Es war Arglosigkeit, die Eva auf die Schlange hereinfallen ließ. Proportional zur Zunahme antifeministischen Schrifttums, so läßt sich beobachten, nimmt auch die Evasentschuldigung zu. Der "Sitz im Leben" solcher Reaktionen ist evident.

Moralphilosophisch wird die Evasentschuldigung von italienischen (Lucretia Marinella) und französischen Schriftstellerinnen des 16./17. Jahrhunderts fortgesetzt, ebenso wie die Beschreibung der Vorzüglichkeit des weiblichen Leibes. Durch den Cartesianismus hatte sich die auch im Mittelalter schon nachweisbare Lehre von der Geschlechtslosigkeit des Geistes wieder verstärkt. Aber während die Scholastiker betonten, der Geist könne sich in einem männlichen Leib besser entfalten als in einem weiblichen, wird jetzt die privilegierte Erschaffung der Eva dagegengestellt. So beklagt Suzanne de Nervèze 1642 in ihrer Frauenapologie, daß immer noch das männliche Geschlecht die Stärke der Vernunft für sich in Anspruch nehme, obwohl es gerade dadurch deren Schwäche verrate. Hier finden wir auch schon den Begriff "Evastöchter", der bis heute negativ assoziiert wird, positiv gewendet und auf die Weisheit der biblischen Frauen bezogen.

In ihrem Werk über die französische Sprache (1668) versucht Marguerite Buffet auch den Frauen sprachliche und schriftstellerische Fähigkeiten zu verschaffen. Da die Geschlechtslosigkeit der Geistseele für sie feststeht, beruft sie sich auf die Vorzüglichkeit des weiblichen Leibes, um deren Entfaltungsmöglichkeiten sicherzustellen. "Wem können wir mehr glauben als dem Gott der Wahrheit, der uns versichert, daß die Vollkommenheit der Schöpfung von der Erschaffung der Frau abhing, dem letzten seiner Werke und deren Krönung. Ohne diese exzellente Kreatur hätte die Welt nicht das ganze Ausmaß ihrer Schönheit und Harmonie erhalten."[21]

Im Laufe der Zeit stiegen auch Männer, die an theologische Schulen weniger gebunden waren und Frauen Gerechtigkeit zukommen lassen wollten, in diese seit dem Mittelalter bestehende Frauentradition ein, was die gegenwärtige Romanistik aus Unkenntnis zu der Behauptung geführt hat, die ersten Feministen seien Männer gewesen. Diese Männer schreiben aber zunächst noch höchst ambivalent, indem sie misogyne Bibelauslegungen neben die aus der Frauentradition entnommenen stellen. Immerhin konnte es den Frauen nützen, wenn sich Männer wie Henricus Cornelius Agrippa von Nettesheim oder Poullain de la Barre für die Aufhebung der Beschränkungen weiblichen Handelns einsetzten. Das Arsenal an Argumenten liefern nach wie vor besonders die drei ersten Kapitel der Genesis in ihrer frauenfreundlichen Deutung.[22]

Der Widerstand gegen das "Gehorsamsgebot" für Frauen nimmt bei Renaissanceschriftstellerinnen, besonders aus dem Hochadel Frankreichs, sehr zu. Es ist von der "Usurpation des Mannes" die Rede, der den Frauen die ihnen ursprünglich eigene Macht genommen habe. Dies muß als Widerstand gegen die Lex Salica gesehen werden, die in Frankreich Frauen von der Thronfolge ausschloß.

Besonders originell ist in ihrer auf das Leben bezogenen Auslegung von Gen 2 und 3 die italienische Nonne Arcangela Tarabotti (1604-1652), die sich auch für die im Ehestand lebenden Frauen eingesetzt hat. Arcangela deutet die göttliche Weisheit, die "Ersterschaffene vor aller Kreatur" (Sir 24,3.9), als eine Art platonischer Idee für die Erschaffung der Frau, die in Maria am vollkommensten erfüllt sei. Dies ist eines der vielen

21 Zu Nervèze und Buffet vgl. Elisabeth Gössmann, "Das Gottes- und Menschenbild in der Frauentradition als Korrektiv und Replik zur männlichen Schultheologie" in: *Jahrbuch für Volkskunde* 14 (1991), 127-142.

22 Zu diesen beiden vgl. Archiv (wie Anm. 11) Bd. 4 und Bd. 6.

Zeugnisse für die Mariologie der Frauen, die alle Frauen mit Maria ebenso verbindet wie mit einer positiv gedeuteten Eva und die von den Zügen einer unterdrückerischen Männer-Mariologie nichts an sich hat. Maria ist wie schon bei Christine de Pizan die Verteidigerin des weiblichen Geschlechts.

Arcangela betont, daß nach Gottes Wort (Gen 1,26ff.) beide Geschlechter die Erde beherrschen sollen. Sie legt Wert auf die Willensfreiheit der Frau und damit auch auf ihre Freiheit zu sündigen. Die Ursünde Evas bezeichnet sie aber als einen einfachen Irrtum, der keineswegs "Ursache für unser aller Sterblichkeit" sei. Indem sie jede verheiratete Frau anspricht, paraphrasiert sie das Wort Gottes an Eva: "Weil Du zu leichtgläubig warst, 'werde ich Deine Mühsale vermehren und Deine Schwangerschaften, und Du wirst in Schmerzen Kinder gebären.' Und es paßt gut zu einem so undankbaren Wesen wie dem Mann, daß er sich auch der eigenen Gebärerin gegenüber sehr undankbar zeigt (...) Im Gegensatz dazu sehe ich voraus, daß Du (...) von der ehelichen Liebe zu sehr berauscht bist und den falschen Gefährten zum Herrn über Deinen Willen machst; daß Du es zuläßt, daß er Dir in seiner Gier alle Autorität nimmt; und weil Du ihm zu sehr glaubst oder nachgibst, kann man von Dir sagen: 'Unter der Macht des Mannes wirst Du sein, und er wird über Dich herrschen', nicht als verdientes Strafurteil, sondern weil Du einmal von Versprechungen, ein andermal von Drohungen oder Bitten besiegt wirst, wirst Du in die Fallen gehen, die Dir dieses Ungeheuer stellen wird."[23]

Auf vielfältige Weise haben sich so Frauen gegen die androzentrische Deutung von Gen 2 und 3 abgearbeitet, um einander zu ermutigen, zu ermächtigen und "consciousness raising" zu betreiben.

---

23 Vgl. Archiv (wie Anm. 11) Bd. 6, Kap. 3.

3 Frau und Amt

a. bei männlichen Autoren:

Trotz des negativen Bescheids ist es bemerkenswert, daß die Frage der Ordination der Frau in Mittelalter und früher Neuzeit diskutiert wurde.[24] Positive Argumente waren etwa die altkirchlichen Diakonissen, die Stärke der Frau im Martyrium oder die Eignung der Frau für die Seelsorge. Die negativen Argumente gaben jedoch den Ausschlag. Bei Thomas von Aquin ist es der "Defekt der Natur" im weiblichen Geschlecht,—und hier versagt die Unterscheidung von Geschlechtergleichheit im gnadenhaften und Unterordnung der Frau im natürlichen Bereich—denn dieser "Naturdefekt" erlaubt es nicht, den "Grad der Exzellenz" zu repräsentieren, den ein Priester durch die sakramentale Gnade der Ordination empfängt. Der untergeordnete Stand (status subiectionis) der Frau verhindert es. Diese Meinung hatte Zukunft, nicht dagegen die des franziskanischen Zeitgenossen Bonaventura, der bezeugt, daß die Frauenordination zwar verboten war, aber offenließ, ob eine solche nicht doch gültig sein könne. Schließlich folgten die Franziskaner ja nicht dem aristotelischen Aktiv-Passiv-Schema für die beiden Geschlechter.

Meine Forschungen zur Rezeptionsgeschichte einer mutmaßlichen Päpstin[25] haben zutage gefördert, was vom 13. bis ins 20. Jahrhundert gegen das weibliche Amt angeführt wurde. Nachdem anfänglich das Papsttum der Frau als unerlaubt, aber gültig und sehr schädlich für die Kirche angesehen wurde, hieß es: Wenn eine Frau sich die Priesterweihe erschleicht, ist sie ungültig wie die eines Häretikers oder Juden. Eine Frau im Amt unterbricht die apostolische Sukzession. Eine Frau im Lehramt verfälscht die christliche Tradition. Eine Frau ist ebenso weiheunfähig wie Hermaphroditen, Monstren (Behinderte!) und Wahnsinnige. Wer sich heute auf Tradition beruft, sollte wenigstens wissen, daß es darin auch derartiges aus der Feder hoch angesehener Traditionszeugen gibt.

---

[24] Für das Folgende einschließlich der Zitatangaben vgl. meinen Beitrag "Äußerungen zum Frauenpriestertum in der christlichen Tradition" in: Dietmar Bader (Hg.), *Freiburger Akademiearbeiten 1979 - 1989* (München/Zürich: Schnell und Steiner 1989) 304-321.

[25] Vgl. Archiv (wie Anm. 11) Bd. 5,1994.

b. in der Frauentradition:

Bei ihrem Umgang mit dem Amtsausschluß lassen sich Frauen nicht auf männliche Begründungsversuche wie Intellektschwäche und moralische Unzuverlässigkeit ein. Hildegard sieht die eucharistische Epiklese und Konsekration als Abbild dessen, was bei der Empfängnis Jesu durch den Heiligen Geist in Maria geschah: die Fleischwerdung des Logos, so daß das priesterliche Handeln auf marianischem Vorbild beruht. Die Klosterfrau stellt sie an die Seite ihres himmlischen sponsus Christus, an dessen urbildlichem Priestertum sie teilhat. Der irdische Priester erfüllt nur einen den Bräuten Christi geschuldeten Dienst.[26]

Über solche theologischen Kompensationen geht Gertrud die Große, von der eine reiche seelsorgliche Tätigkeit bekannt ist, weit hinaus. Im Zusammenhang mit ihrer von Christus bezeugten Gottebenbildlichkeit erwähnt sie auch ihre Bevollmächtigung zum Bußgespräch und zur Sündenvergebung sowie die Erfahrung der Erneuerung der Gnade aller sieben Sakramente, also auch der Priesterweihe[27], durch Christus. Auf der Ebene von Charisma und Mystik überwindet sie den Amtsausschluß für ihren Tätigkeitsbereich, ohne Rivalitätsgefühle zu geweihten Priestern.

Daß Gottebenbildlichkeit und Amtsfähigkeit zusammenhängen, bezeugt auch Marie de Jars de Gournay[28], die empört fragt, da doch die Frauen taufen können und die Befähigung zur Sakramentenspendung eine einzige sei, warum die Frauen die anderen Sakramente nicht spenden dürften. Die Antwort gibt sie sich selbst: weil Männer nicht bereit seien, Macht mit Frauen zu teilen.

III Folgerungen

Wir haben die Frauentradition als Rückendeckung, also benutzen wir sie auch als Zeichen des kontinuierlichen Widerspruchs von Frauen gegen den christlichen Androzentrismus! Viele Namen mußten hier ungenannt bleiben, aber die Kontinuität ist gesichert. Verlangen wir die Anerkennung der Frauentradition als gleichberechtigte christliche Tradition, die sich trotz Lehrverbot und Schweigegebot für Frauen bilden konnte, weil Frauen sich nicht alles bieten ließen; eine Tradition schließlich auch, die

---

26 Vgl. Archiv (Anm. 11).

27 Vgl. a.a.O. (Anm. 14), 43. 163.

28 Vgl. oben Anm. 16.

vieles wieder zurechtrückte, was die androzentrische Sicht am Christentum verfehlt hatte. Im Geiste dieser Tradition und in ihr verwurzelt, weiterzumachen, gibt Feministischer Theologie Heimat.

Freilich ist die Frauentradition den Bedingungen der jeweiligen Zeit unterworfen wie die männliche. Sie reagierte auf der jeweiligen theologischen Ebene, aber transzendierte diese auch zugleich, weil die Lebenserfahrungen von Frauen kontinuierlich die männliche Sicht nicht bestätigen konnten. Zum Verhältnis von Lehramt und anderen Glaubensinstanzen wie Theologie und Glaubensbewußtsein der nicht mit Theologie befaßten Gläubigen kann folgendes gefordert werden: Die jüngsten Ergebnisse der theologischen Forschung, denen der feministische Aspekt integriert sein muß, sollen via Verkündigung allen vermittelt werden, denn die simplices, die einfältigen Gläubigen, die auf Autorität hin glauben, gibt es bald nicht mehr. Dabei müssen die "Kirchenmütter" bzw. -lehrerinnen insgesamt (und nicht nur 2 oder 3) sich gleicher Zitierwürdigkeit erfreuen dürfen wie die "Kirchenväter", ebenso die heutigen Theologinnen wie die Theologen und nicht weniger künftige Generationen in beiden Geschlechtern.

Die letzten offiziellen römischen Verlautbarungen berufen sich auf die Tradition, die eine Erweiterung weiblicher Funktionen nicht zulasse. Es ist wohl deutlich geworden, um welche Tradition es sich dabei handelt und um welche nicht. Wenn Tradition auch Kritik einschließt und wenn Zustimmungsverweigerung eine römische Vorlage "töten" kann[29], dann kann auch "Ordinatio sacerdotalis" von einem solchen Schicksal ereilt werden. Solange eine Sonderposition von kirchlichem Lehramt erhalten bleibt, können Frauen jedenfalls nicht zulassen, darin nicht vertreten zu sein.

---

[29] Siehe oben im Text unter *Stimmen der Zeit* bei Beinert.

Abstracts

Elisabeth GÖSSMANN explores the Catholic understanding of "tradition" since the 19th century, asking whether women's traditions are included. Concluding that they are not, she suggests a contrastive method of research into theological writing by women with the aim of reconstructing a women's counter-tradition. Applying this method to three themes (woman as God's image, interpretation of the stories of creation and fall, and the question of the ordination of women), she concludes that it is possible to establish a woman's tradition which supports our own endeavours as feminist theologians.

Elisabeth GÖSSMANN analyse la conception catholique de la "tradition" depuis le XIXe siècle en essayant de voir si les traditions féminines y sont représentées. Constatant que ce n'est pas le cas, elle propose une méthode de recherche contrastive pour les écrits théologiques des femmes, dans le but de reconstruire une contre-tradition féminine. En appliquant cette méthode à trois thèmes (la femme en tant qu'image de Dieu, l'interprétation des histoires de la création et de la chute, la question de l'ordination des femmes), elle arrive à la conclusion qu'il est possible d'établir une tradition féminine qui conforte nos propres efforts en tant que théologiennes féministes.

Dr. theol. Dr. phil. habil, Dr. theol h.c., Dr. phil. h.c. Elisabeth GÖSSMANN lehrt seit 1968 als Professorin (seit 1989 als Ehrenprofessorin) an der Seishin-Frauenuniversität Tokyo. Nachdem ihr 1962 die Habilitation der Katholisch-Theologischen Fakultät der Universität München verweigert wurde, wurde sie 1978 an der der Philosophischen Fakultät der Universität München habilitiert und ist dort seit 1990 apl. Professorin. Zahlreiche Veröffentlichungen zur Theologie und Philosophie des Mittelalters und der Frühen Neuzeit, Lehraufträge in Österreich, der Schweiz und Deutschland.

Grace M. JANTZEN

Devenir Divin(e)s: La Raison, et les Buts d'une Philosophie Feministe de la Religion

> L'amour de Dieu... indique un chemin... Dieu ne nous oblige à rien, sinon *devenir*. Aucune tâche, aucune obligation ne nous incombe que celle-là: devenir divin(e)s, devenir parfaitement, ne pas nous laisser amputer des parties de nous que nous pouvons épanouir..[1]

Quelle est la tâche fondamentale de la raison? Les réponses à cette question seront très différentes, selon que l'on adoptera une perspective traditionnelle, anglo-américaine de la philosophie de la religion, ou une approche féministe nourrie par la pensée européenne contemporaine. En outre, des buts différents auront manifestement des implications très différentes quant à la manière dont chaque sujet d'étude au sein de cette discipline sera abordé, et quant aux sujets d'études eux-mêmes. Pour Luce Irigaray, notre devoir moral fondamental est de devenir divin(e)s, et la tâche de la philosophie de la religion consiste à permettre ce devenir, sinon elle n'est en fin de compte qu'une discipline inutile.[2] « Philosophie » dans son sens le plus ancien signifie « l'amour de la sagesse », sophia, qui en grec (tout comme en hébreu et dans d'autres langues) est féminin et divin. Selon Irigaray, la sagesse dont les femmes et les hommes ont le plus besoin dans le monde post-moderne est la sagesse qui permet de devenir divin(e)s, sans laquelle nous « ne pouvons nous épanouir ».

Une telle conception a peu de choses en commun avec les objectifs définis normalement par la philosophie de la religion anglo-américaine, mais elle se distingue tout autant des opinions professées par de nombreu-

---

1 Luce Irigaray, *Sexes et parentés* (Paris: Minuit 1987), 81

2 Même alors, il nous faut éviter de lui accorder trop d'importance. C'est l'*amour* de Dieu qui nous montre la voie, et non les discours philosophiques sur Dieu qui caractérisent la philosophie anglo-américaine de la religion.

ses féministes, séculières ou religieuses. Dans cet article, je souhaite d'abord tenter d'expliquer ce que Luce Irigaray entend par « devenir divin(e)s » et souligner en quoi sa conception diffère des buts poursuivis par la philosophie traditionnelle de la religion. Dans la mesure où ce devenir divin(e)s est en effet un but valable, j'essayerai de montrer à quel point le contenu de la philosophie de la religion peut s'en trouver modifié, permettant ainsi de développer une philosophie de la religion féministe et créative.

Toutefois, il convient d'abord de se pencher sur la résistance qu'opposent les féministes elles-mêmes à cette conception. Si bon nombre d'entre elles dénonce sans hésiter la stérilité de la philosophie traditionnelle de la religion, elles sont encore loin d'accepter l'importance que Luce Irigaray attribue à ce devoir de « devenir divin(e)s », ainsi que la centralité qu'elle accorde à l'amour de Dieu, et ce, même parmi les féministes qui reconnaissent la créativité de la pensée d'Irigaray.[3] Et que peut-elle vouloir dire? Deux types de résistance coexistent. D'un côté, il y a les féministes que j'appellerai, par souci de commodité, les féministes « séculières »: elles estiment que la religion a déjà causé assez de dégâts et que les féministes feraient mieux de s'en débarrasser. Au lieu de se vouer à une quelconque quête liée à ce « devenir divin(e)s », les féministes devraient se consacrer à des luttes pratiques et théoriques pour une plus grande justice. Au vu des effets incalculables de la religion occidentale—et principalement du christianisme—en termes de colonialisme, racisme, homophobie et sexisme, un tel refus de prendre la religion en ligne de compte, même dans une perspective de contestation, est totalement compréhensible et respectable de la part de féministes. Certes, une contestation qui ne fait que repasser sur une terre déjà bien piétinée ne fait que la rendre plus dure, comme je l'expliquerai plus loin. En reconnaissant l'existence d'un lieu de l'oppression religieuse, ce qui semble en être une critique permet, en réalité, une récupération de cette même reconnais-

3 Parmi les commentatrices les plus fines de Irigaray, certaines ne font guère allusion à cette question ou en minimisent la portée: voir Tina Chanter, *Ethics of Eros: Irigaray's rewriting of the philosophers* (London: Routledge, 1995), Margaret Whitford, *Luce Irigaray: philosophy in the feminine* (London: Routledge 1991), Caroline Burke, *Engaging with Irigaray*. New York: Columbia University, 1994). Rosi Braidotti s'en distancie explicitement [« Forward » in Adriana Cavarero *In Spite of Plato: A feminist rewriting of ancient philosophy* (Cambridge: Polity, 1995), xvi-xvii].

sance. Une alternative plus créative s'impose. Luce Irigaray en offre-t-elle une en insistant sur ce « devenir divin(e)s »?

De l'autre côté, celles que l'on appelle conventionnellement les féministes « chrétiennes » trouveront peut-être aussi l'idée de Luce Irigaray rebutante. Non pas que les féministes chrétiennes acceptent l'histoire patriarcale du Big Daddy au plus haut des Cieux, du Dieu le Père unique, omnipotent, séparé de l'univers auquel « il » préside—le concept de Dieu tel qu'on l'a toujours retrouvé au coeur des conceptions occidentales d'une déité. Quelle que soit la manière de penser le divin, elle devra être différente. Néanmoins, l'idée de devoir *devenir* divin(e)s, que cela puisse être conçu comme une tâche pour les femmes et les hommes, peut sembler déplaisant tant d'un point de vue moral que religieux. Bien trop d'hommes ont causé bien trop de dégâts en jouant aux petits dieux pour que les féministes puissent trouver à cette idée un quelconque attrait. Le premier des dix commandements, « Tu n'auras pas d'autres dieux que moi » a déjà été amplement justifié; la religion interdit de jouer au dieu et un tel interdit aurait dû bien plus souvent être respecté. Et pourtant, posons-nous à nouveau la question, cette fois dans une perspective religieuse: est-ce là ce que veut dire Luce Irigaray?

En réponse aux approches tant « séculière » que « religieuse » ainsi définies, je souhaite suggérer une alternative. Au lieu de considérer le séculier et le religieux comme antithétiques, tels que les présente conventionnellement la modernité et comme en témoignent les objections ci-dessus, je suggère de les envisager comme les deux faces d'une même pièce, pièce d'une monnaie particulièrement moderne. Depuis que la « voûte sacrée » du monde médiéval s'est effondrée, le sécularisme et la religion se sont souvent définis l'un contre l'autre. Pourtant, au sein des discours de la modernité, l'un et l'autre sont profondément impliqués l'un dans l'autre, ce que laissent apparaître plus particulièrement les techniques du pouvoir dans leur relation aux notions de genre et de « race », au colonialisme, et à la sexualité. Mais si, en effet, le sécularisme et la religion doivent se repenser de façon radicale comme étant imbriqués l'un dans l'autre au sein du projet moderne, et ce, dans ce qu'il a pu avoir de plus condamnable, alors tant les féministes « séculières » que les féministes « religieuses » devront repenser leurs positions les unes par rapport aux autres. De plus, une philosophie féministe de la religion fondée sur ce but: le « devenir divin(e) », fait bien plus que de contester les objectifs et méthodes traditionnels de la philosophie de la religion: elle nous permet de dépasser le projet de la modernité lui-même et offre un nouvel horizon au devenir humain, un « nouveau matin du monde ». [4]

Mais n'allons pas trop vite et revenons même un peu en arrière pour examiner, d'abord, ce que Irigaray entend elle-même par ce « devenir divin ». Luce Irigaray est une psychanalyste et philosophe française dont les écrits doivent se comprendre dans le contexte de ce qu'on appelle aujourd'hui le post-structuralisme, ce courant de pensée créatif et provocant qui s'est développé entre les mouvements étudiants de 1968 et cette fin de millénaire. Afin de comprendre comment elle conçoit la tâche de la philosophie de la religion (qui est de permettre aux femmes et aux hommes de devenir divin(e)s), il nous faut brièvement nous pencher sur l'arrière-plan psychanalytique dérivé de Freud et introduit dans la pensée française par Jacques Lacan, car ce sont eux qui ont évoqué les périls et dangers entraînés par le devenir sujet humain (sans parler d'un devenir divin). Un bref survol nous révèle déjà la différence de buts entre l'approche féministe de Irigaray et la manière dont les philosophes anglo-américains de la religion ont habituellement considéré leur tâche.

Le fait que la subjectivité humaine n'ait rien d'un postulat, ne soit pas donnée au départ, est l'une des idées fondamentales des psychanalystes qui les écarte de la tradition religieuse et philosophique de Saint-Augustin, de Descartes et de Locke. Les personnes ne sont pas des âmes que Dieu glisse toutes faites dans un corps, ni des esprits qui pourraient être mûrs et totalement indépendants de l'histoire physique de l'individu (et qui pourraient survivre après la mort du corps). Au contraire, la personne humaine *se construit*, et se construit à grands frais. Un bébé humain vient au monde avec une foule de désirs conflictuels. Afin de devenir un sujet unifié, certains de ces désirs doivent être refoulés. Ce refoulement des désirs contribue à former l'inconscient et, de cet inconscient, les désirs refoulés menacent toujours de resurgir. Des stratégies sont ainsi mises en place afin de contrôler la pensée, les sentiments et le comportement, sans quoi le fragile sujet se désintègre à nouveau. La religion a été l'une des sources de quelques-unes de ces stratégies parmi les plus efficaces.

En outre, l'unification du sujet, si elle vise à son intégration dans la société, se devra de refléter les normes de cette société: dans le contexte de la modernité occidentale, elles seront très masculines et hétéro-

4 Irigaray, *Sexes et parentés*.

sexuelles. Ainsi, dans son évocation du stade oedipien, Freud nous dit que le jeune homme, sous la menace de la castration, réprime le désir qu'il éprouve pour sa mère et essaye de devenir comme son père, dans l'espoir de finalement prendre sa place dans la société. Toutefois, le coût en sera le déni de quelques-uns de ses désirs les plus essentiels, particulièrement celui qu'il éprouve pour la mère. Un tel déni peut être si douloureux qu'il engendrera colère, peur ou haine envers quiconque le rappellera: de là, la misogynie et l 'homophobie de la modernité occidentale et leur renforcement par les doctrines et rituels religieux.

Irigaray accepte (moyennant certaines réserves) la doctrine psychanalytique selon laquelle la subjectivité n'est pas donnée mais construite, et résulte plutôt d'un processus social et historique. Cependant, dans ses livres *Speculum, de l'autre femme*[5] et *Ce sexe qui n'en est pas un,*[6] elle montre que, lorsqu'ils parlent de cette construction de la subjectivité, Freud et Lacan parlent de sujets *masculins*. Pour Freud, le féminin se définit par un manque: la petite fille est un petit homme, mais privé de pénis. Similairement, Lacan dit de la femme qu'elle est le « pas tout ». La subjectivité n'est possible que pour le masculin.[7] Donc, pour Irigaray, comme pour toute féministe qui prend la psychanalyse au sérieux, une double question se pose: les femmes peuvent-elles être des sujets? et comment les femmes peuvent-elle avoir accès à cette subjectivité *en tant que femmes*, et non en disparaissant dans le paysage masculin ou en essayant d'être « égales » aux hommes (qui, de la sorte, constituent la norme à laquelle les femmes doivent se conformer), en devenant donc ce qu'*elles* sont elles-mêmes et non en se définissant par rapport aux hommes?

Afin de comprendre la réponse de Irigaray à ces questions, et le rôle qu'y joue la religion, souvenons-nous du fait que, selon la théorie freudienne revisitée par Lacan, l'accomplissement de la subjectivité (et le refoulement de désirs inacceptables) se fait selon ce que Lacan nomme, en un écho délibéré de la liturgie catholique, la Loi ou le Nom du Père. Cette formule religieuse à peine voilée expose la nature autoritaire de l'exigence

5 Luce Irigaray, *Speculum, de l'autre femme* (Paris: Minuit, 1974).

6 Luce Irigaray, *Ce sexe qui n'en est pas un* (Paris: Minuit, 1977).

7 Jacques Lacan dans Juliet Mitchell and Jacqueline Rose (eds), *Feminine Sexuality: Jacques Lacan and the école freudienne* (Basingstoke: Macmillan/New York: Pantheon, 1982), 144

sociale, son caractère patriarcal ainsi que sa structure religieuse. Côté pile: refoulement du désir qu'éprouve le garçon pour la mère; côté face: accès au langage, à la civilisation et au monde social des pères, ce que Lacan nomme « le symbolique ». Dans la pensée française, le « symbolique » désigne bien plus que ce que nous appelons traditionnellement les symboles. Il inclut le langage dans sa totalité ainsi que des formes non-linguistiques telles que la musique, l'art, les rituels. En fait, le terme peut s'utiliser pour renvoyer aux structures conceptuelles de la civilisation. De plus, le symbolique est structuré en discours dont l'influence est incalculable: dans l'occident moderne, les discours légaux, scientifiques, économiques et, bien sûr, religieux ont été particulièrement formateurs.

Dans cette perspective, la religion (et par conséquent la philosophie de la religion qui la légitimise) est d'une importance cruciale, puisqu'une conception de Dieu comme Père Divin—un Dieu qui est aussi Verbe et qui dans sa désincarnation, son omnipotence et son omniscience définit les valeurs—sous-tend le symbolique masculiniste occidental. Même dans une société relativement sécularisée, ces attributs traditionnels du divin représentent encore les valeurs les plus élevées. En d'autres termes, même les athées estiment que, si Dieu existait, « il » devrait se conformer à ce modèle: ceci transparaît, par exemple, dans les débats sans fin sur l'existence de Dieu, débats au sein desquels théistes et athées s'accordent tacitement à reconnaître la nature masculinisée du Dieu dont ils disputent de l'existence. Donc, que l'on accepte ou non l'existence de Dieu, le *concept* du divin sert à valoriser la puissance et la rationalité désincarnées. En effet, le divin est ce qui garantit le sens. Selon la terminologie de Derrida, c'est l'hypothèse de la présence divine (même lorsque cette présence est tenue pour absente, comme dans le sécularisme) qui, finalement, fonde le système des signes et permet l'ancrage de signifiants sans cesse flottants en les maintenant tous ensemble au sein d'une unité onto-théologique.[8] La déconstruction selon Derrida offre une perspective importante en ce qu'elle cherche à faire apparaître l' « autre » refoulé, dénié, lequel est pourtant essentiel au discours en question. Et, en ce sens précis, la religion peut être vue comme l'autre refoulé du discours séculariste de la modernité, et donc comme le pivot de la civilisation occidentale

8 Jacques Derrida, *Marges - de la philosophie* (Paris: Minuit, 1972); Kevin Hart, *The Trespass of the Sign: deconstruction, theology and philosophy* (Cambridge: Cambridge University Press, 1989).

moderne. Si c'est le cas, rejeter la religion en faveur du sécularisme ne serait pas plus efficace que de fustiger l'écriture et louer la parole (pour reprendre un des exemples favoris de Derrida: son existence devra être toujours déjà présupposée, même dans son rejet).

Donc, puisque selon la théorie psychanalytique la subjectivité s'accomplit par le refoulement de désirs inacceptables et par l'accès au langage (et au symbolique plus généralement), lequel s'identifie au Nom du Père, les positions de sujets seront, par inhérence, masculines. Les petits garçons deviennent des hommes. Et les petites filles? Selon Lacan, dans la mesure où les femmes peuvent occuper une position de sujet, ayant accès au symbolique, aux discours de la civilisation occidentale, dans cette mesure donc les femmes deviennent aussi masculinisées. Soit nous apprenons à jouer des rôles d'hommes selon les règles posées par les hommes, soit nous adoptons les rôles « féminins » structurés pour nous par les hommes: être mères et domestiques. Il apparaît clairement que, à l'instar des discours légaux, scientifiques et économiques, la religion telle qu'elle a été constituée en Occident a beaucoup contribué à maintenir en place de telles positions de sujets (subjectivité et sujétion). Et la philosophie de la religion n'a pas jugé bon de remettre tout cela en question.

Mais alors, comment une femme peut-elle parler, ou même avoir accès au symbolique? Et quelle cataclysme une femme engendrerait-elle en prenant la parole? Pour Irigaray (comme pour d'autres psychanalystes français), la question de la parole féminine est manifestement très liée à la question de l'accomplissement d'une subjectivité féminine. Si devenir sujet signifie avoir accès au langage, et si le langage est toujours déjà masculin, une femme ne peut accomplir sa subjectivité, si tant est qu'elle le puisse, que dans la mesure où elle se masculinise, s'intègre dans des structures masculinistes fondées sur la rationalité et le discours, et ... ne fait surtout pas de vagues! Irigaray nous signale toutefois que les choses ne sont pas si simples. La raison pour laquelle Freud et Lacan n'ont pu découvrir de réponse à leur question, « que veulent les femmes? », la raison pour laquelle ils ne pouvaient admettre que les femmes puissent parler, réside dans le fait qu'ils n'*écoutaient* pas: d'abord, ils réduisaient la femme au silence en définissant le langage comme masculin; ensuite, ils se plaignaient de ce que les femmes n'aient rien à dire. Irigaray se fait l'avocate d'une stratégie différente, aux multiples aspects, afin de faire entendre les voix des femmes, en cherchant à écouter les silences, les lacunes, les sons surgis de la marge, en n'écoutant pas seulement les pères et les fils, mais aussi les mères et les filles. Manifestement, une telle stratégie suscite un projet d'analyse et de développement du langage religieux immensément différent du projet traditionnel de la philosophie de la religion.

Pour l'heure, l'important réside en ce que Luce Irigaray insiste sur la nécessité de perturber l'ordre symbolique afin que les femmes puissent développer une subjectivité qui soit leur et ne se contentent pas d'adopter des positions de sujets masculinisés. Pour ce faire, elle propose de substituer aux structures masculinistes du symbolique un nouvel imaginaire qui ne soit pas fondé sur le Nom du Père, un nouveau mode d'être et de concevoir qui permette aux femmes d'être sujets *en tant que femmes*. Et comme le discours religieux sert de point d'ancrage au symbolique occidental, c'est le religieux avant tout qu'il faut perturber.

Irigaray s'oppose ainsi à une grande part de la pensée religieuse en affirmant que la religion ne peut être simplement ignorée ou abandonnée: il faut la transformer. Dans son essai « Femmes divines », elle soutient que « afin de devenir », c'est-à-dire d'accéder à la subjectivité, il est nécessaire de se donner un « horizon », d'aspirer à un idéal d'unité.[9] L'ordre symbolique offert par la religion, et en particulier l'idée de Dieu, a pu fournir un tel horizon au devenir, et ce, quels qu'aient pu être ses autres effets. Il a servi d'idéal de perfection, « le lieu de l'absolu *pour nous*, son chemin, l'espoir de son accomplissement. »[10] Le divin représente donc un but pour les humains, ce à l'aune de quoi la pensée et la conduite humaines doivent se mesurer. En tant que tel, il reste indispensable à l'accomplissement de la subjectivité.

> (Le divin est) ce dont nous avons besoin pour devenir libres, autonomes, souveraines. Aucune constitution de subjectivité ni de société humaines ne s'est élaborée sans assistance du divin. Il est des temps de destruction. Mais, pour détruire, il faut que le Dieu ou les dieux existent.[11]

Irigaray est loin de défendre l'acceptation des doctrines et pratiques de la religion patriarcale; mais, dans sa conception du devenir « libre, autonome, souverain », de notre *devenir* en tant que individus humains et

---

9 Irigaray, *Sexes et parentés* 73; la dette envers Feuerbach est manifeste.

10 *Ibid.*, 75

11 *Ibid.*, 74

société humaine, nous ne pouvons nous passer de l'idéal divin. Selon elle, le devenir humain est intrinsèquement lié à l'aspiration au devenir divin.

> Tout homme (selon Feuerbach) et toute femme, à moins de rester soumise à la logique de l'essence de l'homme, doivent s'imaginer un Dieu, un lieu ou chemin objectif et subjectif de possible rassemblement de soi dans l'espace et le temps: unité de l'instinct, du coeur et de la connaissance, unité de la nature et de l'esprit, condition de la demeure et de la sainteté. Seul un Dieu peut nous sauver, nous sauvegarder... Le religieux est seul, en nous et hors de nous, assez fondamental pour nous permettre de découvrir, affirmer, accomplir des buts...[12]

Dans cet ordre d'idées, sa dette envers Nietzsche et Feuerbach mérite d'être un peu plus profondément étudiée car Irigaray est une lectrice attentive, même si créative, de leurs oeuvres.[13] Dans la célèbre parabole de Nietzsche, l'insensé s'exclame:

> Où est allé Dieu? ... je vais vous le dire. *Nous l'avons tué*,... vous et moi! c'est nous, nous tous, qui sommes ses assassins! Mais comment avons-nous fait cela? Comment avons-nous pu vider la mer? Qui nous a donné une éponge pour effacer tout l'horizon? ... La grandeur de cet acte est trop grande pour nous. Ne faut-il pas devenir dieux nous-mêmes pour, simplement, avoir l'air dignes d'elle?[14]

Nous voici en présence d'un thème parallèle à celui du « devenir divin(e)s » que développe Irigaray: « Ne devons-nous pas devenir dieux nous-mêmes? » Ce passage a souvent été interprété comme le récit d'une usurpation du savoir et du pouvoir—le statut de la divinité—par les maîtres de la modernité, comme si, après sa sécularisation, l'homme moderne (et l'emploi du masculin est délibéré) devait prendre la place de Dieu. Toutefois, ce ne peut être ce que Nietzsche a voulu dire, car c'est précisément parmi les incrédules de la modernité que l'insensé cherche Dieu, c'est précisément parmi eux qu'il pleure la tragédie de la mort de Dieu. Au contraire, bien qu'il s'agisse là, en effet, des hommes sécularisés et si plein d'assurance de ce monde—de petits dieux, en effet—ils ne sont en rien devenus dieux comme le concevait Nietzsche.

Dans « Ainsi parlait Zarathoustra », Nietzsche évoque à nouveau le devenir divin. Il écrit que:

---

12 *Ibid.*, 79-80

13 Je suis reconnaissante envers Joanna Hodge d'avoir attiré mon attention sur ce point.

14 Friedrich Nietzsche, *Le gai savoir* (Paris: Folio-Gallimard, 1950), 166-167.

Dieu est une conjecture; mais ce que je veux est que n'aille votre conjecture plus loin que votre pouvoir créateur.

Un dieu, seriez-vous capables de le créer? -- Sur tous les dieux faites-moi donc alors silence! Mais de créer le surhomme bien vous seriez capables (den Übermenschen schaffen).

Non vous-mêmes peut-être, ô mes frères! Mais vous pourriez vous recréer pour être pères et aïeux du surhomme: et que cela soit votre meilleur création![15]

Ce passage, à l'instar du précédent, a souvent été considéré comme une preuve d'athéisme arrogant, même blasphématoire: et, en effet, Nietzsche n'était pas vraiment un fanatique du christianisme sous aucune de ses formes. Toutefois, si l'on relit ces deux passages ensemble, il n'est pas impossible d'interpréter Nietzsche de façon plus créative, en repensant tant le sécularisme que la religion, et suivant en cela la voie déjà tracée par Feuerbach, voie que Luce Irigaray suggère explicitement.

Dans son essai, « L'Essence du Christianisme », Feuerbach soutient que, dans ce qu'elle a de meilleur, la religion tend un miroir à l'humanité dans lequel les humains peuvent voir une image idéale d'eux-mêmes qu'ils chercheront ensuite à refléter.

« ... Dans la religion, l'homme place nécessairement sa nature hors de lui-même, considère sa nature comme une nature distincte... Dieu est son *alter ego*, son autre moitié perdue; Dieu est son complément; en Dieu, il est d'abord homme parfait. Dieu lui est un besoin; quelque chose lui manque dont il ne sait ce que c'est -- Dieu est ce quelque chose qui lui manque, qui lui est indispensable; Dieu participe de sa nature. » (Ndt)

Dieu est donc l'horizon du devenir humain, l'horizon dont Nietzsche craint qu'il ait été effacé. Afin qu'il y ait un devenir, un horizon divin est nécessaire, non au sens réaliste ou empirique remis en question par les critiques de la modernité, mais en tant que miroir du « Dieu qui est en chacun », cette image idéale que nous pouvons à la fois projeter et refléter.

Par la révélation, la nature latente de l'homme lui apparaît, en se faisant objet pour lui. Il est déterminé, influencé par sa propre nature comme par un autre être; il reçoit des mains de Dieu ce que sa propre nature méconnue lui impose

15 Friedrich Nietzsche, *Ainsi parlait Zarathoustra* (Paris: Folio-Gallimard, 1971), 110.

comme une nécessité, sous certaines conditions liées au temps et aux circonstances.[16] (Ndt)

La modernité séculière arrache à l'homme cette dimension religieuse nécessaire, fait de l'homme un petit dieu dans un univers désenchanté, mais, au-delà de sa maîtrise et de sa technique, elle le prive de lui-même, le prive de toute possibilité de devenir un « surhomme »... et ignore complètement la femme—ce qui n'a jamais dû beaucoup troubler ni Nietzsche ni Feuerbach.

Même si elle déforme l'intention originale de Nietzsche et de Feuerbach dans sa conception féministe du devenir divin(e)s,[17] Irigaray le fait de façon à ouvrir des perspectives fécondes. En effet, selon elle, cette projection d'un horizon divin a toujours existé. Quoique la société occidentale soit très sécularisée, au moins en ce sens qu'une grande partie de la population ne respecte pas les observances religieuses, l'imaginaire occidental est saturé d'images, valeurs et symboles dérivés de l'héritage judéo-chrétien. Et c'est de cela que traite la philosophie de la religion. Toutefois, comme je l'ai déjà souligné, le symbolique religieux occidental n'aide en rien les *femmes* a devenir « libres, autonomes, souveraines ». Selon Irigaray, nous ne pouvons nous contenter de simplement reconnaître ce fait. Il nous faut aussi « nous demander pourquoi nous avons été arrêtées dans notre devenir *divines.* »[18] Pourquoi le symbolique religieux oeuvre-t-il à l'encontre des femmes plutôt qu'en leur faveur? Et comment remédier à cela?

Selon Irigaray, la raison en est que les seuls dieux qui ont existé jusqu'à aujourd'hui, en Occident du moins, sont des dieux masculins, et surtout Dieu le Père, celui de la tradition judéo-chrétienne, qui est devenu le Seul et Unique, l'Un, le Seigneur conquérant de tous. Suivant Feuerbach, Irigaray voit en lui une projection masculine.

> ... l'homme l'a cherché dans un Dieu unique *masculin*. Le Dieu, il l'a créé de son genre... A peine se limite-t-il en Lui, entre Lui: il est père, fils, esprit.

---

16 Voir Marx W. Wartofsky, *Feuerbach* (Cambridge: Cambridge University Press, 1977), ch.IX et p.283.

17 Voir Nick Land, « Shamanic Nietzsche » dans Peter Sedgwick (ed.): *Nietzsche: A Critical Reader* (Oxford: Blackwell, 1995). Pour une lecture alternative qui suit au moins partiellement la voie tracée par Irigaray, voir Gregory Bruce Smith, *Nietzsche, Heidegger and the Transition to Postmodernity* (Chicago/London: University of Chicago Press, 1996), 71-72.

18 Irigaray, *Sexes et parentés*, 72; je me permets d'ajouter les premières italiques.

> L'homme ne s'est pas laissé définir par un autre genre: féminin. Son Dieu unique correspondrait au genre humain dont nous savons qu'il n'est pas neutre du point de vue de la différence des sexes.[19]

Par conséquent, dans la perspective adoptée par Irigaray, ce Dieu peut servir au mieux d'horizon divin pour le devenir *masculin*, et pour une masculinité normative qui s'est définie à l'image de l' « un » et a constitué tout le reste en « autre » selon une économie fastidieuse où le même toujours se répète. Irigaray accuse la religion en Occident de constituer un système patriarcal qui « a enlevé le divin aux femmes. Il s'en est emparé dans des lieux de l'entre-hommes et il soupçonne souvent le religieux des femmes de diablerie. »[20] Souvenons-nous, par exemple, des milliers de femmes brûlées comme sorcière au début de l'époque moderne.[21]

Il est certes vrai que les femmes sont souvent attirées par la religion; en fait, dans la plupart des sociétés modernes, plus de femmes que d'hommes participent régulièrement à des rituels religieux, telles les messes. Pourtant, les religions occidentales, avec leur(s) Dieu(x) masculins ne nous offrent aucune possibilité, à nous femmes, d'accomplir notre subjectivité par rapport à un horizon divin. Comme l'écrivait Irigaray,

> La trinité féminine nous manque. Mais, sans divin qui lui convienne, la femme ne peut accomplir sa subjectivité selon un objectif qui lui correspond. Elle manque d'idéal qui lui soit un but et un chemin pour devenir... Pour devenir femme, pour accomplir sa subjectivité féminine, la femme a besoin d'un dieu qui figure la perfection de *sa* subjectivité.[22]

L'ordre symbolique religieux masculiniste doit être subverti. Un espace doit s'ouvrir au divin féminin. « Sommes-nous capables, ce Dieu, de l'imaginer femme? Pouvons-nous le pressentir comme la perfection de notre subjectivité? » [23]

---

19 *Ibid.*, 74.

20 *Ibid.*, 205. Ceci s'applique, *mutatis mutandis*, à tous les « autres Autres »: noirs, homosexuel(le)s, peuples colonisés, ... Irigaray en parle très peu et ses rares remarques sont peu satisfaisantes; voir « J'aime à toi » (1992): Irigaray y écarte la question raciale comme un « problème secondaire ». Toutefois, il semble évident que la subversion qu'elle prône ne devrait pas impliquer uniquement les blancs hétérosexuels.

21 Grace M Jantzen, *Power, Gender and Christian Mysticism* (Cambridge: Cambridge University Press, 1995).

22 Irigaray, *Sexes et parentés*, 76.

23 *Ibid.*, 75.

Ce que Luce Irigaray propose, c'est que les femmes projettent délibérément le divin selon leur genre, comme les hommes l'ont toujours fait selon le leur. Aujourd'hui, les hommes construisent non seulement le symbolique du divin, mais aussi le symbolique du rôle des femmes et leur relation au divin: les femmes sont appelées à être les servantes de l'humanité, avec la souffrance que cela implique, en permettant au monde de se reproduire, et elles seront d'autant plus saintes qu'elles accepteront cette position avec humilité et modestie. Mais cette manière de contraindre la femme à accepter un rôle construit pour elle par l'homme n'aboutit finalement qu'à un déficit pour les deux sexes.

> Pourquoi les femmes n'auraient-elles pas de Dieu leur permettant d'accomplir leur *genre*? Pour que le ciel n'advienne pas sur la terre? Pour rester celles qui accouchent le dieu enfant, le dieu souffrant, le fils rédempteur? Deviennent-elles ainsi divines en leur genre? Et l'homme? Il manque à l'un et à l'autre de grandir jusqu'à l'âge adulte ensemble. Il manque à la femme de devenir Dieu pour elle et pour la communauté. Peut-être pour Dieu.[24]

Renverser ce déficit implique une subversion délibérée du symbolique religieux masculiniste, un effort d'imagination et un passage à l'action par et pour les femmes.

Par conséquent, il s'impose d'examiner en détail comment ceci peut se réaliser dans divers domaines habituellement attribués à la philosophie de la religion: le langage religieux, les questions de la souffrance et du mal, la conception de Dieu, ... Chaque fois, il apparaîtra alors que la séparation séculier/religieux est peu judicieuse, mais aussi que chacune de ces deux positions repose sur des présupposés de race, genre et sexualité qu'il a toujours importé aux féministes de remettre en question. Le compte-rendu qu'a consacré Irigaray au livre de Elisabeth Schüssler Fiorenza, « In Memory of Her »[25] offre un bel avant-goût d'un tel travail.

La thèse de Schüssler Fiorenza consiste en ce que la femme était en réalité bien plus centrale au sein des premiers mouvements chrétiens que ne l'admettent les textes ultérieurs. Elles furent exclues de l'histoire à cause des préjugés masculinistes du monde gréco-romain auquel le Nouveau Testament fut présenté. Irigaray apprécie énormément comment Schüssler Fiorenza a retrouvé les femmes volontairement oubliées du christianisme primitif et juge son livre de loin préférable aux interpréta-

24 *Ibid.*, 83.

25 Elisabeth Schüssler Fiorenza, *In Memory of Her* (London: SCM, 1983).

tions neutres/asexuées du message chrétien. Toutefois, la question subsiste de l'identité de cet homme nommé Jésus, au centre des Evangiles? Dans quelle mesure un Jésus masculin peut-il permettre aux femmes d'accomplir leur subjectivité? Ou n'est-il lui aussi qu'une manière pour Dieu le Père de restreindre l'horizon du devenir des femmes? C'est à ce niveau que le livre de Schüssler Fiorenza déçoit finalement Luce Irigaray: il ne remet pas suffisamment en question ou ne déplace pas assez le symbolique religieux masculiniste traditionnel. Comme l'écrit Irigaray, « les religions monothéistes nous parlent de Dieu le Père et Dieu fait homme; rien n'est dit d'un Dieu la Mère ni de Dieu fait femme, ni même de Dieu en tant que couple ou couples. »[26] Si, à un niveau sociologique, elle soulève des questions importantes concernant les femmes dans le christianisme primitif, Schüssler Fiorenza ne s'affranchit pas, au niveau ontologique, d'un système doctrinal monothéiste et trinitaire qui affirme tant la masculinité que l'unicité du Christ, même si elle adopte une position critique et affiche un certain malaise à ce propos. Et comme l'écrit encore Irigaray, « la sociologie m'ennuye vite lorsque j'attends le divin. »[27]

Toutefois, au lieu de s'en tenir à cette simple critique, Irigaray va plus loin et suggère comment Jésus pourrait, en fait, être interprété de façon à permettre le devenir divin des femmes. Elle commence par une exploration imaginative du concept d' « incarnation »—l'idée que Jésus est Dieu fait chair—concept amplement illustré dans les Evangiles: « chaque étape dans la vie du Christ est reprise dans les Evangiles et décrite comme un événement du corps »[28] de la conception et la naissance jusqu'à la mort en passant par le jeûne, la guérison, les noces, la souffrance. Jésus ne peut se réduire à de la parole ou à des abstractions. Il est présence physique et cette présence physique est toujours centrale. Or, la chair, le corps, du moins le corps humain, sont toujours sexualisés, et le corps de Jésus est masculin. « Pourquoi, se demande Irigaray, son incar-

26 Luce Irigaray, « Equal to whom? » Trad. Robert L. Mazzola, dans *Differences*, Vol.1 N°2, 59-76, ici 71 (Ndt = traductions proposées par le traducteur).

27 *Ibid.*, 74 (Ndt).

28 *Ibid.*, 65 (Ndt).

nation physique est-elle niée ou traitée uniquement sur un plan humain? »[29]

Au premier abord, la question peut paraître terriblement déplacée: au sein du christianisme occidental, la masculinité de Jésus n'a-t-elle pas été continuellement utilisée pour soutenir le symbolique masculin, garantissant ainsi la supériorité des hommes, pour interdire le sacerdoce des femmes et pour projeter sur elles la faute d'Eve, face à un Christ masculin qui est le second Adam? Irigaray ne nie rien de tout cela. Sa question porte plutôt sur quelque chose de plus profond. Après tout, le masculin n'est qu'*un* des sexes: il ne renvoie qu'à une partie de l'humanité et non à l'ensemble. Si Jésus est Dieu fait chair, il n'en est que l'incarnation *partielle*. Il ne peut être le tout, le seul et unique, puisqu'il ne contient pas toute l'humanité. Ainsi, au lieu de ne voir dans l'incarnation qu'une acceptation de Jésus le Seul et unique, Irigaray affirme que « l'incarnation de tous les corps (des hommes et des femmes) est potentiellement divine, chaque homme et chaque femme n'étant ni plus ni moins que des dieux virtuels. »[30] Sinon, si Jésus est unique, comme dans le christianisme traditionnel, il « est véritablement la réalisation du patriarcat, l'apparence du pouvoir du père et du Père »[31] et les féministes n'ont plus à le défendre. Par contre, s'il n'est qu'incarnation partielle, d'autres incarnations, d'autres trinités, d'autres sexualités sont possibles. Le symbolique traditionnel est subverti de l'intérieur, et un espace s'ouvre aux femmes pour développer un nouvel imaginaire religieux qui leur offrira un devenir sexué.[32]

Bien que Luce Irigaray n'aborde pas spécifiquement la philosophie de la religion en tant que discipline universitaire, elle estime manifeste-

29 *Ibid.*, 69 (Ndt).

30 *Ibid.*, 64 (Ndt).

31 *Ibid.*, 70 (Ndt).

32 Irigaray ne va pas jusque là, mais il est aisé d'établir un parallèle avec la dimension « raciale ». Jésus était juif. De ce point de vue, il était donc tout aussi partiel, comme tout être humain: personne ne peut appartenir à toutes les « races » simultanément. Mais le raisonnement d'Irigaray permet d'autres incarnations, permet à d'autres corps particuliers d'un point de vue « racial » de devenir divins. Différents courants de la théologie de la libération ont abordé la question en proposant par exemple un Messie noir, même si aucun ne va jusqu'à la conséquence logique qu'en tire Irigaray: « chaque homme et chaque femme sont virtuellement divins, ni plus ni moins. »

ment que c'est ce type de travail de réflexion et d'imagination qui devrait en constituer le contenu le plus approprié. Selon elle, la philosophie s'est constituée en discours-maître (*master discourse*) par excellence. Par conséquent, nous dit-elle, « c'est précisément le discours philosophique qu'il nous faut contester, et *perturber*, dans la mesure où il constitue le discours sur le discours. »[33] La philosophie de la religion se pose donc comme discours sur le discours religieux, déterminant ce qui peut être dit, et par qui, à propos du divin. Une philosophie féministe de la religion se doit dès lors de révéler les partis pris et la stérilité de l'activité intellectuelle masculiniste (soi-disant neutre) au sein de cette discipline. Toutefois, elle cherchera aussi de façon créative à développer un imaginaire féministe qui permettra le « devenir divines » des femmes: « non seulement *oppositions à, critiques de*, mais *positions de nouvelles valeurs*, essentiellement divines. »[34]

> « "Dieu est le miroir de l'homme" (Feuerbach). Il manque à la femme un miroir pour devenir femme. Avoir un Dieu et devenir son genre vont de pair. Dieu est l'autre dont nous avons absolument besoin. Nous avons besoin du pressentiment d'un accomplissement pour *devenir*, non d'un objectif figé, d'un Un postulé immuable, mais d'une cohésion et d'un horizon qui assurent, pour nous, le passage entre passé et futur... »[35]

Pour Irigaray, le « devenir divin(e) » n'est ni le projet récupérateur de la religion masculiniste que craignent avec raison les féministes séculières, ni le désir de jouer à dieu qui répugne aux féministes chrétiennes. « Il est indispensable que nous soyons Dieu *pour nous* afin d'être divines pour l'autre, et non idoles, fétiche, images déjà profilées ou déterminées. »[36]

Concevoir la philosophie de la religion—et la religion elle-même—de la sorte pose manifestement de nombreuses questions: questions de langage et de référence, de vérité, de moralité, d'égalité et de différence, de culture et de sexualité, auxquelles devrait faire face toute analyse féministe du rôle de la raison dans la religion. Je ne prétends pas que la pensée de Luce Irigaray ne contienne aucune difficulté, encore moins que l'on puisse les ignorer. Mais on peut aussi voir dans ces difficultés des occasions à saisir: occasions de repenser la religion et le sécularisme, de

33 Irigaray, *Ce sexe qui n'en est pas un*; Ndt.

34 Irigaray, *Sexes et parentés*, 80.

35 *Ibid.*, 79.

36 *Ibid.*, 84.

reconsidérer le langage et le sujet parlant dans l'expression religieuse, de refuser le piège des « religions du monde » vues uniquement en tant que doctrines et dogmes, et de s'ouvrir au contraire à des horizons plus vastes ainsi qu'à la possibilité du devenir divin(e)s. Ce qui apparaît surtout clairement, et il s'agit là d'un élément crucial pour une philosophie féministe de la religion, c'est l'immense différence de *but* entre une telle philosophie et la pratique dominante contemporaine au sein de la philosophie de la religion. Irigaray insiste sur le fait que nous—femmes et hommes—devons « devenir divin(e)s »: c'est là notre projet humain et religieux. Et soit la philosophie de la religion visera à explorer ce que cela signifie et à faciliter ce projet, soit, comme à présent, elle lui fera obstacle.

Pourquoi agissent-ils de la sorte?

On ne peut difficilement imaginer plus grand contraste au sein de la philosophie de la religion que lorsqu'on quitte l'oeuvre de Luce Irigaray pour se tourner vers les auteurs anglais contemporains. Où elle se montre passionnée, ils restent froids, réservés, apparemment neutres. Où elle insiste sur l'imagination, ils préfèrent la rigueur logique. Alors que, pour elle, importe surtout le devenir divin(e), ils se préoccupent de justifier des dogmes (truth claims) et d'assurer les fidèles du bien-fondé de leurs croyances (beliefs). En outre, les croyances qu'ils visent à défendre sont celles du Christianisme: voilà donc, selon eux, ce qu'il importe uniquement d'étudier. Dans la mesure où ils ont affaire à d' « autres religions du monde », ils chercheront habituellement à discuter si ou comment les dogmes ou croyances liés à ces religions peuvent être compatibles les uns avec les autres, et surtout avec les doctrines chrétiennes fondamentales, peut-être à un « méta-niveau ». Que l'on puisse imaginer de nouvelles idées religieuses, un nouveau Dieu, ou de nouveaux dieux au féminin, ou en tant que couple(s) ou quoi que ce soit d'autre, n'apparaît jamais dans leurs pages.

Mais que croient-ils donc faire, ces philosophes anglo-américains de la religion, et quels sont leurs buts? Lorsque l'on passe en revue toute une série d'oeuvres en ayant ces deux questions en tête, on est immédiatement frappé par le peu d'attention explicite prêtée à la question des buts poursuivis, et par la superficialité des commentaires sur la nature de ces livres et leur visée. Quelques-uns même ne s'embarrassent d'aucune explication. Ainsi, par exemple, dans sa classique « Introduction to the Philosophy of

Religion », Brian Davies ne dit rien des raisons qui l'ont poussé à l'écrire, ni même de la façon dont il conçoit le but de la philosophie de la religion, sauf comme suit: « Mon intention est d'examiner quelques-unes des questions qui sont traditionnellement estimées être de son ressort »,[37] soit les arguments en faveur de l'existence de Dieu, le concept de miracle, l'idée de vie après la mort. Nulle part l'auteur n'indique qu'il se soit demandé *pourquoi* il juge ces questions centrales plutôt que d'autres, ni de qui il sert les intérêts en se penchant sur elles. De plus, bien qu'il assume explicitement que le lecteur ne possède que des connaissances limitées, ou nulles, en philosophie, il n'estime pas nécessaire de mentionner *pourquoi* nous devrions continuer à philosopher d'une manière devenue conventionnelle. Il dit simplement que, dans son livre, « la méthode de travail adoptée est en grande partie dictée par la manière dont les philosophes ont récemment examiné de nombreuses doctrines religieuses »,[38] comme si le fait que ce soit la méthode habituelle suffit à justifier qu'elle soit conservée. Les quelques commentaires de Davies ne rassureront certes pas quiconque suspecte la philosophie de la religion de ne servir qu'à étayer un symbolique religieux masculiniste.

De nombreux philosophes de la religion sont au moins un peu plus explicites que Davies lorsqu'ils expliquent l'intention et la valeur de leur oeuvre: généralement, ils l'expriment en termes de justifications rationnelles de l'un ou l'autre dogme religieux. Ainsi, par exemple, Richard Swinburne, dans son Introduction à « The Existence of God » affirme que:

> ce qui a préoccupé les hommes [sic] ordinaires depuis des siècles est de savoir si le témoignage de l'expérience humaine prouve que l'affirmation [de l'existence de Dieu] est vraie ou qu'elle est fausse... Ce livre a été écrit avec la conviction profonde qu'il est possible d'arriver à des conclusions relativement bien étayées par une argumentation rationnelle quant à cette question, peut-être la plus importante des questions fondamentales qui stimulent l'esprit humain.[39]

Manifestement, donc, Swinburne estime qu'il s'est voué à une Oeuvre Cruciale, laquelle soulagera les hommes ordinaires de leur préoccupation par cette question des plus fondamentales. Pourtant, les hommes ordinai-

---

37 Brian Davies, *An Introduction to the Philosophy of Religion* (Oxford: Oxford University Press, [2]1982), ix (Ndt).

38 *Ibid.*, x (Ndt).

39 Richard Swinburne, *The Existence of God* (Oxford: Clarendon Press, 1979), 1 (Ndt).

res—sans parler des femmes ordinaires—se sont-ils *vraiment* inquiétés depuis des siècles de l'existence de Dieu (le dieu très précis du théisme classique occidental)? Pour sa plus grande part, l'histoire a été écrite par et à propos des puissants. Il n'est donc pas facile de déterminer ce qui préoccupait ou non les masses. Toutefois, il semble vraisemblable que les gens « ordinaires » (en tout cas en Occident) aient estimé l'existence de Dieu comme allant de soi, ou aient évité de se poser la question (si l'on en juge par la pression qui était nécessaire pour que les fidèles viennent à l'église), consacrant plutôt leurs angoisses aux incertitudes quotidiennes de la vie et de la mort.

Mais quoi qu'il en soit, qui *sont* ces hommes « ordinaires » dont Swinburne désire soulager les inquiétudes? En quoi sont-ils « ordinaires », et ce par rapport à qui? Les hommes « extraordinaires »—les philosophes tels Swinburne?—ne nourrissent probablement pas de telles inquiétudes, puisqu'ils peuvent user d'une argumentation rationnelle, incluant des techniques mathématiques complexes comme le Théorème de Bayes (lequel sert à calculer la probabilité de l'existence de Dieu). On ne voit toutefois pas très clairement comment cela pourrait soulager l' « homme ordinaire » sans faire appel à l'autorité du Très Intelligent Philosophe. Difficile d'imaginer quoi que ce soit de plus éloigné de l'exhortation passionnée de Luce Irigaray, exhortation à accomplir la vocation du devenir « virtuellement divin(e)s », sacré(e)s, tant à nos propres yeux qu'aux yeux les uns des autres.

Ce que Swinburne et bien d'autres considèrent comme de première importance sont des *croyances*, croyances dont il faut prouver qu'elles sont *justifiées*—c'est-à-dire conceptuellement cohérentes et, au moins probablement, vraies. Entretenir des croyances correctes à propos de Dieu, et d'autres questions religieuses telles la vie après la mort, les miracles et la révélation, est jugé d'importance capitale. La tâche du philosophe de la religion est d'examiner ces croyances, de les soumettre au « microscope philosophique. »[40] Dans un récent recueil de vingt essais par des philosophes de la religion américains dans lesquels chacun était invité à relater son itinéraire spirituel personnel, quasi tous ont choisi comme fil conducteur l'évolution de leur attitude face aux croyances: l'acceptation de ces

40 Richard Swinburne, *The Coherence of Theism* (Oxford: Clarendon Press, 1977), 6.

croyances, leur remise en question, leur justification.[41] De fait, certains affirment explicitement que Dieu impose « la punition de la damnation à ceux qui ne croient pas » correctement.[42] Cette façon de placer les croyances au centre de la religion est tout aussi courante en Grande-Bretagne: David Pailin, en dépit de grandes différences entre lui et Swinburne ou Davies, insiste lui aussi sur la justification des croyances comme tâche centrale de la philosophie de la religion:

> Par conséquent, la philosophie de la religion joue un rôle important pour les croyants dans la mesure où elle examine, tant dans la théorie que dans la pratique, comment le consentement à la foi peut se justifier rationnellement... Le but de l'analyse et des relectures produites par la philosophie de la religion est d'établir ce que l'on pourra nommer « la croyance juste ». D'un point de vue négatif, cela implique de poser des questions quant à la vérité, le sens, et l'effet des systèmes de croyances dont nous avons hérité... D'un point de vue positif, nous dirons que le philosophe de la religion cherche à établir un système de croyances que des personnes conscientes d'elles-mêmes et qui vivent dans le monde contemporain pourront accepter comme justifié et porteur de sens. »[43]

Donc, la religion est essentiellement affaire de croyances.[44] En outre, la validité et la valeur de ces croyances s'établissent par leur justification rationnelle, c'est-à-dire leur cohérence conceptuelle et leur vérité probable, le mot « vérité » étant compris comme « correspondance à la réalité. »

Les lecteurs anglo-américains, particulièrement ceux qui ont quelque savoir dans le domaine de la philosophie de la religion, sont si habitués à cette façon d'aborder la religion comme essentiellement un problème de croyances dont la vérité ou la fausseté est d'importance majeure que ce n'est qu'au contact d'une approche aussi différente que celle d'Irigaray qu'ils penseraient à la remettre en question. Mais pourquoi une adhésion

---

41 Thomas V. Morris (ed.), *God and the Philosophers: the reconciliation of faith and reason* (Oxford: Oxford University Press, 1994).

42 Michael Murray, « Seek and you will find »dans Morris (ed.), *God and the Philosophers*, 70 (Ndt).

43 David Pailin, *Groundwork of the Philosophy of Religion* (London: Epworth Press, 1986), 5 (Ndt).

44 Mais pas uniquement: Pailin, comme bon nombre de collaborateurs à ce recueil américain (Morris (ed.), *God and the Philosophers*), ajouterait rapidement que comportement et action sont aussi importants. Mais, chose typique, ils en feraient les conséquences logiques de la foi, plutôt que sa source ou son impulsion, par exemple.

si aveugle? Et dans l'intérêt de qui? Une telle conception confère-t-elle plus ou moins de pouvoir à l' « homme ordinaire » de Swinburne, par exemple? Permet-elle aux femmes de se construire une subjectivité? Ces questions ne sont pas simplement rhétoriques: elles dénoncent, au contraire, une véritable opposition conceptuelle quant à la définition de la religion, une rupture exacerbée par un désaccord quant à la nature et au statut des croyances.

Les philosophes anglo-américains de la religion tels ceux cités précédemment tendent à penser que les croyances vraies, en religion comme ailleurs, confèrent en effet plus de pouvoir, que « la vérité te libèrera », alors que les croyances incorrectes mènent à la superstition. Dans ce contexte, s'appliquer à un examen rigoureux des « dogmes » de la religion ne doit pas être considéré comme une forme d'arrogance, mais bien comme un devoir moral pour les philosophes de la religion. Bon nombre de ceux qui relatent leur « itinéraire spirituel » personnel[45] estiment manifestement que leur étude de la religion est une vocation ou un devoir. En outre, les philosophes traditionnels de la religion éprouvent probablement le sentiment qu'il incombe aux croyants d'essayer de convaincre les sceptiques du bien-fondé de leur foi: Swinburne, par exemple, parle d'un « devoir de convertir les autres » à l'aide de la justification philosophique des croyances.[46]

Par opposition, les philosophes européens comme Irigaray prennent bien plus au sérieux la conception psychanalytique du symbolique, ce système de discours qui inclut la religion, discours construits par la conscience occidentale et qu'ils forment simultanément en retour. Le symbolique occidental après les Lumières, en particulier tel que façonné par le Protestantisme, accorde une importance énorme à la vérité (dans la religion ou dans les sciences), non pas dans le sens de véracité et intégrité, mais dans le sens de vraie croyance, de croyance correspondant à la « réalité ». Si, par contre, nous adoptons la perspective psychanalytique, il nous faudra nous demander comment et moyennant quels refoulements individuels et sociaux ce symbolique fait de croyances et lié à la conscience occidentale depuis les Lumières a-t-il pu se former? Quelles compulsions ce souci de vérité trahit-il? La pensée dominante des philo-

45 Morris (ed.), *God and the Philosophers*.

46 Swinburne, *The Coherence of Theism*, 6 (Ndt).

sophes anglo-américains de la religion a généralement ignoré la psychanalyse, et même la philosophie européenne plus globalement, parce qu'elles se complairaient dans « une argumentation quelque peu désinvolte, auraient tendance à décrire l'univers de façon floue et générale, sans détails clairs et précis ni justification complète, telles une sorte de philosophie plus proche de la littérature que des sciences. »[47]

Ces deux approches s'opposent particulièrement en ce que les philosophes européens considèrent le souci de justification et de vérité de la philosophie anglo-américaine comme participant déjà d'une structure symbolique particulière. En outre, les féministes souligneront qu'il s'agit d'une structure symbolique créée par et pour les hommes blancs occidentaux au pouvoir. Accepter de construire la philosophie de la religion autour d'une réflexion méticuleuse, élaborée et rigoureuse sur la cohérence et la vérité des dogmes religieux ne fait que renforcer l'ordre symbolique patriarcal au lieu de le remettre en question, ou d'apprendre à penser autrement. Mais si le discours religieux au sein de la modernité participe d'un grand mythe de la rationalité, avec les sciences, l'économie et le droit, et si (comme le montre l'effet destructeur de cette rationalité sur les femmes, la terre et la dignité humaine) ce mythe doit être déconstruit et d'autres modes de pensée doivent être inventés, la danse si noble et si respectable des arguments et contre-arguments dans la philosophie anglo-américaine de la religion nous est inutile.

Elle a peut-être même quelque chose d'irréligieux. Bien sûr, la religion devrait alors être entendue comme autre chose qu'une simple question de croyances vraies. Mais si le discours religieux et le symbolique auquel il appartient sont une manière de construire la réalité humaine, un grand mythe ou un ensemble de mythes dont nous vivons (où « mythe » n'aurait pas « vérité » comme opposé), il devient d'importance cruciale de restructurer ce mythe de façon à favoriser la dignité humaine—peut-être de manière à nous forcer à, et à nous permettre de, devenir divin(e)s? Rien d'étonnant à ce qu'il puisse s'agir « d'une sorte de philosophie plus proche de la littérature que des sciences », puisque la littérature, plus souvent que les sciences, a tenté de penser autrement, d'offrir des modèles différents de devenir humain, de remettre en question

47 Richard Swinburne, « Intellectual Autobiography » dans Alan G. Padgett (ed.) *Reason and the Christian Religion: essays in honour of Richard Swinburne* (Oxford: Oxford University Press, 1994), 2 (Ndt).

le rationalisme surtout utilitariste de la conception contemporaine scientifique du monde.

Ce n'est pas un hasard si les philosophes anglo-américains de la religion font si largement appel aux sciences. Après tout, du moins aux niveaux du public et de la technique, la science telle qu'elle se pratique dans l'occident moderne lie intimement l'idée de vérité aux qualités réelles du monde: les dogmes reflètent la réalité. C'est pour cette raison que, dans son livre intitulé « Belief Policies », Paul Helm recommande aux philosophes de la religion l'approche épistémologique des sciences: il estime en effet que les progrès et succès de la science moderne démontrent que les scientifiques « n'ont pu suivre une méthode totalement erronée dans l'acquisition de leurs croyances. »[48] Helm préconise cette approche épistémologique même si le plus gros de son livre vise à expliquer « l'élément volontariste dans la foi. »[49] De même, dans son « Intellectual Autobiography », Richard Swinburne parle de sa dette envers la science moderne, en particulier envers l'idée d'une justification de la théorie par les principes de simplicité et par la prédictabilité de phénomènes qui autrement seraient inattendus. Swinburne continue ainsi:

> Une fois [ces principes scientifiques] examinés, mon programme était établi: il s'agissait d'utiliser les critères des sciences naturelles modernes, analysés avec la rigueur attentive de la philosophie moderne, pour prouver que la théologie chrétienne avait un sens et pouvait être justifiée.[50]

Peter Van Inwegen va plus loin encore. Pour lui, la méthode scientifique n'est pas qu'un outil; la science s'intègre dans une défense du christianisme contre l'athéisme des Lumières:

> Tout comme la rationalité « n'apparut » qu'une fois au cours de la vie terrestre (à la différence des visions), la science « n'apparut » qu'une fois dans l'histoire de la vie humaine (à la différence de l'écriture ou du calendrier). Et cette apparition unique de la science—la science *réelle*, qui ne s'arrête pas aux descriptions précises et systématiques de phénomènes, mais en recherche les causes sous-jacentes—ne s'est produite qu'au sein d'une civilisation qui s'est bâtie sur l'Eglise.[51]

---

48 *Ibid.*, 1 (Ndt).

49 *Ibid.*, 4 (Ndt).

50 *Ibid.*, 8 (Ndt).

51 *Ibid.*, 53 (Ndt).

Dans cette perspective, la Chine, l'Inde et le monde arabe ne possèdent pas la science « réelle » car celle-ci n'a pu se développer qu'à l'intérieur d'un système d'hypothèses chrétiennes (dont la vérité s'en trouve renforcée).

Mais si, comme le suggèrent les philosophes européens, la « vision scientifique du monde » est elle-même un grand récit de la modernité particulièrement suspect et dont les conséquences pour l'humanité et la terre sont bien plus ambiguës que ne semblent le supposer des auteurs comme Van Inwegen, ce lien intime établi entre la religion et le projet scientifique ne nous est utile en rien! En fait, si la méthodologie scientifique sert de modèle pour l'épistémologie religieuse, le fait que la science occidentale soit un Bien devient un article de foi; or un tel point de vue ne peut admettre l'idée que la méthodologie même de la science occidentale (et non simplement de mauvaises applications) puisse être responsable de bon nombre des horreurs de la modernité. Il est pourtant difficile d'ignorer comment l'alliance de la science et de la religion ont pu être les outils d'un patriarcat, outils qui ont encouragé le racisme, le sexisme et toute forme d'exploitation de l'humanité et de la terre.[52] Tous les « autres »—les femmes, les noirs, les homosexuels, ...—ont été fermement maintenus dans un rôle de soumission passive aux hommes au pouvoir, lesquels peuvent définir et délimiter la « vérité » scientifique. Dans la mesure où la philosophie de la religion s'inspire de la méthodologie scientifique issue de la modernité, elle renforce le symbolique occidental, opérant en tant que Loi du Père, au nom de Dieu.

La manière dont la philosophie de la religion telle qu'elle existe aujourd'hui fonctionne en tant que technique de pouvoir apparaît clairement lorsque sont définis son champ d'investigation et les différentes disciplines qu'elle comprend. Les mêmes disciplines reviennent avec une régularité prévisible: comme le dit Brian Davies, la philosophie de la religion, c'est ce que font habituellement les philosophes de la religion! Son livre, ni d'ailleurs aucun de ceux que j'ai mentionnés, ne suggère nulle part que cette discipline puisse avoir une histoire, qu'il puisse s'agir d'une construction sociale qui n'a pas toujours été construite comme aujourd'hui

52 Londa Schiebinger, *Nature's Body* (Boston: Beacon Press, 1993); Val Plumwood, *Feminism and the Mastery of Nature* (London: Routledge, 1993); Ann McClintock, *Imperial Leather: Race, Gender & Sexuality in the Colonial Conquest* (London: Routledge, 1995).

et que ce qui importe dans la philosophie de la religion (et en fait dans la religion elle-même) dépend de celui qui a la parole. Cette manière de concevoir la philosophie de la religion entraîne deux conséquences importantes, lesquelles offrent un contraste frappant avec l'approche de Luce Irigaray.

La première est que les frontières de cette discipline sont dessinées de sorte que, alors que la science et les mathématiques sont prises au sérieux (comme nous l'avons vu), la littérature, la psychanalyse, la théorie sociale ou politique sont généralement ignorées ou traitées avec mépris. Ainsi, par exemple, lorsqu'il défend la position volontariste dans son « Belief Policies », Paul Helm ne prend jamais en considération le rôle des désirs inconscients dans la formation de la volonté, du désir ou du choix de croire.[53] Dans « The Evolution of the Soul » de Richard Swinburne, l'inconscient n'apparaît qu'à la fin du livre sous la forme d'un possible sous-système de croyances qui complique quelque peu le point de vue fondamental selon lequel « l'âme possède une structure de croyances et désirs intrinsèquement propositionnels. »[54] Rien n'est dit sur le développement ou la constitution d'un moi unifié en relation avec le symbolique imposé par la Loi du Père, comme si la théorie psychanalytique était totalement hors de propos pour comprendre le développement du sujet humain. Rien n'est dit sur les implications politiques de spéculations philosophiques aussi détachées. L'hypothèse implicite est généralement que la philosophie de la religion n'a rien à voir avec la politique—ce qui bien sûr renforce le status quo. Les féministes qui examinent les questions de la philosophie de la religion dans leur impact sur les problèmes de justice se voient accusées de « déraper » dans la sociologie ou la politique, et de ne pas s'en tenir aux limites prescrites de la discipline.

A nouveau, de telles différences entre l'approche d'Irigaray et le point de vue des philosophes de la religion anglo-américains se résument à une différence de buts. Si le but est de codifier un système de croyances vraies et justifiées, il n'est peut-être pas surprenant que la littérature ou la théorie psychanalytique, en ce qu'elles subvertissent la crédibilité de l'idée même d'un tel système unifié et cohérent, ne puissent être admises. En outre, une analyse sociale et politique qui montre comment de tels

53 Paul Helm, *Belief Policies* (Cambridge: Cambridge University Press, 1994).

54 Richard Swinburne, *The Evolution of the Soul* (Oxford: Clarendon Press, 1994), 292 (Ndt).

systèmes ont servi à opprimer et déshumaniser déstabilise les philosophes qui cherchent à justifier le dogme selon lequel un Dieu bon peut permettre le mal et la souffrance. Mais si, au contraire, le but de la philosophie de la religion est de permettre le devenir divin(e), le devenir de notre moi sacré et sexué en relation avec la terre et les un(e)s avec les autres, les mathématiques et les applications rigoureuses de théories de l'épistémologie scientifique deviennent sans doute moins pertinentes que la théorie psychanalytique, les possibilités créatives du devenir humain offertes par la littérature et les arts, ou une analyse sociale et politique scrupuleuse.

La seconde différence frappante entre Irigaray et la plupart des philosophes anglo-américains de la religion (à la remarquable exception de penseurs tels William Wainwright[55]) réside en ce que l'approche de ces derniers se focalise sur les articles de foi du christianisme occidental. Tandis que Irigaray se tourne vers d'autres traditions religieuses et vers des sources « païennes » pour décrire le divin différemment, et invite à imaginer autrement, les courants dominants de la philosophie de la religion suivent les sillons creusés pour elle par la théologie chrétienne, une théologie surtout protestante et plutôt conservatrice. La conception médiévale occidentale de la philosophie comme *ancilla theologiae*, servante de la reine des sciences, est souvent mentionnée (même si dans une contextualisation historique douteuse) et, de fait, plusieurs traités classiques de la philosophie de la religion sont explicitement décrits comme « une introduction à la recherche conceptuelle, principalement à l'usage des théologiens. »[56] Rien d'étonnant à ce qu'elle remette peu en question les dogmes chrétiens centraux. Thomas Tracey, dans son compte-rendu sur « God and the Philosophers », approuve le fait que ses auteurs se concentrent sur les articles de foi du christianisme occidental:

> Ces dernières années, la philosophie de la religion a fait connaître des voix nouvelles qui usent d'un talent philosophique admirable pour explorer de manière plus ouverte les idées religieuses. L'éventail des sujets considérés s'est trouvé très enrichi dès lors que les philosophes ont dépassé les discussions classiques au sein du débat sur le théisme, débat issu des Lumières, pour se pencher sur des sujets théologiques traditionnels et s'inspirer de l'héritage des

55 William Wainwright, « Skepticism, Romanticism, & Faith » dans Thomas V. Morris (ed.), *God and the Philosophers*.

56 Vincent Brümmer, *Theology and Philosophical Inquiry: an Introduction* (London: Macmillan, 1981), 4 (Ndt).

> grands philosophes chrétiens du moyen-âge. Ce débat en rapide évolution a engendré des formes de pensée qui constituent véritablement une nouvelle théologie philosophique.[57]

Tracey juge cette identification de la philosophie de la religion à la théologie philosophique chrétienne tout à fait admirable. Mais comment pourrait-elle éviter de renforcer le symbolique religieux masculiniste occidental si un tel point de vue n'est pas subverti par des tentatives de penser différemment, selon une optique définie par d'autres religions et perspectives?

Soyons justes: il existe quelques philosophes de la religion contemporains, dont John Hick est peut-être le plus éminent représentant, qui accordent une importance appréciable aux traditions religieuses autres que le Christianisme. Une grande partie de l'oeuvre de Hick traite du pluralisme religieux, et son livre récent intitulé « An Interpretation of Religion » rassemble bon nombre de ses idées. Tout en reconnaissant l'impossibilité de la chose pour un individu, Hick prône l'idéal suivant: « le philosophe de la religion doit aujourd'hui prendre en ligne de compte non seulement la pensée et l'histoire de la tradition au sein de laquelle il ou elle oeuvre, mais aussi, en principe, l'histoire et la pensée religieuses de toute la race humaine. »[58] Cependant, le but d'un tel élargissement reste la justification de croyances. Bien que ces croyances acquièrent ainsi une dimension plus vaste que celles de toute religion particulière, et bien que Hick espère voir se dissiper les tensions religieuses entre divers groupes « sur notre petite et fragile planète » (xv; Ndt) en trouvant une solution aux problèmes d'incompatibilité apparente, son oeuvre se fonde à nouveau sur l'hypothèse que des croyances justifiées rationnellement ont un rôle central et qu'il appartient aux philosophes de la religion de les examiner. Sans aucun doute, Hick va beaucoup plus loin dans la reconnaissance et le respect de l'altérité que bon nombre de philosophes anglo-américains de la religion. Il reste néanmoins à l'intérieur du projet de la modernité et de son ordre symbolique patriarcal.

---

57 Thomas Tracey, « Review of Thomas V. Morris (ed.) *God and the Philosophers: the reconciliation of faith and reason* » dans *Modern Theology*, Vol.12 n°1 (1996), 127 (Ndt).

58 John Hick, *An Interpretation of Religion: human responses to the transcendent* (London: Macmillan, 1989) xiii (Ndt).

D'un point de vue féministe, il va de soi qu'une critique de la philosophie de la religion anglo-américaine se fait attendre depuis longtemps. Je pense toutefois qu'une telle critique peut être contre-productive si elle ne découle d'une alternative créative. En effet, rester au niveau de la critique signifie rester au même vieux niveau que ceux que nous critiquons: nous ne déplaçons guère le débat. Mais si le débat n'est guère déplacé, il reste stérile, même si là n'est pas notre intention. La raison en est que, dans toute situation d'oppression, c'est l'oppresseur qui peut choisir le cadre original du débat. « Le privilège de l'oppresseur réside en ce qu'il peut décider ce qu'il sera » et, dans une large mesure, non seulement ce qu' « il » sera, mais aussi ce que seront ceux qu' « il » oppresse. Ainsi, comme le fait remarquer Terry Eagleton, « toute identité "d'opposition" est autant fonction de l'oppression que résistance à celle-ci; et, dans ce sens, ce que nous pouvons devenir ne peut se lire simplement dans ce que nous sommes maintenant. »[59] Développer des alternatives créatives signifie à la fois revendiquer le droit d'épanouir notre propre identité plutôt que d'accepter qu'elle nous soit imposée, et déplacer le cadre du débat de façon à ce qu'il puisse être émancipateur.

C'est pour de telles raisons que, dans un plaidoyer pour que les femmes créent de nouvelles stratégies et attitudes, Elizabeth Grosz nous met en garde vis-à-vis d'une activité, même critique, à l'intérieur des modèles dominants:

> Si elle n'est que réactive, simple critique, elle confirme en fin de compte ces théories mêmes qu'elle désire dépasser. Elle reste nécessairement dans le cadre qu'elle vise à contester. Dire que quelque chose est faux, inutile ou sans valeur sans proposer d'alternatives, c'est paradoxalement affirmer que cette chose est vraie, etc...[60]

Il ne s'agit pas pour Grosz de minimiser l'importance de la critique, mais bien de souligner la nécessité de développer des approches créatives qui dépassent celles qui préexistent. De telles approches créatives, lorsque développées par les féministes, seront intrinsèquement liées à des questions de justice, questions fondées non sur une économie du même,

---

59 Terry Eagleton, *The Ideology of the Aesthetic*. Oxford: Blackwell, 1990), 414 (Ndt).

60 Elizabeth Grosz, « Contemporary Theories of Power and Subjectivity » dans Sneja Gunew (ed.), *Feminist Knowledge: critique and construct* (New York/London: Routledge, 1990), 59 (Ndt).

mais sur la reconnaissance de la diversité: diversité des genres, races et sexualités autant que différences d'opportunités et de bien-être matériel.

Les féministes se doivent dès lors de continuer à trouver de nouvelles manières de « parler la vérité face au pouvoir », de nouvelles manières aussi d'oeuvrer avec une énergie revitalisée et les ressources intellectuelles nécessaires. Comme l'écrivait Michel Foucault,

> Il y a des moments dans la vie où la question de savoir si on peut penser autrement qu'on ne pense et percevoir autrement qu'on ne voit est indispensable pour continuer à regarder où à réfléchir... Mais qu'est-ce donc que la philosophie aujourd'hui... si elle n'est pas le travail critique de la pensée sur ellemême? Et si elle ne consiste pas, au lieu de légitimer ce qu'on sait déjà, à entreprendre de savoir comment et jusqu'où il serait possible de penser autrement?[61]

Pour les philosophes féministes de la religion, l'effort de développer des manières de « penser autrement » n'est pas un luxe: nous y sommes contraintes si nous voulons survivre en tant que femmes/philosophes de la religion. Il s'agit là d'une « nécessité absolue » qui s'impose si nous voulons trouver comment la philosophie de la religion peut nous aider à devenir divin(e)s, plutôt que de nous enfermer dans ses traditions moribondes. Toutefois, cette nécessité est aussi une occasion, non seulement pour épanouir notre pensée créative, mais aussi pour assurer la rédemption de notre sujet, lequel se sédimente et se pétrifie si les eaux ne sont pas remuées de cette manière nouvelle.

traduit de l'Anglais par Yves Cantraine

61 Michel Foucault, *L'usage des plaisirs*: Vol 2 de *L'histoire de la sexualité* (Paris: Gallimard, 1984), 14-15.

Abstracts

Following Feuerbach, Luce Irigaray describes the divine horizon as the horizon for human becoming. But human becoming is inseparable from language and is always gendered; and up to now, the divine horizon has been gendered masculine.Thus the aim of a feminist philosophy of religion is to develop the understanding of female subjectivity and language, and a god according to our gender, to enable us to 'become divine'. By contrast, when we ask why men do philosophy of religion, they frequently speak in terms of the importance of justifying religious truth claims concerning the existence and nature of God. They take physical science as their conceptual model, draw the boundaries of the discipline tightly, and are concerned to a very large extend with the claims of christian theology only.

Luce Irigaray folgt Feuerbach, indem sie den göttlichen Horizont als den Horizont menschlichen Werdens beschreibt. Doch menschliches Werden ist untrennbar verbunden mit Sprache und stets geschlechtlich differenziertes Werden. Allerdings wurde bis heute der göttliche Horizont männlich verstanden. Daher ist es Ziel einer feministischen Religionsphilosophie, das Verständnis weiblicher Subjektivität und Sprache, eines Gottes entsprechend unserem Geschlecht zu entwickeln, uns zu befähigen 'göttlich zu werden'. Im Gegensatz dazu betonen männliche Religionsphilosophen häufig die Bedeutung religöser Wahrheitsansprüche, die die Existenz und das Wesen Gottes betreffen. Ihre Begrifflichkeit orientiert sich an naturwissenschaftlichen Modellen, zieht die Grenzen der Disziplin eng und bezieht sich weitgehend auf die christlicher Theologie.

Grace JANTZEN was born and raised in a Mennonite community in Western Canada. She holds a doctorate in philosophy from the University of Calgary and a doctorate in theology from the University of Oxford. She was a member of hte Canadian Royal Commission on New Reproductive Technologies. She is Professorial Research Fellow in the Department of Religions and Theology, University of Manchester, and joint director of the Centre for Religion, Culture and Gender. Her interests are mysticism, feminism and theorizing religion in(post) modernity. She is a member of the Religious Society of Friends (Quakers).

Monika JAKOBS

Auf der Suche nach dem verlorenen Paradies? Zur Hermeneutik von Ursprüngen in der feministischen Theologie.

I Die Frage

> Obwohl wir zwischen hohen Stahlbetonbauten, kunststoffbeschichteten Arbeitsplatten und elektronischen Bildschirmen leben, gibt es in uns allen, Männern wie Frauen, etwas, das uns zutiefst mit der Vergangenheit verbindet. Vielleicht ist es die überraschende Feuchtigkeit einer Höhle am Strand oder es sind die Strahlen des Sonnenlichts, die das feine Spitzenmuster der Blätter einer alten Baumkrone durchbrechen, und die es vermögen, in den verborgenen Nischen unserer Seelen entfernte Echos einer entlegenen, alten Zeit zum Klingen zu bringen und uns zu den Uranfängen menschlichen Lebens zurückzuführen.(..) Am Anfang beteten die Menschen zur Schöpferin des Lebens, zur Himmelskönigin. Am Anfang der Religion war Gott eine Frau. Erinnerst du dich?[1]

Dieser Text stammt von Merlin Stone, einer prominenten Vertreterin einer weiblichen Spiritualität, die sich auf den Kult der "Alten Göttin" bezieht, einer Figur, die sich in vielen weiblichen Gottheiten spiegelt. Obwohl Stone in ihrem Buch den Ausdruck "Matriarchat" vermeidet, so ist sie doch davon überzeugt, daß es in der Vorzeit einen weiblichen Kult gegeben hat, der mit einer großen gesellschaftlichen Bedeutsamkeit weiblicher Fähigkeiten und Tätigkeiten einherging. Obwohl diese Zeit dem heutigen Zugriff entzogen ist, legt das Zitat nahe, daß die Verbindung zwischen der ältesten Vergangenheit und der Gegenwart erspürt werden kann, zum Beispiel in einem intensiven Naturerlebnis wie oben beschrieben. In diesem Gefühl offenbart sich das Erinnern.

Sicherlich kann man dem Text eine unreflektierte und suggestiv verstandene Naturromantik vorwerfen, die nicht nach den Bedingungen von Naturvorstellungen und Naturerleben fragt; man kann ihn abgrenzen gegen eine feministische Theologie, die nicht einzelne und ihr Erleben, sondern menschliche Beziehung in den Vordergrund stellt. Diese Kritik

---

1 Merlin Stone, *The Paradise Papers* (London: Virago 1976), 17.

bleibt aber die Antwort auf die Frage schuldig, woher wir kommen, wo unser Ursprung liegt.

Die Frage nach einem Ursprung hat mindestens zwei Dimensionen:
- sie dient zur Klärung der eigenen Identität, der Zugehörigkeit, der Suche nach den Wurzeln.
- sie drückt die Sehnsucht nach einem unverfälschten, "eigentlichen" Zustand aus, in dem alles so ist, wie es sein soll.

Beide Dimensionen gründen in der Erfahrung der Entfremdung. Der Feminismus hat die Entfremdung der Frauen zur Sprache gebracht, indem er männlich-gesellschaftliche Fremdzuschreibungen und Definitionen als solche bewußt gemacht hat. Er hat Frauen damit vor die schwierige, da ungewohnte, Aufgabe gestellt, nämlich weibliche Identität, Integrität und Unabhängigkeit zusammen zu denken. Der feministische Prozeß hat aber auch die Entfremdungen der gesamtgesellschaftlichen Konstruktion bewußt gemacht, die als patriarchal erfahren und qualifiziert werden. Die Hoffnung auf eine schnelle positive Veränderung hat sich jedoch nicht erfüllt; die feministische Vision zielt nach wie vor auf eine U-topie, auf etwas, das (noch) keinen Ort hat und, wie es aussieht, so bald keinen in dieser Welt bekommen wird. Anscheinend reicht es aber nicht aus, eine solche Utopie in der fernen, ungewissen Zukunft zu sehen, sie scheint auch in der fernen, gewissen (?) Vergangenheit angesiedelt zu sein.

Die historisch-kritische Exegese hat uns gelehrt, bestimmte Texte als Ätiologie zu deuten, d.h. als eine Form des Rückgriffs auf einen Ursprung, der eine gegenwärtige Situation deutet und keine historische Sachbeschreibung ist. Diese Einordnung trifft beispielsweise auf die biblischen Schöpfungsgeschichten zu.

Entsprechend ist Stones Rückgriff auf eine Vorzeit zu verstehen, die in historischen Zeugnissen kaum noch greifbar und vorstellbar ist, und deren Zeugnisse zudem aus heutiger Sicht äußerst schwer zu interpretieren sind. So ist auch das von ihr angesprochene Erinnern nur im Absehen von einem neuzeitlich-wissenschaftlichen Zugang zu deuten, eben nicht als historisches.

Folgt man aber der Argumentation des Buches, sieht sie keineswegs von dem historischen Anspruch ab, sondern bedient sich der Interpretation historischer Zeugnisse, meist von Frauenfigurinen. Die Rekonstruktion der Geschichte ist hier ein Mittel zu dem Zweck, die Bedeutung der beschriebenen Zeit für die Wertschätzung von Frauen und von sog. weiblichen Werten in der heutigen Zeit zu postulieren.

Die Rekonstruktion eines authentischen, reinen und unverdorbenen Anfangs ist kein Spezifikum feministischer Spiritualität, sondern religionsgeschichtlich weit verbreitet. Offensichtlich eignen sich die schon bekannten, z.B. biblischen Ursprungserzählungen aber nicht für ein feministisches Interesse, denn schon diese Anfänge werden als patriarchal verfälscht entlarvt. Gerade die Wirkungsgeschichte von Gen 2-3 ist ja ein unrühmliches Beispiel für Frauenfeindlichkeit.

Die ideologische Kritik an patriarchalen Mythen ist der eine Schritt,[2] der andere ist die historische Kritik: vor den patriarchalen Ursprüngen gibt es ältere und authentischere matriarchale. Meine Argumentation ist dahingehend, daß eine unreflektierte Verquickung dieser beiden Argumentationsstränge wiederum ein beträchtliches Ideologiepotential hat.

Mary Daly hat schon früh die weibliche Erfahrung der Entfremdung pointiert formuliert und ihre Konsequenzen beschrieben:

> "Dieses Werden-was-wir-wirklich-Sind erfordert den existentiellen Mut, sich der Erfahrung des Nichts zu stellen."[3]

Auch sie sah den Zusammenhang zwischen gegenwärtigen Ritualen und der ideologischen Inanspruchnahme der Vergangenheit: "Ein Grund für die Bedrohlichkeit liegt darin, daß das religiöse Ritual eine Kontinuität zwischen der Gegenwart und der religiösen Tradition aufrechterhält. *Die Tradition ist ihrem Wesen nach ein Erinnern. Das sexistische Ritual aber ist falsches Erinnern*(...). Antikirche heißt, diesem Erinnern ein Nein entgegenzusetzen."[4] Da die feministische Bewegung etwas gänzlich Neues sei und keine Vorbilder habe, brauche sie keine Erinnerung. Was zählt,

---

2 Vergleichbar das Vorgehen von Heide Göttner-Abendroth bei der Kritik des Zeus-Athene Mythos; dagegen z.B. Phyllis Trible, für die der jahwistische Schöpfungsbericht keineswegs patriarchal ist, sondern der bisherige Zugang dazu. Vgl. Heide Göttner-Abendroth, "Die Eule der Athene fliegt um Mitternacht: Zum Verhältnis von Mythologie und Philosophie" in: Ruth Großmaß/Christiane Schmerl (Hg.), *Philosophische Beiträge zur Frauenforschung* (Bochum: Germinal 1981), 51-66; Phyllis Trible, "Gegen das patriarchalische Prinzip in Bibelinterpretationen" in: Elisabeth Moltmann-Wendel (Hg.), *Frauenbefreiung: Biblische und theologische Argumente* (München: Kaiser [3]1982), 93-117.

3 Mary Daly, *Jenseits von Gottvater, Sohn & Co* (München: Frauenoffensive 1980), 37

4 Ebd., 162-3.

ist einzig die aktive "Teilnahme am Sein". Diese Radikalität nicht nur der Fragestellung, sondern der Antwort Mary Dalys bringt eine Religiosität hervor, die aus Angst von Ideologisierung bildfrei und traditionslos bleiben muß, aber gerade deshalb kaum lebbar ist, sondern als ein reines und faszinierendes Schema theologischer Abstraktion verharrt. Gerade aber weil die geschichtliche Dimension immer eine der Verwurzelung und der Identität ist, ist sie in der Theologie wie in der religiösen Praxis unverzichtbar,[5] denn sie beinhaltet auch den Horizont der Gegenwart und der Zukunft.

Auf welche Tradition, auf welche Ursprünge, kann sich feministische Theologie beziehen, und in welcher Weise soll sie es tun? Gibt es eine Frauentradition vor, neben oder nach der patriarchalen? Kann sie eine Quelle heutiger Frauenspiritualität sein?

II Geschichtstheoretische Überlegungen

Die Geschichtslosigkeit der Frau wird durch die Geschichte hergestellt.[6]

Die Historiographie ist bis zur Gegenwart—mit wenigen Ausnahmen—eine Beschreibung aus der Sicht von Männern mit Blick auf Mächtige gewesen. Frauen sind darin nur dann von Bedeutung, wenn es ihnen gelang, männliche Machtpositionen zu übernehmen—etwa als Königin, oder wenn ihnen ein außerordentlicher Einfluß auf mächtige Männer zugeschrieben wurde.

Diese Sicht ist nicht nur deshalb skandalös, weil mindestens die Hälfte der Menschheit nicht berücksichtigt worden ist und sie deshalb unvollständig ist. Geschichtsschreibung ist auch ein Mittel der Herrschaft; für Janssen-Jurreit ist sie "die wirksamste Form der Herrschaft überhaupt."[7] Geschichtsschreibung ist nicht nur eine möglichst genaue Rekonstruktion der Vergangenheit, sondern deutet die Gegenwart immer mit, sie schafft Traditionen und Identitäten. Männliche Geschichte ist "der große Tank, aus dem die männliche Identität gezapft wird, und dient der

5 Das wird an einem Negativbeispiel deutlich. Die Schwierigkeiten der Deutschen in der Auseinandersetzung mit dem Nationalsozialismus haben darin ihre Wurzel, daß die Vergangenheits- und die Gegenwartsbewältigung untrennbar miteinander verquickt sind.

6 Marie-Luise Janssen-Jurreit, *Sexismus* (Frankfurt/M.: Fischer ^{3}1978), 28.

7 Ebd., 55.

Mythologisierung großer Männer. Das Bild, das von ihm entsteht, ist eine Komposition, die auf die psychologischen Bedürfnisse der männlichen Geschichtskonsumenten zugeschnitten ist."[8] Janssen-Jurreit weist darauf hin, daß auch mündliche Traditionen primitiver Völker zum großen Teil Frauen ausschließen. Inhalt und Perspektive der Geschichten werden von Männern definiert, und Frauen haben keine Möglichkeit, ihre eigenen Mythen dagegenzusetzen.

Die Diskussion um feministische Geschichtsschreibung hat erkannt, daß eine kompensatorische Perspektive, die die androzentrische nur um das Weggelassene im Sinne einer Geschichte weiblicher Prominenz ergänzt, einem positivistischen und an traditionellen Kategorien von Macht orientierten Geschichtsbild aufsitzt.[9] Aber auch bei einer kontributorischen Auffassung (Beitrag der Frauen zu Leistungen wie Antisklavereibewegung, Arbeiterbewegung etc.) werden die historischen Kriterien, die auf Männer zugeschnitten sind, nicht in Frage gestellt. In dieser Perspektive bleiben Frauen allzuoft nur die Opfer der Geschichte. Der Beitrag der Frauen zur menschlichen Kultur kann aber nur dann aufgedeckt werden, wenn sie nicht mehr ausschließlich als patriarchale Objekte betrachtet werden.[10]

Das Skandalon patriarchaler Geschichtsschreibung ist die Vereinzelung von Frauen,"da sie sich geschichtlich an nichts orientieren kann, was ihre persönlichen Erfahrungen in eine Kontinuität mit der Vergangenheit bringen könnte."[11] Die Rückseite der Vereinzelung ist die Subsummierung unter die diffuse und wandelbare Kategorie Geschlecht, die sich an männliche Standards anpaßt (ob nun im Sinne von Komplementarität oder Gleichwertigkeit) und Differenzierungen nicht zuläßt.

---

8 Ebd., 55-6.

9 Vgl. Gerda Lerner, "Welchen Platz nehmen Frauen in der Geschichte ein? Alte Definitionen und neue Aufgaben" in: Elisabeth List/Herlinde Studer (Hg.), *Denkverhältnisse: Feminismus und Kritik* (Frankfurt/M.: Suhrkamp 1989), 334-52, hier: 334; Elisabeth Gössmann, "Die Rezeption von Frauengelehrsamkeit aus Antike, Mittelalter und Renaissance im 17. und 18. Jahrhundert" in: dies. (Hg.), *Eva Gottes Meisterwerk*, Archiv für philosophie- und theologiegeschichtliche Frauenforschung 2 (München: Iudicium 1985), 7.

10 Vgl. Lerner, "Welchen Platz nehmen Frauen in der Geschichte ein?" (wie Anm. 9), 336.

11 Janssen-Jurreit, *Sexismus* (wie Anm. 6), 64.

Die Verwurzelung in der Geschichte berührt die existenzielle Frage der individuellen und kollektiven Identität. Dies trifft auch den Kern einer feministischen Hermeneutik.

III Göttintheologie und weibliche Spiritualität

Bei ihrer Suche nach den Anfängen der Geschichte hat die Göttintheologie auf Matriarchatstheorien des 19. Jahrhunderts zurückgegriffen.[12] Die patriarchale Tendenz der Autoren wird an dieser Stelle hier nicht diskutiert.[13] Es geht hier auch nicht um eine erschöpfende Diskussion von Matriarchatstheorien, sondern um die Bedeutung, die diese Ursprünge für eine feministisch orientierte Spiritualität haben.

Für Elizabeth Gould Davis ist das Matriarchat ein "goldenes Zeitalter": die wichtigsten Kulturtechniken wie Landbewirtschaftung, Spinnen, Weben, Töpfern und Kochen seien hier erfunden worden. Die Menschen seien friedlich und nicht kriegerisch gewesen und waren schöpferisch tätig; überhaupt sei im Matriarchat nicht im uns bekannten "männlichen" Sinne von Frauen geherrscht worden. Die Frauen waren jedoch Dreh- und Angelpunkt der Gesellschaft, auch der Religion.

Auf die Schwierigkeit, ein solches Matriarchat historisch zu belegen, weisen Archäologinnen mit dem Verweis auf die begrenzte Aussagekraft archäologischer Zeugnisse wie Scherben, Gräber, Reste von Siedlungen hin.[14] Demgegenüber argumentieren die Befürworterinnen der Matriarchatsthese, daß für die Rekonstruktion des Matriarchates herkömmliche wissenschaftliche Methoden nicht ausreichen. Interpretierte schon Bachofen den Amazonenmythos und die Orestie, so greift auch Heide Göttner-Abendroth auf antike Mythen und Zaubermärchen zurück, um damit Hinweise auf die religiösen Strukturen des Matriarchats zu erhalten.[15] In die-

---

12 Zur Matriarchatsdebatte s. Themaheft *Schlangenbrut* 11 (1993), Nr. 42; auch Beiträge von Ulla Henze, Christiane Schmerl und Cordula Ritter in: Ruth Großmaß/Christiane Schmerl (Hg.), *Philosophische Beiträge zur Frauenforschung* (wie Anm. 2).

13 Siehe dazu: Uwe Wesel, *Der Mythos vom Matriarchat* (Frankfurt/M.: Suhrkamp 1980); Janssen-Jurreit, *Sexismus* (wie Anm. 6), bes. Kap. 6-10.

14 Vgl. Sybille Kästner, "Vom Mythos zur Realität?" in: *Schlangenbrut* 11 (1993), Nr. 42, 14-16.

15 Heide Göttner-Abendroth, *Die Göttin und ihr Heros: Die matriarchalen Religion in Mythos, Märchen und Dichtung* (München: Frauenoffensive 1980).

sen seien viele Spuren des Matriarchates noch sichtbar, wenn auch in patriarchal verzerrter Form. So wurde die Mädchengöttin zum naiven Kind (Artemis), die Große Göttin degenerierte zur Hure (Aphrodite), und die Fähigkeit, Leben und Heilung zu bringen, wird im Bild der Hexe dämonisiert, oder auf Männer übertragen (Zeus). Nach Göttner-Abendroth hat die patriarchale Ideologie schon die Anfänge der Mythographie und der Geschichtsschreibung geprägt. Ihr Ziel ist es, hinter die patriarchale Fassade zu sehen, und zum Matriarchat als einer verdrängten Epoche der Menschheit vorzustoßen. So ist Athene beispielsweise keineswegs die aus dem Vater Zeus Geborene, sondern eine Weisheitsgöttin, deren Weisheit im Patriarchat männlich umgedeutet werden mußte.[16] Athene stellt in dieser Deutung eine "Superfrau" dar: "Athene ist also nicht nur Kämpferin, Schöpferin, Mutter, Erfinderin und Weise in einer Person(...)."[17] Darüber hinaus vertritt sie ein "nichtpatriarchales" Konzept von Kunst und Wissenschaft, die nicht in der "Sphäre des schönen Scheins" angesiedelt ist und keines methodischen Korsetts bedarf, sondern praktisches Wissen und Lebensweisheit verkörpert.

Die von Göttner-Abendroth skizzierte Weisheitsgöttin Athene, die durch das Patriarchat verstümmelt wurde, entspricht in mehrfacher Hinsicht dem Bedürfnis heutiger Frauen. Sie deutet alle weiblichen Lebensphasen positiv, sie beinhaltet eine alternative, "unmännliche" Perspektive der Wissenschaft und der Kunst und sie scheint als "Superfrau" ein von männlichen Fremdbestimmungen unberührtes Ideal für Frauen zu sein. Sie verkörpert das, was Frauen als ihre Errungenschaft beanspruchen, nämlich praktisches Wissen und Lebensweisheit. Damit füllt dieses Bild ohne Zweifel eine Lücke, denn selbstbestimmte, positive, kraftvolle Bilder von Frauen sind kultur- und religionsgeschichtlich äußerst rar.

Andererseits ist das Bild der Athene nicht frei von Anklängen an eine tüchtige (und patriarchal angepaßte) Hausfrau, die sich der Sorge um das Leben in Form von Kindern und der Natur widmet und sogar in der Ästhetik der Pragmatik verhaftet ist; und es ist ein Frauenbild, das ohne Mütter-

---

16 Vgl. Heide Göttner-Abendroth, "Die Eule der Athene fliegt um Mitternacht" (wie Anm. 2), 51-66.

17 Ebd., 59.

lichkeit und sog. mütterliche Werthaltungen unvollkommen wäre.[18] Insofern ist es nicht frei von Vorstellungen, die weibliche Lebensentwürfe und -formen durchaus behindern können.

Angesichts der Übermacht des Patriarchats ist es nicht verwunderlich, daß eine Vorstellung wie das Matriarchat äußerst attraktiv ist, weil sie geeignet ist, "die scheinbare Naturwüchsigkeit patriarchaler Gesellschaften zu durchbrechen."[19] Sie beinhaltet nicht nur ein alternatives Frauenbild, sondern dient als Sammelbecken für jegliche Art von Kulturkritik, am häufigsten an der Naturferne und Destruktivität männlicher Wissenschaft und männlichen Erfindergeistes. Nach Starhawk basiert die von ihr so bezeichnete "Alte Religion" nicht auf einem Dogma oder einer Reihe von Glaubenssätzen, sondern lernt aus der Natur und läßt sich von Sonne, Mond und Sternen, vom Vogelflug, dem Wachsen der Bäume und dem Wechsel der Jahreszeiten inspirieren.[20]

Nach Beate Wagner-Hasel kann die Renaissance von Matriarchatstheorien verunsichernde und beängstigende gesellschaftliche Entwicklungen kompensieren. Schon Bachofen hatte die Widersprüche zwischen der alten Lebensform und der heraufziehenden Industriekultur zu verarbeiten, ähnlich waren es bei der ersten Bachofen-Renaissance in den 20er Jahren unseres Jahrhunderts.[21] Matriarchatsvorstellungen also als Reflex von Modernisierungskrisen. Heute ist ein Postulat wie Naturnähe und Ganzheitlichkeit eine beruhigende Abwehr gegen die drängender werdenden Probleme der Umweltzerstörung.

Abgesichert wird die Behauptung vom Matriarchat durch einen unbedingten historischen Anspruch. Starhawk wie auch andere weisen immer wieder auf das Alter und die Vorgängigkeit des Matriarchates bzw.

---

18 Zur Problematik der Geschlechterrollen in matriarchal begründeten religiösen Formen s. Monika Jakobs, *Frauen auf der Suche nach dem Göttlichen: Zur Gottesfrage in der Feministischen Theologie* (Münster: 1993), 123-41.

19 Ulla Henze, "Bornemann und Wesel—zwei Klärungsansätze zum Thema 'Matriarchat'," in: Großmaß/Schmerl, *Philosophische Beiträge zur Frauenforschung* (wie Anm. 2), 69.

20 Starhawk, *The Spiral Dance: A Rebirth of the Ancient Religion of the Great Goddess* (San Francisco: Harper 1979), 3.

21 Vgl. Beate Wagner-Hasel, *Schlangenbrut* 11 (1993), Nr. 42, 9.

des Göttinkultes hin.[22] Dies scheint implizit auch ein Argument für ihre Überlegenheit zu sein.

Die Frage nach dem Matriarchat hat Identifikationsfunktion bekommen. Sie dient "1. als Rückversicherung eigener nicht sub-alterner Lebenstraditionen, 2. als Materialfolie für eigene Machtwünsche und -phantasien."[23] Die historische Rückversicherung scheint notwendig, um die Arroganz und Unüberwindlichkeit des Patriarchats in Frage stellen zu können; und sie ist ein Reflex auf einen wissenschaftlichen und gesellschaftlichen Diskurs, der feministischen Positionen nicht ernsthaft einen Platz einräumt.

Die Göttintheologie übt wegen ihrer radikalen Trennung von der als patriarchal empfundenen Religion und dem Angebot einer spirituellen Alternative eine große Anziehungskraft aus, auch für Christinnen. Ihr Dreh- und Angelpunkt sind Images von Frauen, weibliche Lebensmöglichkeiten und Bewertung weiblichen Tuns sowie das Bemühen um eine ganzheitliche Religion, die weder Körperlichkeit noch die natürliche Umwelt unterdrückt.

Problematisch erscheint mir jedoch der Versuch, dies mit historischen Argumenten zu untermauern; in einer Vision eines vorzeitlichen Matriarchats, das unhinterfragbar ist, können sich allzuschnell auch sehr traditionelle und einengende Frauenbilder mit dem Label der "guten Frau" einnisten. Selbstreflexion ist hier dringend geboten.

IV Bibelhermeneutik

Schon Elizabeth Cady Stantons Projekt, eine "bereinigte" Fassung der Bibel vorzulegen, ist der Versuch, die Bibel als einen für Frauen akzeptablen Ursprungstext zu rehabilitieren.[24] Das Spannungsfeld, aus dem die Women's Bible letztlich entstanden ist, bildet bis heute den Hintergrund für feministische Christinnen. Die Wahrnehmung von Sexismus in Kirche und Theologie hat für diese nicht die zwingende Konsequenz, das

22 Vgl. ebd., 2.

23 Henze, "Bornemann und Wesel," (wie Anm. 19), 69.

24 Zur Entstehungsgeschichte der Women's Bible vgl. Elisabeth Schüssler Fiorenza, *Zu ihrem Gedächtnis* (München: Kaiser 1988), 33-42; Bibliographie in: Luise Schottroff/Silvia Schroer/Marie-Theres Wacker, *Feministische Exegese: Forschungserträge der Bibel aus der Perspektive von Frauen* (Darmstadt: Wissenschaftliche Buchgesellschaft 1995), 5-7.

Christentum ganz zu verwerfen, sondern den Beweis anzutreten, daß die christliche Botschaft in ihrem Kern nicht-patriarchal sei. Ähnliches gilt auch für das Judentum.

Die Beweisführung hat unterschiedliche Wege eingeschlagen: so spricht Phyllis Trible von einem nicht-patriarchalischen Prinzip der Bibelinterpretation, Rosemary Radford Ruether von der prophetisch-befreienden Tradition innerhalb der Bibel.[25] Für gut befundene Wertvorstellungen und Ideale bilden die Folie, auf der die Bibel gelesen wird. Dies ist aber keineswegs eine spezifisch feministische Fragestellung. So korrespondiert z.B. auch die Idealisierung der Jerusalemer Urgemeinde mit den gesellschaftskritischen, kommunitären Denkansätzen der 60er und 70er Jahre.[26] Es geht in unserem Zusammenhang auch nicht um die historische Angemessenheit der Methoden.

Gemeinsam ist allen die Verwobenheit von historischer Rekonstruktion und religiöser Identität. Dabei ist die Schwierigkeit festzustellen, ob ein ganzes religiöses System "unrettbar patriarchal" oder frauenbefreiend ist, angesichts einer Soziologie des Wissens nahezu unlösbar. Der redliche Umgang mit dem eigenen Erkenntnisinteresse verbietet es, universale Normen aus bestimmten historischen Phasen, die als Offenbarung gedeutet werden können, abzuleiten.

Schon einer der frühesten Sammelbände zur feministischen Theologie, "Womanspirit Rising",[27] thematisiert das Verhältnis zwischen religiöser Tradition und religiöser Identität. Unter der Kapitelüberschrift "Reconstructing Tradition", finden sich u.a. Beiträge von jüdischen Autorinnen, die feministisches Denken in jüdische Strukturen integrieren.[28]

---

25 Vgl. Phyllis Trible, "Gegen das patriarchalische Prinzip in Bibelinterpretationen," in: Elisabeth Moltmann-Wendel (Hg.), *Frauenbefreiung* (wie Anm. 2), 93-117; ebenso Helen Schüngel-Straumann, "Gott als Mutter in Hosea 11" in *ThQ* 166 (1986), 119-134; Vgl. Rosemary Radford Ruether, *Sexismus und die Rede von Gott* (Gütersloh: Mohn 1985), 25; Ebd., "Leicht zugänglich" in: Maria Kassel (Hg.), *Feministische Theologie: Perspektiven zur Orientierung* (Stuttgart: Kreuzberg 1988), 13-44.

26 Ursprünglich schon bei Friedrich Engels, vgl. Ludger Schenke, *Die Urgemeinde* (Stuttgart: Kohlhammer 1990).

27 Carol P. Christ and Judith Plaskow (eds), *Womanspirit Rising* (San Francisco: Harper 1979).

28 Vgl. die Beiträge von R. Gross, Naomi Janowitz/Maggie Wenig und von Judith Plaskow in Christ/Plaskow*Womanspirit Rising* (wie Anm. 27), 167-184.

Judith Plaskow begründet die Kreation eines jüdischen Initiationsritus für Mädchen wie folgt: "In insisting that girl children are also the heirs and guarantors of tradition, it reminds us that—just as they are excluded from brit milah—they have in fact been excluded from much of Jewish religious life."[29]

Sie schlägt damit einen Weg ein, der sich auch in der neutestamentlichen Hermeneutik von Elisabeth Schüssler Fiorenza findet.[30] Die feministische Hermeneutik betrachtet demnach das NT nicht als ein System von Normen, zu dem vom Standpunkt des Feminismus aus eine angemessene Bewertung gefunden werden soll, sondern bezieht sich auf die Geschichte christlicher Frauen und rehabilitiert sie als Subjekte von Theologie. Diese Offenlegung bringt sowohl das Ausmaß der Unterdrückung wie die Handlungsmöglichkeiten von Frauen zum Vorschein. So werden rigide Vorschriften (Schweigegebot 1 Kor 14,34) als Indikatoren für Konflikte und nicht als überzeitliche Normen gedeutet.

Solchermaßen feministische Zugänge zur Bibel sind häufig als "reformerisch" bezeichnet worden (gegenüber der "radikaleren" vollkommenen Ablehnung der Bibel wie in der Göttintheologie). Das ist mitnichten der Fall. Wird einerseits die Schrift als theologische Grundlage ernst genommen, so werden andererseits die Maßstäbe ihres Verstehens radikal offengelegt. Für feministische Theologie bedeutet dies ein Abschied von einem—von Schüssler Fiorenza so bezeichneten—neo-orthodoxen Zugang zur Bibel, der den eigenen Standpunkt apodiktisch voraussetzt und ihn nicht reflektiert. Es bedeutet eine klare Unterscheidung zwischen historisch Rekonstruierbarem und den Inhalten der Verkündigung, die nicht direkt abgeleitet, sondern diskursiv legitimiert werden müssen.

V Zwischen Relativismus und Neo-Fundamentalismus

Bei der Hermeneutik der Ursprünge wurden zwei unterschiedliche Dinge untersucht: einerseits eine Ursprungs*theorie* (das Matriarchat), andererseits eine heilige Schrift. Einmal haben wir es mit der Anfangsära der Menschheit zu tun, ein anderes Mal mit einer Schrift, die ein offenbartes Ereignis bezeugt. Beide repräsentieren auf je eigene Weise ideale Ur-

29 Judith Plaskow, "Bringing a Daughter into the Covenant" in: Christ/Plaskow, *Womanspirit Rising* (wie Anm. 27), 180.

30 Vgl. Elisabeth Schüssler Fiorenza, *Zu ihrem Gedächtnis* (wie Anm. 24).

sprungssituationen und sie sind Quellen einer Religiösität, die sich zeitlich gewissermaßen unerreichbar weit von diesen Ursprüngen entfernt hat. Diese Ursprünge sind aber insofern nah, als sie nach wie vor zur Legitimation und Identifikation einer Gruppe und ihres Handelns dienen.

Wie die beiden Beispielen gezeigt haben, erfordert der Umgang mit solchen Quellen eine Hermeneutik, die sowohl den Abstand wie die Nähe zur heutigen Zeit reflektiert und zum Ausdruck bringt. Das Alter oder die Vorgängigkeit sind dabei weder Argumente für noch gegen eine bestimmte Religion. Wenn man ernsthaft zu der Auffassung kommen würde, daß das Christentum eine menschen- und lebensfeindliche Religion sei, dann würde die Disqualifikation dieser Religion auch nicht durch eine noch so lange, alte Tradition wettgemacht.

Eine Hermeneutik der Ursprünge erfordert einen offenen Umgang mit Normativität. Inwieweit werden heutige, wünschenswerte Ideale in eine historische Situation hineininterpretiert, damit genau diese Historie wieder zur Legitimierung herangezogen werden kann?

Was bedeutet es, wenn es keine Matriarchate gegeben hat? Werden dann die Ziele, Werte und Symbole einer Göttinreligion obsolet? Wird ein christlicher Feminismus in Frage gestellt, wenn Jesus kein "Feminist" (im heutigen Sinne) war?

Die stärkste Herausforderung in einer Hermeneutik nach der Prägung Schüssler Fiorenzas liegt in ihrem Verzicht auf apodiktisch gesetzte Normen, die durch die Offenbarung legitimiert werden. Die Spannung zwischen Gegenwart und Ursprung muß offen gehalten werden und gewinnt immer wieder verschiedene Facetten. Es liegt aber auch die Befürchtung nahe, daß die identitätsstiftende Funktion darunter leidet. Eine Gegenbewegung dazu ist eine neo-fundamentalistische Einstellung, die -je nach Couleur- die Bibel oder eine mehr oder weniger daraus abzuleitende historische Situation als einmaliges und letztgültiges Offenbarungsereignis definiert. In dieser Gefahr steht auch die Göttintheologie, wenn sie die historische Begründung des Matriarchats unkritisch zum Maßstab weiblicher Spiritualität macht.

VI Neue Quellen—alte Paradiese?

Die Macht patriarchaler Geschichtsschreibung hat Frauen entmachtet. Es ist nicht erstaunlich, daß eine feministische Geschichtsschreibung versucht, die Macht und die Verdienste von Frauen zurückzugewinnen und ihre Unterdrückung offenzulegen. Dieses Vorgehen ist für eine neue, authentische Selbstdefinition von Frauen unabdingbar.

> Was braucht denn eine Frau an Wissen, um ein selbstbewußter, selbstbestimmter Mensch zu werden? Braucht sie nicht ein Wissen von ihrer Geschichte, von ihrem ach so politisierten Frauenkörper, von dem kreativen Genius der Frauen vergangener Zeiten—den Kenntnissen, Fähigkeiten und Visionen, welche Frauen anderer Zeiten und Kulturen besaßen—und davon, wie all dies in Anonymität getaucht, daß nicht die weibliche Anatomie, sondern erzwungene Ignoranz ein entscheidender Schlüssel zu unserer Machtlosigkeit ist.[31]

Die Gefahr besteht darin, den Prozeß der weiblichen Selbstdefinition aus einem Spannungsfeld herauszunehmen und in ein vorzeitliches Paradies zu verlagern. Mit der Matriarchatstheorie einher geht ein radikaler Bezug zur eigenen Erfahrung und die Ablehnung äußerer Autoritäten.[32] Dies ist die Voraussetzung für authentische weibliche Religiosität. Unreflektiert entbindet sie aber von der Aufgabe, das Patriarchat und die Frauen darin in ihrer Mehrdeutigkeit zu betrachten. Dies kann zu einer neuerlichen Enteignung der Frauen von ihrer Geschichte führen.

Gesellschaftliche Lebensformen ohne Sexismus im allgemeinen und weibliche Spiritualität im besonderen brauchen die Wiederaneignung der Geschichte von Frauen (als Opfer, als Heldinnen, als Mitläuferinnen und Mitttäterinnen), aber nicht im Sinne einer Rückversicherung. Dieser Problematik ist sich auch Starhawk bewußt, wenn sie schreibt: "Witchcraft is indeed the Old Religion, but it is undergoing so much change and development at present that, in essence, is is being recreated rather than revived. The feminist religion of the future is presently being formed."[33] Das heißt: Kreative Neuerschaffung statt pseudohistorische Neubelebung.

Die Bedeutung von Geschichte für die Identität ist hier betont worden. Neue religiöse Entwürfe müssen aber die Gegenwartsdimension als Eingebundenheit in einen gesellschaftlichen und theologischen Diskurs ebenso ernst nehmen wie den Vergangenheitsbezug. Die Suche nach einem verlorenen Paradies und das Benennen von Sündenböcken ("das

---

31 Adrienne Rich, zit. nach Claudia Opitz, "Der 'andere Blick' der Frauen in die Geschichte: Überlegungen zu Analyse- und Darstellungsmethoden feministischer Geschichtsforschung," in: *beiträge zur feministischen theorie und praxis* 11 (1984), 66.

32 So z.B. ausdrücklich bei Starhawk, *The Spiral Dance* (wie Anm. 20), 187.

33 Starhawk, *The Spiral Dance* (wie Anm. 20), 188.

Patriarchat") wiederholt die Fehler ebendieses patriarchalen Denkens und entbindet nicht von politischem Handeln. Verantwortlichkeit in Gegenwart und Geschichte—und das ist nichts anderes als die Subjektwerdung der Frauen—bedeutet aber auch den schmerzlichen Verzicht auf eine generelle Unschuldsvermutung von Frauen oder des Postulates biologisch begründeter "besserer" Werte.

Abstracts

Dans son souci de retracer les commencements de l'histoire, la théologie de la Déesse s'inspire des théories du matriarcat du XIXe siècle pour proposer l'idée d'une "origine idéale". De manière similaire, certaines approches féministes des Ecritures s'efforcent de prouver que le noyau de l'Evangile n'est pas patriarcal. Monika Jakobs questionne la façon dont cette "herméneutique des origines" tente de légitimer et d'établir l'identité d'un groupe et de ses actions, et elle insiste sur la nécessité de reconnaître la complexité des relations entre le passé et le présent; elle se demande également s'il faut absolument inventer un passé idéal pour légitimer des préoccupations actuelles.

In its search for the beginnings of history, goddess theology turns to nineteenth century theories of matriarchy to supply a view of an "ideal origin". In a similar way, feminist approaches to the Scriptures seek to prove that the core of the gospel is not patriarchal. Monika Jakobs questions the way in which such "hermeneutics of origins" seek to legitimate and establish the identity of a group and its actions, arguing that it is necessary to recognise the complexity of relationships between the past and the present and asking whether it is necessary to construct a past ideal to legitimise present concerns

Monika JAKOBS (1959), Studium in Katholischer Theologie, Germanistik und Sozialkunde in Saarbrücken und Cardiff. Promotion 1993. Nach verschiedenen Tätigkeiten in Kirche und Schule seit 1993 Dozentin für Religionspädagogik an der Universität Landau/Pfalz. Von 1991-1995 Sekretärin der ESWTR.

Channa SAFRAI

Feminist Theology in a Jewish Context

Superficially I have been described as a Jewish Feminist Theologian and as such was invited to respond to Monika Jakobs. I found myself in a great dilemma since almost all the relevant elements for my religious feminist perspective are either totally missing or subjected to a sense of triumphalistic white Christian vision. In the light of her article I feel myself obliged to define my own premises better, and wish to start with the three components: theologian, feminist, Jewish.

'Theology' does not seem to fit. It is a well known fact that the term theology does not exist in Hebrew and is not found in the traditional sources. Existing partial equivalents would serve the feminist critic much better: 'Jewish thought', 'Jewish tradition', 'Jewish ideas', 'Jewish community and its faith', or 'Jewish community in its relation to the Divine'. All are expressions found in the Jewish tradition and sources[1] which seem to avoid two critical elements evoked in the term theology. First, they are somewhat more fragmentary, less inclusive and enable a variety of propositions; they are less systematic or dogmatic by their own definition. And second, these formulations carve a greater space for human aspects. They are preoccupied more with the community in faith, and less with Divine definitions. Such a basic attention to the communal presentation should be more open to re-evaluation, namely to human/feminist considerations.

Similarly 'feminist' is problematic. Once more this is not a question of keeping pace with long-standing terminological debates, but rather of trying to avoid new pitfalls. Feminism is a militant objective term when it is presented as if neutral, but in fact it is the fruit of a specific tradition striving for abstract absolute truth. If one is reluctant to discuss faith outside a concrete community, it is more helpful to resort to another terminology, women or womanism, which unfortunately received scarce attention

1 For a recent summary of this quest see: Jonathan Sacks, *One People? Tradition, Modernity and Jewish Unity* (London: Littman 1993), in particular 1-18 and bibliography there.

from Monika. Yet this black women's coinage seems to fit me better. It expresses a reluctance to be totally submerged in the current waves of white female Christians' objections to the formation of their history and faith. It has been argued that this rejected history is an essential part of black women's self-definition, and indeed, that of Jewish women as well. Take it away and an important part of their/our experience vanishes, to our loss.[2] Furthermore, the term women (as opposed to females) implies a concrete community, families and relations; the love and suffering, struggle and achievements of living people.[3] It is thus a preferable term.

The third element 'Jewish' is not less complex. Bearing in mind that the Jewish concrete world of ideas is comprised of a variety of communities, some more faith-oriented than others, every responsible student must define the type of orientations he or she brings into the discussion. This response is inspired by modern Jewish orthodoxy with a basic commitment to observation of Rabbinic Halakha. For many this would by definition contradict any feminist possibility, even that of a womanist critique, since neither the Rabbis nor their Halakha are understood to be women-friendly. Nonetheless it is for me an obvious choice of commitment for my Jewishness. I could not join those who maintain that there is Jewish tradition or Jewish thought and history apart from Halakha; similarly, I oppose many of the present orthodox Rabbis, who either reject all those who are not committed to Halakha or fear and reject any responsible criticism, including feminist criticism. I am feminist/womanist, post-modern in a certain sense. My commitment to Halakhic tradition creates a specific arena for the present debate, and lends our discussion specific Halakhic and Jewish premises. It enables a free use of past traditions and texts, and at the same time perpetuates many issues of critique long since solved by other Jewish denominations. It carries its own characteristics.

Bearing these three elements in mind, there is no space for any radical thinking or a comprehensive abstract solution, no call for radical new beginnings.[4] Rather, there is a perpetual search for needed changes, a continuous resistance of injustice within the tradition, even if success can

2 Katie G. Cannon, *Black Womanist Ethics* (Atlanta: Scholars Press 1988), 84-90

3 *Ibid.*, 59-66. See also Carole Boyce Davies, *Black Women, Writing and Identity* (London: Routledge 1994), 38-58.

4 Judith Plaskov, *Standing again at Sinai* (San Francisco: Harper 1991).

at best be partial.[5] There is a permanent sensitivity to growth—developments or transformations of consciousness—and the search for means and modes of appropriate acceptable adaptations.

In the last three decades scholars, theologians, anthropologists, sociologists and philosophers have come up with a variety of what then seemed to be solutions and remedies to the feminist issue. A few decades later the search has not ceased, and society has not come up with the final answer, neither theoretically nor practically. Christian Theology does not seem to differ from all other critical approaches, I would argue that in my 'Jewish' search all of them are a part, though never a sufficient part, of the whole quest. The question is not whether a solution has been found, but rather what are the ways and means by which small or large critical measurements can be absorbed or responded to.[6]

In Jewish terms, then, the question would be: if one were to apply a women-oriented critic to Jewish social and religious norms, would the tradition be able to respond? Or, from another perspective, did the tradition ever develop relevant tools for such social or ideological changes? Are there already existing, non-feminist modes of thought and behavior that could be activated if one was to try and respond to these new social psychological challenges? I consider these to be two aspects of crucial relevance in the Jewish realm and found very little sympathy in this respect in the presentation of Monika Jakobs.

Defining the tools for the women's agenda in Jewish terms is a crucial task, and it derives its ideas from all areas of feminist critique.[7] As such, once again, it is not a closed, organized task but rather a quest for all new sensitivities as they seem to develop.[8] My personal experience is that the Jewish tradition, though neither 'feminist' nor necessarily women-friendly, is theoretically capable of rising to many of the challenges, and serves the seeker with much traditional Jewish terminology and many possibilities. It would seem that some examples are here in order.

---

5 Sharon D. Welch, *A Feminist Ethics of Risk* (Minneapolis: Fortress 1992), 67-82.; Cannon, *Black Womanist Ethics* (as note 2), 169 ff.

6 Davies, *Black Women, Writing and Identity* (as note 3), 152-64.

7 Welch speaks of ethics of control and theology of resistance and hope, *A Feminist Ethics of Risk* (as note 5), 23 ff. and 153 ff.

8 Eva F. Kittay and Diana T Meyers (eds), *Women and Moral Theory* (Totowa NJ: Rowman & Littlefield 1987).

Feminist critique maintains that male religious literature has subordinated and ignored female activities and interests. As a result a major focus of the theological search is the rediscovery of these lost aspects, regaining their role, status and relevance or creating an alternative respectful religious herstory. This task is no less relevant in the Jewish story, but two specific Jewish aspects are of interest. The chances of finding hidden womens' stories, taken for granted in Christian Feminist Theology, are limited, because from the Rabbinic period (from the second century) there are no monarchs, Temple or capital city with their associated high societies; furthermore there are no convents or great armies, potential sources of stories concerning ladies of power. Jewish society is politically low-ranked, and the majority of stories concern the Rabbis and study, traditionally a male activity. On the other hand, the Rabbinic literature, the main source for the Rabbinic information, religion and ideology, defines itself as an oral literature, conceived as a collection of sayings, statements, stories and biblical interpretations from past generations. Even if one accepts the most rigid literary criticism and reads the books as literary units, one can hardly ignore the implication of these previous stages of existing written literature. Once one begins not to follow the formal Rabbinic interests but to devise new focal points, namely women, their involvement, their commitments, their Halakhic relevance and their rejection, one is bound to find hitherto neglected but extremely illuminating traces of long-forgotten women. These refer not to high and mighty women but rather to the common type of female religious preoccupations and limitations. These are the perfect role models, relevant examples for contemporary modern theology. Jewish womanists do not have to struggle with christological models, but rather to unearth available hidden common women.

Furthermore, the Rabbinic Jewish tradition has for generations been busy adapting its religious ideas and praxis to changing realities. It has an inbuilt system for change and development. No, it has never applied itself to women, but it has continually been busy with social equality and religious 'democracy'. The Rabbis in the first centuries developed a personal, individual and communal religiosity from the basis of a priestly Bible. They created new institutions while mourning the loss and destruction of the old ones.[9] Their tradition is adapted to social challenges, and

9 Avot de rabbi Nathan, Version A ch. 4. Version B ch. 8. Where charity replaces the Temple. and many others.

the womanist call is just that—a social challenge. The inclusion of those who were excluded, lay males in the priestly role and females with males, is an old new religious requirement, an expansion or variation of the ancient known challenge.

The various discussions of 'female writing'[10] or 'women's voice'[11] struggle to define literary forms and presentations advantageous for women. For Jewish womanists it has been helpful to note that many of the characteristically relevant phenomena are to be detected in traditional Rabbinic literature, although again with no specific benefit for women's equality or presentation. Thus Rabbinic literature is fragmentary; it seems to develop small details rather than grand theoretical ideas. One finds in it a keen interest in the individual case and particular circumstances together with a contemplative religious approach to the physical, the practical and the concrete. Thus when Hillel takes a bath it is understood as an act of worship.[12] Similarlay, according to some Rabbis, a Nazerite who refrains from drinking wine and cutting his hair must bring a sin offering because he thereby refrains from enjoying the divine pleasures of this earthly world.[13] The Jewish tradition does not have to learn to appreciate these 'typically female' characteristics. It has, though, to learn to apply them for the benefit of women believers, and this is the task of the womanist.

One could refer here to recent discussions on purity and females. This theme has been subjected to heavy criticism, tied in with the question of the dualisms male-female, good-evil, physical-spiritual. As was pointed out long ago, in the Jewish tradition the dualism body-spirit is of lesser interest; the body, the earthly is mostly conceived as a shrine, or even as an opportunity for spiritual contemplative divine elements.[14] The school of Hillel argues from scripture that earth was created first (Gen 2:4), though the school of Shammai has it the other way around (Gen

10 Hélène Cixous, *La* (Paris: Gallimard 1976). For an analysis of the feminist elements of writing see: Ingeborg Weber (ed.), *Weiblichkeit und weibliches Schreiben* (Darmstadt: Wissenschaftliche Buchgesellschaft 1994), 15-50.

11 Fokkelien van Dijk-Hemmes, *Sporen van vrouwenteksten in de Hebreeuwse Bijbel,* (Utrecht: Utrecht University Press 1992), 161-244.

12 Lev Raba, 34:3.

13 BT Nedarim 10a; JT Nedarim 1 [36d] and parallels.

14 Daniel Boyarin, *Carnal Israel, Reading Sex in Talmudic Culture* (Berkeley: University of California Press 1993), 31-60.

1:1).[15] Hillel's philosophy was the more popular and gained the sanction of the Jewish community and authority. Nonetheless in the concrete experience of women the purity regulations were experienced quite often as social control and religious inferiority. The question here would be, not whether this tradition had or still has this particular function which is hostile to women, but whether one could turn these Halakhic structures to the advantage of women in the community of faith. Some have called this apologetics; Welch calls it very appropriately ethics of control. Modern feminism calls for women rituals and celebration. Women/society/community could and should take it upon themselves to translate existing traditional rituals into a religious affirmations of womanhood, which transform the woman-cycle and the act of sex into part of the divine experience and the home into a small private mutual shrine of love.

Such a transformation of attitude, or such a psychological and exegetical effort, is only possible in a self-conscious community of men and women. It requires a strong need and a sense of authority within the community of believers. I missed in Monika Jakobs' presentation this important sense of communal commitment, which for Jewish womanists is a crucial traditional element. Women's issues and critiques may be new but the authority of the community is a long formulated theme in Jewish tradition. No Rabbi should impose a prohibition on a community if the community is not ready to accept his ruling,[16] and one even finds a Halakhic precept which argues: "Not that it is an obligation, but in order to please women."[17] Circumstances, willingness, appreciation and possibilities are not extraneous to religious life but can become an intrinsic part of the Halakhic requirements. The womanist desires consciously to resort to this traditional language. Furthermore, the fact that this tradition carries this element with pride should make it possible to expound on it, and to develop with new sensitivities new terms and vocabulary appropriate for modern ever renewed questions. No tradition is alive if it resorts only to copying, and does not make full use of its own opportunities. That the Jewish version of womanism is a call for a perpetual creativity, a quest for new possibilities based on past experience and a tradition of criticism.

15 TB Hagiga 12 a and many parallels.

16 TB Baba Kama 79b and parallels.

17 Channa Safrai, "Women and Temple" (dissertation KTUA 1991), 104-123.

Susan Sered argues that female religious organizations carry specific characteristics and seem to be more oral and less centralized.[18] This is a serious drawback for western women with their long literary tradition with its strong textual authority, including highly centralized institutions. Women experience the Jewish tradition as text and as Rabbinic-centered in a way which is similar to all other western religions. Nevertheless, one detects in the growth of the Rabbinic tradition various elements that correspond to this advantageous element for women's expression. Thus the Pharisees and latter the early Rabbis insisted on an oral tradition alongside Scripture.[19] This oral tradition is a product of a dispersed decentralized process of study occurring in groups and schools each with its own Rabbi. The strong elements of the group and the oral transmission, are not mere technicalities but dictate an atmosphere of involvement, commitment, interchange and comradery, all of which have been defined by various critics as feminine. When women enter with their critical approach they are bound to find this tradition inherently fitting to their supposedly particular psychology.

The most obvious of these characteristics is surely the so-called culture of controversy. The Rabbinic ability to accept more than one opinion or decision as Halakhic and legitimate is directly connected with the decentralized character of that tradition. If the Rabbinic tradition is orally transmitted, and everyone is encouraged to participate, then differences are unavoidable. And indeed, the Rabbinic tradition recognized this fact, legitimized and glorified it: "Both are the words of the living God."[20] If God is to be alive there should be more than one opinion. Diversity of opinion and acceptence of oppositions is thus embedded in the tradition, though forgotten by recent more centralized western Jewish communities. The various opinions and decisions quite often hold in themselves friendlier approaches to women issues, and besides this they contain an additional important element: the possibility of recreating and reusing this traditional language for the benefit of new agendas, thus combining new critique with old revived habits.

---

18 Susan Starr Sered, *Priestess, Mother, Sacred Sister: Religions dominated by Women* (Oxford: OUP 1994), 243 ff.

19 TB Gittin 60a and many parallels.

20 TB Erubin 13b.

This Jewish traditional concept leads us to the last general point. Many have argued (and is this argument not lurking in Monika's presentation as well?) that the feminist critique is so radical and all-encompassing that no previous structure could possibly survive it. In this argument is inherent a strong belief that criticism is by definition destructive; theologically it is a deviation from the absolute unity of God. It carries with it the notion that the new ideology has to replace the old and become the next absolute, one-and-only possibility. The legitimacy of discussion implies a variant on this old theme. The Jewish Rabbinical tradition legitimates a fierce constructive criticism and makes it welcome. Thus criticism is not a failure, but rather a proof of faith and commitment. Variety is no threat but rather enrichment.

The obligation of the creative Jewish womanist is to apply on a regular basis new sensitivities to existing standard thoughts and praxis, to continue forever to question, criticize, and explore possible innovative avenues. She can never assume that the road has reached its end, but rather must approach the crossroads again and again and try to develop new bye-ways leading from within the tradition with the tradition toward a better sensitized world.

In summary, I would prefer not to call myself a theologian, but rather a student within a perpetual learning process of Jewish thought, throughout the generations within variety of communities, in search of a meaningful Jewish life with women and for women. I demand for us the right to use our old vocabulary and thus create a relevant womanist milieu. Though I am sure Monika would not object, I doubt if she is truly aware of this need.

Abstracts

Chana SAFRAI aborde plusieurs problèmes relatifs aux termes "juif", "féministe" et "théologie". Aucun de ces termes n'est abstrait; mais c'est seulement lorsqu'ils sont ancrés dans une communauté et une situation particulière qu'ils prennent toute leur signification. C'est pourquoi l'idée d'un recommencement radical est illogique, car le changement doit s'inscrire dans la continuité de la tradition d'une communauté. Or, dans la tradition juive, il existe des éléments qui répondent parfaitement aux besoins des femmes et aux projets de changement. Traditionnellement d'ailleurs, le judaïsme rabbinique a toujours su s'adapter aux situations nouvelles et proposer des réponses variées aux circonstances extérieures.

Chana SAFRAI problematisiert das Verständnis der Begriffe "jüdisch", "feministisch" und "Theologie". Keiner ist ein Abstraktum, vielmehr erhalten sie ihre Bedeutung durch ihre Verwurzelung in einer bestimmten Gemeinscahft und in bestimmten Situationen. Jede Forderung nach einem radikalen Neuanfang ist unangemessen, da Veränderungen in der Kontinuität der Traditionen einer Gemeinschaft stehen müssen. Es gibt sehr wohl Elemente innerhalb der jüdischen Tradition, die den Bedürfnissen von Frauen und ihren veränderten Entwürfen entsprechen. Mehr noch, das rabbinische Judentum zeichnet sich durch eine Tradition der Anpassung an neue Gegebenheiten und durch eine Bandbreite von Antworten auf vorgegebene Umstände aus. Allerdings bedeutet dies nicht notwendigerweise, daß sie bisher zugunsten von Frauen genutzt werden. Sie jedoch bieten eine theoretische Möglichkeit .

Chana SAFRAI holds a Ph.D from the Katholieke Theologische Universiteit Amsterdam with a dissertation on "The Status and the Role of Women in the Second Temnple of Jerusalem" and teaches Talmudica at the Katholieke Theologische Universiteit te Utrecht. She is engaged in numerous research programmmes in Israel and the Netherlands, participates in rabbinic conferences and in the Jewish- Christian dialogue.

Marcella ALTHAUS-REID

I know how to make a death spell, but I cannot change history

I know how to make a death spell. A poor indigenous woman from my country, Argentina, told me one day how to perform the intense, if brief, traditional death spell as it has been performed by her people for centuries. We were living at that time under the power of a cruel dictatorship which during the 1970s exterminated nearly 30,000 women, men and children accused of communism in my country. Poverty, political persecution and strong censorship in all areas of philosophy, sociology and theology were the everyday reality, with universities closed and books burnt in police quarters. I asked that woman how the death spell worked with people in power. Could it eliminate a criminal Junta in power? She answered that in her opinion, the death spell worked reasonably well with individuals but couldn't change the unjust laws of the country. At that point, I decided to challenge her, expressing my doubts, not in the power of the death spell she taught me, but in its utility. It was not so much the individuals who needed to be changed but whole structures of oppression that needed to be overturned. In reply to my comments, she looked at me enigmatically and said: "Ah, Señorita, but how do you think we have survived during 500 years of colonisation?"

The spirituality of poor women as a hermeneutics of origins

I have never used the ritual of the death spell, but I learned from that woman that the spirituality of survival of poor women in my country is a hermeneutical spirituality. It comprises some of the key elements of what Jakobs calls a hermeneutics of origins (identity, history and a present dimension) but it comes from a style of doing feminist theology in Latin America. The first distinctive point to emphasise here is that this paper is an issue-based response to Jakobs. Second: that this reflection is nurtured from a community of poor, oppressed indigenous women. Third: that I recognise their death spell rituals as a theological referent in the present response to Jakobs, because "death" is an important issue amongst the poor, especially amongst poor women in my country. As Stone goes back to a mythological past of caves and goddesses of heaven, so the oppressed always go back to invasions and colonisation, and the death of dreams, civilisations and people. I hope that this crucial theme of a hermeneutics of origins, rather than being a response from me in terms of agreements and disagreements, will help in establishing a dialogue with the plurality which exists in our lives as women, and breaking away from the imposed homogeneity of the historical patriarchal project of oppression. Such a project is both idealist and univocal. The feminist project I advocate is, in contrast, materialist and plural.

The hermeneutics of origins in "death spells"

The woman who shared some of her rituals with me was very concrete in the sense of establishing what she meant by origins. She implied in her discourse that the origins of life and its present meaning come from a spirituality which allowed tribal survival. Death spells, so common in popular religiosity both rural and urban in my country, are in themselves a discourse of the origins of oppression and disempowerment which people suffered with the coming of Christianity to Latin America. Ritual magic is based on an identity in struggle, not with "nothingness", as Mary Daly claims (cited by Jakobs), but with the concrete things in the lives of oppressed indigenous women, such as hunger, political oppression and the multiple forms of the body's colonisation (rape, forced marriages and procreation, lack of sexual options, the politics of motherhood as vocation etc.). Nothingness is not a problem for us as Latinas. Hunger is quite something. Deprived of elemental forms of law and order for centuries, the indigenous Latinas do not want to remember Persian paradises memorised from texts brought by elite Anglo-Saxon men; they want to remember the origins of suffering in rituals which became the only way to operate in a world which excluded them completely for the purposes of economic exploitation. They express the origins of disempowerment through ritual responses rather than political ones, and these need to be interpreted in order to decolonise the epistemological implications hidden in any search for collective and individual identity.

The important theological point for a hermeneutics of survival is that, as the woman said to me, it is easier to consider the elimination of individuals than of structures of sinful power. Metaphorically speaking, in feminist theology we take the risk that we can easily "kill" individual patriarchal interpretations of the Bible; we consider if Jesus was feminist or if Genesis, according to Trible,[1] has been misinterpreted. We unmask the individuality in the Scriptures, because we are still using the epistemological project of authority from patriarchalism. Why do we consider Genesis as an account of our origins? Why do we not consider, for instance, the origins of monotheism in Israel, more in tune with Luce Irigaray's analysis of the "economy of the same",[2] which results in one king, one God, and one penis? Unfortunately Jakobs does not challenge the consideration of origins from an idealist perspective of "where do we come from?" type of questions. She forgets that in reality the most important knowledge we have is that we come from complex relations of production and politics of reproduction. Israel's political programme of monotheism and monarchy while oppressing and demonising the Canaanite culture (thus, giving sacred status to oppression) is more relevant from a feminist identity point of view than the beginnings from ribs or dust.

Why it is easy to kill one individual

We can change exegesis and make liberative re-readings of the whole Scriptures, as Trible does, or we can achieve at least a combination between prophetic denunciation of irredeemable texts and re-appropriation of chauvinist interpretations, more in tune with Radford Ruether's hermeneutics of liberation.[3] We can kill patriarchal exegesis as if we were using death spells, but unfortunately we cannot change the structures of symbolic systems, or even really challenge our methodological presuppositions. If killing one bad character in the Scripture through rearticulating the re-reading process liberates the subversive feminist power of the Scriptures (as Fiorenza would claim[4]), one could hope that

1 Phyllis Trible, *God and the Rhetoric of Sexuality* (Philadelphia: Fortress, 1978) 12-21.

2 See Luce Irigaray, *The Speculum of the Other Women* (Ithaca: Cornell University Press 1985).

3 See Rosemary Radford Ruether, *Sexism and God Talk: Towards a Feminist Theology* (Boston: Beacon Press, 1983)

4 Elizabeth Schüssler Fiorenza, *Searching the Scriptures: A Feminist Introduction* (London: SCM 1994).

this would have changed the patriarchal system. If liberative exegesis has the power to change history, I think we should now be living in a post-patriarchal era, with the goddess walking in the streets at night without fear of rape. However, this is not the case, and the theological reflection on spirituality, origins and power that the indigenous woman shared with me is true. We can kill an individual but not a structure of oppression. Paul can be redeemed, and Jesus crowned the goddess's Messiah but the structures of sacred power/knowledge which sustain both Paul and Jesus are those which need to be "killed", that is, deconstructed. However, symbolic systems change slowly and with difficulty, and are mainly communitarian processes; the change of symbolic systems is not a task for an individual theologian, but for whole communities through their search for the origins of oppression and structures of sacred injustice. This is far more important in the search for an everyday women's identity in the struggle than is reflecting on goddesses and caves.

The hermeneutics of origins of Jakobs seems in a sense to belong to the kind of project that I am proposing here. She believes that we should not comfort ourselves with matriarchal paradises, while emphasising the need for engagement with social and theological discourses of the present. When Merlin Stone, in the text quoted by Jakobs, asks us to travel from "high concrete and steel buildings" and "electronic screens" to an ancient time when people venerated the Goddess of Heaven, Jakobs argues that there is a lack of historical evidence in this process, and it is therefore difficult to explain and understand. However, where I think I take a different perspective is from Jakobs' concept of history, which seems to be based here on a supposed chronological facticity instead of an accomodated ideology which finds facts suitable for its own justification. We need to recognise that the past is organised from the present in a genealogical fashion in which we choose significative elements to sustain our present ideological situation and trace back a false chronology in which a false order establishes "normality". We discipline history and believe in its logic. Thus, in the politics of "common sense" in which the patriarchal order flourishes and women wither, we do, as Jakobs claims, need origins to clarify our identity and the way things should be. This explains the bitter aftertaste of homogenisation I had after reading Stone's opening paragraph. She presupposes that all of us come from "plastic-covered work spaces and electronic screens" and from high buildings. In fact, many of us come from cardboard slums, from huts made of mud with roofs made of the heavy branches of a tree, or , even in "First World" countries such as Britain, from blankets and bags in the railway stations at night. Because unemployment is rampant in the First World, even the phrase "work spaces" does not make sense for thousands of women struggling for their identity.

Origins: one God, one currency, one penis

The hermeneutics of origins presented here is elitist. Stone is concerned with matriarchy and female cults in so called pre-historic times (what does this mean? surely all times are historic). These are concerns inherited from the patriarchal foundations of authority as knowledge, and knowledge as hierarchical knowledge. Thus, the female cult *needs* to be either older or supreme, or a combination of both; unfortunately, we are still killing individuals rather than the frame of thought which teaches us that if we are to validate the goddess spirituality as part of a hermeneutics of origins, we need to proceed through the same classist processes of supremacy by age or by uniqueness.

Meanwhile, Jakobs is concerned with the historicity (not genealogy) of such facts, while I am concerned with the construction of history and the origins of monotheism, economic monopoly, monogamy and only one mode of sexuality. One God, one currency and one penis are concepts so inextricably related that unless you undo one, you cannot undo the others. For a hermeneutics of origins in the Scriptures, apart from the origins of hegemonic sacred orders, I want to know the origins of prescribed heterosexuality from the intertextuality of the theosocial, economic discourses of the Bible. The biblical hermeneuticians quoted by Jakobs do not consider that. Jakobs only mentions European and United States theologians. There is not a single mention of Asian, Latina or African feminist hermeneuticians.

This is perhaps, after all, not a coincidence. In reality, the paradise of origins of Stone is the counter-discourse of life in a middle-class white Anglo-Saxon context. What do professional women working with electronic screens want during the heavy summer of the big cities? A beach, old witch trees, and dark caves where they can remember how to sing hallelujah to the goddess. From one hegemonic group conception of women's lives one can go to its projection into the past, projecting unsuspecting hegemonic thoughts. Rather than finding this surprising, I consider it to be the normal procedure of colonial patriarchalism in its search for normality based in univocal discourses of false chronological traditions. Jakobs does not challenge this point, and therefore does not see the connection between this and the feminist vision as utopia (which term she uses in a negative sense). The point is that this colonial patriarchal ideology, located in the past and articulated in the present by a normative sacred symbolic system, can never produce an effective utopia (I use the term in a positive way; utopia and strategy are different things). Or can it? If the historical method is used for this homogenisation process, the utopia (ideology projected into the future) must be projected to avoid challenges. Perhaps we have a clue here as to why some feminist utopias are, as Paul Ricoeur calls them, "schizophrenic";[5] that is, they do not have a clear strategy of action attached to them. This is what in Latin America we consider to be a faith *without* an ideology, and therefore a dead faith.[6] However, Jakobs claims that an "utopia must also be seen as having *colonised* the distant past" (my italics). The use of the verb "to colonise" in the positive sense of "envisioning the distant past" implies a process of possessing and imposing to the past an utopia born of the high buildings of Stone. This is where as Third World hermeneuticians we can be useful, because a hermeneutics of origins needs to start with a process of de-colonising our feminist theologies of structures of alienation, and of a current epistemology of alienation.

The goddess and the beauty contest

In Perú, when asked about God, some people will still ask which God we are referring to. Are we talking of the old God?[7] By that, they refer to Pachamama, the "Mother of Cosmic Time" of the ancient Inca religion. Her worship, far from extinct, is performed actively to the point that some Catholic parishes have incorporated the Pachamama together with the Virgin Mary (whose worship in Latin America is built upon the great Goddesses of the continent). This has happened because the spirituality of survival and resistance tends to be always female. The gods either died or

---

5 Paul Ricoeur, in Richard Kerney, *Dialogues with Contemporary Continental Thinkers* (Manchester: Manchester University Press 1984), 30.

6 Juan Luis Segundo, *La Liberación de la Teología* (Buenos Aires: Lohlé 1975), 158ff.

7 Gustavo Gutiérrez, "Entre Las Calandrias," in *Paginas* 100 (1989), 91-125.

were domesticated; the goddesses are tough cookies. However, from a materialist perspective we will say that good ideas do not fall from heaven, but are rather the product of the social constructions of the elite in power. And gods and goddesses are always good ideas, supporting phallocratic discourses of origins to establish hierarchies, functions, and a cultural order based on possessions, properties and social roles. Thoughts about matriarchy do not escape from this pattern either. The question is which god/dess? Do we need to deconstruct god/desses and leave the referent open? Why does the goddess need to always be a famous Greek marble beauty, the winning candidate of the European Beauty Contest? After all, Christianity, as interpreted from the Western theological hegemony, drank in the wells of Greek thought as the epitome of culture. We are unable to think god/dess outside the lines of patriarchal discourses of class and race supremacy.

Subverting hermeneutics to change history

A theological project in subverted order implies a hermeneutics from the underside of history. This means that we are not going to be concerned with people praying "in the beginning", as Stone says, to the Goddess of Heaven, but with the women themselves and their historical project as reflected in their theology. The challenge, then, is not to find matriarchies but to see the goddess in the drunk woman sleeping in the streets of Edinburgh, or to recognise the goddess who is a child prostitute in the streets of Rio. If we cannot do that, it is because we are still drinking in the wells of patriarchal theophanies: gods and their power, beauty and invincible strength; the politics of the all-mighties and the compassion of the disembodied beings towards the pains of physical pain. Does Athenea have the callused hands of women peasants? The hermeneutics of origins I would like to apply here must begin by finding out where a theologian starts to assume a theological agitator role. How can we as a community of feminist theologians become collective strategists and organisers towards the realisation of our utopias? This requires us to theologise dialectically, incorporating a much needed sense of methodological inexactitude and change in order to deconstruct systematic thinking in theology. We need to start from a basic materialist approach, considering that god/desses do not have a separate existence from the bag lady in the park. What is the bag lady's spiritual project? A room for the night and a cup of tea? Who is the God/dess then, the bag lady or the cup of tea? I would say that She is the meaning in between.

My main point here is that a hermeneutics of origins needs to come from the anti-paradises and from the historical consciousness of the dialectic, male oppression and female guerrilla. As the woman who told me how to perform a death spell said, we have survived but we have not lived. We are still preoccupied with individualities in feminist theologies, re-interpreting one passage, or finding an alternative to a text, but we are falling short on structures, not only theological structures, but our own structure as a body of women theologians. We do not have either common strategies or a clear idea of the stages of development of our struggle. Dreams we have a-plenty, common tactics none, and although there is an inevitability of the historical processes in our favour, unless we realise that doing theology with poor women in our countries is the first step towards effective, material theosocial subversion, nothing will change. The hermeneutics of origins needs to read the streets first, then accept its methodological inexactitude (contextually challenged) and find a strategy. This is a project for theologians and agitators. I agree with Jakobs that religious forms need to be rooted in a social discourse and furthermore, that they are always thus rooted, whether we like it or not, but Jakobs does not make explicit that any hermeneutics implies action. Interpretations do visible things and have material consequences in the world, but one *molotov* does not change a government. It might contribute, but serious analysis and planned strategies are what are needed now. This is what I miss in our feminist hermeneutics, because, as my indigenous friend would say, it has been relatively easy till now to eliminate particular theological features (a chauvinist reading of Genesis, for instance), but still we are a group of dispersed feminist theologians who cannot change the course of history. That is for me a very important hermeneutical clue which we must explore in community in order to understand the theological inefficacy which characterises our present reflection and to be able to start a praxis of transformation so much needed in our theosocial discourses.

Abstracts

Cet exposé constitue une réponse à Monika Jakobs, et ce dans une optique post-coloniale et féministe matérialiste. Selon l'auteure, seule est valable une herméneutique des origines qui se base sur les origines du système de production monothéiste. A défaut de cela, la théologie demeure l'affaire d'une élite occidentale. D'autre part, l'exégèse féministe ne peut pas modifier le cours de la religion patriarcale. Livrée à elle-même, elle a pour fonction d'accomplir des petits actes rituels: une espèce de sortilège de mort qui peut symboliquement tuer un aspect patriarcal de la Bible par le biais de la critique littéraire féministe, mais n'est pas à même de changer les structures historiques du pouvoir et du savoir sacrés qui sous-tendent ce discours. La tâche de l'herméneutique féministe est donc d'élaborer des stratégies de résistance pour une théologie efficace, qui puisse finalement changer le cours de l'histoire et de la religion patriarcales.

Der Beitrag stellt eine Erwiderung auf Jakobs aus postkolonialer und feministisch-materialistischer Sicht dar. Die Verfasserin vertritt die These, eine gültige Hermeneutik der Ursprünge müsse auf die Entstehung des Systems des Monotheismus rekurrieren, sofern die Theologie nicht westlich und elitär bleiben wolle. Zum zweiten könne feministische Exegese nicht den Lauf der patriarchalen Religion verändern. Auf sich selbst gestellt, hat sie die Funktion kleinerer ritueller Aktionen; eines Todeszaubers, der symbolisch patriarchale biblische Charaktere durch feministische Literaturkritik tötet, aber nicht die historischen Strukturen geheiligter Macht/geheiligten Wissens verändern kann, die diesen Diskurs stützen. Aufgabe feministische Hermeneutik sei es, Strategien des Widerstandes für eine Theologie hervorzubringen, die schließlich den Lauf der patriarchalen Geschichte und Religion ändern kann.

Dr *Marcella Maria ALTHAUS-REID* is an Argentinian theologian, currently a lecturer in the Faculty of Divinity of Edinburgh University, Scotland. Her field of research is Post-Colonial Feminist Hermeneutics. Besides numerous articles published in journals and books, with Dr R. S. Suggirtharajah she has written *Negotiating the Narratives: Hermeneutical Practices of Asian and Latin American Interpreters*. (Forthcoming; Sheffield: Sheffield University Press). Marcella is a Quaker.

Joyce Muhindo TSONGO et Marie Bagalet TABU
avec Emma WILD

Etouffement des Droits ou Union Vitale? La Femme, la Culture et le Christianisme au Zaïre

Introduction

La voix des femmes en Afrique est souvent étouffée. Ce n'est que pendant cette décennie que certaines femmes africaines ont eu l'occasion d'expliquer leur vie et leur foi au monde. Parfois l'Occident est resté sourd à la voix africaine. Parfois la culture, les hommes et la lutte quotidienne pour la vie ont empêché le cri des Africaines d'être entendu.

Ci-dessous, Joyce Muhindo Tsongo et Marie Bagalet Tabu, deux zaïroises, parlent d'une façon familière de leurs expériences personnelles en tant que femmes éduquées, étudiantes de théologie et membres engagés de l'église chrétienne. Elles réfléchissent sur la culture, le mariage, et l'interprétation de la Bible dans leur contexte. Elles terminent en jetant un coup d'oeil sur les théologies africaines et féministes. Marie et Joyce sont en train de se préparer au ministère de l'église anglicane au Zaïre. Cependant leur situation dans l'église à la fin de leurs études sera ambiguë parce que la question de l'ordination des femmes n'est pas résolue.

Les féministes occidentales pourraient trouver étonnantes certaines réponses aux questions posées. La compréhension de la responsabilité et du rôle de la femme, par exemple, ou l'idée qu'être servante est un aspect positif de la culture n'apparaît pas dans la littérature féministe récente en Europe et en Amérique du Nord. Marie et Joyce montrent clairement la différence entre la voix africaine et la voix occidentale. Leurs pensées reflètent, je crois, les sentiments de la majorité des zaïroises éduquées, c'est-à-dire, elles critiquent leur église, leurs hommes et leurs cultures mais d'une façon fortement tempérée par une loyauté pour ces derniers. Elle se sentent insatisfaites dans leur position humble. Elles voudraient le changement; non pas par une révolution mais par une réforme profonde. Cette attitude modeste reflète, je crois, l'harmonie dont Marie et Joyce parlent à la fin de leur discours. L'harmonie et l'union sont des idées vitales aux cultures africaines. On les voit dans les relations quotidiennes et elles sont intégrales aux femmes comme aux hommes. Marie et Joyce ont cherché une harmonie entre la théologie africaine et la théologie féministe. Généralement la théologie africaine soutient les cultures africaines tandis que la théologie féministe est bien connue pour sa forte critique de la culture dominante (et masculine). Elles ont tâché de faire quelques réflexions théologiques qui mettent en harmonie ce paradoxe suivant l'angle où on regarde la culture. D'abord elles se présenteront et expliqueront leur vie et leurs pensées en tant que femmes zaïroises:-

Trialogue.

J. Je suis zaïroise, étudiante en théologie pour devenir ministre de l'église anglicane. J'ai eu la chance de grandir dans une famille chrétienne. Papa, étant pasteur, était convaincu de l'égalité des sexes à cause de l'enseignement biblique qu'il a reçu. Alors il a scolarisé tous ces enfants, quelque chose d'assez rare à cette époque. Après mes études je suis devenue directrice dans une école où tous les autres enseignants étaient des hommes. Etre une femme supérieure hiérarchique d'hommes pose un problème selon certaines personnes. Mais mon travail a bien marché, plus qu'au temps de mes prédécesseurs hommes.

M. J'ai eu une expérience pareille. Dans la famille j'étais l'unique fille parmi les garçons avec un père qui ne faisait pas de distinction entre filles et garçons. Mon père a fait des études universitaires. Il a vu que les femmes devraient étudier aussi. Je n'ai pas senti de complexe devant les garçons car j'ai passé assez de temps avec eux à l'école secondaire et à l'université. Quand je suis devenue directrice, mon travail a été plus apprécié par les inspecteurs que celui de mon prefet malgré son ancienneté. J'ai su maintenir l'ordre et la discipline.

E. Quelles sont les choses qui vous ont facilité le travail dans ce domaine?

M. Ceci est dû d'abord à l'honnêteté des femmes.

J. L'instinct maternel influence le service, c'est-à-dire que la femme s'attache à son travail comme on s'attacherait à son enfant ou à sa famille. On accorde beaucoup plus de temps au service qu'aux loisirs.

E. Comment trouvez-vous le milieu et les études à l'institut théologique?

M. Ici à l'institut c'est seulement le sujet des cours qui constitue un changement non l'auditoire. Cependant, dans la vie sociale je suis un peu indignée de voir mes collègues réfuter mes propos parce que je suis femme. La femme ne peut pas être pasteur, disent ils, elle doit rester clouée à la cuisine.

J. Je n'ai pas de complexe devant des hommes car mon père me considérait comme un garçon et j'assumais les mêmes responsabilités que mes frères aînés de sorte qu'ils ont regretté mon départ aux études. Cependant ici à l'institut les collègues étudiants sont jaloux de la promotion des femmes parce qu'ils sont influencés par la culture africaine qui rabaisse la femme. Par exemple nos hommes disent qu'ils doivent payer pour se marier, et donc que la femme est la propriété de son mari. Néanmoins quand nous sommes en classe, Marie et moi, nous ne manquons pas de courage et on n'est pas étouffées par la voix des hommes. Aussi le directeur et des autres membres de l'équipe soutiennent nos études ici.

E. Est-ce qu'il y a une différence de statut dans les yeux des autres entre Marie, qui est mariée, et Joyce, qui est célibataire?

M. Il y a une différence pour nous plutôt que pour les autres. La femme africaine intellectuelle continue à se sentir fière de sa position dans la famille, sauf que la liberté d'une femme mariée est limitée par le fait que son mari doit intervenir dans ses décisions et programme d'action.

J. Mes parents ne veulent pas que j'épouse un homme de différente confession à la nôtre et ils préfèrent que j'étudie plutôt que de me "donner" a un mari fortuné. Aussi je vois que le mari constitue un poids, on n'est pas libre.

M. Quand on étudie on voit qu'il vaut mieux rester célibataire car on a double travail. Il faut d'abord satisfaire son mari et le reste après.

E. Je vois que vos pères vous ont encouragées à étudier et il y a des hommes dans l'église qui sont en faveur de l'instruction des femmes. Mais d'autres, comme vos collègues, doutent de la participation des femmes dans la formation théologique et le ministère pastoral. Est-ce qu'on voit ceci partout dans l'église du Zaïre?

J. Oui, les deux positions sont partout, il y a ceux qui sont pour et ceux qui sont contre.

M. Les hommes souffrent de la jalousie parce que les hommes en Afrique ne sont pas convaincus que les femmes puissent faire des exploits. Souvent à l'église on dit que l'homme est la tête de la femme alors que certains hommes se comportent en irresponsables.

On dit aussi que la femme doit appeler son mari “Seigneur”, comme Sara dans l’Ancien Testament. Ce passage, d’après nous, est mal interprété par les hommes car ce n’est pas dans le sens d’assujettir sa femme que le mari est appelé Seigneur mais plutôt pour montrer le respect. Quand on dit que Jésus est la tête de l’église on compare aussi l’homme à Jésus mais l’homme est faillible et pécheur. De même la femme peut avoir ses qualités et ses défauts.

E. Comment, pensez-vous, peut-on s’attaquer à ce problème?

M. Je suis toujours pour l’égalité, pas dans le sens de prendre la place de l’homme, et vice versa, mais dans le sens que chacun a ses responsabilités. Une telle chose n’entraînerait pas la division mais signifierait l’entraide mutuelle, pas la dictature mais la compréhension. Il faut qu’ils trouvent un accord en discutant les problèmes de leur foyer et non pas en l’imposition par la force. Que l’homme sache que son épouse est créée à l’image de Dieu ainsi que lui. La relation de fraternité doit régner dans leur vie quotidienne.
La responsabilité de la femme, par exemple, est d’élever les enfants et leur apprendre les premieres notions de la vie. C’est pourquoi il est dit que quand on éduque une femme on éduque toute une nation. La responsabilité de l’homme est de pourvoir aux besoins de la famille. Ces responsabilités sont interdépendantes et doivent être assumées par les deux conjoints.

J. L’intention de Dieu est que l’homme et la femme soient des partenaires, se prêtent assistance et se soutiennent l’un l’autre. Ils doivent vivre en corrélation car ils sont héritiers de la grâce de Dieu. Mais nous voyons que l’homme africain n’a pas mis en considération le dessin de Dieu et la femme est devenue la propriété de son mari.

E. Alors, vous voudriez voir un grand changement dans le mariage, c’est-à-dire le respect mutuel.

J. & M. Oui, c’est ça.

E. D’où vient cette idée de la femme qu’on trouve dans l’église? De la Bible ou de la culture?

M. De la façon dont la culture africaine utilise les passages bibliques, c’est-à-dire, de l’interprétation de l’homme africain. Par exemple les Africains brandissent le verset biblique où Paul dit que la femme ne peut pas parler dans l’assemblée des hommes (1 Cor.14: 34,35). En disant ceci ils étouffent le droit d’expression de la femme et ils oublient des autres passages bibliques, tel que l’histoire de Marthe et

Marie (Luc 10: 38-42). Une telle idée est soutenue par la culture mais nous vivons dans un monde en évolution. La culture a changé et changera encore. La femme ne devrait pas rester en arrière. Les études de la femme constituent un moyen de se promouvoir. Mon souci est de voir que l'église n'en parle pas, ou que l'église soutient la fausse conception de la femme tout en sachant que homme et femme sont les créatures de Dieu.

J. Dans la société africaine la naissance d'un garçon donne beaucoup plus de joie, que celle d'une fille. Nous savons que Dieu ne regarde pas le sexe mais le fond du coeur de chacun.

M. Certaines gens disent que le fait que Jésus était du sexe masculin prouve l'importance de l'homme dans la société, car si Jésus avait été une femme il n'aurait pas pu mener à bien mission. Cette conception juive est soutenue par la culture africaine. Cependant c'est l'appel de Dieu qui est important plutôt que le sexe.

J. Ce que la société doit savoir, ce que la foi chrétienne devrait montre à la société, est que homme et femme ont une même importance. C'est seulement la position et le devoir qui font leur distinction. Leurs caracères, leurs capacités et leurs dons se complètent.

E. Quelle est la position de la femme en pratique dans l'église du Zaïre?

J. Ce qu'on remarque dans nos églises c'est qu'on consulte les hommes pour la prise de décisions. Les femmes sont interpellées en premier lieu quand il y a des travaux manuels.

M. C'est ça. Pour la cuisine, pour servir les gens ce sont toujours les femmes. Dans notre Union de Mères de Kisangani ce qui m'a frappé le plus est que les enseignements se basaient toujours sur la bonne relation avec le mari. Quel est le but de l'Union? Est-ce que pour aider la femme à se bien comporter dans son foyer ou bien un département qui peut aider l'église dans d'autres domaines, tel que l'Ecole du Dimanche et l'évangélisation?

E. Vous deux, vous serez peut-être dirigeants de l'Union de Mères un jour. Que voyez-vous comme autres choses qui peuvent être traitée dans les réunions?

J. Moi, je peux dire ce que maman racontait lors qu'elle avait participé à un groupe de mères dans l'une des paroisses de Nord-Kivu. On apprenait la broderie et la cuisine pour que les mères puissent être financièrement indépendantes au lieu d'être toujours un fardeau pour leur mari et qu'elles puissent nourrir la famille car les soins pour le mari ne peuvent pas primer les soins de la famille parce que si le mari l'abondonne elles restent seules avec les enfants.

E. Voyez-vous une place pour les femmes dans la direction de l'église?

M. Bien sûr. Mais nous n'avons pas encore vu une femme diriger une église. Même dans l'Union des Mères il y a des aumôniers qui dirigent les activités.

J. J'envisage que si l'église pouvait encourager les mamans à s'occuper de l'Ecole du Dimanche on aurait de bonnes écoles parce que dans la Bible il est dit que les femmes seront sauvées grâce à leurs enfants (1 Tim. 2:15). On peut comprendre ceci quand on élève les enfants dans la Parole de Dieu.

E. Quand vous parlez de la culture vous parlez des attitudes traditionnelles africaines, n'est pas? Quelles sont les coutumes importantes qui touchent la vie d'une femme et qui explique les problèmes que vous voyez dans des attitudes culturelles?

M. Dans la plupart des tribus qu'on rencontre à Kisangani la circoncision des hommes se passe dans la forêt. Ils y passent un mois et y recevront l'initiation à la vie. Alors, la personne qui s'occupe de leur cuisine est, soit un homme soit une vieille maman qui a passé la ménopause. Les filles, ou les jeunes mamans qui en leurs règles sont considérées comme impures. Ces circoncis, une fois rentrés au village ne peuvent pas coucher avec leur femme avant que la plaie se soit cicatrisée. Une femme ne peut même pas regarder la plaie ce qui l'empêcherait de se cicatriser.
On voit cette idée de l'impureté de la femme dans l'église aussi. Chez les Catholiques quand une soeur a ses règles elle ne peut pas assister à la messe. Cependant c'est Dieu qui nous a créées ainsi et nous devons être fière de notre condition féminine. Nous sommes déjà purifiées par sang de notre Sauveur Jésus Christ, mort sur la croix, et nous devons le servir avec cet état biologique qui d'ailleurs joue un rôle vital dans la production de la race humaine.

J. Dans la tradition de la chasse les femmes sont vues comme des éléments de la mal chance. C'est ainsi que la veille de la chasse tous les hommes passent la nuit loin de leur toit conjugal. Quiconque va contre ce règlement en subit les conséquences graves allant même à la mort.

M. On regarde les femmes comme les portes du malheur dans la tradition. Il y a une conception qu'un bébé ne doit pas passer entre les mains de n'importe quelle mère qui a ses règles si on veut éviter certaines maladies, tels que la gale, la toux, ainsi de suite.

E. Je crois qu'il y a aussi les interdits sur l'alimentation.

J. Oui, mais on ne s'explique pas pourquoi. Par exemple on interdit à la femme de consommer la viande de la poule. Pourquoi? On n'en sait rien. Cependant certains arguments sont avancés surtout pour les femmes enceintes. Si une femme enceinte se hasarde à prendre les aliments interdits par la coutume les méfaits retombent sur son bébé. Le bébé alors peut sortir du sein de sa mère avec certaines déformités; six doigts ou deux, lèvre déchirée, etc..

M. Dans une tribu que je connais une femme ne consomme pas la viande du singe de peur de ne pas trouver de mari ou que son enfant ait la forme d'un singe. Il y a certaines parties de la viande réservées uniquement aux hommes (p. ex. le gésier d'une poule) et une femme ne peut pas la consommer sinon elle aura des problèmes.

E. Quelles sont les bonnes choses dans la culture qui peuvent aider la femme africaine?

J. Il y en a certainement. La première chose que nous rencontrons est le service. Car dans la coutume trouver un mari était conditionné par le labeur. Une fille paresseuse ne pouvait pas trouver un foyer. Cette exigence influence la vie spirituelle des mamans. Celles-ci habituées dès le bas âge à travailler, sont alors aptes à servir le Seigneur sans réticence. La deuxième chose; le respect dû aux supérieurs de la famille se voit dans la vie de nos filles au service. C'est rare qu'elles aient des problèmes avec leurs chefs de service car elles les respectent comme elles respectaient leur propres parents.

E. C'est à dire que les femmes entretiennent des rapports avec les autres d'une façon plus respectueuse que les hommes?

M. Oui. Nous pouvons ajouter le problème de la responsabilité envers les enfants. Dans la coutume c'est la maman qui se soucie des enfants. Elle doit se démener pour trouver ne fut-ce qu'un petit rien pour les servir. Alors cet esprit se manifeste dans l'église lorsqu'on demande un service la femme se sent plus concernée et n'est tranquille qu'après avoir accompli ce service demandé par les dirigeants de l'église.

Autre chose positive de la culture est le métier. Si une femme a appris à tisser les nattes elle peut développer ce talent et en leur profit. Tandis que les filles qui grandissent en ville sont plus attachées à l'intellectualisme qu'aux métiers de sorte qu'elles ne peuvent pas directement rapporter quelque chose. Alors il faut éduquer les filles à la culture ainsi qu'à l'école.

E. En fin, pouvons-nous dire que vous ne voudriez pas effacer la culture africaine que vous connaissez mais vous y voyez certaines difficultés pour la femme et vous voudriez améliorer cette situation.

M. & J. Oui, c'est ça.

E. Etant donné ceci et étant donné que vous êtes étudiantes en théologie, quelle est la relation, croyez-vous, entre la théologie africaine et la théologie féministe.

M. La théologie africaine met l'accent sur la culture et la relation entre les cultures africaines et le christianisme. En bref, la théologie africaine accepte, plus ou moins, la hiérarchie de la société africaine. On a une chaîne des ancêtres, les chefs, les aînés, les hommes, les femmes, les enfants. Parfois on compare Jésus Christ à l'ancêtre, ou même au chef suprême.

J. Tous les membres de cette chaîne hiérarchique constituent une force, une union vitale. Quand on perd un membre la force diminue aussi. On ne considère pas l'individu, c'est le groupe qui est important. Cependant la femme est rarement considérée comme membre effectif de l'union vitale. Elle n'est pas considérée comme responsable dans les décisions, le conseil et la réconciliation.

M. La théologie féministe met au contraire l'accent sur l'égalité entre homme et femme. La femme affirme qu'elle est créée a l'image de Dieu et qu'elle possède toute sorte de dons. Alors elle revendique ses droits et elle réclame le pouvoir d'agir en tant qu'être humain. Cette théologie féministe est née dans une théologie de la libération. La femme qui est opprimée par l'insistance sur la culture traditionnelle cherche à se libérer dans la théologie féministe. Néanmoins, il faut dire qu'il y a des femmes africaines qui préfèrent la tradition et qui n'aiment pas que la femme prenne une position publique.

J. Toutefois, on ne peut pas nier l'importance de la théologie africaine. Cette union vitale pourrait être bonne si on permet a la femme d'être membre actif avec les responsabilités publiques. L'unité est un concept chrétien. En Jean 15 nous voyons l'unité entre le Christ et ses fidèles. Le cep et les sarments produisent ensemble le bon fruit. En 1 Cor. 12, Paul parle de l'image d'un corps avec plusieurs membres qui sont interdépendants les uns des autres. L'unité chrétienne est une force plus puissante que l'unité africaine. Alors, l'église doit être une seule entité. Cette unité est évidente surtout dans les sectes et les églises indépendantes d'Afrique. Les membres partagent la joie et la peine; ils accueillent chaleureusement et ils s'aident mutuellement quand ils souffrent. Ce style de vie est plus proche de la tradition africaine.

M. Je vois qu'ici il y a une tension entre la théologie africaine et la théologie féministe. Souvent le résultat du féminisme est l'individualisme; chacune développe ses propre talents. Cet individualisme est contraire à la communauté africaine. Mais, de l'autre côté, il ne faut pas limiter la domaine de la femme aux rôles déjà désignés dans la culture.

J. Oui, elles sont capables de tout faire. Et si nous acceptons ceci les femmes auront des rôles divers selon leurs propres dons.

E. Moi, je vois que l'idée de la diversité est aussi biblique. Le passage que Joyce a cité, 1 Cor. 12, parle de la diversité dans l'unité. L'esprit uni tous les membres en un seul corps, mais qu'est-ce qu'il uni? Il uni les individus divers et les dons divers.

M. Comme ça on peut essayer de mettre les deux idées ensemble. On voit que l'expression libre de la femme ne casse pas nécessairement l'unité de la société africaine. Cependant cette société doit s'adapter à la diversité que les femmes peuvent lui offrir quand chacune a la liberté de choisir son propre domaine.

J. On peut faire une synthèse entre les éléments positifs dans la théologie africaine et la théologie féministe pour répondre aux besoins de la femme africaine chrétienne.

Emma WILD est professeur de l'Histoire de lÉglise et de la Théologie Systematique á lInstitut Supérieur Théologique Anglican á Bunia, nord-est Zaïre depuis 1993. Avant d'arivée à l'ISThA *Joyce Muhindo TSONGU* était directrice d'une ecole secondaire et comptable du service medical dans la region de Kiru. *Marie Bagalet TABU* était aussi directrice d'une ecole secondaire à Kisangani.

Pendant le pillage et la guèrre au Zaïre la communauté de l'ISThA a suspendu les cours, et pour quelques semaines, a pris réfuge dans un village. Joyce et Marie espèrent terminer leurs diplomes fin août et rentrer chez eux pour le travail pastoral.

Esperanza BAUTISTA PAREJO

Femmes en Espagne: Réalité Sociale et Réalité Théologique

A l'instar de ce qui se passe dans d'autres pays occidentaux, l'opinion sur la théologie féministe en Espagne se traduit généralement par des clichés qui parlent de femmes revendiquant, violemment parfois, leurs droits. Or, dans une société de classes se définissant comme juridiquement égalitaire, les femmes et les hommes ont effectivement été considérés de façon manifestement inégale dans les textes de loi: ainsi, certains droits ont été et sont déniés aux femmes simplement parce qu'elles sont femmes. Et, trop souvent encore, l'application de ces droits stipulés par la loi n'est pas respectée dans la pratique sociale. C'est pourquoi, avant d'aborder notre sujet—les femmes et la théologie en Espagne—il nous faut d'abord évoquer deux points importants: leur situation sociale et le rôle qu'y a joué le mouvement féministe; après quoi nous donnerons un bref aperçu de l'état et de l'évolution des droits de la femme en Espagne, pour ensuite nous pencher sur la théologie féministe proprement dite. Ce n'est qu'ainsi que nous pourrons mieux comprendre les aspects positifs et négatifs de ses relations avec la théologie en général.

I Les Droits de la Femme: Evolution Juridique et Réalité Sociale

La situation actuelle de la femme en Espagne est étroitement liée à l'avènement de la démocratie dans notre pays ainsi qu'à l'évolution juridique de ses droits. Mais en disant cela, il convient de rappeler le long chemin parcouru pour conquérir ces droits et l'évolution juridique qui s'est avérée nécessaire jusqu'à ce qu'ils soient stipulés dans les différents textes de loi. Pour cette raison—et aussi parce que la mémoire historique nous permet d'éviter la répétition de nos propres erreurs—nous allons d'abord évoquer la situation juridique des femmes en Espagne à une époque qui n'est pas si lointaine, même si aux yeux de la femme espagnole actuelle cela peut sembler remonter à la nuit des temps.[1]

---

1 Esperanza Bautista Parejo, *Mujer y Democracia en España: Evolución Jurídica y*

Depuis le siècle dernier, d'éminentes femmes juristes espagnoles comme Concepción Arenal, des politiciennes comme Clara Campoamor ou des femmes écrivains telles qu'Emilia Pardo Bazán ont lutté pour les droits de la femme. En dépit de cela, nous les femmes avons dû attendre longtemps, pratiquement jusqu'à l'avènement de la démocratie, pour voir nos droits pleinement reconnus par la loi. Cette lutte se concrétise dans quatre domaines particulièrement significatifs: le droit à l'éducation, le droit au travail, les droits politiques et les droits au sein de l'institution familiale. Dans ce sens, il reste essentiel que la femme prenne conscience de soi en tant que personne car, comme le pensait déjà Concepción Arenal, la plénitude de la vie de la conscience permet d'espérer l'émancipation des individus et le progrès des sociétés. Une notion qui continue à être valable et précieuse pour le mouvement féministe et pour le travail de la théologie féministe. Cette idée nourrit également les réflexions de l'écrivain Emilia Pardo Bazán qui, confrontée à ce complexe d'infériorité si profondément ancré dans le coeur des femmes, nous dit: "S'il y avait lieu ici de donner des conseils, je ne cesserais de rappeler aux femmes que c'est en elles que résident la vertu et la force rédemptrices. Davantage que sur nos discours et nos études, nous devons nous appuyer sur l'exercice de notre propre volonté et sur la rectitude de notre ligne de conduite. La femme se croit faible et désarmée parce qu'elle est toujours influencée par l'idée de son infériorité. C'est une erreur gravissime: la femme dispose d'une force incontestable et doit seulement se décider à s'en servir sans crainte"[2].

Nous nous contenterons d'un bref aperçu: dans le domaine de l'éducation, le droit légal de la femme de participer à tous les niveaux de l'enseignement ne fut pas reconnu avant le 5 mars 1910. Or, à la fin du XIXe siècle, 10% des femmes seulement savaient lire et écrire. Dans les premières années du XXe siècle, garçons et filles commencent à fréquenter ensemble les salles de classe, mais leurs activités diffèrent en fonction du sexe. Cependant, en ce début de siècle, on perçoit l'émergence d'une nouvelle mentalité en matière d'égalité des sexes et de participation des

---

Realidad Social, Documentación Social n° 105, 1996.

2 Emilia Pardo Bazán, "La educación del hombre y de la mujer. Sus relaciones y diferencias". Mémoire lu au Congreso Pedagógico de 1892, *La mujer española y otros artículos feministas*. Sélection et prologue de Leda Schiavo (Madrid: Real Academia Gallega, Editora Nacional 1993).

femmes au développement de la société. Le souci d'une éducation et d'une formation personnelle, culturelle et professionnelle de la femme aboutit à des institutions telles que la Institución Libre de Enseñanza (laïque) ou la Institución Teresiana (religieuse) et l'association Juventud Universitaria Femenina, fondée en 1920 par Clara Campoamor. Ce sont les premiers pas pour ouvrir le monde du travail aux femmes: dans les centres de formation professionnelle, on crée des cours à leur intention. La Universidad Profesional de Acción Católica, la Escuela Central de Idiomas et le Real Conservatorio de Música y Declamación sont d'importants foyers de formation professionnelle où les femmes sont préparées à exercer un métier public. L'enseignemnt trouve son espace officiel dans la Escuela Normal Central et dans la Escuela de Estudios Superiores del Magisterio. Mais la lutte pour la liberté et l'égalité des chances dut attendre l'arrivée de temps meilleurs, peut-être parce qu'on continuait à ne pas tenir compte de la situation d'infériorité dans laquelle se trouvait la femme, tant au niveau de l'éducation que dans le domaine social et culturel en général.

Clara Campoamor, avocate et député au Parlement, lutta avec beaucoup d'abnégation pour la défense des droits de la femme en tant que personne, pour son égalité, sa liberté et sa capacité de participation. Elle parvint à faire concéder le droit de vote aux femmes, le seul droit qui fut maintenu lors de l'instauration de la dictature en Espagne. Tout comme dans d'autres pays européens, les normes du Code Napoléon donnèrent lieu en Espagne à des situations restrictives pour les femmes, de sorte que la différence de sexe constituait non seulement une situation de fait dans la société espagnole, mais fut aussi renforcée par la loi.

Les possibilités d'emploi se trouvaient principalement dans le travail domestique, dans l'artisanat, la confection et, bien entendu, dans la prostitution. Mais l'inégalité des salaires de la main d'oeuvre féminine a toujours existé[3], une situation acceptée par la société et par les femmes elles-mêmes comme relevant de "l'ordre naturel". Sous la dictature, la femme fut privée des rares droits qu'elle avait pu obtenir et l'égalité juridique des sexes stipulée dans la Constitution républicaine antérieure fut jetée aux oubliettes. Sous prétexte de les protéger, la dictature allait en fait exclure

3 Une statistique de 1841 sur l'industrie du coton en Galice établit que les hommes recevaient 65% du salaire total, tandis qu'un nombre équivalent de femmes ne recevait que 20,7%.

les femmes mariées du monde du travail; l'exercice de diverses professions fut interdit aux femmes et, dans les cas où elles pouvaient travailler, il leur fallait une autorisation du mari, lequel pouvait même obtenir le droit d'encaisser le salaire de son épouse.

Le droit de la famille est le domaine qui offre le plus de résistances quand il s'agit d'éliminer la discrimination sexiste. Les réformes antérieures à notre époque ne firent rien d'autre que consolider une situation d'éternelle minorité d'âge de la femme et surtout de la femme mariée. En réalité, jusqu'au 13 mai 1981, date de la révision du Code civil espagnol, le législateur n'a jamais pu supprimer toutes les différentes catégories de discrimination sexiste existant dans le ménage. Dans les Codes antérieurs, le mari était traité avec beaucoup d'égards et de complaisance, protégé et chaperonné au maximum par la loi. Le fait d'être le représentant légal de son épouse et l'administrateur des biens de la communauté conjugale, conjugué à d'autres dispositions, revenait à donner au mari la possibilité de vivre confortablement grâce aux biens de son épouse et, pour légitimer cette spoliation légale de la femme mariée, tout cela se faisait au nom de l'honneur et de l'autorité.

Dans le droit pénal, un des grands problèmes réside dans la manière d'appliquer les principes, voire l'absence d'application de certaines normes légales. Le domaine pénal s'est toujours distingué par sa dureté vis-à-vis de la femme, justement parce qu'elle est considérée comme la garante stabilisatrice de la famille patriarcale et de la pureté de la descendance. Au fond, tout tourne autour de l'honneur et de la réputation, tantôt de la femme, tantôt de l'homme. Mais comme partout dans la culture patriarcale occidentale, certaines catégories du droit semblent surtout refléter l'opinion que les hommes se font des femmes. Nous connaissons l'importance de l'honneur en la matière. On nous a souvent présenté la femme comme étant extrêmement soucieuse de son honneur, mais la conception de cet honneur est très symptomatique: en définitive, elle sert à occulter la situation d'abandon et de marginalisation de la femme, le manque d'appui personnel et économique, tant de la part des institutions que de sa propre famille. Ce qu'on nous cache aussi, c'est que si la femme se préoccupe tant de son honneur, c'est parce que la société définit l'honneur et la réputation des femmes en fonction de leur conduite sexuelle: ce n'est pas la femme qui est obsédée par son honneur, elle reflète plutôt l'obsession de la société qui fait et défait les réputations, quelque chose qui nous rappelle Mary Daly et sa "Société miroir". Un prestigieux juriste du droit pénal espagnol le confirme: "... on protège l'homme s'évertuant à défendre la sphère de son soi-disant honneur et l'on ne tient absolument pas compte de l'autre homme, celui qui a osé porter atteinte à l'honneur d'un père (en déshonorant sa fille). La femme assiste en témoin silencieux à toute cette distribution de privilèges et sa tragédie à elle n'intéresse personne"[4].

Ceci rejoint le délit d'adultère et la "vengeance du sang". L'adultère était considéré comme un délit commis par la femme mariée, sans qu'il n'existe de concept correspondant pour l'adultère du mari. Durant une bonne partie de notre siècle, le devoir de fidélité conjugale exigé des deux conjoints est demeuré nettement différencié: seule l'infidélité de l'épouse était considérée comme adultère et sévèrement punie; l'infidélité de l'époux équivalait à un concubinage qui n'était puni que si le mari entrenait sa concubine dans le domicile conjugal ou, trop notoirement, à l'extérieur. Au-delà du principe, on voulait surtout protéger la certitude de la paternité, et ce encore une fois au nom de l'honneur.

Par ailleurs, il y avait la question de la "vengeance du sang", un pouvoir concédé aux pères et aux maris qui leur permettait de tuer leurs filles ou épouses et les hommes qui couchaient avec elles, pouvoir dont les antécédents remontent jusqu'au droit familial romain. Cet "extraordinaire privilège" fut réinstauré sous la dictature, mais révisé en 1963 pour être définitivement banni du Code pénal.

L'avènement de la démocratie

Du point de vue formel, nous pouvons et devons affirmer que la démocratie est bonne pour les femmes. Un fait qu'il est important de souligner alors que certaines tendances ultra-conservatrices et fondamentalistes refont surface un peu partout dans le monde, parfois avec une virulence inquiétante. Les réformes introduites dans notre législation depuis l'avènement de la démocratie ont établi une égalité formelle des femmes et des hommes devant la loi. Mais il a fallu passer par plusieurs réformes du Code civil pour qu'en 1975 l'article 62 du nouveau Code déclare enfin (!) que "Le mariage ne restreint pas la capacité d'agir de l'un ou l'autre conjoint". Ce n'est qu'à partir de 1961, quand une loi sur les droits politiques et professionnels de la femme a supprimé toute forme de discrimination

4 Enrique Gimbernat, "La mujer y el Código Penal Español", dans *Estudios de Derecho Penal,* (Madrid: Tecnos 1990).

sexiste et promulgué l'égalité des salaires, que le monde du travail a définitivement ouvert ses portes aux femmes.

Enfin, avec l'instauration de la démocratie en Espagne, la non-discrimination en raison du sexe est légalement garantie par la Constitution du 27 décembre 1978. L'article 9.2 donne mandat aux pouvoirs publics de réaliser l'égalité effective et réelle des individus et des groupes auxquels ils appartiennent; la non-discrimination légale est garantie en formulant ce principe dans l'article 14 de la Constitution, repris en ces mêmes termes à l'article 32 relatif au mariage et à l'article 35 relatif au travail. Le Tribunal constitutionnel a interprété en diverses sentences le principe contenu dans l'article 9.2 (et dans l'article 14) en déclarant que ce principe "trouve sa justification concrète dans la volonté du pouvoir constituant de mettre fin à la situation historique d'infériorité dans laquelle la vie sociale et juridique avait placé la population féminine, une situation qui, sous l'angle qui nous intéresse ici, se traduit par les difficultés spécifiques que rencontre la femme lorsqu'elle veut accéder au travail et avoir droit aux promotions correspondantes".

Réalité sociale

Avec la démocratie, la femme peut enfin commencer à croire qu'on la considère comme une personne libre et responsable de ses actes qui n'a pas besoin de tutelle extérieure ni de paternalisme protecteur. On peut dire que, pour la première fois dans son histoire, la femme espagnole a obtenu un maximum d'égalité juridique. Mais si ceci est bien vrai sur le plan formel, la réalité sociale laisse encore beaucoup à désirer. Il existe un proverbe espagnol qui dit: "du dire au faire il y a un fameux bout de chemin"; c'est sur ce chemin qu'il reste beaucoup à faire. Et la femme continue à y être la principale protagoniste.

Impossible d'oublier à quel point il est difficile de surmonter les barrières de l'habitude et, pire encore, les attitudes mentales patriarcales. Et nous ne devons pas oublier non plus que l'égalité juridique stipulée par la loi ne signifie pas grand chose si elle n'est pas acceptée par la société, c'est-à-dire si elle ne se traduit pas par une réelle égalité sociale. Au cours des deux dernières décennies, l'Espagne a connu une profonde transformation de la réalité sociale féminine; néanmoins, nous sommes encore loin d'atteindre à une égalité pleine et effective puisque cela présuppose une volonté démocratique qui n'est pas toujours présente chez tous les membres de la société.

L'appréciation tendancieuse de certains délits commis à l'encontre de la femme et la manière dont s'appliquent et s'interprètent les normes induisent une réalité qui n'a guère de rapport avec la volonté démocratique nécessaire pour accepter et assumer l'égalité juridique et sociale. Les femmes juristes espagnoles ont dénoncé et condamné le fait qu'on impute aux femmes la faute de certaines agressions sexuelles qui seraient provoquées par leur propre conduite, leur façon de s'habiller, leur présence accrue dans les rues et l'absence de contrôle paternel (comme l'ont prétendu certains magistrats dans leurs sentences); elles ont également dénoncé et condamné le fait que d'aucuns se soient prononcés contre le divorce et l'avortement (même dans leurs aspects actuellement réglementés par la loi) ainsi que contre les relations homosexuelles, tout ceci au nom d'une loi naturelle qui n'est pas acceptée par tous/toutes les juristes. Plus fréquemment qu'on ne pourrait le croire, certaines sentences s'appuyent sur des jugements de valeur sexistes pour soutenir une décision judiciaire défavorable à la femme et l'on voit même ressurgir le thème de l'honneur, un fait qui ne se limite pas seulement à l'Espagne. Un jugement récent prononcé par les tribunaux italiens a justifié le fait qu'un mari puisse faire subir des mauvais traitements physiques à sa femme pour cause de jalousie.

En ce qui concerne la réalité socio-professionnelle de la femme espagnole, les changements sont considérables. Les femmes sont entrées dans le monde du travail et n'ont plus tendance à abandonner leurs activités professionnelles en cas de maternité (hormis pour les congés légaux), de mariage etc. Il n'en reste pas moins que le taux de chômage est beaucoup plus élevé chez les femmes; celles-ci sont surtout entrées dans le secteur des services (à salaire inférieur) et, outre le problème du chômage, leurs contrats de travail sont plus précaires; davantage que les hommes elles occupent des emplois à temps partiel (non pas pour combiner leur activité professionnelle aux activités domestiques mais en raison de la ségrégation professionnelle et occupationnelle) et les différences de salaire par rapport aux hommes continuent àêtre scandaleuses; tout cela malgré l'importance des changements législatifs obtenus.

II La Femme et la Théologie en Espagne

Au vu de ce panorama, il est facile d'imaginer les difficultés auxquelles se heurte la femme espagnole dans le domaine de la théologie, et d'autant plus si l'on considère le fait qu'en Espagne, on peut seulement faire des études théologiques universitaires dans les facultés de théologie—qui, jusqu'à présent, ont toujours relevé de l'Eglise—et dans les séminaires ou centres d'études qui en dépendent; c'est-à-dire qu'il n'existe pas de facultés publiques ou d'Etat où étudier la théologie.

Les difficultés

E. Schüssler Fiorenza a défini un problème qui correspond assez exactement à la situation actuelle de la femme espagnole dans la théologie: "les femmes peuvent étudier la théologie, mais il est rare qu'on leur permette d'enseigner dans les écoles et les facultés de théologie. Nous sommes exclues de la prêtrise et nous ne pouvons pas organiser l'administration de l'Eglise ni formuler sa doctrine (...) Aucune théologienne féministe ne peut s'appuyer sur un soutien émanant des autorités de l'enseignement officiel et aucune d'entre nous n'appartient à une commission internationale ou pontificale (...) Les manuels et les études de théologie, les controverses et les débats théologiques et même les représentants de la théologie de la libération ignorent notre travail théologique"[5].

En Espagne, l'accès des femmes aux études théologiques universitaires est assez récent. C'est seulement au début des années 70 que les femmes ont été autorisées à étudier cette discipline; à l'heure actuelle cependant, et en dépit des difficultés, on constate qu'il existe un véritable mouvement en faveur de l'étude et des recherches théologiques féministes dont la force et la vigueur sont attestées par un fait très significatif: dans maintes facultés de théologie espagnoles, approximativement 45% des étudiants sont des femmes.

Outre les difficultés qu' implique l'absence de facultés publiques de théologie, les femmes espagnoles ont dû en surmonter d'autres qui sont probablement communes à toutes les femmes intéressées par la théologie. En un premier temps, les cours de théologie étaient strictement interdits aux femmes. Quand, dans une seconde étape, on nous y donna accès, les difficultés furent liées à l'insuffisance des systèmes de scolarisation, par exemple le manque de facilités pour combiner les horaires et l'absence de patrons de thèse, ce qui a contraint bon nombre de femmes à abandonner les études théologiques universitaires. Dans la troisième étape et du fait de l'accroissement des femmes admises dans les facultés de théologie, on a

5 E. Schüssler Fiorenza, "Romper el Silencio" dans *Concilium*, 202 (1985).

pu résoudre certains problèmes. Mais l'orientation des matières d'enseignement, le langage et les contenus ne tiennent pas suffisamment compte de l'expérience des femmes. De fait, il n'existe aucune chaire de théologie féministe en Espagne; jusqu'à présent nous avons seulement pu organiser des petits séminaires portant sur un thème relatif aux femmes et des "noyaux féministes" qui ont pris l'habitude d'inviter à leur propre compte des femmes professeurs dans les cours.

Les possibilités d'emploi étant assez rares, la majorité des femmes doivent combiner leurs études et activités théologiques avec une activité civile rémunérée. Donner des cours de religion dans des collèges privés et des instituts devient de plus en plus difficile et ce pour deux raisons: d'une part de nombreux diocèses refusent, plus ou moins ouvertement, de donner les postes de professeur de religion aux femmes (on donne la préférence aux prêtres); d'autre part, la nouvelle législation a mis fin aux cours de religion obligatoires, même si l'on discerne ces derniers temps une demande accrue en la matière. Théoriquement, les facultés et les séminaires ou centres qui en dépendent acceptent des femmes dans leur professorat. Mais pour l'année 1981-82 par exemple, aucune femme n'enseignait la théologie dans les facultés de Barcelone, Universidad Pontificia Comillas (Madrid), Deusto, Salamanque et Instituto Superior de Pastoral (dépendant du séminaire de Madrid). Pour 1986-87, seule une femme sur 37 professeurs enseignait la Bible à la U.P.C. Actuellement, il y a de plus en plus de femmes qui deviennent professeur dans les facultés de théologie ou qui enseignent la théologie dans d'autres facultés relevant des universités privées catholiques; la proportion par rapport aux hommes continue cependant à être de 1/30 ou 1/40. Et bien sûr, aucune femme n'occupe une chaire. Inutile de dire qu'en Espagne l'Eglise est en retard par rapport aux facultés enseignant d'autres disciplines dans les universités d'Etat et même dans les universités privées catholiques, où les chaires occupées par des femmes éminentes sont fréquentes.

Les problèmes avec la hiérarchie ecclésiastique sont vraisemblablement les mêmes que ceux rencontrés par les théologiennes féministes catholiques dans le monde entier, mais, outre ceux que nous venons d'évoquer, certains de ces problèmes risquent aujourd'hui de devenir un obstacle insurmontable puisque la tendance de la hiérarchie est d'entraver l'accès aux études de théologie, non seulement pour les femmes mais pour les laïcs en général, hommes et femmes. Actuellement, on interdit aux laïcs, et aux religieuses, de fréquenter les séminaires pour mener à bien leurs études -comme ils le faisaient jusqu'à présent. Les séminaires sont redevenus un lieu exclusif où seuls les futurs prêtres sont admis. Les centres d'études théologiques continuent à admettre les femmes et les laïcs en général, mais comme dans la plupart des cas ils dépendent des séminaires, ils ont de gros problèmes pour subsister. De fait, on a déjà commencé à en fermer certains par faute de moyens, et toutes les personnes qui y ont suivi des cours de théologie—ou souhaitent le faire—ne peuvent plus les poursuivre, sauf dans les villes où il existe une université dépendant de l'Eglise -Salamanque, Madrid, Barcelone, Bilbao par exemple—avec ses facultés de théologie correspondantes.

Les facultés de théologie continuent à être ouvertes à tous et toutes, et c'est un point important, notamment parce que l'enseignement y est d'un niveau supérieur à celui des séminaires; et, comme il s'agit d'universités qui doivent assurer l'équivalence des diplômes sanctionnant les études proposées avec les diplômes des universités publiques, la législation en vigueur interdit toute forme de discrimination; à moins que les facultés de théologie ne disparaissent en tant que telles ou ne prennent une autre appellation... Pour les femmes, ceci serait l'ultime et la plus grave menace, mais cette perspective reste encore lointaine, même si elle est effectivement dans l'air. Ce serait le coup de grâce pour l'accès des femmes à la théologie.

Comment nous organisons-nous?

Voilà les problèmes, mais qu'ont fait les théologiennes féministes espagnoles pour répondre à cette situation? Nous nous sommes associées et regroupées. Et, périodiquement, nous prenons contact avec les femmes des différentes églises protestantes implantées en Espagne, par le biais de rencontres, de colloques etc. Sous certains aspects, leurs problèmes à elles sont les mêmes que ceux des femmes catholiques, voire pire encore en matière de formation et d'études théologiques, phénomène qui pourrait être dû à des raisons historiques. La société espagnole reconnaît et admet assez bien ces églises chrétiennes, mais on ne peut nier que, même si cela ne concerne qu'une minorité, l'ignorance religieuse et les couches sociales les plus conservatrices font obstacle à la compréhension d'un fait fondamental: la fraternité de toutes les églises chrétiennes. Ou alors cela leur est indifférent. Mais cette indifférence et cette ignorance affectent souvent l'Eglise catholique elle-même.

Toutefois, la force réelle de la théologie féministe en Espagne a favorisé la formation de divers groupes et associations de femmes qui travaillent à partir et en faveur de la théologie féministe. En résumé, ceux-ci se présentent comme suit:

Foro de Estudios sobre la Mujer (F.E.M), fondé en novembre 1986 à l'initiative de Pilar Bellosillo qui a invité des femmes catholiques ayant des choix de vie et de profession variés mais qui sont unies par une préoccupation concrète pour la situation de la femme dans la société et plus spécialement dans l'Eglise. Son but est de promouvoir une réflexion visant à faciliter et à renforcer la participation active des femmes à la vie de l'Eglise. Collaborer à la transformation du savoir théologique en y apportant les réflexions et les expériences des femmes. Soutenir celles qui occupent des postes de responsabilité dans l'Eglise, ainsi que celles qui n'ont pas encore compris la discrimination dont elles font l'objet. Dialoguer avec la hiérarchie ecclésiastique pour lui faire connaître nos préoccupations et nos propositions. Le F.E.M. est membre du Forum Oecuménique des Femmes Chrétiennes d'Europe et est officiellement reconnu par l'Instituto de la Mujer.

Mujeres y Teología voit également le jour en novembre 1986; parmi ses objectifs figurent notamment la reconnaissance de la pleine participation des femmes à la vie ecclésiastique et l'exercice de tous ses ministères. Pratiquer la théologie en prenant le parti des personnes les plus défavorisées, avec une attitude d'écoute et de service. Employer un langage clair, simple et créatif. Connaître la théologie pratiquée par les femmes et créer des canaux pour sa diffusion. Cheminer avec et dans les mouvements féministes.

Asociación de Teólogas Españolas (A.T.E.), fondée le 2 juillet 1992; ses objectifs sont l'étude et la recherche théologiques en interaction avec d'autres disciplines universitaires et d'autres confessions religieuses, ainsi qu'avoir des contacts étroits avec les mouvements féministes. Les membres ordinaires sont des femmes diplômées en théologie, mais en tant que membres extraordinaires on y accueille également des hommes et des femmes titulaires de diplômes dans des disciplines proches de la théologie. En juin 1993 l'association a tenu à Madrid son 1er colloque Théologie et Femme sur le thème de "L'éthique fondamentale et la femme", à l'Universidad Pontificia Comillas; en octobre 1996, un 2e colloque sur le thème de "Changement de paradigme: genre et ecclésiologie" s'est tenu à Bilbao, dans l'Universidad Deusto. L'A.T.E. est membre du Forum Oecuménique des Femmes Chrétiennes d'Europe et est officiellement reconnue par l'Instituto de la Mujer.

Centro Ecuménico de las Misioneras de la Unidad est un collectif qui a démarré en 1968 en Catalogne en misant sur un des signes les plus clairs de notre temps: la femme a "découvert" sa propre dignité en tant que personne et il faut par conséquent lui donner de nouvelles perspectives dans la société ecclésiale. Son objectif le plus immédiat est de sensibiliser un maximum de personnes, surtout les femmes, à propos de la situation d'inégalité et d'infériorité que celles-ci subissent au sein de l'Eglise catholique.

Arnasatu est un nouveau groupe de femmes d'Eglise créé en Biscaye en avril 1996. Il s'est formé autour de femmes chrétiennes désireuses d'assister au 1er Synode européen des Femmes en Autriche. Il ne s'intéresse pas seulement à la théologie, même si celle-ci est capitale pour le groupe, mais aussi aux questions plus générales concernant l'Eglise et la société; se définit clairement comme chrétien, d'inspiration féministe et avec un intérêt commun: faire bouger les choses au Pays Basque et encourager le dialogue oecuménique et interconfessionnel. Officiellement reconnu par l'Instituto de la Mujer du Pays Basque (Emakunde).

Cristianas y Feministas est un groupe de femmes, majoritairement jeunes, appartenant à des communautés de base et implanté à Bilbao. Vocation prononcée pour le groupe et une réflexion commune. Travaille en relation étroite avec le groupe *Mujeres y Teología* et, comme ce dernier, ne vise pas à une reconnaissance officielle par l'Instituto de la Mujer et d'autres organismes. Se définit comme un groupe résolument chrétien et féministe[6].

Il faut souligner que l'objectif commun de tous ces groupes et associations est la collaboration mutuelle, le maintien d'une relation étroite entre tous, la diffusion d'informations relatives aux diverses activités, le travail en équipe lorsque le sujet concerné l'exige etc.; de fait, de nombreuses femmes sont des membres actifs, ou assurent une présence active, dans les divers groupes et associations.

6 Informations empruntées à Maria Salas et M.-José Arana dans *Recordamos Juntas el Futuro*, cahier n° 1 (Madrid: Publicaciones Claretianas 1995).

A partir d'où se pratique la théologie féministe en Espagne?

Voilà une question qu'il nous faut aborder maintenant. La réponse est vaste car, s'il s'agit bien évidemment d'une théologie pratiquée par des femmes blanches, occidentales, issues de la classe moyenne et souvent dotées d'une formation universitaire, nous sommes loin d'avoir oublié la discrimination socio-juridique dont nous avons, jusqu'à récemment encore, fait l'objet (comme nous avons pu le constater dans les pages qui précèdent). Ce qui nous permet d'évoquer certains traits communs avec la théologie de toutes les femmes; en effet:

1) Il s'agit d'une théologie visant à surmonter et franchir les barrières entre l'Occident et le Tiers Monde. Les distances et les difficultés économiques sont un obstacle de taille, mais les rencontres et les échanges d'expériences et de travaux de recherche constituent un espoir pour l'avenir. Nous pensons que les théologiennes espagnoles ont une grande responsabilité, celle de servir de "pont" ou de "charnière" entre l'Europe et l'Amérique latine.

2) La volonté de travailler en équipe est très présente car nous croyons à la force et à la richesse d'un travail en commun.

3) C'est une théologie plus inductive que déductive car, en général, elle se base moins sur des principes dogmatiques que sur la réalité, c'est-à-dire qu'elle se fonde plutôt sur des éléments concrets et sur l'expérience en s'efforçant d'en comprendre le sens par rapport à la Parole divine.

4) Elle s'accompagne d'un puissant sentiment de libération qui procède de notre propre expérience de la discrimination; nous croyons que la théologie ne doit pas rester étrangère à ces situations et peut actualiser les gestes de Jésus en faveur des exclus et des femmes en particulier.

5) Elle remet en question les paramètres androcentriques et patriarcaux qui prédominent dans le domaine du savoir, de l'histoire, de l'exégèse biblique et des structures.

6) C'est une théologie intégratrice. Elle fait vraiment recours à une démarche interdisciplinaire; il est courant que, outre leurs titres universitaires en théologie, les théologiennes détiennent d'autres diplômes de l'enseignement universitaire public.

7) Elle est oecuménique, non seulement parce qu'elle recherche et encourage les rencontres avec des femmes de différentes confessions, mais aussi parce qu'elle s'intéresse à la vie, à l'écologie et à l'univers.

8) Elle veut construire, déconstruire, reconstruire et, en définitive, resituer et réinterpréter les concepts fondamentaux de la théologie.

9) Elle vise également à une relecture de l'Histoire afin de mettre en évidence l'histoire des femmes, toujours passée sous silence.

10) Il y a le désir et la ferme résolution de transformer les structures de l'Eglise afin qu'elles intègrent d'autres modes de vie et d'expression de l'expérience divine et de la solidarité avec son prochain[7].

En guise de conclusion nous voudrions nous joindre à María José Arana pour dire:

> "Notre propre expérience personnelle et un regard attentif sur la réalité environnante nous permettent de concevoir la théologie comme l'offrande d'un verre d'eau fraîche donné gratuitement aux assoiffés/ées qui passent à côté de nous. Nous constatons avec tristesse qu'au fil des siècles, une partie de la théologie s'est convertie en eau de bouteille tièdasse, avec des étiquettes illisibles et un goût rance qui n'apaise pas la soif.[8]"

traduit d'Espagnol par J R

Esperanza BAUTISTA PAREJO est licenciée en théologie (dogmatique) de l'Universidad Pontificia Comillas (Madrid); sa thèse est consacrée au "Statut de la femme dans l'Eglise primitive"; elle est également titulaire d'une licence en droit de l'Universidad Complutense de Madrid. Elle est professeur de théologie à l'U.P.C. (ICAI) où elle enseigne une "Introduction au fait religieux et à la christologie" et dirige un séminaire bi-annuel consacré à "La femme dans la pensée chrétienne (Ier—IVe siècle)" auprès de la faculté de théologie. Membre fondateur de l'Asociación de Teólogas españolas (A.T.E.) et membre du Foro de Estudios sobre la Mujer (F.E.M.). Publications: *La Mujer en la Iglesia Primitiva,* (Estella: Verbo Divino 1993); en collaboration avec d'autres théologiennes, *Diez Mujeres escriben Teología* (Estella: Verbo Divino 1993), *Para Comprender el Cuerpo de la Mujer*, (Estella: Verbo Divino 1996) et *Recordamos juntas el Futuro* (Madrid: Publicaciones Claretianas 1995).

---

7 Cette synthèse s'inspire de la réflexion de Marifé Ramos et M.-José Arana, "Mujeres y Teología" dans *Recordamos Juntas el Futuro,* cahier n° 9 (Madrid: Publicaciones Claretianas 1995).

8 Ibid, 7.

Maaike de HAARDT

The body as profile, the profile of the body: women's studies in the Netherlands

In 1995 Anne-Marie Korte wrote an article in this Yearbook on the developments in feminist theology as a 'different academic discipline'.[1] She used the situation in the Netherlands as a case study to describe the different kind of 'struggles' feminist theology has to go through in order to establish itself as a recognisable and academically respected discipline. Two important conditions were set out. First, the necessity for an institutional incorporated research programme in women's studies in theology and, second, a strong thematic component that would distinguish our theological research as women's studies and would give us a higher profile.

Although academic reorganisations, restructuring of the research organisations and declining financial resources are still a feature of Dutch university life (and not only Dutch), and although we do not have any more women professors than three years ago, this does not mean that nothing new has happened. In this article I shall give a report on the developments in the Netherlands with regard to the two points mentioned above: the way we are working to reach the *institutional incorporation* of women studies in theology and the way we are gradually developing a *visible content* through a national research programme. I shall concentrate on a recent development in Dutch theological women's studies, the 'Corporeality project', or, to be more precise, the project 'Corporeality, Religion and Gender'.[2]

---

1 Anne-Marie Korte, "High Standards: Ideals and Reality of Feminist Theology as a "'Different Academic Discipline'," in: Angela Berlis, Julie Hopkins, Hedwig Meyer-Wilmes, Caroline Vander Stichele (eds.), *Women Churches: Networking and Reflections in the European Context*, ESWTR Yearbook 3 (Kampen/Mainz: Kok Pharos/Grünewald 1995),113-125.

2 Jonneke Bekkenkamp and I have been appointed by the Dutch National Organisation for Scientific Research and the University of Groningen as co-ordinators of this national research programme. At the ESWTR conference at

In December 1993 two half-time senior researchers were appointed to initiate, stimulate and co-ordinate a national research programme in Women Studies in Theology. The main reason for the development of a national feminist research programme is the fact that in most of our universities—as is probably the case everywhere in Europe—only one or two senior researchers are working in the field of feminist theology. At the same time all individual researchers/faculty members are obliged to participate in more extensive programmes. These programmes are for the most part structured and organised according to discipline. Some of us feel very uncomfortable in this situation because feminist research reaches beyond the borders of this traditional classifications. Therefore these position of feminist theologians is complex compared to other theologians in the same field. We require multi-levelled strategies to reach the goal of being recognised as an academic discipline and not considered only a hobby of some feminists.

We still have to fight for a feminist approach in the traditional departments. But then, when we do have a place in these programmes—which some of us indeed have—we become totally invisible as women studies researchers because we have to fit in. Important as this strategy of integration is, it also means that most of the time we can only 'react' to traditional theology because we have to defend or explain our feminist approach within one discipline. The price of integration is that it leaves us no space and no structural opportunity to set out our own feminist discussions fields on our own terms. We are not free to set our own theological agenda within the existing academic theological structures. This means that if we want to develop our own discussions, and thus to develop feminist theology as an autonomous discipline, we require other frameworks. And there is where our project started: to work on the development of a research programme in which feminist theologians really could work together, where we could cross the boundaries of traditional disciplines while at the same time using our individual academic and disciplinary skills.

Before turning to the theme and the content of the programme I want to indicate the institutional aspects of the project. As one of its co-ordinators I have become increasingly convinced that content and

Höör, Sweden (August 1995) we gave a first international presentation on this programme.

institutional incorporation are equally important but that they have to be strongly intertwined to be successful. The corporeality project explicitly aims at the integration of women's studies in theology at the various academic research institutions, while at the same time it seeks to highlight, strengthen and connect the diversity of feminist theological research in these institutions as *feminist*. The thoughts behind this project are in fact practical elaborations of the two conditions mentioned above: first the conviction of the importance and the necessity of making visible the feminist theological research that was already going on in the institutions but that was not identifiable as such. Second, the necessity of creating a framework to establish and elaborate the meaning of the feminist perspective as a distinct or autonomous 'discipline' throughout the different theological disciplines and within the context of Dutch theological research. One can understand these goals simply as an effort to gain official and institutional acknowledgement of the already existing forms of feminist theological co-operation. From this perspective the project is an important effort to gain institutional acknowledgement of the autonomy strategy for research in women studies in theology.[3]

But there is more to say on the goals of the project. To make them more productive for ourselves, these goals can also be considered as a challenge to women's studies in theology. That is to say, they offer us a challenge to structure and intensify our own informal feminist-theological meetings and discussions, and to give them a context that is less free. Therefore the project also can be regarded as an effort to give our own discussions a public academic platform and with that to give them a qualitative impulse in the search for our own profile. It is one thing to state that women's studies in theology needs a face of its own and a higher profile; it is quite another to set out such a profile in a common deliberation, especially if this profile will have consequences for the individual research of the participants. On this point it becomes clear that content and structure cannot be distinguished if women's studies in theo-

---

3 This 'double strategy' of integration and autonomy in women's studies is very common in most of the academic disciplines in the Netherlands. However, in theology it seems that this double strategy has become a division between education and research, in which autonomy seems to be reserved only for education and integration is best realised in research. In my opinion the power of this double strategy is strongly undermined by this development.

logy wants to survive as a strong and visible field in academic theology. The fact that in the project we see the elements of institutionalisation as closely connected to internal feminist-theological discussions, so that we connect the structure with the content, with the intention of mutual reinforcement and consolidation, is, therefore, characteristic of the corporeality project and makes it unique among the strategies followed in the Netherlands until now.

For the participants the most important aspect of such an enterprise is its content, the relevance of its central theme, and its appeal to all who want to work on the subject. Since the project implies that it should be possible to make contributions to the programme from different disciplines in the study of religion, this main theme must be specific enough to serve as a focus.

In the light of recent developments in theoretical questions the steering committee of our project chose 'corporeality' or 'embodiment' as the fundamental concept for this feminist research programme. This means that 'the body' functions as the central starting point for further explication and exploration of the specific epistemological and hermeneutical contribution of feminist theology to theology and religious studies. To be more concrete: What does it mean for feminist theologians to say that we are embodied beings and that our thinking is an embodied thinking? What are the gender-specific implications of these statements? How does the context, the particular situation of each participant in the debate, relate to these observations? What are the implications and consequences of these insights for our methods and our theology? And above all: what is this 'body' about which we are speaking? Because of the growing emphasis on the importance of the body not only for political action but also for philosophical reflection, it is becoming urgent to explain more precisely what we, as feminist theologians, mean when we constantly emphasise the embodied character of all (theological) knowledge and thinking. It all seems so self-evident, yet one of the first questions we have to pose is: what do we mean by body? A study of the literature brings us to the conclusion that much of the contemporary emphasis on the body serves primarily as a means of overcoming a number of dualisms, notably the mind-body split.[4] The body is for the

4 See: Maaike de Haardt and Jonneke Bekkenkamp, "Feministische theologie en het lichaam" in: *Godsdienst en Maatschappij* 19 (1994) 6, 3-6; Jonneke Bekkenkamp

most part a reaction against and a symbol countering abstract rationalism. Overall it seems to represent a synonym for a plea for concreteness, materiality, vulnerability, and the importance of daily life. But then it must be asked: what are the theological implications of this approach and what kind of theological knowledge follows from these insights? For this reason the official name of the programme is 'Corporeality, Religion and Gender', stressing not only the women's studies perspective but also the theological.

As a group of twenty senior and junior researchers we are working together to grasp the meaning and the implications of this cluster of interrelated questions in relation to our own research.[5] We meet regularly to discuss not only well-known contemporary philosophical and theological texts on the body, but also to present our own research on the subject.[6]

The members of the group are willing to formulate their individual research projects not only in relation to the subject of 'corporeality' but also in collaboration with the others members of the project, most of whom are working in different theological fields. However difficult this may sometimes be, it offers at the same time a great opportunity to exercise real multi- and interdisciplinary co-operation while developing the common project of women studies in theology. Gradually we are developing a shared framework and a set of questions to which all participants relate in one way or another. Central to our current debates on the body is the question of whether and how both 'the body' and 'religion' could be characterised in an analogical and polysemic way in a feminist theological approach. Religion is described as binding and

---

and Maaike de Haardt, "Lichamelijkheid, Subjectiviteit en Transcendentie" in: Anne-Marie Korte, Marian Papvoine, Jonneke Bekkenkamp, Freda Dröes (eds.), *Proeven van Vrouwenstudies Theologie Deel* IV, Zoetermeer 1996,185-203.

5 Here we have the advantage of being a small country where travelling is easy, not too expensive and seldom too far.

6 To give just an impression, we have discussed not only Carol P. Christ' "Embodied Thinking", an article well known in feminist theological circles, but also contemporary classics such as Judith Butler's *Bodies that Matter* and Paula Cooey's *Religious Imagination and the Body*. We have also considered Martha Hewitt's criticism of Butler, Christ and Haraway. The works of Luce Irigaray, Donna Haraway, Teresa of Avila, Mary Daly and many others have shaped our discussion of these authors and our presentations of research, whether directly or via their reception in the works of others we studied. The same can be said of the paintings of Frida Kahlo, Marlene Dumas and the photographs of Cindy Sherman.

unbinding, as bonding and liberating, as a core concern addressing the sacred and as disclosing a transcendent focus linked to ultimate value. Feminist discourses on the body and subjectivity show a remarkable similarity to these descriptions of 'religion' when they point to the body as vehicle and generator of meaning, as giving and undermining sense, as makable and breakable, as cultural and biological, while at the same time escaping or transcending all these categories. Is it possible to exchange or transfer the descriptions of religion and body? Further, can these reflections give a meaningful framework for the ambivalent, bodily or material experiences of change, vulnerability and finitude? And can they in the end provide us with tools for the critical analysis of political and theological powers? In our project we are exploring these questions in case-studies where we, starting with the body, seek our way between the Scylla and Charybdis of essentialism and constructivism to a transforming theology. It is probably no coincidence that the majority of the participants use so-called 'indirect communication' (that is: poems, novels, rituals, films, modern art, and the reception of biblical themes in art) in addition to more traditional theological sources, that they are engaged in deconstruction as well as reconstruction of theological concepts and imagination. For the moment this seems a fruitful and convincing way to establish women studies in theology as a 'different theological discipline'.

Maaike DE HAARDT (1954) studied Theology in Tilburg (The Netherlands) with a Ph.D. in Death in Feminist Theology. She is a lecturer at the Tilburg Faculty of Theology and a Co-Director of the research project 'Corporeality, Religion and Gender' at the University of Groningen. Her main interest is women's studies in systematic theology.

Leonore SIEGELE-WENSCHKEWITZ

Die Verankerung von feministischer Theologie und theologischer Frauenforschung im akademischen Lehr- und Forschungsbetrieb—ein Projekt*

Im November 1996 hat die EKD-Synode, die auf Borkum tagte, über den Abschlußbericht einer vom Rat der EKD eingesetzten Kommission "Förderung theologischer Frauenforschung" beraten ebenso wie über ein Sondervotum zu diesem Bericht. Zwölf Mitglieder der Kommission haben den Abschlußbericht verabschiedet, vier ein Sondervotum vorgelegt.[1] Die Einsetzung der Kommission ging auf folgenden Beschluß der Synode vom November 1989 zum Schwerpunktthema "Die Gemeinschaft von Frauen und Männern in der Kirche" zurück:

> Die Synode hält es für notwendig, die Perspektive von Frauen in theologischer Forschung und Studienarbeit aller Disziplinen einzubeziehen sowie neue Ansätze theologischer Frauenforschung zu fördern. Die Synode bittet den Rat der EKD, einen Ausschuß zu berufen, der Vertreterinnen der theologischen Frauenforschung, Vertreter/innen der theologischen Ausbildungsstätten und der Kirchen umfaßt. Der Ausschuß soll ein Konzept vorlegen, wie die Frauenforschung in die Einrichtungen theologischer Forschung und Lehre integriert werden kann.[2]

Damit hat die EKD ihr Interesse bekundet, daß die an theologischen Fakultäten für den kirchlichen Dienst erworbene Kompetenz theologische Frauenforschung in sich schließt. Das Vorgehen der Kommission war davon bestimmt, bereits an den evangelisch-theologischen Fakultäten und Kirchlichen Hochschulen realisierte Schritte der Institutionalisierung so umfassend wie möglich zu erkunden. Deshalb hat eine Befragung der verschiedenen universitären Statusgruppen—von den feministisch-

---

* zuerst erschienen in: *Evangelische Theologie* 57/2, (1977), 172-175.

1 Die Texte liegen vor in: EKD-Synode Borkum 3, *epd-Dokumentation* 49/96 vom 18. November 1996.

2 Synode der Evangelischen Kirche in Deutschland, *Die Gemeinschaft von Frauen und Männern in der Kirche*. Im Auftrag des Rates der Evangelischen Kirche in Deutschland herausgegeben vom Kirchenamt der EKD, Gütersloh 1990, 25.

theologischen Frauenforen über die zumeist dem akademischen Mittelbau entstammenden Frauenbeauftragten bis hin zu den Dekanen und Rektoren, unter ihnen eine Rektorin,—stattgefunden. Dies Anknüpfen an die von den universitären Bildungseinrichtungen selbst vorgenommenen Maßnahmen hatte einen einfachen Grund: Selbstverständlich will und kann der erarbeitete Vorschlag der Kommission nicht in die den Hochschulen verbriefte Freiheit von Forschung und Lehre eingreifen. Die Kommission hat allerdings ihre Aufgabe darin gesehen, darauf aufmerksam zu machen, daß die theologische Wissenschaft eine neue Forschungsrichtung hervorgebracht hat, die verdient, in die Arbeit der theologischen Fakultäten integriert zu werden. Welcher Richtung die Fakultäten Geltung verschaffen wollen, ob feministischer Theologie, ob theologischer Frauenforschung, ob Gender Studies, werden die Bildungseinrichtungen selbst entscheiden bei der Gewährung von Lehraufträgen sowie durch die personal-politische Auswahl bei der Stellenbesetzung.

Hinsichtlich der Frage, was denn im akademischen Lehr- und Forschungsbetrieb verankert werden solle, gibt der Abschlußbericht eine Orientierung, indem er drei Begriffe ins Spiel bringt: Feministische Theologie, theologische Frauenforschung und Gender Studies; sie führen die Gender-Kategorie als analytische und theoretische in die Theologie ein.[3] Sie hat teil an der Vielfalt der Ansätze der allgemeinen Frauenforschung. Damit ergibt sich derzeit folgendes Spektrum an Zugangsweisen: Theologische Frauenforschung, Feministische Theologie und Gender Studies

1. sind Forschung *über Frauen*, deren Erfahrungen, Motivationen und Lebens-situationen in der Geschichte der Kirche und der von ihr mitgeprägten Gesellschaft;
2. sind Forschung *aus der Sicht von Frauen*, insofern darin ihre historisch geprägten Perspektiven auf und Zugangsweisen zu Themen des Glaubens und der Theologie zum Ausdruck kommen;
3. untersuchen, inwieweit die gesellschaftlichen *Konstruktionen der Geschlechter* Theologie und Kirche auf der Symbolebene, der strukturellen Ebene und der Ebene der Individualität beeinflußt haben, und umgekehrt: inwieweit Theologie und Kirche die gesellschaftlichen

[3] Hadumod Bußmann/Renate Hof (Hg.), *Genus, Zur Geschlechterdifferenz in den Kulturwissenschaften*, Stuttgart 1995.

Konstruktionen der Geschlechter geprägt, legitimiert, kritisiert oder verändert haben;

4. implizieren *Wissenschaftskritik.* Darin haben sie teil an der neueren Wissenschaftssoziologie, die Wissenschaft konsequent als "gesellschaftliche Tätigkeit" begreift. Sie verweisen insbesondere auf die Perspektivität und Kontextualität jeglichen Erkenntnisprozesses und decken die Androzentrik bisheriger Themenbestimmung und Theoriebilder auf. Sie setzen dagegen eine bewußte Forschungstätigkeit zur Überwindung androzentrischen Denkens und patriarchaler Strukturen;
5. sind im *Kontext der Frauenbewegung* entstanden. Die Wechselwirkung von Forschung und sozialer Bewegung gehört zu ihren konstitutiven Merkmalen. Dementsprechend suchen sie nach Methoden und Arbeitsformen, die den Zusammenhang von Lebenswelt und Wissenschaft, subjektiver Befindlichkeit und Theoriebildung reflektieren.

Was empfiehlt der Abschlußbericht?

Auf dem Hintergrund solcher theologischer und begrifflicher Überlegungen, der Würdigung des bislang an den Fakultäten Gewachsenen und Erreichten und grundsätzlicher Erwägungen zur Frauenforschung und Gleichstellung von Frauen in Wissenschaft und Universität kommt der Abschlußbericht der Kommission zu folgenden Empfehlungen zur Integration und Institutionalisierung feministischer Theologie, theologischer Frauenforschung und Gender Studies:

- Die feministische Dimension in jeder theologischen Disziplin zur Geltung bringen: Fragestellungen der feministischen Theologie, der theologischen Frauenforschung und Gender Studies entstehen in und richten sich an jede der traditionellen theologischen Disziplinen. Sachgemäß muß also nach Wegen gesucht werden, die die feministische Dimension in jede Disziplin integrieren und Fragestellungen und Inhalte im Rahmen wissenschaftlicher Forschung und Lehre bearbeiten.
- Lehrstühle bzw. Professuren in den theologischen Fachdisziplinen mit ausgewiesenem Schwerpunkt "feministische Theologie, theologische Frauen-forschung und Gender Studies" bereitzustellen.
- Feministische Theologie, theologische Frauenforschung und Gender Studies als mögliche Prüfungsinhalte in den Studien- und Prüfungsordnungen zu verankern. Prüfungsrelevanz setzt voraus:

- die Bereitstellung qualifizierter Lehrangebote im Bereich feministischer Theologie, theologischer Frauenforschung und Gender Studies;
- die Förderung von akademischem Nachwuchs mit Qualifikationen für feministische Theologie, theologische Frauenforschung und Gender Studies mittelfristig unter Gleichstellungsgesichtspunkten: Förderung von Frauen (Promotions-, Habilitationsförderung, qualifizierte Quotierung) und schließlich
- allgemeine Ansätze der Hochschulreform wie die Förderung von Interdisziplinarität und die Reflexion der Interdependenz zwischen Theorie und Praxis zu stärken oder formale Zugangs- und Abschlußvoraussetzungen im Blick auf weibliche Lebensplanung zu flexibilisieren.

Worin besteht das Strittige dieses Projekts?

Ich sehe drei unterschiedliche Problemkreise, die einem jeweils unterschiedlichen Kontext und Interesse entstammen:

Ein Einwand, der gegenüber feministischer Theologie vorgebracht wird, seit es sie gibt, heißt: sie widerstreite Schrift und Bekenntnis. Damit zieht feministische Theologie den nicht beendeten Streit zwischen Gemeindetheologie und wissenschaftlicher, historisch-kritisch arbeitender Theologie auf sich. In eminenter Weise hat feministisch-theologische Arbeit sich Fragen der Hermeneutik gewidmet, vor allem dem Problem, wie Schrift und Bekenntnis so verstanden und angeeignet werden können, daß die befreiende Botschaft des Evangeliums explizit allen Menschen zugute kommt, auch Frauen in ihrem weiblichen Lebenszusammenhang. Die Anwendung eines geschlechts-spezifischen Ansatzes macht Frauenerfahrung nicht zu einer Offenbarungsquelle. Als Mann und Frau, also unterschiedlichen Geschlechts geschaffen zu sein, ist Teil der Reflexion des Kontextes, die in die Hermeneutik gehört und nicht in die Glaubenslehre.

Ein zweiter Einwand gegen dieses Projekt kommt aus den Fakultäten, die an dieser Frage dezidiert eine kirchliche Einflußnahme, ja Bevormundung zurückweisen, um so die Freiheit von Forschung und Lehre zu verteidigen. Gleichwohl gibt die Kirche bei verschiedenen Gelegenheiten ihr Interesse an der theologischen Ausbildung zu erkennen: z.B. bei der Mitwirkung am 1. Theologischen Examen oder in der Zusammenarbeit in der sogenannten Gemischten Kommission. Es erschient mir legitim, daß die Kirche aus ekklesiologischen, ethischen wie seelsorgerlichen Gründen

—wie sonst—auch in diesem Fall ihr Interesse artikuliert. Die Freiheit der Fakultäten ist weder durch die Befragung noch gar durch den Abschlußbericht angetastet worden. Denn den Fakultäten bleibt uneingeschränkt das Recht der Selbstergänzung. Sie werden gebeten, Frauen dafür heranzuziehen—um ihrer eigenen Bereicherung willen.

Ein drittes Konfliktfeld berührt ein allgemeines gesellschaftliches Problem, das auch an den Universtitäten zum Vorschein kommt. Allerdings ist die Lage an den theo-logischen Fakultäten insofern verschärft, als hier—anders als in anderen Wissen-schaftsdisziplinen—unter den Hochschullehrern nur 4,3% Frauen sind. Es wird als eine Tabuverletzung erlebt, wenn feministische Theologinnen—seien es Studentinnen oder Hochschullehrerinnen—den unübersehbaren Sexismus, Androzentrismus und Patriarchalismus an evangelisch-theologischen Fakultäten benennen und kritisieren. Dies widerspricht dem Comment des Männerbunds auf der einen Seite, es kränkt das Selbstbild des frauenfreundlichen, frauenförderungswilligen Hochschullehrers auf der anderen Seite.

So sehr es mich reizen würde, ausführlicher argumentativ auf diese drei Punkte einzugehen, kann dieser kurze Beitrag doch nur zur Diskussion einladen, die in der Arbeit der Kommission und bei der Beratung der Synode bereits begonnen hat. Mir erscheint die Verankerung von feministischer Theologie, theologischer Frauen- und Geschlechterforschung im akademischem Lehr- und Forschungsbetrieb als ein Desiderat und Postulat, um ihre unfreiwillige Ghettoexistenz zu beenden und sie in lebendigem Pro und Contra der akademischen Gemeinschaft zur Geltung zu bringen und weiterzuentwickeln.

Pfarrein PD Dr. Leonore SIEGELE-WENSCHKEWITZ ist Studienleiterin und seit 1996 Direktorin der Evangelischen Akademie Arnoldshain. Von 1990-1996 war sie Vorsitzende der EKD-Kommission "Förderung theologischer Frauenforschung".

Anke E. PASSENIER

Der Lustgarten des Leibes und die Freiheit der Seele: Wege der Mittelalterlichen Frauenspiritualität*

Einführung

Die Spiritualität mittelalterlicher 'religiöser Frauen'[1] wurde in den letzten Jahrzehnten zu einem vielbearbeiteten Forschungsthema, das auch außerhalb der akademischen Welt, bei einem breiten Publikum zunehmend Beachtung findet. Mystikerinnen wie Hadewijch, Mechthild von Magdeburg und Marguerite Porete sind aus der Klausur der spezialisierten literaturwissenschaftlichen und spiritualitätsgeschichtlichen Forschung herausgetreten. Eine Vielfalt an Disziplinen bemüht sich um die Bearbeitung und Interpretation ihrer Texte, die überdies zu manchen Spiritualitätskursen und Frauengruppen ihren Weg gefunden haben.[2]

Eine auffallende Tendenz in der modernen—vor allem auch feministischen—Forschung ist die positive Einschätzung der mittelalterlichen

---

* Die Forschungsarbeit für diesen Artikel wurde ermöglicht von der *Stichting voor Filosofie en Theologie* des niederländischen Forschungsinstituts *NWO* (Nederlandse Organisatie voor Wetenschappelijk Onderzoek). Eine kürzere und popularisierende Version dieses Artikels ist: "Het lijdend lichaam en de vrije ziel. Middeleeuwse mystica's op zoek naar God" in: *Lover. Literatuuroverzicht over feminisme, cultuur en wetenschap*, 23 (1996) 1, 15-22. Meiner Kusine Heidi Zimmermann danke ich für die Korrektur des Deutschen.

1 'Religiöse Frauen' (mulieres religiosae) ist ein Sammelbegriff, der sowohl Nonnen, Beginen, Klausnerinnen als auch Hospitalschwestern bezeichnen kann, d.h. Frauen, die sich für ein 'religiöses Leben' (vita religiosa) einer bestimmten geordneten Form entschieden und dazu ihre weltliche Position (Ehe, Familie, Besitz) aufgaben.

2 Für eine Übersicht siehe z.B. Gertrud Jaron Lewis, *Bibliographie zur deutschen Frauenmystik des Mittelalters* (Berlin: Schmidt 1989); Kurt Ruh, *Geschichte der abendländischen Mystik. Band II: Frauenmystik und Franziskanische Mystik der Frühzeit* (München: Beck 1993); Peter Dinzelbacher, *Mittelalterliche Frauenmystik* (Paderborn u.a.: Schöningh 1993); Elizabeth A. Petroff, *Body and Soul: Essays on Medieval Women and Mysticism* (Oxford: OUP 1994); Elizabeth A. Petroff (ed.), *Medieval Women's Visionary Literature* (Oxford: OUP 1986).

Frauenmystik als Exponent einer eigenständigen, spezifischen Frauenspiritualität, die sich durch eine starke Betonung von Leiblichkeit und Affektivität auszeichne. Gegen diese Einschätzung wurde in letzter Zeit schon mehrmals Einspruch erhoben, vor allem da sie den spezifischen historischen Kontext, in dem die frauenmystischen Texte entstanden sind, wenig zu berücksichtigen scheint.[3] Dieser Kritik möchte ich mich in diesem Artikel mit einigen weiteren Überlegungen anschließen. Ausgangspunkt meiner Argumentation sind einige Beobachtungen hinsichtlich der 'Verketzerung' von bestimmten religiösen Frauen einerseits und der Wirksamkeit von Stereotypen des Weiblichen in der Darstellung mittelalterlicher Frauenspiritualität andererseits, so wie diese sich aus meiner Forschung über die Mystikerin Marguerite Porete ergeben haben. Bei einer Auffassung der mittelalterlichen Frauenmystik als leiblich und affektiv orientiert scheinen 'verketzerte', anders ausgerichtete Traditionen kaum berücksichtigt zu werden und uralte Stereotypen des Weiblichen wieder aufzuleben. Es scheint mir an der Zeit, eine Lanze einzulegen für die Vielfältigkeit der Weisen in denen mittelalterliche Frauen eine Verbindung zum Göttlichen erstrebt haben und Spuren der Uneinigkeit sichtbar zu machen.

Eine 'weibliche (Gottes)erfahrung'?

Wer die mittelalterlichen Lebensbeschreibungen religiöser Frauen liest, wird sich nur schwer dem Eindruck entziehen können, daß in der Spiritualität dieser Frauen Körper, Blut, Leiden, Ekstase, Gefühl und Affekt eine große Rolle spielten. Nehmen wir z.B. die *Vita* der Maria von Oignies (1177?-1213), geschrieben von ihrem geistlichen Freund und Berater Jakob von Vitry.[4] Dort ist zu lesen, daß Maria kein Kreuzbild sehen konnte, ohne darüber in Ekstase zu geraten. Ihre Betrachtung der Leiden Christi konnte heftige Gefühlsausbrüche auslösen und hätte einen solchen Ekel vor ihrem eigenen Körper provoziert, daß sie eines Tages Stücke davon abgeschnitten und beerdigt hätte. Jakob schreibt Maria auch eine besondere Erkenntnis der göttlichen Geheimnisse und der Heiligen Schrift zu: Auf ihrem Sterbebett habe sie auf Grund einer speziellen göttlichen Offenbarung einige Schriftstellen ganz neu erklärt. Nicht dem Studium,

3 Literaturangaben zu dieser Kritik werden im Laufe des Artikels folgen.

4 Jakob war jahrelang der engste Vertrauter Marias und betrachtete sie als seine geistliche Führerin und Mutter.

sondern einer ekstatischen Erleuchtung habe Maria ihre besonderen Erkenntnisse zu verdanken.[5]

Maria von Oignies war eine der vielen Frauen im nordeuropäischen Bereich, die seit Ende des 12. Jahrhunderts Ehe, Besitz und Familie aufgaben, um in der Nachfolge Christi ein 'religiöses Leben' (vita religiosa) von Armut, Gebet, Meditation und Dienstbarkeit zu führen. Ein Teil dieser Frauen schloß sich den Klosterorden an, die dem enormen Zulauf bald nicht mehr gewachsen waren; viele andere lebten als sogenannte 'Beginen' alleine im eigenen Haus oder in einer Gemeinschaft ohne Klosterregel. Vor allem in Flandern, Brabant und im Rheinland erreichte die religiöse Frauenbewegung einen beträchtlichen Umfang und von dort breitete sie sich im Laufe des 13. Jahrhunderts nach Süd-Deutschland, die Schweiz und Italien aus.[6] Maria von Oignies, eine Vorläuferin der Beginen, die ihre Ehe und ihren Besitz aufgab, um sich den Aussätzigen zu widmen, und die später eine kleine Frauengruppe um sich sammelte, ist ein Prototyp der religiösen Frauen, die vor allem in der Diözese Lüttich sehr zahlreich waren. Das Porträt, das Jakob von Vitry von ihr zeichnet, ist noch immer bestimmend für das Bild der mittelalterlichen Frauenspiritualität.[7]

Die Ausstellung *Hooglied* (Brüssel 1994) über die Bilderwelt religiöser Frauen in den südlichen Niederlanden hätte wahrscheinlich in mehreren Hinsichten Jakobs Zustimmung gefunden.[8] Die Atmosphäre und Ausrichtung dieser Ausstellung bestätigten mir den Eindruck, daß mittelalterliche Frauenmystik nicht selten voreilig mit Körperlichkeit, Affektivität und Ekstase assoziiert wird und, daß man zudem geneigt ist, dies als 'typisch weiblich' zu präsentieren. Dies zeigt sich an manchen Ver-

---

5 Jakob von Vitry, *Vita Mariae Oigniacensis (VMO)* (ed. D. Papebroeck), *Acta Sanctorum 23. Juni IV* (Antwerpen 1707), 630-666.

6 Siehe z.B. Ernest W. McDonnell, *The Beguines and Beghards in Medieval Culture* (New York 1969); Brigitte Degler-Spengler, "Die religiöse Frauenbewegung des Mittelalters: Konversen, Nonnen, Beginen" in: *Rottenburger Jahrbuch für Kirchengeschichte* 3 (1984), 75-88; Ute Weinmann, *Mittelalterliche Frauenbewegungen. Ihre Beziehungen zur Orthodoxie und Häresie* (Pfaffenweiler: Centaurus 1990), 145vv (mit Forschungsüberblick).

7 Siehe Brenda M. Bolton, "Vitae Matrum: A further Aspect of the Frauenfrage" in: Derek Baker (ed.), *Medieval Women* (Oxford 1978), 253-273.

8 Ausstellungskatalog: *Hooglied. De Beeldwereld van Religieuze Vrouwen in de Zuidelijke Nederlanden, vanaf de 13de eeuw.* Paleis voor Schone Kunsten Brussel (25. Februar - 22. Mai 1994).

öffentlichungen zu diesem Thema, von sowohl wissenschaftlicher als popularisierender Art. So spielt in den einflußreichen Studien von Caroline Walker Bynum der Gedanke, daß die Spiritualität mittelalterlicher religiöser Frauen ein 'female concern' zum Ausdruck bringe, eine wichtige Rolle. Die besondere Devotion mittelalterlicher Nonnen und Beginen zum menschlichen Christus und zu seinem Leib in der Eucharistie würde mit ihrer spezifischen Situation als Frauen zusammenhängen. Gerade als Frauen, traditionell mit dem Leib, dem Irdischen und Materiellen assoziiert, hätten sie eine Spiritualität und theologische Artikulation entwickelt, in denen Leiblichkeit, Sinnlichkeit und Inkarnation des Göttlichen im Mittelpunkt stehen.[9] Ähnlich behauptet Peter Dinzelbacher, daß ekstatisches Erleben, Vision und Erscheinung als Typikum der mittelalterlichen Frauenmystik zu betrachten sind, auch wenn er immerhin nicht ausschließen möchte, daß dies damit zusammenhängt, daß Frauen eine wissenschaftlich-theologische Ausbildung entbehren mußten und daher andere Ausdrucksmöglichkeiten erprobt haben.[10] Die Betonung des Affektiven und Visuellen findet sich auch in den Arbeiten Elizabeth Petroffs: '... die Mystikerin sah und fühlte die Wahrheit, sah Gott oder Christus oder die Heiligen und wurde von Liebe überflutet für das, was sie sah'.[11]

---

9 Siehe vor allem Caroline Walker Bynum, "Women Mystics and Eucharistic Devotion in the Thirteenth Century" in: *Women's Studies* (1984)11, 179-214; idem, *Holy Feast and Holy Fast: The Religious Significance of Food to Medieval Women* (Berkeley: University of California Press 1987); idem, *Fragmentation and Redemption: Essays on Gender and the Human Body in Medieval Religion* (New York: Urzone Publishers 1991).

10 Peter Dinzelbacher und Dieter R. Bauer (ed.), *Frauenmystik im Mittelalter* (Ostfildern: Schwabenverlag 1985); idem, *Religiöse Frauenbewegung und mystische Frömmigkeit im Mittelalter* (Köln/Wien: Böhlau 1988); Peter Dinzelbacher, *Mittelalterliche Frauenmystik* (Paderborn u.a.: Schöningh 1993) 19, `Ekstatisches Erleben, Vision und Erscheinung, tiefstes Fühlen mit allen Kräften von Leib und Seele: dies möchte ein, wenn nicht vielleicht *das* Typikum der Frauenmystik des Mittelalters sein...'

11 Elizabeth Alvilda Petroff, *Body & Soul. Essays on Medieval Women and Mysticism* (New York/Oxford: Oxford University Press 1994), 6. In popularisierenden Veröffentlichungen ist die Verbindung von Frauen mit Leib und Gefühl oft noch massiver und weniger nuanciert, so lässt es sich auf jeden Fall für den holländischen Bereich feststellen. Vergl. z.B. Martie Dieperink, *Dochters naar mijn hart. Spiritualiteit van vrouwen in de Middeleeuwen* (Kampen: Kok 1995), 11, oder Peter Bot, *Dochters van Deborah. Het profetisch optreden van vrouwen in de middeleeuwse kerk* (Kampen: Kok Agora 1994), 115.

Der Gedanke einer spezifischen Frauenspiritualität, die sich in den Texten mittelalterlicher Mystikerinnen vorfinden ließe, ist oft in irgendeiner Weise verbunden mit dem Begriff der sexuellen Differenz, nach dem die Erfahrungsmöglichkeiten von Männern und Frauen grundsätzlich verschieden sind. Das Differenz-Denken findet sich in manchen traditionellen, oft mit religiösen und biologischen Argumenten begründeten Auffassungen der Geschlechterrollen. Gegenwärtige, vor allem von feministischen Forscherinnen vorgetragene Auffassungen der sexuellen Differenz richten sich gegen einseitige kulturelle Definierungen des Weiblichen als abgeleitet von dem Männlichen, als das Nicht-Männliche, und erstreben eine positive Benennung des Weiblichen. In dieser Neu-Definierung spielt die mittelalterliche Frauenmystik, als Quelle artikulierter weiblicher Erfahrung eine wichtige Rolle. In prägnanter Form wird dieser neue Differenz-Begriff von Luce Irigaray in einem Beitrag 'Der Weg des Weiblichen' für den Katalog der Ausstellung *Hooglied* dargestellt, in dem sie Gemälde und Skulpturen, die das Verhältnis religiöser Frauen zum leidenden Christus zum Thema haben, interpretiert.[12] Nach Irigaray seien diese Abbildungen, obwohl meist von Männern angefertigt, als Ausdrucksformen einer wesentlich anthropomorphen, weiblichen Spiritualität aufzufassen. Während der Mann seinen Gott in einer anderen Welt suche, über das leibliche Hier-und-Jetzt hinaus und an dem Gegenwärtig-Sein bei sich, der Welt und den Anderen vorbei, würden Frauen das Göttliche im Zwischen-uns und im leiblichen Sein erfahren: die 'Liebe in ihrer weiblichen Gestalt'. Nach Irigaray wird auf diesen Bildern eine spezifisch weibliche Form der Gottesbegegnung sichtbar und eine Erfahrungsweise, deren Artikulierung im männlich geprägten religiösen Diskurs in den Hintergrund gedrängt wäre.

Gegen eine solche Auffassung der mittelalterlichen Frauenspiritualität möchte ich einige Bedenken vorbringen. Erstens, weil sie m.E. die Variabilität an Formen, die es in der mittelalterlichen Frauenspiritualität gegeben hat, zu wenig berücksichtigt. Zweitens, weil die Charakterisierung der Frauenspiritualität als leiblich-affektiv die Gefahr einer Wiederbelebung und Instandhaltung uralter traditioneller Stereotypen des Weiblichen in sich birgt.

Die leibliche und affektive Frauenmystik war im Mittelalter keine unterdrückte Tradition, sondern vielmehr konnte sie von mächtigen

12 Luce Irigaray, "De weg van het vrouwelijke" in: *Hooglied* 155-166.

Geistlichen unterstützt und gefördert werden. Frauen, die andere, eher spiritualisierende Wege der Gottesbegegnung propagierten, waren jedoch im Allgemeinen den führenden kirchlichen Institutionen zuwider und konnten der 'Ketzerei' angeklagt werden. Anhand einer Konfrontierung zweier Frauentexte aus dem späten Mittelalter will ich aufzeigen, daß die mystischen Texte mittelalterlicher religiöser Frauen zwar bestimmte Themen und Vorstellungen gemeinsam haben, aber auch in manchen Hinsichten als grundverschieden erscheinen. Es handelt sich zum einen um den *Mirouer des simples ames anienties* der Marguerite Porete, eine Begine aus dem Hennegau (Nord-Frankreich), die im Jahre 1310 in Paris als 'Ketzerin' verbrannt wurde, und zum anderen um die *Offenbarungen* einer Dominikanernonne aus Medingen, Margaretha Ebner (±1291-1351), die auf Antrieb ihres Beichtvaters, Heinrich von Nördlingen, ihre spirituelle Biographie aufzeichnete.[13]

Liebeslust und Leibespein bei Margaretha Ebner

Im Mittelpunkt der Aufzeichnungen Margaretha Ebners steht die leidenschaftliche Liebesbeziehung zum leidenden Christus am Kreuz, der vor allem ein leiblicher, fühl- und greifbarer Jesus ist. Die ekstatisch erlebte Einheit mit Christus, die von Margaretha Ebner erstrebt wird, ist nicht das Ergebnis blutloser mystischer Spekulation, sondern realisiert sich im Berühren, Umarmen, Küssen, Trinken. An einer Stelle beschreibt Margaretha wie sie ein Evangeliar mit einer Abbildung des Gekreuzigten auf ihren nackten Busen trägt und nachts unter ihr Kopfkissen legt. Eine wunderbare Freude und Süßigkeit durchströmt sie dabei. Oft ist ihr aber auch der Anblick eines Kreuzbildes unerträglich, weil er zu schlimmen Schmerzanfällen führt. Auch die Kommunion provoziert heftige Gefühlsreaktionen, von brennender Sehnsucht und Begierde bis zur höchsten Freude.[14] Das Aufessen der Hostie erlebt Margaretha als eine sehr konkrete Einswerdung mit dem Mann Jesus:

---

13 Philipp Strauch, *Margaretha Ebner und Heinrich von Nördlingen. Ein Beitrag zur Geschichte der deutschen Mystik* (1882; Amsterdam 1966). Siehe für Margaretha Ebner: Georg Schwaiger, "Ebner, Margaretha." in: Ruh, Kurt e.a. (ed.), *Die deutsche Literatur des Mittelalters. Verfasserlexikon* II (1980), Kol. 303-306.

14 Siehe, z.B. Strauch, *Margaretha Ebner* 9; 11; 20-22; 47-48; 61-62. Da eine moderne Übersetzung fehlt, zitiere ich nach Josef Prestel *Die Offenbarungen der Margaretha Ebner und der Adelheid Langmann* (Weimar: Böhlaus 1939), 12-13; 19; 43-44; 35-36.

> Und wieder danach schaute ich ganz klar und lauter eines Mannes Leib, der lag vor mir ganz bloß. Von diesem Leibe kam mir größte Süßigkeit und Gnade, denn er war ganz Glast und Glanz. Da wurde mir gegeben, daß wir ihn genießen sollten. Da hatte ich große Hoffnung, daß man den Leib verteilen und verkosten werde. Doch meine Schwester sprach: "Er kommt, der ihn teilen soll," und danach ward mir kund, daß es der zarte Fronleichnam wäre unsers Herrn; denn kurz darauf empfingen wir unsern Herrn.[15]

An anderer Stelle sagt Margaretha, daß ihr die Gnade gewährt sei, daß sie im Sakrament 'nicht mehr die Materie des Brotes verspüre,' und, daß sie die Wahrheit in der er sein heilig Fleisch und Blut gegeben hat, so gegenwärtiglich empfunden hat, als ob sie 'es leiblich sähe und esse und trinke'.[16]

Die leibliche Identifizierung, die in Margarethas Buch zentral ist, kommt auch in vielen sonderbaren Krankheiten und psychosomatischen Erscheinungen sichtbar zum Ausdruck. Fürchterliche Schmerzanfälle, Lähmungen und Krämpfe quälen die Mystikerin oft jahrelang. Die Lust am leiblichen Miterleben von Christi Leiden äußert sich auch in einer brennenden Sehnsucht nach dem Empfang der Stigmata, die Wundmale des Gekreuzigten, an ihrem eigenen Körper, ein Verlangen, das sie eines Nachts im Traum erfüllt sieht. Die Einheit mit Christi Leiden beherrscht auch Margarethas Lebensführung und ihre religiösen Übungen. Sie fastet oft lange Zeit und ißt mit Vorliebe nur die unappetitlichsten Speisen. Selbst bei schwerer Krankheit weigert sie sich, auf einem Kissen zu liegen, weil dies für eine Braut Christi unpassend sei. Auch berichtet sie, wie sie sich über dreißig Jahre nicht gewaschen oder gebadet habe. Auch in der täglichen Christusnachfolge (imitatio Christi) dreht sich alles um den Körper und um die leibliche Symbiose mit dem Gott-Menschen.[17]

Obwohl der Gekreuzigte in den *Offenbarungen* immer im Mittelpunkt ist, kann die Verbindung mit dem Menschen Jesus mehrere Gestalten annehmen. Der körperliche Aspekt ist aber immer von wesentlicher Bedeutung. Neben dem schönen Mann und dem leidenden Gekreuzigten hat Margaretha auch eine besondere Beziehung zum Christuskind. Außer seinem Leiden am Kreuz und seinem Tod sind die Konzeption, die Geburt, die Abhängigkeit von der Mutterbrust und die schmerzliche Beschneidung weitere Zeugen der wahrhaftigen Menschlichkeit Christi.

15 Strauch, *Margaretha Ebner* 50 (Prestel 37).

16 Strauch, *Margaretha Ebner* 105 (Prestel 71).

17 Strauch, *Margaretha Ebner* 1-4; 19; 46; 50; 78-80 (Prestel 7-9; 18; 34; 37; 54-55).

Margaretha berichtet, wie, als sie ihr Buch zur Hälfte geschrieben hatte, ihr 'ein allergrößtes Gelüsten nach der Kindheit unsers Herrn' überkam und sie durch eine Puppe des Christuskindes Gottes Gegenwart empfindet.[18] Daß die Empfindung der Gnade vom Christuskind sich noch steigern kann zur körperlichen Erfahrung, zeigt sich an folgender Stelle:

> Da überkam mir wieder große Lust zur Kindheit unsers Herrn, ich nahm das kindliche Bild und drückt es an mein bloßes Herz aus allen meinen Kräften. Dabei verspürt ich menschliche Berührung seines Mundes an meinem bloßen Herzen.[19]

Der Traum einer Mitschwester bestätigt später die göttliche Herkunft dieser Empfindung:

> Die sprach zu mir: "Ich bot dir heut in dieser Nacht in einem Traum dein Kind und das war ein lebendes Kind und das nahmst du von mir mit grosser Begierde und legtest es an dein Herz und wolltest es säugen und dessen wunderte mich, so schüchtern schamhaft als du bist, daß du dich nicht schämtest."[20]

Aus diesen Stellen wird ersichtlich, daß die Abbildungen des Herrn wie das Sakrament in den wirklichen, menschlichen Christus transformiert werden, mit dem man sich konkret-sinnlich vereinigen kann. Margarethas Christus ist der Geliebte, den sie umarmen und küssen kann, das Kind, das sie säugen kann und auch die Mutter aus deren Brust sie trinken kann.[21] In Träumen und Visionen erscheint er ihr in menschlicher Gestalt, um ihre Sehnsucht zu stillen und ihre Lust nach ihm zu befriedigen. In körperlichen Empfindungen, wie Berührung und Geschmack, spürt sie seine Gegenwart. Vor allem ist er der sakramentale Christus, der Leib, dessen Substanz in die eigene Substanz übergehen kann. Die Kommunikation mit dem Göttlichen ist wesentlich Kommunion: Essen, Trinken, Ineinanderfließen und Austausch von Substanzen. Durch die Vereinigung mit dem

---

18 Die Beschneidung interessiert Margaretha am meisten in der Kindheitsgeschichte Christi, weil er hier schon der Leidende ist und sein Blut vergossen wird. Vgl. Strauch, *Margaretha Ebner* 87 (Prestel 59-60).

19 Strauch, *Margaretha Ebner* 89 (Prestel 61).

20 Strauch, *Margaretha Ebner* 90 (Prestel 62).

21 Das Trinken aus dem geöffneten Herz Christi, aus der Seitenwunde, wird von Margaretha auch umschrieben als Trinken 'us den süezzen brüsten Jhesu Christi'. (Strauch, *Margaretha Ebner* 74 (Prestel 52). Zu diesem weitverbreiteten mystischen Motiv, siehe: Caroline Walker Bynum, *Jesus as a Mother. Studies in the Spirituality of the High Middle Ages* (Berkeley etc.: University of California Press 1982).

göttlichen Körper erfährt auch der eigene Körper eine Transformation oder Transsubstantiation. Margarethas Körper wird selbst zum Christusleib und zum Zeichen der Gegenwart Gottes unter den Menschen, eine Gegenwart, von der ihre *Offenbarungen* Zeugnis ablegen sollen, den Leser(inne)n zum Trost. Das in der Liturgie gefeierte Mysterium der realen, leiblichen Gottespräsenz wiederholt sich in Leib und Leben der Mystikerin. Eine Heilige wie Margaretha gewährleistet mehr oder weniger die Wirklichkeit der 'spirituellen Wahrheiten', ihre beständige Inkarnierung. Sie gibt selbst den klaren Hinweis, daß ihre konkreten Erfahrungen einen geistlichen, symbolischen Sinn haben. Das Säugen des Christuskindes bedeutet, daß sie durch seine lautere Menschlichkeit gereinigt, mit seiner süßen Gnade durchgossen und in den Genuss seines göttlichen Wesens gezogen werde, so erklärt Margaretha.[22] Derartige theologische Aussagen gehen weit über harmloses Puppenspiel hinaus! Kern der *Offenbarungen* ist jedoch, daß die Theologie sichtbar, handgreiflich und fühlbar wird und sich vollzieht an und in einem menschlichen Körper als Ort der Gegenwärtigkeit Gottes. Die Berührung mit dem Göttlichen kann nicht anders als leiblich sein.

Die *Offenbarungen* der Margaretha Ebner erscheinen in ihrer durch und durch 'erotischen' Beschreibung der Liebesvereinigung mit Gott als ein typisches Beispiel der sogenannten 'weiblichen' Spiritualität, so wie diese in manchen modernen Arbeiten dargestellt wird. Im Falle Margaretha Ebners ist es offensichtlich, daß es sich hier um eine Spiritualitätsform handelt, die bei den kirchlichen Autoritäten unverdächtig war. Der Weltgeistliche Heinrich von Nördlingen,[23] der ein großes Interesse für mystisch begabte Frauen wie Margaretha hegte, hat sie zur Aufzeichnung ihrer *Offenbarungen* ermuntert. Seine Briefe an sie, in denen er selbst hervortritt als ihr engster Vertrauter, der sie wegen ihrer göttlichen Leiden und Gnaden bewundert, suggerieren eine enge Zusammenarbeit bei der Entstehung ihrer 'hailig(en) geschrift,' die der Erbauung der 'Gottesfreunde'[24] dienen soll.

---

22 Strauch, *Margaretha Ebner* 86-87 (Prestel 60).

23 Über Margarethas Beziehung zu Heinrich siehe z.B.: Ursula Peters, *Religiöse Erfahrung als literarisches Faktum. Zur Vorgeschichte und Genese frauenmystischer Texte des 13. und 14. Jahrhunderts* (Tübingen: Niemeyer 1988), 142-155.

24 Über die 'Gottesfreunde', Gruppen Geistlicher und Laien, die zur geistlichen Erbauung Kontakte miteinander pflegen und an geistliche Unterweisungsliteratur

Margarethas *Offenbarungen* waren offenbar für die kirchlichen Autoritäten durchaus akzeptabel. Die Frömmigkeit der deutschen Dominikanerinnen wurde öffentlich gefördert und ihre Schriften waren verbreitet in frommen Leserkreisen, die die Frauen als Heilige verehrten.

Lustlosigkeit und Freiheit zur Lust bei Marguerite Porete

Anders verhält es sich mit Marguerite Porete, eine nordfranzösische Begine, die im Jahre 1310 in Paris als 'Ketzerin' verbrannt wurde. Sie hatte ein mystisches Lehrbuch geschrieben und verbreitet, das im Auftrag des dominikanischen Inquisitors Wilhelm von Paris von einem erlauchten Gremium aus 21 Theologen als 'ketzerisch' verurteilt wurde. Marguerite verweigerte jedoch dem Inquisitionstribunal jede Aussage und war nicht zur Widerrufung ihrer 'Irrlehren' bereit, weshalb sie nach zirka anderthalbjähriger Haft in den Kerkern der Inquisition der weltlichen Macht ausgeliefert und am 1. Juni 1310 auf der Place de Grèves verbrannt wurde. Auch ihr Buch übergab man den Flammen und noch existierende Exemplare wurden beschlagnahmt, so daß man es lange Zeit verloren wähnte. Im Jahre 1946 machte aber die italienische Gelehrte Romana Guarnieri die aufsehenerregende Entdeckung, daß Marguerites Schrift mit dem anonym überlieferten *Mirouer des simples ames* identisch sein müsse.[25] Einige von der Inquisition verurteilten Sätze aus Margaretha's Buch, die in den Prozeßakten aufgezeichnet wurden, ließen sich in dem

interessiert sind, siehe z.B. Angelus Walz, "Gottesfreunde um Margaretha Ebner" in: *Historisches Jahrbuch der Görres-Gesellschaft* 72 (1953), 253-265.

25 Romana Guarnieri, "Il movimento del Libero Spirito. Testi e documenti. 2.Teil: Il'Miroir des simples âmes' di Margherita Porete" in: *Archivio italiano per la storia della pietà* (1965) 4, 501-635. Eine Doppelausgabe mit dem altfranzösischen und dem lateinischen Text wurde 1986 in der Continuatio Medievalis des Corpus Christianorum herausgebracht: Marguerite Porete, *Le mirouer des simples ames*, ed. par Romana Guarnieri; Margaretae Porete, *Speculum simplicium animarum*, cura et studio Paul Verdeyen (CC. Cont. Med. 69) (Turnhout 1986). (Ich zitiere nach dieser Ausgabe die Kapitel und deren Zeilen). Deutsche Übersetzung: *Margareta Porete, Der Spiegel der einfachen Seelen*, aus dem Altfranzösischen übertragen und mit einem Nachwort und Anmerkungen von Louise Gnädinger (Zürich/München 1987). Über Marguerite Porete siehe z.B. Kurt Ruh, *Geschichte der abendländischen Mystik II* 338-371; Anke E. Passenier, "Heilige Kerk-de-Kleine in de Spiegel van Marguerite Porete" in: Dorothée van Paassen en Anke E. Passenier (ed.), *Op zoek naar vrouwen in ketterij en sekte* (Kampen: Kok 1993) 95-115. Über den Inquisitionsprozess gegen Marguerite: Paul Verdeyen, "Le procès d'inquisition contre Marguerite Porete et Guiard de Cressonessart (1309-1310)" in: *Revue d'histoire ecclésiastique* 81 (1986), 47-94.

Mirouer fast buchstäblich wiederfinden. Der *Mirouer*, der schon im Mittelalter eine außerordentliche Verbreitung fand und in sechs Sprachen überliefert wurde, hatte jahrhundertelang vor allem in klösterlichem Milieu zirkuliert. Daß er einmal als häretisch verurteilt worden war, war oft nicht mehr bekannt und in England wurde lange Zeit der berühmte Ruusbroec für den Verfasser gehalten. Der *Spiegel* der Marguerite Porete ist ein Unikum, weil die Texte verketzerter Personen in den meisten Fällen vernichtet sind. Dieser Traktat verschafft uns die Möglichkeit, verketzerte Auffassungen aus erster Hand kennenzulernen und nicht nur aus den tendenziösen Berichten ihrer Gegner, den sogenannten polemischen Quellen.

Bemerkenswert ist es nun, daß in dem *Spiegel* eine Auffassung der Einheit mit dem Göttlichen vertreten wird, die stark abweicht von der leiblichen, affektiven Mystik einer Margaretha Ebner. Marguerite unterscheidet sieben Seinsweisen oder Stände (estaz, estres, degrez) auf dem Weg zur Einheit mit Gott und zur spirituellen Vollkommenheit. Nur die ersten Phasen stehen im Zeichen der Nachfolge des menschlichen Christus. Die Seele steht unter der strengen Herrschaft der Tugenden—vor allem der Vernunft—, die sie zwingen ohne Unterlaß den Willen Gottes zu vollbringen, das heißt die Gebote zu halten und Christus nachzufolgen im Verzicht auf Ehre, Reichtum, Luxus und die Abtötung leiblicher Begierde.[26] Marguerite beschreibt in ihrem Buch vor allem eine Stufe, die sie das Leben der 'vernichteten' und 'befreiten' Seele nennt, und in der man schon auf Erden, auch neben den flüchtigen Augenblicken ekstatischer Entrückung, mit Gott vereinigt ist. Diese Stufe wird erreicht, wenn die Seele in ein und demselben Augenblick, wie von einem

26 Die verschiedenen Stufen beschreibt Marguerite erst gegen Ende ihres Buches (*Mirouer* 118, Gnädinger 169-177). Kurz zusammengefasst beinhalten sie: 1. Das Halten der Gebote; 2. Die Befolgung der evangelischen Anweisungen für Gottes besondere Freunde: die Abtötung der Natur und die Verachtung von Reichtum, Ehre und Besitz nach dem Beispiel Jesu Christi; 3. Das Aufgeben der Werke; statt den eigenen den Willen eines Anderen vollbringen; 4. Sich üben in Betrachtungen und Meditationen; Ablassen von äußeren Werken; von Minne überwältigt werden und sich ganz dem Genießen der Minne übergeben; 5. Gott und sich selbst schauen; Vernichtung durch die Erkenntnis der eigenen Nichtigkeit; Rückkehr in Gott; nur den göttlichen Willen wollen; 6. Augenblicke der Entrückung, in der die Seele wie von einem Blitz erleuchtet ihre künftige Herrlichkeit sieht; 7. Ewige Herrlichkeit im Paradies; völliger Besitz der Vollkommenheit. Eine kurze Besprechung der sieben Stufen gibt z.B. Kurt Ruh in *Geschichte der abendländischen Mystik II* 346-349.

Blitzstrahl erleuchtet, sich selbst und Gott erkennt und gegenüber der unermeßlichen Größe Gottes ihre eigene Nichtigkeit erfährt.[27] In der Erkenntnis von Gottes allumfassendem Sein zeigt sich die Beschränktheit und die völlige Abhängigkeit alles menschlichen Seins. An dieser Einsicht zerbricht jede Eigen- und Selbständigkeit. Die Orientierung verschiebt sich von dem eigenen Willen, der eigenen Erkenntnis und dem eigenen Handeln auf das umfassende Wollen, Wissen und Wirken Gottes. Nun, behauptet Marguerite, ist es Gott, der in der Seele wirkt,[28] und das bedeutet eine Befreiung von jeder menschlichen Begrenzung und Beschränkung.

Auch die Identifizierung mit dem menschlichen Christus gehört zu jenen Beschränkungen, die die vernichtete Seele durchbricht und aufgibt. Die Identifikation mit dem menschlichen Christus ist nicht wie bei Margaretha Ebner der zentrale Weg zur Gotteseinheit so lange der Mensch auf Erden lebt, sondern ist vielmehr eine Lehre die man abschließen kann. Marguerite spornt ihre Leser(innen) an, von dem menschlichen Christus zum Göttlichen zu gehen und nicht bei dem irdischen Jesus stehenzubleiben. Sie verweist in diesem Zusammenhang auf das Beispiel der Jünger, die Christus nicht zum Himmel fahren lassen wollten, weil sie ihn 'zu sehr liebten nach seiner menschlichen Natur', eine Haltung die dem Kommen des Geistes im Wege ist. Auch Maria Magdalena, ein beliebtes Identifikationsmodell für viele mittelalterliche Frauen, hat in Marguerites Sicht Christus zu sehr in einer menschlichen, affektiven Weise geliebt, als sie ihn suchte beim Grab. Sie hatte noch nicht eingesehen, daß sie ihn in sich selbst finden sollte.[29]

Marguerite richtet sich gegen die Tendenz, das Göttliche zu lokalisieren und zu stark an den menschlichen Jesus zu binden. Der göttliche

---

27 Zentral im *Mirouer* sind die fünfte und sechste Stufe, von denen die sechste (die ekstatische Entrückung) auch aus anderen Einteilungen des mystischen Weges bekannt ist. Die fünfte Stufe ist jedoch originell und charakteristisch für den *Mirouer*.
Über diese Erkenntnis siehe z.B. Blanca Garì, "Der Weg zum 'Land der Freiheit' im Spiegel der einfachen Seelen von Margareta Porete" in: Andrea Günter und Ulrike Wagener, *Was bedeutet es heute feministische Theologin zu sein?* Jahrbuch der Europäischen Gesellschaft für theologische Forschung von Frauen 4 (Mainz: Grünewald/Kampen: Kok Pharos 1996), 140-154.

28 Z.B. *Mirouer* 11, 54-56; 71, 3-7.

29 *Mirouer* 123-124, (Gnädinger 186-191).

Geliebte, der in ihrem Buch zentral ist, ist nicht so sehr Christus, sondern Frau Liebe (Dame Amour), die auch mit Gott selbst und mit dem Heiligen Geist gleichgestellt wird.[30] An die Stelle einer greifbaren Gestalt tritt die unbegreifliche Liebe, der unfassbare Geist, der weht wohin er will und nicht festgelegt werden kann. Den unbekannten Geliebten kann man nur finden, indem man ihn losläßt und aufgibt. Nach Marguerite könnte er nie an bestimmte Orte und Gegenstände gebunden sein. Sie nennt diejenigen, die Gott in Kirchen, Klöstern, Gebeten, Worten und Schriften suchen 'Esel', weil sie nicht einsehen, daß Gott überall ist:

> DIE SEELE: Solche Leute, spricht diese Seele, die ich Esel nenne, suchen Gott in den Geschöpfen, durch Gebete in den Kirchen, im geschaffenen Paradies, in Menschenworten und in Schriften. ... Den Unerfahrenen scheint es, daß solche Leute, die ihn auf Bergen und in Tälern suchen, in der Annahme lebten, daß Gott seinen Sakramenten und seinen Werken unterworfen sei. Ach weh! Was schaffen sie sich für Beschwerden, es ist zum Erbarmen! ... Doch jene haben gute und gewinnreiche Zeiten, die Gott nicht allein in Kirchen und Münstern, sondern an allen Orten anbeten durch die Übereinstimmung mit dem göttlichen Willen.[31]

Es wird nicht verwundern, daß eine spezielle Devotion zur Eucharistie im *Spiegel* fehlt, obwohl Marguerite die Präsenz Christi im Altarsakrament voraussetzt. Die Bedeutung und Funktion der Sakramente ist beschränkt; sie gehören zur göttlichen Pädagogik, zur Übungsschule, die die Seele durchlaufen muss, bevor sie Gott in sich selbst gefunden hat und der Heilige Geist selbst sie unterrichtet. Mit großer Dreistigkeit behauptet Marguerite, daß Messen und Predigten für die freie Seele nicht länger von Bedeutung sind; sie geht zur Messe nur aufgrund guter Gewohnheit oder der Vorschriften der Kirche.[32]

Daß Marguerites Aussagen manchen kirchlichen Autoritäten nicht gefällig waren, läßt sich denken. Marguerite war sich dessen offenbar bewußt, wie der Aufbau ihres Buches, das größtenteils die Form einer Disputation zwischen Liebe, Vernunft und der Seele hat, aufweist. Bedeutungsvoll ist, daß Vernunft nicht nur auftritt als eine der Tugenden, sondern auch als die Lehrerin der irdischen, institutionellen Kirche, von Mar-

30 Vgl. *Mirouer* 21, 44-46: 'Je suis Dieu, dit Amour, car Amour est Dieu, et Dieu est amour, et ceste Ame est Dieu par condicion d'amour...' (Gnädinger 51) und 110, 34-35: '... Amour, qui est le Saint Esperit...'(Gnädinger 161).

31 *Mirouer* 69, 35-48 (Gnädinger 108).

32 *Mirouer* 7, 29-32 (Gnädinger 25); 9, 19-20 (Gnädinger 27); 85, 17-25 (Gnädinger 131).

guerite Heilige Kirche-die-Kleine (Saincte Eglise-la-Petite) genannt. Mehrmals ruft Vernunft im Laufe der Dialoge verzweifelt aus, daß eine Seele die solches behauptet wie in diesem Buch in die Irre geht und wohl wahnsinnig sein muß.[33] Liebe, die die Heilige Kirche-die-Grosse (Saincte Eglise-la-Grande) leitet, die unsichtbare Gemeinschaft der freien Seelen, siegt jedoch immer wieder über Vernunft und bringt sie zum Schweigen.[34]

Daß Frau Liebe die Vernunft besiegt, könnte den Eindruck wecken, daß Gefühl, Affekt und Emotion den Vorrang haben in der Liebeseinheit mit dem Göttlichen. Ganz im Gegenteil: Begehren, Verlangen, Affekte und Liebesgefühle gehören zur Lehrschule der Vernunft. Auch diese soll die Seele lassen, weil sie die Liebe binden und die Seele versklaven statt sie zu befreien:

> DIE VERNUNFT: Nun denn, Liebe!, spricht die Vernunft. Wann befinden sich solche Seelen in der richtigen Freiheit der reinen Liebe?
>
> DIE LIEBE: Wenn sie keinerlei Begehren, auch keinerlei Empfinden und zu keiner Zeit irgendwelche geistige Anhänglichkeiten haben. Denn eine derartige Lebensgewohnheit würde sie in Knechtschaft bringen, weil sie zu weit entfernt ist vom Frieden der Freiheit, in dem nur wenige Leute sich niederlassen.[35]

Die Süßigkeit von Tröstungen und Liebesgefühlen, die in Margaretha Ebners *Offenbarungen* zutiefst ersehnte, handgreifliche Beweise der göttlichen Liebe sind, haben für die freie Seele im *Spiegel* ihre Bedeutung verloren. Sie hat den Schenker gefunden und sehnt sich nicht mehr nach den Geschenken.

Einer der revolutionärsten Sätze Marguerites, der sich mit offizieller Kirchenlehre nur schwer vereinbaren ließ, betrifft die Freiheit der vernichteten Seele 'der Natur zu geben, was sie verlangt', das heisst: ihre 'natürlichen Bedürfnisse' zu befriedigen. In den ersten Stadien des mystischen Lebens wird die Seele, ganz wie es auch Margaretha beschreibt, alles, was dem Leibe Lust und Behagen verschafft nach dem Beispiel Jesu Christi vermeiden müssen. Wenn die Seele jedoch von Frau Liebe aus der Sklaverei der Tugenden befreit ist, kann sie tun, was sie will. Sie kann sich aller 'geschaffenen Dinge' bedienen, weil sie nach ihrer harten und langen

33 Z.B. *Mirouer* 8, 4-10 (Gnädinger 25).

34 Über die zwei Kirchen siehe z.B. *Mirouer* 19 (Gnädinger 47, 48) and 43, 1-19 (Gnädinger 76, 77).

35 *Mirouer* 24, 3-9 (Gnädinger 54-55).

Übung die natürlichen Triebe unter Kontrolle hat und der 'Natur' frei gegenüber steht. Mit Marguerites Worten:

> (DAS GÖTTLICHE RECHT):... weshalb sollten sich solche Seelen ein Gewissen daraus machen, das zu nehmen, was ihnen fehlt, wenn die Not es verlangt? Dies bedeutete für solche Seelen einen Mangel an Unschuld und ein Hindernis zum Frieden, in dem diese Seele sich ausruht von allen Dingen. Wer wäre das, der sich ein Gewissen daraus machen müsste, von den vier Elementen das zu beanspruchen, dessen er bedarf, wie das Licht des Himmels, die Wärme des Feuers, der Tau des Wassers und die Erde, die uns erhält? Wir beanspruchen den Dienst der vier Elemente in jeder Weise, in der die Natur ihrer bedarf, ohne den Einspruch der Vernunft. Diese freigebigen Elemente wurden von Gott erschaffen wie die anderen Dinge. Und daher machen solche Seelen von allen gemachten und erschaffenen Dingen Gebrauch, so wie die Natur ihrer bedarf, in einem solchen Herzensfrieden, wie sie ihn der Erde gegenüber einhalten, auf der sie gehen.[36]

Die Aussagen Marguerite Poretes über die freie Befriedigung natürlicher Bedürfnisse an Schlaf, Nahrung, Kleidung und dergleichen befinden sich in schroffem Gegensatz zur allgemeinen asketischen Tendenz des mittelalterlichen religiösen Lebens. Sie bedeuten soviel wie eine Befreiung des Körpers. Die leibliche Identifikation mit Christus im körperlichen Leiden durch Krankheit und Selbstkasteiung, die den Text Margaretha Ebners weithin beherrscht, spielt bei Marguerite kaum eine Rolle. Nur die noch unfreie Seele wird die körperlichen Triebe zähmen und bekämpfen müssen, aber wenn sie die Natur besiegt hat, kann sie dem Körper zugestehen was er braucht. Er ist nun dem Leiden enthoben und vor Krankheiten bewahrt, weil er geübt ist und weil die Freiheit der Seele sich mit Krankheit nicht verträgt. Nicht nur ist die Seele zurückgekehrt zu ihrem ursprünglichen Zustand, auch der Körper hat den Stand der Unschuld des Paradieses wiedergewonnen und ist ein gehorsames Instrument der Seele, die frei über ihn verfügen kann. Marguerite durchbricht damit die Überzeugung, daß die wahre schuldlose Leiblichkeit ausschließlich an dem Leib Christi gebunden ist und, daß der Körper nur in der Gleichförmigkeit an diesem leidenden Leib der Gnade teilhaftig wird. Bei Marguerite wird die Bindung des Körpers an den menschlichen Christus zu einer begrenzten Stufe des spirituellen Lebens, die abgelöst wird von einem Stand körperlicher Unschuld, der jeden weiteren Zwang überflüssig macht. Damit lehnt sie den vor allem Frauen empfohlenen Leidenskult ab.[37] Für die von

---

36 *Mirouer* 17, 37-50 (Gnädinger 46).

37 So auch: Amy Hollywood, "Suffering Transformed: Marguerite Porete, Meister

der Inquisition beauftragten Begutachter des *Mirouer* war diese Auffassung offenbar nicht zulässig. Die Freiheit körperliche Bedürfnisse zu befriedigen wurde unvermeidlich mit sexueller Zügellosigkeit assoziiert. Marguerites sorgfältige Erklärung, daß eine freie Seele nie etwas unternehmen wird, was Gott verboten hat,[38] wurde offensichtlich von ihren Gegnern übersehen.

Es ist jedoch nicht wahrscheinlich, daß nur die moralische Entrüstung kirchlicher Würdenträger Marguerites Verurteilung herbeigeführt hat. Die Aufrechterhaltung der Bindung der Spiritualität an den Leib Christi war für die Kirche von größtem Interesse. Beginen wie Marguerite Porete, die diesen Spiritualitätstypus vertraten und die leibliche Identifizierung mit Christus relativierten, wurden der Häresie verdächtigt und verfolgt. Daß es viele Frauen gegeben hat, die in ihrem Geiste ein religiöses Leben praktizierten und theologisierten, läßt sich aus den Verurteilungen von Beginen (und ihrer männlichen Variante, den Begarden) als sogenannte 'Ketzer des Freien Geistes' schließen. Kurz nach Marguerites Hinrichtung wurden auf dem Vienner Konzil in der Bulle *Ad Nostrum* 'Irrtümer' gewisser Beginen und Begarden bezüglich der Vollkommenheit (dem höchsten Stand des mystischen Lebens) formuliert, die zu Verfolgungen der Beginen bis ins 15. Jahrhundert führten. Die Häretiker hätten laut der Bulle u.a. gelehrt, daß der Mensch in diesem Leben einen solchen Grad der Vollkommenheit erreichen kann, daß er nicht mehr sündigen könne, die Übung der Tugenden und die Enthaltsamkeit aufgeben kann und dem natürlichen Geschlechtstrieb folgen soll. Den Leib Christi bräuchten sie nicht zu ehren und kirchlichen Vorschriften seien sie nicht länger unterworfen, denn 'wo der Geist des Herrn ist, ist Freiheit'. In anderen polemischen Berichten von Bekämpfern der 'Brüder und Schwester des Freien Geistes' heißt es, daß diese aus der Überzeugung, daß Gott selbst in ihnen wirke, gefolgert hätten, daß ihnen jede Freveltat erlaubt sei. Vor allem könnten sie ohne Scham und Skrupel ihre sexuellen

---

Eckhart and the Problem of Women's Spirituality" in: Bernard McGinn (ed.), *Meister Eckhart and the Beguine Mystics* (New York: Continuum 1994), 87-113. Die Untersuchungen Caroline Walker Bynums haben gezeigt, daß die Teilnahme an Christi Leiden in Krankheitszuständen und durch Selbstkasteiung (bis zur Verstümmelung) sowie die Nahrungsverweigerung aus dem Verlangen, nur von der Hostie als Leib Christi zu leben, vor allem in Texten von und über Frauen vorkommen und als typische 'Frauenthemen' zu betrachten sind [Vergl. Anm. 9].

38 *Mirouer* 9, 22-25.

Lüste ausleben, was sie auch in ihren geheimen Zusammenkünften getan hätten.[39] Da das Schreckensbild von Libertinismus, Anarchismus und sexueller Zügellosigkeit sich schon in den Ketzerbeschreibungen der alten Kirche befindet und auch im Mittelalter zu den festen Bestandteilen der Ketzerpolemik gehört, ist die Glaubwürdigkeit dieser Beschuldigungen von Anarchismus und Immoralität zweifelhaft. Die Vergöttlichungsmystik, die auch manche Beginen offenbar vertraten und vielleicht wie Marguerite in Texten erörtert haben, erscheint in den Darstellungen ihrer Gegner im Zerrbild der Orgie. Die Furcht, daß die Beginen insgesamt von dieser Häresie angesteckt seien, führte zur Aufhebung zahlreicher Beginengemeinschaften vor allem im Rheinland und zur Überprüfung der Rechtgläubigkeit selbst der streng beaufsichtigten belgischen Beginenhöfe.

Die Stereotypen des Weiblichen und die Disziplinierung der religiösen Frauen

Obwohl die Zeugnisse verketzerter Gruppen wegen deren Marginalisierung spärlich sind, dürfen die Äusserungen religiöser Frauen, die andere Spiritualitäten vertraten als die von der Kirche sanktionierten, nicht außer Betracht gelassen werden. Jede Auswertung der mittelalterlichen Frauenspiritualität sollte damit rechnen, daß den Betätigungen religiöser Frauen bestimmte Grenzen gesetzt waren und, daß diese Grenzen im Laufe der Zeit verschärft wurden. Es handelt sich dabei m.E. nicht nur um kirchliche Maßnahmen die anti-häretischen Motiven entsprossen, sondern auch um Begrenzungen, die mit bestimmten stereotypen Auffassungen 'des Weiblichen' und der Geschlechterrollen zusammenhängen. Stereotypen des Weiblichen fungierten schon in der Griechisch-Römischen Welt als strukturierendes Prinzip der Gesellschaft und des Weltbildes und haben ihren Einfluß in der abendländischen Kultur nicht verloren. Oppositionen wie Geist-Körper, Vernunft-Gefühl sind als Konstruktionen der sexuellen Differenz bis auf den heutigen Tag wirksam und waren es auch im Mittelalter.[40]

---

[39] Über die Ketzerei des Freien Geistes, siehe vor allem: Robert E. Lerner, *The Heresy of the Free Spirit in the Later Middle Ages* (Berkeley usw. 1972).

[40] Über Stereotypen des Weiblichen in verschiedenen religiösen Traditionen, siehe: Ria Kloppenborg and Wouter J. Hanegraaff, *Female Stereotypes in Religious Traditons* (Leiden: Brill 1995). Siehe auch: Caroline Walker Bynum e.a. (ed.),

Für die mittelalterlichen Vitenschreiber waren diese Oppositionen eine Selbstverständlichkeit, die sie häufig anwandten, um die verschiedenen religiösen Aufgaben von Männern und Frauen zu umschreiben. So behauptet Abt Philipp von Clairvaux, der um 1267 seine Biographie der Elisabeth von Spalbeek aufzeichnete, daß Männer durch Schreiben und Predigen das Evangelium verkünden sollen.[41] Frauen aber hätten eine spezielle Begabung Christus in seiner Menschlichkeit nachzufolgen, nämlich durch die Abbildung seines Leidens in ihren Körpern in einer visuellen, dramatischen Darstellung.[42] Auch in anderen Biographien von religiösen Frauen in den südlichen Niederlanden fällt auf, daß Tätigkeiten, Haltungen und Eigenschaften, die als typisch weiblich galten, in den Vordergrund gestellt werden. Was die Vitenschreiber in hohem Maße an ihren Heldinnen bewundern, ist ihre besondere Begabung zur Ekstase, ihre emotionelle und leibliche Expression und ihre strenge leibliche Askese. Ihnen wird eine spezielle Fähigkeit zum Enthusiasmus (in-Gott-sein) zur Verkörperung und Inkarnation (Maria!) zugeschrieben, das dem Mann fehlt oder das er von der Frau lernen muß. Zur gleichen Zeit weisen die Hagiographen immer wieder darauf hin, daß solche Frauen, die im religiösen Leben ihrer Zeit einen großen Einfluß ausübten, die Kompetenz des männlichen Klerus in keiner Weise bedrohten. So wird oft behauptet, daß die heilige Frau in ekstatischer Entrückung Latein gesprochen hätte, ohne jedoch diese Sprache jemals gelernt zu haben. Mehrfach wird den Leser(inne)n beteuert, daß die heiligen Frauen zwar die Schrift auslegen konnten, aber daß sie dies nur zur Not und mit Widerwillen taten, weil es in ihren Augen die Aufgabe der gelehrten Geistlichkeit war.[43] Die Oppo-

Gender and Religion: On the Complexity of Symbols (Boston: Beacon Press 1986).

41 Siehe: Walter Simons and Johanna Ziegler, "Phenomenal Religion in the Thirteenth Century and its Image: Elisabeth of Spalbeek and the Passion Cult" in: W.J. Sheils and Diana Wood (ed.), *Women in the Church* (Oxford: Blackwell 1990), 117-126.

42 Für diesen Hagiographen ist Elisabeth eine Christusikone. Sie hätte auch ein Holzgemälde in ihrem Besitz auf dem der gekreuzigte Christus abgebildet ist und an das sie sich klammert, ähnlich wie Margaretha Ebner das Kruzifix umarmt. In Augenblicken der Ekstase würden ihre Lippen so fest an diesem Bild haften, daß kein Mensch sie davon hätte loslösen können.

43 Siehe z.B. Bolton, "Vitae Matrum" 269,270 und Anke Passenier, "'Women on the Loose': Stereotypes of Women in the Story of the Medieval Beguines" in: Kloppenborg en Hanegraaff, *Female stereotypes* 75-81.

sition von der Ekstatikerin, die das Göttliche auf Grund einer speziellen Offenbarung verkündet, und dem gelehrten Geistlichen, der dies auf Grund seines Amtes und Studiums macht, gehört zu den Topoi der Hagiographie.

Das Gleiche gilt m.E. für den damit verbundenen Gegensatz zwischen der heiligen Frau, die sich in ihrem Körper mit Christus identifiziert, und dem heiligen Mann, der Christus in einem besitzlosen Wanderleben, predigend und unterrichtend in der Öffentlichkeit nachfolgt. Aus den Lebensbeschreibungen der belgischen religiösen Frauen geht jedoch zugleich hervor, daß sie die Nachfolge Christi in der Öffentlichkeit manchmal doch erstrebten. Jakob von Vitry berichtet, daß Maria von Oignies gerne gepredigt hätte, aber daß ihr das als Frau nicht zukam. Sie gibt sich deshalb damit zufrieden als Jakobs unermüdliche Beraterin und Seelenführerin aufzutreten, durch die ihm die Inspiration zur Predigt zufließt.[44] Auch berichtet er an anderer Stelle wie Maria sich entschlossen hatte wegzuziehen um ein Wanderleben in der Nachfolge Christi zu führen und für ihren Lebensunterhalt zu betteln. Nur die dringenden Bitten ihrer Verwandten, diesen Vorsatz aufzugeben, konnten sie zurückhalten.[45] Offenbar hatten religiöse Frauen, die von dem Streben nach einem Leben in den Fußspuren Christi ergriffen waren, oft die gleichen Wünsche wie ihre männlichen Gefährten. Diese Wünsche mußten sie jedoch im Laufe der Institutionalisierung der religiösen Bewegung wegen ihres Geschlechtes aufgeben.

Aus kirchlichen Anordnungen und Maßnahmen wird ersichtlich, daß es viele Beginen gab, die sich den Frauen gesetzten Schranken nicht fügten.[46] Manche führten ein Wanderleben oder widmeten sich—wie Marguerite Porete—der religiös-mystischen Unterrichtung anderer in lehrhaften Schriften. Daß vor allem die theologische Betätigung mancher Beginen den Autoritäten ein Dorn im Auge war, geht aus der auf dem Vienner Konzil aufgestellten Bulle *Cum de quibusdam mulieribus* hervor. Das Konzil hatte sich laut dieser Bulle dazu entschlossen, den ganzen Beginenstand aufzuheben, weil Beginen ein religiöses Leben führten ohne Gehorsamkeitsgelübde und ohne anerkannte Regel. Zudem würden man-

---

44 *VMO* 654.

45 *VMO* 648.

46 Über diese kirchlichen Anordnungen, siehe: Passenier, "Women on the Loose" (wie Anm. 55).

che Beginen wie Wahnsinnige über die Trinität und das Wesen Gottes disputieren und predigen, und Auffassungen bezüglich den Glaubensartikeln und den Sakramenten der Kirche verbreiten, die sich mit dem katholischen Glauben nicht vereinbaren ließen. Deshalb müsse der Beginenstand für immer verboten und die Beginen ganz und gar aus der Kirche verbannt werden. Nach einer Zeit vielfacher Verfolgungen und Belästigungen durch kirchliche und weltliche Obrigkeiten war der unstete Teil der Beginenbewegung letzten Endes gebändigt.[47] Schließlich stand für Frauen fast nur noch die Möglichkeit einer klösterlichen Lebensweise innerhalb einer Abtei, eines Drittordenskonvents oder eines vom Klerus beaufsichtigten Beginenhofes offen.[48] Ihre Identifikation mit Christus sollte eine private sein in der Abgeschlossenheit der klausurierten Gemeinschaft und in dem 'geschlossenen Garten' (hortus conclusus) ihres Körpers.[49] Ihre theologische Betätigung wurde begrenzt auf das Gebiet der Privatoffenbarung, der Ekstase, der Visionen und Erscheinungen.

Auffassungen bezüglich der Geschlechterrollen und Vorstellungen von Weiblichkeit und Männlichkeit haben zweiffellos im Prozess der Disziplinierung religiöser Frauen eine Rolle gespielt. Die Heiligenviten und die Maßnahmen gegen verdächtige religiöse Frauen sind getragen von einer Denkart, in der das Männliche mit Geist, Vernunft, Sprechen, Wort, und das Weibliche mit Körper, Gefühl, Schweigen, Bild, assoziiert wird.

---

47 Da diese radikale Anordnung auch Beginen traf, die unter Aufsicht des Klerus ein geregeltes Leben führten und nicht literarisch und theologisch tätig waren, hat man später eine Klausel zugefügt, um die geregelten Beginen, die sich theologischen Disputationen enthielten, von den Maßnahmen auszunehmen.

48 Über den Prozess der Disziplinierung, siehe z.B.: Brenda M. Bolton, "Some Thirteenth Century Women in the Low countries - A Special Case?" in: *Nederlands Archief voor Kerkgeschiedenis* 61 (1981), 7-29.

49 Das vielseitige, im Mittelalter sehr geläufige Bild des 'hortus conclusus' ist u.a. dem biblischen Hohenlied entnommen, wo die Geliebte in den Garten (hortus) des Geliebten eingeladen wird (VI,2), aber auch selbst als Garten angedeutet wird: 'Hortus conclusus amica mea' (IV,12). Auch weist der Garten hin auf den verlorenen Lustgarten des Paradieses, und auf den himmlischen Paradiesgarten, wo der göttliche Geliebte seine Jungfrauen zum Tanz auffordert und zur Hochzeit einlädt. Das von der Welt abgeschlossene Kloster oder die Klausnerzelle konnten auch als 'hortus conclusus' aufgefasst werden. Eine wichtige Rolle spielt das Bild des geschlossenen Gartens auch im *Rosenroman*, wo er vor allem Garten der Verführung ist, in den der Liebhaber einzudringen sucht um seine Geliebte zu verführen und den streng bewachten Rosenknopf zu pflücken. Siehe z.B.: René Louis, *Le Roman de la Rose. Essai d'interprétation de l'allégorisme érotique* (Paris: Honoré Champion 1974), 33-38.

Wo christliche Traditionen über Maria als Mutter Gottes sich mit den traditionellen Stereotypen verbinden, wird die Frau ganz besonders zur Hüterin der Inkarnation. Selbstverständlich ist diese Denkweise nicht beschränkt auf die Darstellungen von Frauen aus männlicher Perspektive. Sie bestimmt auch die Weise in der Frauen sich selbst definieren und präsentieren sowie die literarischen Gattungen, die sie zur Artikulierung ihrer Erfahrungen und Ansichten angewandt haben.[50]

Dies könnte durchaus auch auf die *Offenbarungen* Margaretha Ebners zutreffen. In der älteren Forschung wurde dieser Text oft als das Produkt einer einfältigen, ungebildeten Frau betrachtet.[51] Trotzdem enthält er aber einige, mehr spekulativ ausgerichtete Stellen—z.B. über das Einkehren in 'Gottes wilde Einheit'—, die eine nähere Bekanntschaft mit dem mystisch-theologischen Diskurs voraussetzen.[52] Siegfried Ringler hat gezeigt, daß diese Texte weniger als Erfahrungsberichte, sondern als mystische Lehre in Vitenform konzipiert seien. Es werde von geläufigen literarischen Gattungen und Traditionen Gebrauch gemacht und es gebe eine rhetorische Struktur, die das Ganze beherrscht.[53] Gertrud Jaron Lewis kombiniert diese neuen literarischen Einsichten mit einer Berücksichtigung vom historischen 'Sitz im Leben' der mittelalterlichen Frauenkonvente zu einer ausgeglichenen Sicht.[54] Die Anwendung dieser neuentwickelten Perspektiven auf die *Offenbarungen* legt nahe, daß die Betonung des Leiblich-Affektiven, die diesen Text kennzeichnet, von dem was man von Frauen auf theologischem und literarischen Gebiet erwartete, mitbestimmt wurde.

---

50 Claudia Opitz hat darauf hingewiesen, daß die süddeutschen Nonnen sich in ihren *Nonnenbüchern* oft bestimmter literarischer Gattungen bedienten, die als spezifisch weiblich betrachtet wurden, wahrscheinlich weil diese ihnen zukamen und andere nicht. Sie hätten religiöses Erleben und nicht Lehre in ihren Texten formuliert, weil die Domäne der Spekulation und der theologischen Argumentation Männern vorbehalten war und nicht weil sie als Frauen anders dachten und fühlten. Siehe Claudia Opitz, "'... zu schriben von gutten und selgen schwestern uebung'" in: *Die Frauenfeder* (Weingarten 1986) 75-104.

51 Siehe z.B.: Ludwig Zoepf, *Die Mystikerin Margaretha Ebner (ca. 1291-1351)* (Leipzig und Berlin 1914).

52 Strauch, *Margaretha Ebner* 76.

53 Siegfried Ringler, *Viten- und Offenbarungsliteratur in Frauenklöstern des Mittelalters* (München 1980).

54 Siehe Gertrud Jaron Lewis, *By Women, For Women, About Women: The Fourteenth-Century Sister-Books* (Toronto: Pontifical Institute 1995/6).

Nicht alle Frauen haben sich diesen Erwartungen gefügt. Es waren auch nicht nur Frauen, die sich der Gattung des Erfahrungstextes bedienten. Auch von Männern sind Texte erhalten, in denen sie sich als 'Braut Christi' präsentieren und in denen das Leiblich-Affektive eine große Rolle spielt.[55] Die religiösen und theologischen Artikulierungen von Männern und Frauen waren anscheinend nicht so scharf voneinander getrennt wie die Heiligenleben vermuten lassen. Offenbar präsentieren uns die Hagiographen ein Bild von der religiösen Rollenverteilung, das mit dem was aus den Texten von Männern und Frauen selbst hervorgeht nicht ganz übereinstimmt.

Amy Hollywood hat festgestellt, daß die leibliche Identifikation mit dem leidenden Christus vor allem von der Hagiographie betont wurde. Hollywood weist auf den Unterschied zwischen der anonymen *Vita* der Zisterzienserin Beatrijs von Nazareth (1200-1268), in dem körperliche Vorgänge im Vordergrund stehen, und dem von Beatrijs selbst geschriebenen mystischen Traktat, *Seven Manieren van Minne*, hin. In dem Traktat handelt es sich vielmehr um innere Prozesse, während das Heiligenleben, das die Präsenz Gottes sichtbar machen will, sich traditionell an das Äußere hält und innere Abläufe in äußere Geschehnisse verwandelt.[56] Welche Quellen man bei der Darstellung der mittelalterlichen Frauenspiritualität als Ausgangspunkt wählt, ist also von entscheidender Bedeutung. Dies gilt auch für die Texte, die von Frauen selbst verfaßt wurden und die verschiedener Gattung sein können. So ergibt sich aus den oft als Musterbeispiel der leiblich-affektiven Mystik herangezogenen *Visionen* der brabantischen Mystikerin Hadewijch (13. Jahrhundert), ein ganz anderes Bild als aus ihren *Briefen*.[57] Letztere haben einen mehr argumentierenden Charakter und betonen die Nachfolge Christi in Nächstenliebe und Tugendwerken. Auf jeden Fall treten aus dem mittelalterlichen Quellen-

---

55 Z.B. Friedrich Sunder, Klosterkaplan des Frauenklosters Engelthal, erzählt in seinem Gnadenleben, wie er das Jesuskind an den Brüsten seiner Seele säugt. Text bei Ringler, *Viten- und Offenbarungsliteratur* 391-444.

56 Hollywood, "Suffering transformed" 91-93. Siehe auch: Else Marie Wiberg Pedersen, "Image of God-Image of Mary-Image of Women: On the Theology and Spirituality of Beatrice of Nazareth" in: *Cistercian Studies Quarterly* 29/2 (1994) 209-220.

57 Über Hadewijch siehe z.B.: Paul Mommaers, *Hadewijch. Schrijfster, Begijn, Mystica* (Averbode/Kampen: Kok 1989).

material eine Vielfältigkeit und eine Diskontinuität hervor, woraus sich kein eindeutiges Bild ergibt.[58]

Von dieser Diversität in der modernen Historiographie und Mystikforschung läßt sich kaum eine Spur auffinden. Im Allgemeinen wird Weiblichkeit mit Leiblichkeit und Empfindsamkeit gleichgesetzt, und dies oft im negativen Sinn. Vor allem in der nach-Freudschen religionspsychologisch orientierten Forschung wurden die Nonnenviten negativ bewertet als Niederschlag krankhafter Hysterieanfälle und sexueller Obsessionen. Die strenge Klausur, die den Nonnen auferlegt worden war, hätte zu neurotischen Defekten und psychischer Deformierung geführt und in ihren mystischen Erlebnissen hätten sie verdrängte weibliche Wünsche nach sexueller Erfüllung, Schwanger- und Mutterschaft sublimiert.[59] Auch in der eher theologisch ausgerichteten Mystikforschung herrschte lange Zeit eine negative Einschätzung der Frauenmystik vor. Häufig wurden die Nonnenviten aufgefasst als geschmacklose Dokumente einer entarteten Erlebnismystik oder Pseudo-mystik, in die schaulustige Nonnen die mystischen Lehren ihrer Prediger umgesetzt hätten. Die Frauenmystik sei der Unfähigkeit der Nonnen, die mystischen Spekulationen ihrer gelehrten dominikanischen Prediger und Seelsorger richtig zu verstehen und dem 'verflachten Gefühlsleben' einer Niedergangszeit der Mystik erwachsen.[60] Gegen die bislang negative oder zumindest herablassende Interpretation vieler frauenmystischer Texte in der hauptsächlich von Männern betriebenen Forschung wurde in den letzten Dezennien zunehmend Stellung genommen. Die Leiblichkeit und Emotionalität die als typisch weiblich und zugleich als pathologisch, entartet oder kindlich-naiv abqualifiziert wurden, bekamen in manchen feministischen Studien eine positive Konnotation. Für Luce Irigaray, die sich der 'Hysterie'-Qualifikation männlicher Psychoanalytiker widersetzt, kennzeichnen Körperlichkeit, Innerlichkeit

---

58 Inwiefern Darstellungen der mittelalterlichen Frauenspiritualität mitbestimmt sind durch die Gattung der benutzten Quellen und durch die Topik der Hagiographie, bleibt so vorläufig eine interessante Frage.

59 Siehe z.B. Oskar Pfister, "Hysterie und Mystik bei Margaretha Ebner (1291-1351)" in: *Zentralblatt für Psychoanalyse* 1. Jg. (1911) 10/12, 468-485 und Mela Escherich, "Das Visionenwesen in den mittelalterlichen Frauenklöstern" in: *Deutsche Psychologie* 1 (1918), 153-166.

60 Siehe z.B.: Walter Blank, "Umsetzung der Mystik in den Frauenklöstern" in: Hans H. Hofstätter, *Mystik am Oberrhein und in benachbarten Gebieten* (Freiburg 1977), 25-36.

und Affektivität den weiblichen Weg der (Gottes)erfahrung. Die Frage ist jedoch, ob damit nicht Weiblichkeitsstereotypen wiederbelebt werden, die die Vielfältigkeit des religiösen Lebens und der theologischen Artikulation von mittelalterlichen religiösen Frauen unberücksichtigt lassen.

Schlußbemerkung

Es läßt sich nicht leugnen, daß die Sprache des Körpers und des Bildes für viele mittelalterliche Frauen wichtige Ausdrucksmittel ihrer Gotteserfahrung darstellten. Männer haben sich dieser Mittel viel seltener bedient und manchmal Frauen darum bewundert und beneidet. Im Mittelalter wurden die Erfahrungen religiöser Frauen, wie Margaretha Ebner, nicht als krankhaft abqualifiziert, sondern als eine spezielle Form göttlicher Offenbarung betrachtet, die besonders Frauen vorbehalten war. Man hielt Frauen für fähig, eine spezifische Verbindung mit dem Göttlichen herzustellen, nämlich in der Ekstase und in ihrem Körper. Ihnen wurde eine besondere Begabung zum Enthusiasmus und zur Verkörperung des Göttlichen zugeschrieben. In dieser Rhetorik ist die Frau die Andere (alter) des Mannes und sie kann ihm eine Muse und Seelenführerin sein. Auf diese Weise konnten Frauen sich Anerkennung, Respekt und Autorität erwerben.

Andererseits bedeutet diese Rollenzuweisung auch eine Einschränkung, oft auch im buchstäblichen Sinn. Vor allem aus der Geschichte der Beginenbewegung wird ersichtlich, daß Frauen diese Beschränkung nicht immer akzeptiert haben und Wünsche hegen konnten, die sich in den vorherrschenden Verhältnissen nicht verwirklichen ließen. Die freien Beginen, die in den Fußspuren Christi ohne festen Wohnsitz wanderten und bettelten, wurden nach einiger Zeit gebändigt und verpflichtet in Höfen zu wohnen. Ihre Identifizierung mit Christus sollte sich in dem geschlossenen Garten ihres Körpers vollziehen und konnte nicht die Nachfolge in seinen Fußspuren sein, wie sie Männern vorbehalten blieb. Beginen, die eigene Schriften verfassten und sich an theologischen Diskussionen beteiligten, wurden bald für Ketzerinnen gehalten. Beginen, die eine Freiheit des Geistes über Christus und seinen Leib stellten, konnten verfolgt und sogar verbrannt werden. Vielleicht war ihre Ketzerei auch, und nicht zuletzt, daß sie sündigten gegen die 'Weiblichkeit'.

Abstracts

Modern research often views medieval women's mysticism as a specifically female spirituality, characterised by corporeality and passion. This interpretation is shaped by the concept of sexual difference; Anke Passenier argues that it neglects the spirituality of other medieval women, often labelled 'heretical'. The comparison between the texts of the Dominican nun Margaretha Ebner and the 'heretical' Beguine Marguerite Porete demonstrates that other forms of spirituality did indeed exist. The characterisation of women's spirituality as corporeal is in danger of returning to ancient stereotypes of female which restrict the religious actions of women to visions, ecstatic trances and dramatic expression.

La recherche contemporaine a tendance à considérer la mystique des femmes du Moyen Age comme une spiritualité spécifiquement féminine, caractérisée par la corporalité et la passion. Une interprétation qui dérive du concept de différence sexuelle et qui, comme le démontre Anke Passenier, néglige la spiritualité d'autres femmes médiévales, souvent taxée d'"hérétique". La comparaison entre les écrits de la moniale dominicaine Margaretha Ebner et la béguine "hérétique" Marguerite Porete atteste qu'il existait effectivement d'autres formes de spiritualité. Le fait de définir la spiritualité des femmes comme étant corporelle risque de nous ramener aux vieux stéréotypes du féminin, qui réduisent les actes religieux des femmes à des visions, des transes extatiques et des expressions dramatiques.

Anke PASSENIER (1956) studierte Theologie in Utrecht mit dem Schwerpunkt Kirchengeschichte. Im Moment bereitet sie eine Dissertation vor über Marguerite Porete und die Rolle 'religiöser Frauen' in der spätmittelalterlichen Mystik.

Lesley Orr MACDONALD

A Unique and Glorious Mission? The Work of Presbyterian Women in Victorian Scotland

'She struggles all in vain against a Divine appointment': Womanhood and monstrosity in presbyterian Scotland

In 1898, sixty-one years after Queen Victoria's accession to the throne, an Edinburgh churchwoman gave a stirring address to a parish branch of the Church of Scotland Woman's Guild. It was entitled 'The Rise of Women's Work in the Victorian Era':

> The reign of Victoria has lessons very specially for women. It has opened up in a remarkable manner the sphere of woman's influence and usefulness. It is the fulfilment of the blessing proclaimed at Pentecost, that woman was to come prominently into the work of the Church and the world (Acts 2: 17-18). By its fulfilment we see what this means—to teach, instruct, counsel, to share in the work of the Age. ... It is long past time to apologise for the woman worker, or to argue whether she should be permitted or not. The fact is apparent that she has come into the work of the age—as God's Word foretells—and has come to stay.[1]

The speaker's self-confident assessment of the Victorian era and her bold appropriation of Scriptural prophecy to her own time and situation are typical of the optimistic mood among many upper and middle-class Scottish women at the end of the nineteenth century. Reflecting on the significant and extensive changes which had become possible in their own lives, they believed that women had a distinctive and divinely sanctioned mission to transform society, and usher in a new Golden Age.

Those who exhorted their sisters to assert themselves as agents of human and divine history belonged to a complex process of social and ideological change which affected the industrialising societies of Europe and North America. Especially in the English-speaking Protestant world, the 'Woman Question' was a major defining features of the Victorian era.

---

1 Address reported in *Church of Scotland News of Female Missions* November 1898.

The distinctive religious and cultural context of Scotland has been widely regarded as presenting a somewhat challenging, even intractable environment for those who sought to engage in this contest. In much cultural discourse, it has been maintained that the post-Reformation dominance of Calvinist presbyterianism in particular ways served to subjugate and oppress the women of Scotland. As Barbara Littlewood observes in a recent article:

> In the popular imagination, Scotland is often conceived of as a sexually repressed and repressive culture, with much of the blame put on the special tradition of Protestantism which took root here. Closely linked with this is a misogyny manifest in both violent and non-violent ways, in the burning of witches and the writing out of women from Scottish history.[2]

Of course, witchhunts and misogyny were not peculiar to Scotland, but the Scottish Reformation had the dubious distinction of having been led by a man who achieved enduring notoriety for the intemperate and virulent expression of his views concerning the place of women in church and society. In his *First Blast of the Trumpet Against the Monstrous Regiment of Women* (1558), John Knox declared:

> Nature, I say, doth paint [women] forth to be weak, frail, impatient, feeble and foolish; and experience hath declared them to be unconstant, variable, cruel, and lacking in the spirit of counsel and regiment.[3]

This natural incapacity, believed Knox, was confirmed by the authority of Scripture in Genesis and in the Pastoral Epistles of the New Testament. He was particularly vehement about the curse of Eve:

> After her fall and rebellion committed against God there was put upon her a new necessity, and she was made subject to man by the irrevocable sentence of God...As God should say: "Forasmuch as thou hast abused thy former condition, and because thy free will hath brought thyself and mankind into the bondage of Satan, I therefore will bring thee in bondage to man. For where before thy obedience should have been voluntary, now it shall be by constraint and by necessity; and that because thou hast deceived thy man, thou shalt therefore be no longer mistress over thine own appetites, over thine own will nor desires. For in thee there is neither reason nor discretion which be able to moderate thy affections, and therefore they shall be subject to the desire of thy man. He shall be lord and governor, not only over thy body, but even over thy

2 Barbara Littlewood, "Sex and the Scottish Psyche" in *Cencrastus* 46 (1993) 3.

3 John Knox, "First Blast of the Trumpet Against the Monstrous Regiment of Women" in: Marvin A Breslow, *The Political Writings of John Knox* (Washington: Folger Books 1985) 37-78, here 43.

> appetites and will." This sentence, I say, did God pronounce against Eve and her daughters, as the rest of the Scriptures doth evidently witness. So that no woman can ever presume to reign over man, but the same she must needs do in despite of God and in contempt of his punishment and malediction.[4]

In view of the dangers presented by the daughters of Eve, the Scottish Reformers, and the parochial system of discipline and correction which evolved from the sixteenth century, took very seriously the need to control women's sexual, social and religious lives.[5] It would have been as unthinkable for Knox to imagine women exercising the orderly ministry of teaching and oversight which was so central to the presbyterian ethos as it was distressing for him to contemplate the secular rule of queens.

The religious language and context which shaped the Victorian debate about the 'Woman Question' in Scotland had the distinctive accent of this heritage. As I have noted, it is a truism that the life of this nation was indelibly marked by the post-reformation Kirk, the masculine severity of whose Calvinist doctrines and practices issued in expressions of patriarchy which formalised and encouraged a particularly radical and pernicious oppression of women. But other insights and elements of this heritage were potentially revolutionary resources for women. There was a recognition of spiritual equality; a new emphasis on the participation of the whole people of God (not just a priestly caste) in the liturgy and work of the church; a commitment to literacy so that each person could read and understand the Word of God; and the principle that church organisation was never an end in itself, but as *ecclesia reformata semper reformanda,* had the freedom to change to enable all people to hear the gospel and glorify God.[6] As a Scottish feminist historian, I want to discover whether my own presbyterian tradition served to obstruct or enable the agency and

4 Knox, "First Blast" 45-6.

5 For a brief, illustrated survey of the punishments imposed on women for a range of offences, from gossiping and slander to adultery, harlotry and witchcraft, see Elspeth King, *The Hidden History of Glasgow's Women: The Thenew Factor* (Edinburgh:Mainstream 1993) 25-38. For evidence that there was also widespread resistance and subversion of presbyterian discipline, see Leah Leneman and Rosalind Mitchison, *Sexuality and Social Control* (Oxford: OUP 1990).

6 On the distinctive ethos of Scottish presbyterianism, see eg William Storrar, *Scottish Identity: A Christian Vision* (Edinburgh: 1990); on Calvinist pronouncements and possibilities for women, Jane Dempsey Douglass, *Women, Freedom and Calvin* (Philadelphia: Westminster Press 1986).

empowerment of women in this country. In my search for a 'usable past',[7] the historical task is twofold. First, to research and recover the lives, experiences, ideas and beliefs of 'the voiceless, nameless women...[who] seem to crowd the margin with acts for which there is neither testament nor memorial,'[8] not simply to insert them into otherwise unchanged narratives, but as a basic challenge to historiography, which needs to recognise that all dimensions and structures of the human story have been affected by the diverse experiences of women. And second, to analyse and assess the reality, singularity and extent of the Scottish presbyterian ethos as a source of oppression or liberation in the lives of women in this country.

The Victorian period was a time of social, economic, intellectual, political, religious and psychological upheaval; a period of great change both for women and for the institutional church in Scotland. The rise of evangelicalism; the intellectual legacy of the liberal Enlightenment; challenges to doctrinal orthodoxy; the impact of new studies in physical and social sciences; the human consequences of industrial capitalism: all of these impinged on the 'Woman Question' as they did on presbyterianism. In this article, most of these will remain the unexamined background as I highlight one of the distinctive reformation principles—work—and explore some of the issues for Scottish women who appropriated it to help explain, justify and sanctify their ideas and actions during a period which was marked by a largely new phenomenon in religious and public life: the self-conscious moral and corporate agency of women.[9]

During the Victorian era, the use of the word 'Woman' (singular and capitalised) was very popular in religious, scientific and conversational discourse. It presumed to signify a universal, abstract and stable category, which confidently prescribed all the qualities, defects and characteristics of Woman as a matter of nature and divine intent. One consequence of this essentialism was that individuals who did not conform to the

---

7 Letty M Russell, *Human Liberation in a Feminist Perspective: A Theology* (Philadelphia: Westminster Press 1974) 85.

8 Stevie Davies, *Arms and the Girl* (London: The Women's Press 1992) 69. This powerful novel is set in 1950s rural Scotland.

9 Another important principle, education, was also appropriated by women, but due to lack of space will not be considered here.

definition were conventionally regarded as peculiar, deviant, unsexed or monstrous. In 1871, the Free Church of Scotland *Watchword* magazine contended:

> Ambition, pride, wilfulness or any earthly passion will distort her being. She struggles all in vain against a Divine appointment...Woman's worst enemy is he who would cruelly lift her out of her sphere, and would try to reverse the laws of God and nature on her behalf.[10]

All individual, group and class differences tended to be collapsed into a reified theory of Womanhood, which purported to be timeless and universal, but was actually constructed on a bourgeois model: itself subject to considerable modification. Nevertheless, it encouraged the unfortunate habit of making sweeping assertions about what 'Woman' could or could not do. In particular, Woman was excluded from the public territory of autonomous political and economic agency, and hence, by virtue of her nature, from the making of history.

I want to challenge the assumption that the absence of women from historical accounts is to be ascribed to such a natural order, whereby the biological constitution of the female gender determines all women's roles and functions as essentially private and ahistorical. One of the insights of contemporary contextual and liberation theologies (including those developed by feminists) is that liberation is not simply a goal, but a dynamic process which affirms the possibility of personal and social transformation. That process, by demonstrating the exercise of agency, humanises those who struggle to transcend the givenness, the objectivity, the 'non-being' state of existence. I contend that the real, embodied, complex women of the nineteenth century resisted the confines of archetype and were moral agents with the capacity

> to respond creatively and critically to their environment instead of simply taking it as given. Whether symbolised religiously or otherwise, the exercise [of morality] as a critical response to life is the basic means by which human beings are creatures not simply of nature, but of history and culture. The world is not simply given but constructed.[11]

From the beginning of Victoria's reign, work and education were important components (though not the only ones) of female endeavours to

10 "Woman's Work and Mission", in *The Watchword* (1871) 81.

11 Ruth L Smith, "Moral Transcendence and Moral Space in the Historical Experiences of Women" in *Journal of Feminist Studies in Religion* (Fall 1988) 24.

understand and construct alternative worlds; expanding, transforming and in some instances rejecting altogether the religious and domestic ideology which circumscribed their lives. Protestant women increasingly seized upon the concept of 'Women's Mission' to justify and interpret their moral agency in religious work, philanthropy, social and political campaigns. Other women, both in Scotland and abroad, had to deal with that mission as its objects. They responded to the message and its bearers in a variety of ways which belie facile stereotypes of passive acceptance or belligerent rejection.

'A sentimental priesthood': the work of women in the heavenly home

In post-Reformation Scotland, the institutions, structures and official work of the church were understood to be the exclusive province of men. The supreme Christian duty of women (who no longer had the option of a celibate conventual life) was to fulfil, in submission and obedience, the role of wife, mother and housekeeper. By the nineteenth century, it was a widely accepted convention that the Reformation had been a great benefit to women, because it dignified marriage. The hierarchy of human ranks was regarded as a positive blessing, designed to preserve order against the chaos of rule by the weak or infirm. The Christian ideal for marriage was a kind of loving despotism, founded on such texts as Ephesians 5:22-3.

Enlightenment philosophy challenged some of the more rigorous and austere elements of scholastic Calvinist theology, but confirmed the patriarchal family as the basis for political, legal, economic and personal relationships of inequality between the sexes.[12] During the nineteenth century, the function of the patriarchal family, as the main social unit in relation to the state, underwent considerable change, as the concept of individual citizenship took hold. However, the series of Reform Acts, beginning in 1832, were explicit in formalising the continued exclusion of women from political power in Britain. And the family remained a key

---

12 There is an extensive literature discussing Enlightenment philosophies, liberal politics and gender issues. See eg L M G Clark and L Lange (eds.), *The Sexism of Social and Political Theory* (Toronto: 1979); Susan Moller Okin, *Women in Western Political Thought* (Princeton: Princeton University Press reprint 1992); Anne Phillips, *Engendering Democracy* (Cambridge: CUP 1991); Linda J Nicholson, *Gender and History: The Limits of Social Theory in the Age of the Family* (New York: Columbia University Press 1986); Carol Pateman, *The Sexual Contract* (Oxford: OUP 1988).

ideological building block in modern social democracy. The public sphere of political activity was for men; the private sphere of domestic nurture was for women: and both were under male control.

In economic terms, the doctrine of separate spheres developed in the wake of industrialisation. Rapid growth of factories and towns brought about an increasing separation of remunerated and domestic (unpaid) labour. The Industrial Revolution in Scotland was to a large extent carried on the backs of female and child labourers. Indeed, the early exploitation of their toil threatened the very survival of working-class families. However, at both ideological and practical levels, the division of spheres was increasingly promoted and accepted:

> Home and work were not two separate worlds, and women's participation in the labour market was much more extensive than has previously been assumed. But the reality did little to diminsh the force of the ideology—whose social origins became obscured so that it appeared as a natural phenomenon.[13]

Among the growing urban middle classes, the tendency to regard the home as both analogy and preparation for heaven assumed cult status. The burgeoning prosperity of the bourgeoisie was based on the exercise of competition, aggression and self-interest, and these wrought dreadful poverty and human degradation. In this confusing and contradictory world, the home was presented as a haven from fear and alienation. Physically distant from both the workplace and the miserable masses, and enjoying conspicuous new material comforts, it was worshipped as a place of order, private virtue and spiritual reinforcement. And for most Scottish presbyterians, including artisans and aspiring working-class members, it was these values, rather than radical political solutions, which were regarded as the means to reform social evils. The domestic sphere was abstracted (rhetorically at least) from the harsh public world, and the role of 'Woman' as custodian of Christian principles assumed an increasing and sentimental importance. Women were, in law, the property of their husbands. Their work was not meant to be economic, but reproductive, emotional and religious. It was supposedly motivated, not by the crass standards of the marketplace, but by that self-sacrificial love which was assumed to be part of 'womanly' nature.

---

13 Eleanor Gordon, *Women and the Labour Movement in Scotland 1850 -1914* (Oxford: OUP 1991).

Excluded from active participation in the worship and structures of the Church, women had to assert the spiritual equality promised them by the Reformation within the home. The evangelical revival, which began in the late eighteenth century and which, by the 1830s, was becoming the most influential expression of Scottish presbyterianism, revitalised the family as locus for religious formation and expression. It was to be the centre of the daily struggle against the forces of sin and chaos, for virtue and order. The duties of discipline and self-examination were enthusiastically prescribed, as church courts exercised their right to public control of morals less rigorously. And if the patriarch was to be priest for his family, ensuring the practice of daily household prayer and Bible study, the mother had a special responsibility for instructing children in the precepts of religion, so that what was taught would be 'interwoven gradually with all that is most sweet, sacred, endearing, enduring in the associations of home.'[14]

'A nobler destiny!': Woman's Mission

> We claim for them no less an office than that of instruments under God for the regeneration of the world—restorers of God's image in the human soul. Can any of the warmest advocates of the political rights of woman claim or assert for her a more exalted mission—a nobler destiny![15]

Thus wrote Sarah Lewis in *Woman's Mission* (1839), a widely read contribution to the debate about the nature and role of women. While many elements of the sexual ideology extolled by Lewis and others were not new, they owed their conceptual framework to the evangelical revival. The idea that anyone—let alone a woman—might have a mission which could engage them in anything more strenuous than prayer or pious platitude was rather novel in presbyterian Scotland. But the revival, which emphasised a faith of personal commitment and action, and the perfectability of the redeemed life, presented a dynamic challenge to the Kirk's complacency and social control. In the first decades of the nineteenth century, it inspired reform campaigns which were regarded as a threat to the political and religious establishment, especially in the wake of the French Revolution. The anti-slavery movement, foreign missions,

---

14 *Acts of the General Assembly of the Free Church of Scotland* (1858-1863) 491.

15 Sarah Lewis, *Woman's Mission* (London: 1839) 11-12.

temperance, philanthropic organisations; these and others gave political education and campaigning experience to social groups, including women, which had hitherto been excluded from an active role in church and state. In this context, the concept of woman's mission translated conventional notions of female benevolence and influence into the proposition that the moral power of women was crucial to the evangelical task. For it was those very 'feminine' characteristics, the virtues which blessed the home, which were required to make the grimy wórld a godly place. In the new mythology, 'Womanhood' became a powerful symbol of righteousness and purity, and those dangerous, unruly female traits which presbyterianism had struggled to discipline were regarded as carnal aberrations. Against these, working-class women had to be vigilant, but the essence of their ladylike superiors was held to be an angelic, self-abnegating goodness, which paradoxically was their glorious transforming power.

'A unique and glorious mission': women's work for the church

> The service of Christ in His Church, what is it but the permeating of society with that gentleness, sweetness and tact, and that sympathy with all forms of human need and suffering, which is peculiarly woman's own province, and towards which her tender nature turns as naturally as a flower turns to the sun. Hers is a unique and glorious mission; and today, more than ever, your Saviour and Church are inviting you, my sisters, to arise and fulfil it.[16]

When Rev J F W Grant addressed the 1894 national conference of the Church of Scotland Woman's Guild, his combination of sentimental idealisation and evangelical fervour was characteristic of the methods adopted to encourage the 'Angel in the House' to become an 'Angel in the World'. If women's sphere was the home, how could they, without damage to themselves and the divinely ordained order of things, possibly engage with the public domain? The answer was not to go *beyond* their sphere, but to exert their blessed power in an entirely womanly extension of domestic virtues into the the villages, slums, orphanages, schools and rescue homes of Scotland by their charitable and evangelistic dealings with the poor, the squalid, the inadequate and the degenerate of society. The religious establishment gradually warmed to the idea that the unpaid

16 Address reported in the Church of Scotland's magazine *Life and Work* (1894) 116.

protector of the hearth was entitled to act as voluntary guardian of Christian values and social hierarchy. The fundamental cause of social disorder, it was believed, was individual sinfulness, and a plethora of educational, charitable and visiting organisations developed to engage in an aggressive strategy of home mission work. At the same time, colonial expansion in Africa, Asia and the Caribbean offered much wider horizons for those who felt called to test their religious fervour in foreign mission fields.

In this changing climate, new modes of existence were encouraged for morally serious women:

> Their lives, compared with what they might be, are an almost barren waste, a dead blank in the scale of being... Let them learn to do all with the utmost fidelity, diligence and despatch; and always before retiring, let them call themselves to strict account for the manner in which they have spent the day.[17]

Thousands of presbyterian women took this counsel to heart, as women's work in the churches grew from tentative begininnings to become a major and significant element in Scottish religious and cultural life. Throughout the Victorian era, women worked in local parish societies and district visiting; in mission associations and agencies. Female duties were typically narrowly defined and strictly auxiliary: raising funds for good causes, by collections, or by sale of sewing and other traditional female craft skills. Their associations did have committee and prayer meetings, and sometimes female office-bearers, but they were always under male direction, and this was as far as many churchfolk were prepared to go. Nonetheless there were also opportunities for more direct initiatives. The Female School of Industry run by the Ladies Association for Perth was typical of the class-based interaction between upper class and labouring women. The school aimed to train destitute girls 'not only to habits of moral and religious feeling, but to the kind of industrial exertion which will fit them for their future position in life ... and not, either by dress, food or education, to give them ideas and hopes associated with a higher position.'[18]

In congregations and parishes, women gave their time to approved pastoral and missionary work. By 1884, after years of gathering

---

[17] Rev Hubbard Winslow, "Woman As She Should Be" part III: United Secession Church *Christian Journal* (1840) 209.

[18] *Church of Scotland Home and Foreign Missionary Record* (1845) 13.

information about lay involvement in the parochial work of the Church of Scotland, the convenor of its Life and Work Committee could write:

> When one looks clearly at work done by a congregation in aid of the minister, women obviously get most of it to do...Elders and a few young men who teach in Sunday School are for the most part all the male allies of the minister, whereas the woman-helpers are numerous... The Sunday School itself is mainly taught by women... The Clothing Society and Mother's Meeting...The District Visiting—hardest, most trying, but most effective of all mission agencies—is as a rule entirely done by the minister and his 'lady-visitors'.[19]

From 1887, when the Kirk's National Woman's Guild (including an Order of Deaconesses) was founded, the three main presbyterian denominations implemented schemes to organise women's work within their national structures. These mirrored the presbyterian polity in a kind of subordinate parallelism, which allowed women a measure of experience and autonomy in their decision-making processes. A number worked full time (and often without pay, since their work was supposed to be motivated by love and service rather than money!). They established and ran hospitals, training institutions and rescue homes. They did pioneering social and healing work in slums and mining villages. They led their own meetings, conferences and worship, and some travelled all over Scotland to encourage and train their less confident sisters. Temperance work, extensive writing and publishing also contributed to the growth of a distinctive female culture. Much of the primary source material indicates how important this was in enabling a network of learning, friendship, leadership, self-confidence and solidarity to develop among women whose horizons were expanded geographically, intellectually and politically, beyond the stultifying confines of their genteel parlours.

It is true that most of the initiatives developed by women in response to their sense of mission, could be understood as an extension of the domestic duties which were considered appropriate women's work. In sociological terms, their activities tended to reinforce the dominance of an individualistic evangelical liberalism, and the ascendancy of the domestic ideology as an ideal for all classes. But to criticise their endeavours simply as attempts to secure a compliant working class, or to extol uncomplaining domestic servitude and drudgery as the true emancipation of Christian women, does little justice to the convictions, effort and

19 *Life and Work* (1884) 33.

courage of many. Their concern, strength of character and Christian convictions gave them liberty to act, where they believed they were called to do so, against the conventions of what was seemly or proper female behaviour. In 1901, The National President of the Woman's Guild rallied her members with these rousing words:

> There is a cry on the part of some that it is not good for women, not even good for the causes in which we are interested, that we should come too much to the front. We must not forego opportunities because such an objection is taken, but we can act so as to make it visibly baseless...And so, if the sight of the woes of others call any of you to work beyond what have been hitherto the ordinary limits of women's work, you need not fear surely to listen to the voice, nor think that it calls you beyond a woman's province: "Whatsoever He saith unto you, Do it."[20]

For some women, the call was to foreign mission. They were exhorted, in the light of their elevated status, to take responsibility for spreading the gospel to their poor degraded sisters in the East. This was a crucial task, for without women, converted and domesticated according to the standards of the home church, 'heathen' societies could never be civilised in the image of the evangelising nations. The domestic ideology, which constrained so many in Scotland, was thus paradoxically the basis of outreach and emancipation proclaimed by missionary women. Moreover, the complex dynamics of race, gender, caste and class in very diverse crcumstances, challenged and frequently undermined that underlying ideology. Involvement in foreign mission, especially in the field, but also in home associations, had the practical effect of transforming the lives of many women without necessarily transforming their consciousness. The need to serve the cause of introducing Christian concepts of womanliness provided the rationale for training and qualification in teaching, nursing, medicine, social work, administration and preaching. Because of this, missionaries were among the first truly professional women, but unlike the New Woman of the late nineteenth century, who in the popular view had cast off her femininity to compete with men, the missionaries were apparently motivated by the 'truly womanly' qualities of altruism and self-sacrifice. Missions offered the opportunity of an independent career, with the added glamour (and potential dangers) of travel and adventure, but without condemning agents to the fierce criticism reserved for women

20 *Life and Work: Woman's Guild Supplement* (1901) 56.

whose personal ambition was seen as a fundamental threat to the ordered spheres of society.

One of the main goals of mission work was to build communities which would replicate the values and domestic arrangements of presbyterian culture, and many female missionaries were content to understand their role in this way. Others were never circumscribed by such conventions, either in their own lifestyle, or in their approach to those women among whom they laboured. Individuals like Jane Waterston (the first Scotswoman to qualify as a physician), Mary Slessor and Annie Small were strong and unconventional, innovative and compassionate, and devoted to the freedom and independence of women both in the field and back in Scotland. Physical distance blessed them with a critical perspective on the manners, conventions, and rigidities of their own church and society. Those who experienced obstruction and petty restrictions abroad, and conversely those who felt that Scottish church life compared unfavourably with opportunities in the field, used their considerable influence as female heroines and exemplars to disturb the *status quo*. Some notable ex-missionaries were at the forefront of the reformist Women's Movement which developed in Britain in the latter part of the nineteenth century. The experience of female missionaries in India made a direct impact on the Scottish campaign for the right of women to qualify as medical doctors, because they discovered that women who suffered appalling gender-related health problems were not allowed to be seen by male doctors. During the 1880s, several of the first women medical graduates were employed by Scottish female missionary associations.

By the end of the nineteenth century, however they chose to respond, presbyterian women could not ignore a message which was beginning seriously to challenge the credibility of separate private and public spheres:

> That a woman should never be seen out of her own house is a heathen idea; that a woman should be a fellow-worker with Christ himself, and His apostles and ministers, is New Testament teaching.[21]

But was this brave new world of women workers a sign of equality and liberation achieved? The phenomenon of growing female involvement in

21 *Life and Work: Woman's Guild Supplement* (1898) 48.

the public mission and service of the church certainly led to the significant feminisation of an institution which was overwhelmingly masculine in tone and structure. The evolution of the church as focus for a range of missionary and social inititiatives was inextricably linked with the growing participation of women; and by 1900 Scottish presbyterianism had in many respects a somewhat altered character and public image.

This feminisation was, however, essentially in terms of service rather than of status and authority. The establishment remained solidly patriarchal in structure, decision-making and attitude. From the 1870s especially, there were many orthodox Christians who viewed the secular' movement for women's rights with horror. As a contemporary wrote:

> Was not this novel claim but one of many signs that the world was in a bad case, that the Bible was losing its authority, and that flood-gates were being opened through which fierce, foul streams would rush to whelm everything in chaos and death? After this the deluge, was the mournful, despairing conclusion of many devout souls, who were sure the end could not be far off when such enormities were to be seen as women in pulpits.[22]

In fact, the unthinkable had already happened, and during a new phase of revivalism in Scotland in the 1860s wandering women preachers had been known to appear in the pulpits of sympathetic ministers, upon whom the wrath of the local presbytery would quickly fall.[23] Although such women did not constitute a direct challenge to the official establishment, Olive Anderson concludes that their very existence 'probably provoked dismay and thus stimulated the provision of less disturbing, more controlled outlets for female zeal.'[24] It is surely no coincidence that establishment

22 *United Presbyterian Magazine* (1890) 70.

23 From 1859 until 1873 (when the Edinburgh campaign of the Americans Moody and Sankey ushered in a new style of revivalism), public prayer and preaching by women was a distinctive feature of the religious landscape, especially in working class areas where the simple Arminian message, and freedom from rigid ecclesiastical structures, made most impact. Premillenialist enthusiasm enabled small communities to accept women preachers, whose success in evangelisation was seen as an indication that their gifts were fruits of the Holy Spirit, and one of the signs of the 'last days' prophesied in Joel 2:28-29. The presbyterian establishment could not concur, and condemned any 'inadvertent' incident which occurred within their jurisdiction. (Examples are recorded in Presbytery minutes, eg Brechin April 1867; Orkney, September 1869).

24 Olive Anderson, "Women Preachers in Mid-Victorian Britain" in *Historical Journal* (1969) 468-485, here 481.

churchmen who campaigned for organised women's work became more vociferous and successful during the 1870s. The challenge they saw was to recognise and utilise appropriate models for women's work, while rejecting any possibility that the exercise of official authority in ministries of teaching and oversight should be available to women. Notwithstanding some diehard conservatives who could not accept that Christian women had any function outside the home, the development of a separate and distinctive 'women's ministry' was vigorously promoted, and increasingly accepted. In a church which had a powerful paradigm of domination as its model for ordained ministry, and in a society so defined by the domestic ideology, the phrase 'women's ministry' required careful definition to accommodate prevailing understandings of both women and ministry, and to expunge any possibility of gender parity. The theological premise of this position was that female selfless devotion should be the primary distinguishing characteristic, not just of voluntary activity, but also of those who engaged in full-time ministry. Traditionalists acceded to this as a useful extension of the essentially auxiliary place of women in the divine scheme of things, and encouraged the exploitation of those qualities traditionally ascribed as feminine. In theory, the holy subordination of a distinctive diaconal female ministry did not undermine adherence to the authority of Scripture or the historical practice of the Church Universal. It conformed to their view that the roles of men and women were not interchangeable, and that ultimately it was the task of men to rule and of women to obey.

This view fails to do justice to the paradoxical experience of many women who took up employment or service according to the ethos of 'women's ministry'. These women responded with enthusiasm and imagination to the challenges and interests of unknown territory—in themselves and in their world—and discovered what the theory expressly repudiated: that their gifts, qualities and aspirations were not confined within the modest boundaries of 'woman's sphere', but spilled over and intruded into the erstwhile male arenas of public affairs, political analysis, social critique, organisation, preaching and leadership. Thus from the 1880s, the enormous complexities and injustices of industrial Scotland shook the confidence of some presbyterians in the divine benevolence and inexorability of the political and economic order, and they began to question the conventional evangelical response. Helen Crawfurd, a minister's wife who was later to become a leading suffragette and communist activist was not alone when she wrote:

> To me it seemed all wrong that religion should be so much concerned about heaven and a future life, and so little concerned with the present, where God's creatures were living in slums, many of them owned by the Churches, amidst poverty and disease.[25]

Progressive presbyterians, influenced by socialist politics and a new interest in the Kingdom of God, made use of an ethical familialist, rather than collectivist model to develop their understanding of justice and the role of the state. In this, women workers and their supposedly distinctive female qualities had a key role to play in reproducing 'home values' by intervening in that realm between private and public which was assuming increasing importance—the social dimension. This was actually a somewhat conservative strategy, designed to help preserve the influence of religion in Scottish society, and doomed to failure. In practice, it meant that a few overworked and under-resourced women became virtually the only representatives of the church in some of the most poverty-stricken areas of Scotland. Their courage and compassion was the vicarious and tenuous link between the 'unchurched masses', and those large, prosperous suburban congregations which simply retreated from the perplexing challenges of the time.

The official response to growing evidence that women's work would refuse to remain safely confined was ambivalent. Some churchmen conceded—grudgingly or with patronising grace—that women indeed had it in them to be competent in these ways. But women were not to be given the opportunity, salaries or status to demonstrate this on equal terms with men. The subordinate parallelism whereby women were organised within a separate structure which mirrored the courts and boards of the church, ensured their exclusion from presbyterian polity. They could exercise no effective authority or responsibility outwith their parallel organisation (and were even denied effective internal autonomy). By 1900, women remained clearly defined and confined by their gender to official subordination in an institution which was increasingly reliant upon their services, money and goodwill.

---

25 Helen Crawfurd, unpublished biography, 46 (copy of manuscript held in the William Gallacher Memorial Library, Scottish Trades Union Congress Headquarters, Glasgow).

'For the business of life and the purpose of eternity': interpreting the Bible

Within the Women's Movement, many were actively struggling to reconcile their commitment to emancipation with their religion. Historical criticism introduced the option of an alternative hermeneutical principle to one of the most intransigent and damaging sources of opposition to women's rights: the assertion that the Bible was infallibly inspired and offered unequivocal guidance on every social and moral concern, valid for all times and situations. Now women could countenance the theory that not all biblical statements have equal claim to truth and authority by postulating a canon within the canon. On the whole they appropriated new ways of thinking about the Bible by giving priority to Jesus' own words and example over the culturally conditioned injunctions of Paul and the pastoral epistles. In biblical studies and devotional life Jesus became much more central, not simply as a symbol of comfort and compassion, but also because he was perceived as revealing the quality of right and equal relationship between women and men. Isabella Armstrong, a female preacher, tartly observed:

> The disciples marvelled that Jesus talked with the woman at the well (John 4:27) ... and it is evident that the disciples still marvel, that the great Shepherd speaks so graciously to the female members of his body, though it is to be regretted that they do not evince the same circumspection in allowing Him to manifest in His own time His own God-like purposes.[26]

In reformed, and especially in evangelical, Protestantism, Pauline texts had been paramount in shaping doctrine and practice. Christ was significant above all in his ontological, representative character as sacrifice to atone for human sin, and as Head of the Church. The new interest in him as a historical figure, seeking radical transformation of the world, brought a new freedom and dynamism to many who had felt stifled and oppressed by the harsh Calvinist doctrines of human depravity and election. As Jane Waterston claimed in 1885:

> We have read the Bible with women's eyes, and if Christianity is true at all it is a living thing, growing with the growing years, and not a lifeless form which can at best give us the dead women's clothes of fifty or sixty years after Christ. It is surely not the letter that giveth life, and yet you would give to women letter

26 Isabella Armstrong, *A Plea for Modern Prophetesses* (Glasgow 1867) 3.

> and tradition as their sole portion. Much harm has been done by false ideas of what Christianity taught concerning women.[27]

In spite of the frustrations they often felt, most Victorian women who sought equal rights did not desert the church, because they did not believe that their challenges were inimical to the spirit of the Reformation. Indeed, it was not uncommon for them to assert their Pentecostal right to prophecy in proclaiming that they were part of a movement of the Holy Spirit to call the church back to the central truths of its reformed heritage.

Among those women who strived to break down all barriers of law and custom which prevented them entering into professions and employment of their choice, the issue was one of power and structural change, not just about personal culture and learning. They seemed to many to be in open revolt against the ideal of Womanhood. By asserting their entitlement to choose and exercise authority over their own lives, in open competition with men, they offended the modesty and subordination which were the crown of traditional femininity. In short, they were asking to be considered as individuals with distinctive responsibilities and talents and to be freed from the category 'Woman' which assumed that their life was determined and exhausted by their biological sex. The success of the campaign for higher education (marked by the Act which opened Scottish universities to women in 1894) was due largely to an eventual pragmatic acceptance that the protestant work ethic, expressed in both intellectual and economic labour, might in certain circumstances apply also to women. The underlying social axiom remained that girls should be educated to fulfil their pre-ordained womanly functions according to their station in life, while those few who avowedly pursued intellectual excellence and professional parity for personal satisfaction could no longer truly be considered as women, but had, in effect (either literally or metaphorically), desexed themselves. Women might have gained the right of access to their faith in a different way, but the religious institutions and culture of the time did nothing to challenge these parameters of gender and class as they shaped the educational options and experience of Scottish women.

---

27 Speech quoted in Jane Bean and Elizabeth van Heyningen (eds.), *The Letters of Jane E Waterston* 1866-1905 (Cape Town 1983) 288.

'She must not soar too high': the liberation and limitations of women's work for Scottish presbyterian women

Speaking from the depths of painful personal experience, and years of educating girls, Dr Jane Waterston suggested to a church meeting in 1885 that to thwart the aspiration to work could result in women deserting their faith:

> When she expresses the desire for work, she is told that she has no need for work, and that she should be content and happy... Is it a wonder that in some cases she begins to question the Bible itself. "Can it be true? Can God have given me talents and then expect me to bury them in the earth?"[28]

In 1855, a Scottish journal, the *North British Review*, published an article entitled 'The Non-Existence of Women'. It argued that the right to work was a human right of self-definition, by which it was possible to move from private, passive suffering, into active doing in the 'real' public sphere. The cultural restrictions on women's work denied their human identity and declared their psychological and social non-existence.[29] This is an exposition of the theory that work liberates, through personal dignity, creative production, freeing of aptitude and capacity, the community of sharing a common task, and the engagement of body, mind and soul. For Victorian women in Scotland, work was, perhaps, the main arena in which they expressed their agency; their right and capacity to respond to and change the world in which they lived. At its best, the evangelical concept of women's mission transcended the patriarchal exploitation of female ministration, which women were socialised to accept as natural and virtuous. For many , the opportunities to work (in religious, philanthropic, and eventually professional activity) were welcomed as a matter of decision and choice, rather than compulsion. They might describe their motivations in terms of self-sacrifice and duty, and their hopes for success were often subverted by the chronic religious self-doubt of those who have been convinced of the daily necessity to examine their sinful lives for evidence of God's election, but the humanising value of their productive activity could be a really life-changing experience, especially when it included the possibility of over-

---

28 Waterston, speech1885 , in Bean and Heyningen (eds.), *The Letters of Jane E Waterston* (see note 29), 281

29 J W Kaye, "The Non-Existence of Women" in: *The North British Review* (1855) 559.

coming the psychological or economic dependence which were central to the definition of 'true Womanhood'.

It is necessary, nevertheless, to be cautious about careless use of 'women' as an inclusive category. In Scotland, those who seized upon the liberating potential of such work were rarely those thousands of women who had to grind out long hours in factories and sweatshops, in domestic service or brothels, in the exhausting struggle to maintain the basic conditions of existence. For too many, labour extracted effort which diminished and dehumanised. It did not value and nourish human potential. For women of all classes, but especially for the poor, domestic labour was undervalued, sentimentalised, or presented as the maudlin *sine qua non* of female fulfilment. The church was always ready to judge and condemn those who were found wanting in their roles as wife, mother and housekeeper.

Much of 'women's work for women' was devoted to social and moral progress, but it often had the effect of stereotyping and objectifying other women; of confirming their dependence and inferiority; of underlining that their situation of poverty and servitude was established by the simple, indelible fact of their birth into a certain social class and gender. The freedom to escape the givenness of a situation, to exercise significant life-choices, was severely constrained for most poor women. But there is some evidence that, in the midst of great material hardship, thousands of working women discovered sustenance and enjoyment in the solidarity of each other's company: perhaps a sense of humour and community enabled them to subvert the prescriptions of both social superiors and a judgmental religious culture. There is no reason why history should not acknowledge that women could be oppressed, circumscribed, victimised—yet also 'bold-eyed and loud, lusty and inquiring.'[30] In spite, rather than because, of their religious heritage, they had the potential to transcend the limitations of their lives and affirm their humanity.

I believe that the struggle for women in Scottish church and society has to a great extent been that struggle to realise and celebrate our humanity (individually and collectively) in its embodied particularity,

30 William Walker, *Juteopolos: Dundee and its Textile Workers 1885-1923* (Edinburgh: EUP 1979) 40. A comment on the mill-girl culture of Dundee, where the jute industry was based on extensive female employment.

against a prevailing tendency to reduce real human beings to symbols, stereotypes and archetypes, defined in terms of the services which they are to provide as a matter of biological destiny and divine command. In the processes which wrought change in Victorian Scotland, women were involved in the complex system of interrelated social and cultural structures as both agents and objects. Their struggles for survival, dignity and self-determination often brought those from different circumstances into confrontation with one another. Presbyterianism provided conditions which helped facilitate and shape those processes. But as a patriarchal institution within a hierarchical class society, the church's organisation showed, in relation to women, 'evidence of considerable rigidity which sometimes breaks down but which rarely yields without a real struggle.'[31] As a shaper of Scottish culture, it remained committed to a conservative domestic ideology acting (though not always deliberately) to hinder the full, egalitarian recognition of personhood which has sometimes been proclaimed as a distinctive feature of this protestant tradition. Too many presbyterians have been ardent supporters of that 'perfect Womanhood' which is always defined in terms of its relationship to the male sex, so that, as one minister wrote:

> Nothing so much handicaps a woman as oddity, eccentricity, peculiarity. Nothing assists her so much as that grace, charm and ease of manner which men everywhere and instinctively expect in women.[32]

My work is a modest testament to all those unique and glorious Scotswomen who asserted their right to be odd, eccentric or peculiar, and whose witness to that choice was rooted firmly in their own understanding of religious freedom. Let Jeanie Morison, poet, polemicist and presbyterian, have the last word:

> I am responsible to none but God, and my own conscience, for my opinions. No man can come to me and take my burden of responsibility on his shoulder; and therefore no man has a right to dictate to me in what manner I am to discharge myself of that responsibility.[33]

---

31 *Revised Interim Report of a Study on the Life and Work of Women in the Church* (World Council of Churches: Geneva 1948) 14.

32 David Watson, *Perfect Womanhood* (Edinburgh: 1905) 101.

33 *The Attempt: A Magazine for Ladies* (Edinburgh 1874). *The Attempt* was a publication of the Edinburgh Ladies Debating Society, founded 1865, which

Abstracts

Der Beitrag behandelt die wechselnden Entwürfe und die Praxis der Frauenarbeit in der Schottischen Presbyterianischen Kirche während der viktorianischen Ära. Er vertritt die These, daß Frauen nicht einfach Opfer oder passive Objekte waren, sondern historische Akteure, die sich kritisch und kreativ auf ihre spezifischen Umstände einstellten. Nichtsdestotrotz handelten sie innerhalb eines kulturellen und ideologischen Rahmens, besonders bei Frauen der Arbeiterklasse, deren häusliche und wirtschaftliche Umstände nicht dem stereotypen Ethos christlicher "Frauenarbeit" entsprachen.

Cette étude examine l'évolution des concepts et de la pratique du travail des femmes au sein de l'Eglise presbytérienne d'Ecosse à l'époque victorienne. Elle démontre que les femmes n'y étaient pas simplement des victimes ou des objects passifs, mais bien des acteurs historiques qui répondaient de façon critique et créative aux situations données. Cependant, elles intervenaient au sein d'un cadre culturel, idéologique et structurel précis - particulièrement les femmes de la classe ouvrière, dont la situation domestique et économique ne correspondait pas aux principes stéréotypés du "travail de femme" chrétien.

Lesley ORR MACDONALD MA BD PhD (born 1957) is a feminist historian and theologian, coordinating an action-research project *Out of the Shadows—Christianity and Violence Against Women in Scotland* at the Centre for Theology and Public Issues, University of Edinburgh. Her doctoral thesis explored the relationship between women and presbyterianism in Scotland during the period c1830–1930. A book based on the research will be published shortly.

provided an important forum for discussion and development of many campaigns, especially suffrage and higher education.

Kerstin SÖDERBLOM

Differenzen—Gedanken zum Unterschied zwischen lesbisch-feministischen und feministischen Theologien

Vorbemerkung

Es gibt weder *die* feministische noch *die* lesbisch-feministische Theologie. Ich werde daher überblickshaft verschiedene Aspekte skizzieren, die sich seit den späten siebziger Jahren hinter dem Label »feministische Theologie« verbergen, um einen Orientierungsrahmen für mein Thema abzustecken. Meiner Darstellung liegt eine chronologische Struktur zugrunde, da sich Unterschiede und Gemeinsamkeiten nur vor dem Hintergrund der Entwicklungsprozesse feministisch-theologischer Ansätze seit den siebziger Jahren angemessen entziffern lassen.

Die Bezeichnung lesbisch-feministische Theologie gibt es m. W. lediglich als Arbeitsbegriff. In verschiedenen Arbeitsgruppen des Netzwerks Labrystheia[1] benutzen wir den Begriff, um unsere Arbeit kenntlich zu machen. Ein Vergleich kann letztlich also nur gezogen werden zwischen feministisch-theologisch arbeitenden Gruppen und solchen Gruppen, in denen explizit lesbisch lebende Frauen feministisch-theologisch forschen und zusammenarbeiten. Ich bemühe mich in diesem Aufsatz um einen Vergleich aus meiner persönlichen Sicht: aus der Sicht einer lesbischen, feministischen Theologin.[2]

---

1 Labrystheia ist ein ökumenisches Netzwerk in Deutschland, in dem sich lesbische Frauen seit 1989 zweimal im Jahr auf Gesamttagungen treffen und zu feministisch-theologischen, kirchen- und gesellschaftspolitischen Themen aus lesbischer Perspektive arbeiten. Die Mitarbeiterinnen studieren Theologie, Religionspädagogik o.ä. oder absolvieren Ausbildungen, die sie zur Institution Kirche als Arbeitgeberin führen könnten. Darüberhinaus ist das Netzwerk für alle Interessierten, die nicht (mehr) in der Ausbildung sind und sich lesbisch-feministisch enagagieren wollen, offen. Vgl. Geertje F. Bolle und Christine F. und Evelyn Schwarz, "Lesbische Feministinnen in der Kirche" in: Barbara Kittelberger und Wolfgang Schürger und Wolfgang Heilig-Achneck (Hg.), *Was auf dem Spiel steht: Diskussionsbeiträge zu Homosexualität und Kirche* (München: Claudius 1993), 217-222.

2 Meine eigenen Forschungen gründen sich auf eine im Mai 1996 an der Universität

1 Der Zusammenschluß von feministisch-theologisch arbeitenden Frauen in den siebziger Jahren

Seit den siebziger Jahren treffen sich kirchlich und spirituell interessierte Frauen auf Tagungen und Veranstaltungen, auf denen sie ihre eigene Situation als Frauen in der Institution Kirche thematisieren. Sie gründeten Frauengruppen in vielen Gemeinden, trafen sich in überregionalen feministisch-theologischen Arbeitsgruppen und anläßlich der feministischen Werkstätten, die beispielsweise an der Akademie Bad Boll unter der Initiative von Herta Leistner und Elisabeth Moltmann-Wendel seit 1979 stattfinden.[3] An diesen Orten finden bis heute feministisch-theologisch interessierte Frauen zusammen, die—trotz vieler Zweifel, Frustration und Enttäuschungen—aus ganz unterschiedlichen lebensgeschichtlichen und inhaltlichen Gründen an ihrer Zugehörigkeit zu einer der beiden großen christlichen Kirchen in Deutschland festhalten. Knapp zehn Jahre nach Beginn der »autonomen« neuen Frauenbewegung in Deutschland begann sich folglich Ende der siebziger Jahre auch die kirchliche Frauenbewegung in Deutschland zu formieren. Diese entwickelte sich genauso wenig einheitlich wie die nichtkirchliche Frauenbewegung. Verschiedene feministisch-theologische Ansätze in den unterschiedlichen theologischen Disziplinen wurden auf akademischer und gemeindenaher Ebene entwickelt, an den Universitäten, auf Akademietagungen und feministischen Werkstätten diskutiert, ausprobiert und wieder verworfen. Viele Impulse kamen aus den Vereinigten Staaten. Erste feministisch-theologische Bücher aus den Vereinigten Staaten wurden von deutschen Frauen mitgebracht und auf Englisch gelesen. Einige dieser Bücher wurden Mitte der achtziger Jahre ins Deutsche übersetzt und für den hiesigen Kontext rezipiert.[4]

Hamburg eingereichte Dissertation zum Thema "Grenzgängerinnen. Die Bedeutung von christlicher Religion in Lebensgeschichten lesbischer Frauen in Deutschland." In diesem Rahmen habe ich 20 Interviews mit lesbischen Frauen im Alter zwischen 21 und 72 aus den alten Bundesländern geführt, deren soziale Herkunft, Ausbildung und Erwerbstätigkeit ganz unterschiedlich sind.

3 Vgl. Herta Leistner, "Werkstätten Feministischer Theologie in Bad Boll" in: Christine Schaumberger und Monika Maaßen (Hg.), *Handbuch Feministische Theologie* (Münster: Morgana Frauenbuchverlag [3]1989) 142-147.

4 Zur Entwicklung und zum Zusammenhang amerikanischer und deutscher feministisch-theologischer Ansätze vgl. Rita Burrichter und Claudia Lueg, "Aufbrüche und Umbrüche. Zur Entwicklung Feministischer Theologie in unserem Kontext"

Wichtigste Kennzeichen der Mehrzahl damaliger Ansätze feministischer Theologie waren zum einen, daß sie bewußt nicht den Anspruch hatten und haben, ein geschlossenes dogmatisches System darzustellen. Zum zweiten war die Parteilichkeit für Frauen grundlegend. Darüberhinaus waren folgende Aspekte wichtig:

- Erfahrungs- und kontextbezogenes Arbeiten;
- Kritik an der angeblichen Objektivität männlicher Wissenschaftsprojekte;
- Analyse und Kritik sexistischer Gewaltstrukturen in und außerhalb der Kirchen;
- die enge Verbindung zwischen wissenschaftlicher Arbeit und kritischer gesellschaftlicher und darin kirchlicher Praxis.[5]

Die lesbischen Frauen waren in all diesen Konsolidierungsprozessen von Anfang an dabei. Die wichtige Initiativarbeit von Herta Leistner für die Feministischen Werkstätten in Bad Boll Ende der siebziger Jahre mag hier als Beispiel genügen. Dennoch tauchten sie in den ersten Jahren weder explizit als lesbische Frauen auf noch wurden sie als solche gehört. Ihre Lebensgeschichten, ihre spezifischen Schwierigkeiten in den christlichen Kirchen, ihre Alltagssorgen, Ängste, Diskriminierungs- und Befreiungserfahrungen und ihre inhaltlichen Interessen wurden nicht explizit thematisiert. Ihre Fragen waren eher am Rande und in informellen Gesprächen zwischen den Arbeitsgruppen Thema. Auch in feministisch-theologischen Kreisen, die für sich in Anspruch nahmen, erfahrungsbezogen, kontextuell und parteilich zu arbeiten, kamen lesbische Frauen nicht vor. Lesbische Existnenz blieb als Thema verschwiegen. Allerdings thematisierten die meisten Lesben aus Angst vor negativen Reaktionen ihre Lebenswirklichkeiten und die damit zusammenhängenden Probleme und Herausforderungen lange Zeit auch selbst nicht.

Der feministische Anspruch, den eigenen Kontext transparent zu machen und differenziert darzustellen, wurde in Abgrenzung zu nicht

---

in: ebd., 14-35. Jutta Flatters, "»Probier, den alten weißen Mann aus meinem Kopf zu treiben... jetzt, wo meine Augen aufgehen...«. Feministische Theologie in den USA" in: ebd., 37-50. In diesem Artikel ist eine umfangreiche Literaturliste zum Thema zu finden.

5 Vgl. dazu Christine Schaumberger, "Es geht um jede Minute unseres Lebens! Auf dem Weg zu einer kontextuellen feministischen Befreiungstheologie" in: Renate Jost, Ursula Kubera (Hg.), *Befreiung hat viele Farben* (Gütersloh: Gütersloher Verlagshaus 1991), 15-34.

feministischen Theologinnen und gegenüber Männern zumeist umgesetzt. Eine ausdifferenzierte Kontextbestimmung nach innen—also innerhalb der feministisch-theologischen Gruppierungen—blieb dagegen zu oft aus. Die angenommene Gleichheit unter den Frauen schien diesen Standortbestimmungsprozeß entbehrlich zu machen. Die Konsequenz dieser Gleichheitsannahme beschreibt eine fast siebzigjährige lesbische Pastorin während meines Interviews mit ihr:

> "1983 war es, glaub ich, da hab ich zusammen mit einer anderen Frau einen kleinen Arbeitskreis zur feministischen Theologie gegründet, der noch heute besteht. Auch da war ich zunächst überhaupt keine Lesbe, gar nicht! Und bin es bis heute auch nur gepaart mit Unsicherheit und Verlegenheit. Es ist jedenfalls kein Thema in unserer Gruppe. Sie mögen mich alle gerne. Ich bin da wichtig und gehöre dazu, und wir tagen hier auch immer bei mir. Alle vierzehn Tage sind wir ein Herz und eine Seele, aber Lesbischsein, ja es scheint einerseits so ganz selbstverständlich, aber es ist eben doch kein Thema. Dieses Schweigen ist brutal." (Karla P., 68 Jahre alt)

Tabuisierung und Verschweigen kennzeichnen auch in den Erzählungen der anderen lesbischen Frauen, die ich interviewt habe, am prägnantesten den lang anhaltenden Nicht-Umgang der Frauengruppen mit dem Thema Lesbischsein. Die lebensgeschichtlichen Unterschiede unter den Frauen verunsicherten viele. Differenzen dürfen nicht sein, also redet frau nicht darüber. Die lesbischen Frauen mußten mit ihren Ängsten, Sorgen und Bedürfnissen nach Erfahrungsaustausch und Selbstvergewisserung alleine fertig werden. Die Frauengruppen boten nur wenig Unterstützung. Die ersten Verunsicherungen hinsichtlich der beschworenen einheitlichen Gruppenidentitäten begannen Fragen aufzuwerfen und Unruhe zu stiften. Dennoch schienen die Grundannahmen noch klar: die Kirche ist ein männerbündischer Verein, streng hierarchisch organisiert, und die herkömmlichen Theologien sind frauenfeindlich und auf den männlichen Erfahrungshorizont bezogen. Frauen in kirchlichen Institutionen sind die Opfer, die Männer sind direkte oder indirekte Täter, Verantwortliche oder zumindest Nutznießer des frauenfeindlichen Klimas in den Kirchen. Von den Frauen wurde übergreifende Solidarität unter Frauen ausgerufen, beschworen und auch in die Praxis umzusetzen versucht. Es herrschte Aufbruchstimmung. Die folgenden Themen standen in Arbeitsgruppen und Tagungen im Vordergrund:

- Entwicklung von frauengerechter Sprache, von Gottesdiensten und Predigten, in denen die Erfahrungswelt von Frauen einbezogen und reflektiert wird;

- Gründung von feministischen Liturgiegruppen;
- Forschung über Frauen in der (Kirchen-)Geschichte;
- Diskussionen über weibliche Gottesbilder;
- Auseinandersetzung über Positionen einer feministischen Ethik und Anthropologie;
- Diskussion über Ansätze feministischer Christologie;
- Matriarchatsforschung;
- Gründung von theologischen Frauennetzwerken, um kirchen- und universitätspolitisch Einfluß zu nehmen, beispielsweise um für Frauen auf allen Ebenen der kirchlichen Hierarchie besser bezahlte und einflußreichere Positionen zu fordern.
- Arbeit mit Bibeltexten, in denen die Erfahrungswelten von Frauen rekonstruiert und rekontextualisiert werden konnten.

Auf der Ebene der Kontext- und Methodenklärung erhielten die Begriffe Ganzheitlichkeit, Naturverbundenheit und die Aufwertung der eigenen Weiblichkeit zentrale Bedeutung.

Als ein Beispiel für einen inhaltlichen Schwerpunkt läßt sich die Diskussion über weibliche Gottesbilder anführen. In diesem Zusammenhang wurde von einer Vielzahl von Frauengruppen die Göttin wiederentdeckt, aus alten Quellen ausgegraben oder neugeschaffen. Sie stilisierten die Göttin als heterosexuell lebende Frau, Gattin oder Liebhaberin des männlichen Königs, Fruchtbarkeitsgarantin und Spenderin des Lebens. Dadurch liefen sie Gefahr, auf der Projektionsfläche von archaischen und zeitgenössischen Göttinnenbildern erneut bestimmte altbekannte Vorstellungen von Weiblichkeit zu reproduzieren. Für lesbische Frauen war es oft eine erneute Ausgrenzungserfahrung, von der Göttin als Gattin und Mutter zu hören. Die erklärte These, daß sich Frauen mit weiblichen Gottesbildern besser identifizieren können als mit männlichen, blieb für viele lesbische Frauen völlig unverständlich. Im Gegenteil, es verdeutlichte für viele erneut auf schmerzliche Weise, daß ihre Erfahrungen keinen Platz in den theologischen Überlegungen der meisten Frauengruppen hatten.

Trotz dieser Probleme können die siebziger Jahre bezüglich der säkularen und—knapp 5-10 Jahre verspätet—auch bezüglich der kirchlichen Frauenbewegung als die Zeit des Aufbruchs, der Sammlung und der Zusammenschlüsse bezeichnet werden. Das Zauberwort der Sammlung war: WIR Frauen! Alle sind benachteiligt, alle leiden unter sexistischen Verhältnissen und patriarchalen Strukturen. Alle Frauen sind Opfer dieser strukturellen Ungerechtigkeiten. Unterschiedliche Lebensformen, Alltagskontexte und Herkunftsgeschichten fielen durch die groben Maschen der Einheitsbeschwörung hindurch.

Dennoch stimmte das äußere Erscheinungsbild der WIR-Welt in den siebziger Jahren noch. Das dualistisch in den Außenraum hineinkonstruierte Feindbild war besonders in kirchlich-feministischen Kreisen so gegenwärtig und stark, daß die Außenorientierung zunächst tatsächlich nach innen einte. Unterschiede wurden aus scheinbar strategischen Gründen zurückgestellt. Die Frauen meinten, daß diese angesichts des übermächtigen patriarchalen Feindes nicht so wichtig seien. Die Erfahrungen vieler lesbischer Frauen wurden auf diese Weise ausgeklammert und Kontextbestimmungen zu global formuliert. Subtile Vereinnahmungsprozesse waren die Folge.

2 Die achtziger Jahre

2.1 Die Zeit der Ausdiffenzierungen

Die Risse im Geflecht des großen WIR-Frauen-Kreises wurden in den achtziger Jahren sichtbar: Die achtziger Jahre waren die Zeit der Ausdifferenzierung. Es zeigte sich, daß die lebensgeschichtlichen Ausgangspunkte, inhaltlichen Vorannahmen, theologischen Herangehensweisen und Positionen, das Maß an Kritik an herkömmlichen theologischen Lehren und konventioneller Kirchenpolitik und die Radikalität der Veränderungsbereitschaft sehr unterschiedlich waren. Auch die Methoden, Themenstellungen und Zielperspektiven vervielfältigten sich—je nach inhaltlichen und kirchenpolitischen Positionen.

Zudem begannen immer mehr Frauen, sich gegen Weiblichkeitsvorstellungen und deren unkritische Aufwertung durch Projektionen in Göttinnengestalten, wie oben beschrieben, zu wehren. Die in den siebziger Jahren so wichtigen Schlüsselbegriffe wie die Aufwertung von Weiblichkeit[6] Mütterlichkeit und Ganzheitlichkeit, wurden in den achtziger Jahren immer kontroverser diskutiert. Das große einheitliche WIR-Frauen ist darüber brüchiger geworden. Die Unterschiede sowohl auf inhaltlicher wie auch auf lebensgeschichtlicher Ebene traten deutlicher zutage. Viele Strömungen innerhalb des Sammelbegriffs der feministischen Theologie wurden von den Vertreterinnen jeweils anderer Strömungen und Positionen kritisiert, abgelehnt oder gar heftig angegriffen.

---

6 Vgl. Andrea Bieler, *Konstruktionen des Weiblichen* (Gütersloh: Mohn 1994).

Der Schwesternstreit begann: Ich bin nicht wie Du! Wir sind nicht alle gleich, nur weil wir Frauen sind. Wir entwickeln auch nicht alle die gleiche feministische Theologie, nur weil wir Frauen sind. Folgende Erkenntnisse setzten sich in den Debatten durch:

- Frauen sind unterschiedlich.
- Frauen sind nicht alle in demselben Maß von patriarchalen Strukturen benachteiligt und auch nicht alle in gleicher Weise Opfer derselben.[7]
- Frauen sind nicht nur Opfer, sie sind auch Täterinnen im gesellschaftlichen und lebensgeschichtlichen Kontext. Sie sind verantwortlich für ihr Tun, und genießen in unterschiedlicher Weise—je nach sozialer Herkunft, Nationalität, Hautfarbe, Bildungsweg und Lebensform unterschiedliche Privilegien.[8]

Die Auseinandersetzungen der achtziger Jahre zeigten immer deutlicher: Der Slogan WIR Frauen ist eine Illusion! Die Realität sieht anders aus: Lesben leben nicht heterosexuell, bisexuelle Frauen nicht ausschließlich lesbisch, Mütter sind nicht alle verheiratet und heterosexuell, Frauen sind nicht alle Mütter. Frauen sind schwarz, weiß, in einem spezifischen Kontext Einheimische oder Ausländerinnen, sie sind Christinnen, Zugehörige einer anderen Religion oder Atheistinnen. Sie sind jung, alt, gesund, krank, Akademikerinnen, Angestellte, Arbeiterinnen, Erwerbslose u.v.m.[9]

Kurz: Nicht Gemeinsamkeiten sondern Unterschiede auf allen Ebenen kennzeichnen die Situation von Frauen. Seit den achtziger Jahren wird dies deutlicher benannt und auch theoretisch stärker reflektiert.

2.2 Der Aufbruch der lesbischen Frauen

In den achtziger Jahren, den Jahren der Ausdifferenzierung feministischer Positionen, haben lesbische Frauen im kirchlichen Umfeld in West-

7 Siehe z.B. den Vergleich zwischen Frauen aus den Industrienationen und Frauen aus Ländern der Zweidrittelwelt und das Verhältnis zwischen schwarzen und weißen Frauen. Vgl. Ika Hügel u.a. (Hg.), *Entfernte Verbindungen. Rassismus, Antisemitismus, Klassenunterdrückung* (Berlin: Orlanda 1993).

8 Vgl. dazu Frigga Haug, "Frauen—Opfer oder Täter?", in: *Erinnerungsarbeit* (Hamburg: Argumentverlag 1990), 9-19; Christina Thürmer-Rohr: *Mittäterschaft und Entdeckungslust* (Berlin: Orlanda 1990).

9 Im Zuge dieser Ausdifferenzierung hat sich nicht zuletzt auch die "European Society of Women in Theological Research" 1986 als spezifisches Netzwerk für Frauen, die auf akademischer Ebene in den verschiedenen theologischen Bereichen arbeiten, gegründet.

deutschland begonnen[10], sich zu organisieren. Immer mehr Lesben fühlten sich in feministisch-theologischen Arbeitskreisen und Gruppen nicht mehr aufgehoben. Ihre Lebenswirklichkeiten blieben unbenannt, es sei denn, sie fingen selbst davon an zu erzählen. Die Sorge, auch in feministischen Kreisen nicht als Lesben willkommen zu sein, war bei vielen lesbischen Frauen groß und nicht unberechtigt. Die Abwehr, über »Fremdes« und Verunsicherndes zu reden, war groß und spaltete manch eine Frauengruppe. Lesben suchten also andere lesbische Frauen, die ähnliche Probleme in ihrem Umfeld und in vielerorts homophoben christlichen Kirchen gemacht hatten und die ebenfalls in Frauenkreisen nicht explizit vorkamen. Diese Auseinanderentwicklung kommentiert eine der lesbischen Frauen, die ich in meinen Interviews befragt habe:

> "... die Streitigkeiten zwischen Heteras und Lesben sind anstrengend. Die Heteras fühlen sich von Lesben angepiekst und angemacht, weil sie noch mit Männern ins Bett gehen und nicht feministisch genug sind. Die Lesben sind häufig enttäuscht, daß viele Heteras zwar erwarten, daß Lesben mit auf § 218-Demos kommen, daß sie aber nicht da sind, wenn es darum geht, auf die Rechte von Lesben aufmerksam zu machen und Lesbendiskriminierung anzuprangern. Darüber gibt's oft Streit und die sogenannte Prioritätenfrage steht immer wieder im Mittelpunkt der Debatten, statt konstruktiv mit Unterschieden umzugehen und Bündnisse zu schließen. Die Zersplitterung in der Frauenbewegung kommt ja schließlich vor allem den Herren zugute, die schon an der Macht sind, und alles beim Alten lassen wollen." (Anja T., 35 Jahre)

Eine andere lesbische Frau berichtet dazu:

> "Ich erlebe manchmal in feministischen Zusammenhängen starke Aggressionen. Also beispielsweise denke ich nicht, daß ich mein Lesbischsein andauernd thematisiere. Aber es ist auch schon vorgekommen, daß ich dann, wenn ich es thematisiere, von den anderen Frauen sowas höre wie: oh nein nicht schon wieder! Also daß ich immer wieder als diejenige, die das Thema einbringt, durch unterschwellige Aggressionen angefeindet wurde. Wenn ich es aber nicht anspreche, kommt das Thema gar nicht vor. Verschweigen ist auch eine Form von Diskriminierung, und sie tut mir sehr weh." (Anna B., 30 Jahre)

So begannen lesbische Frauen seit 1985 auf Lesbentagungen,[11] in Lesbengruppen und Netzwerken selbst als Subjekte und Expertinnen ihrer

---

10 Über die diesbezüglichen Entwicklungen in der ehemaligen DDR habe ich keine Informationen. Daher beziehe ich mich im folgenden nur auf Westdeutschland.

11 Die erste Lesbentagung fand 1985 an der Akademie Arnoldshain statt. Sie wurde von Monika Barz, Herta Leistner, Ute Wild und der Studienleiterin der Akademie Arnoldshain, Leonore Siegele-Wenschkewitz, organisiert. Als Referentin war die US-amerikanische Neutestamentlerin Bernadette Brooten eingeladen, die zu jener Zeit in Tübingen arbeitete. Sie war seit 1982 im Rahmen des Forschungsprojekts

Lebensgeschichten Theologie zu treiben, sich über ihre Erfahrungen auszutauschen und Solidaritätsgruppen zu bilden. 1986 gründete sich die erste Regionalgruppe des ökumenischen Arbeitskreises Lesben und Kirche (LuK) in Westberlin. 1986 wurde das Maria-und-Martha-Netzwerk (MuM) gegründet, das ein Unterstützungs- und Solidaritätsnetzwerk für lesbische Frauen ist, die hauptamtlich bei der Institution Kirche arbeiten. 1989 gründete sich Labrystheia. Schließlich gründeten lesbische Frauen aus Ostdeutschland 1992 den Arbeitskreis Lesben in der Kirche (LiK), um zunächst unabhängig von westdeutschen Lesben ihre eigene spezifische Situation als Lesben aus den neuen Bundesländern benennen und austauschen zu können.

In diesen Netzwerken und auf den Lesbentagungen an der Evangelischen Akademie in Bad Boll, an der Heimvolkshochschule in Loccum und in regionalen und überregionalen Lesbengruppen arbeiten seitdem viele Lesben zu Themen biblischer Exegese und hermeneutischen Fragestellungen. Andere beschäftigen sich mit Themen der Anthropologie, der (Sexual-)Ethik, überdenken traditionelle Gottesbilder und kritisieren Ansätze von Göttinnenspiritualität. Wieder andere machen sich Gedanken über ekklesiologische Konsequenzen aufgrund der immer offensiveren Präsenz von Lesben und Schwulen in den Kirchen, erarbeiten Segensrituale zur Segnung gleichgeschlechtlicher Partnerschaften oder besprechen auf kirchenpolitischer Ebene strategische Vorgehensweisen bezüglich der Debatten um das Thema der Lebensformen auf Synoden, in Kirchenvorstandssitzungen oder in ähnlichen Kirchengremien.[12] Auch das Thema der Seelsorge ist für viele lesbische Frauen wichtig. Sie arbeiten daran, Beratungen und Seelsorge für lesbische Frauen so anzubieten und durchzuführen, daß Lesben nicht als Objekte paternalistischer Seelsorge angesehen werden, sondern daß sie als Subjekte ernstgenommen werden.

"Frau und Christentum", das mit Geldern der VW-Stiftung eingerichtet worden war, in Tübingen. Sie schied Ende 1985 allerdings vorzeitig aus dem Projekt aus, da der Projektleiter Prof. Hans Küng und andere nicht akzeptierten, daß Frau Brooten ihren Arbeitsschwerpunkt unter anderem auf das Thema "Liebesbeziehungen unter Frauen bei Paulus und in der griechischen und römischen Umwelt" setzte. Zu dem scharfen Konflikt siehe die Dokumentation von Heinz Blanke, Lisa Napholcz, Anne Simon, Gerd Wild, Ute Wild (Hg.), *»Eigene Fragen stellen«: Dokumentation zum Konflikt um Küng, Wissenschaftsfreiheit und lesbische Liebe* (Tübingen: Selbstverlag 1986).

12 Vgl. Kerstin Söderblom, "Kirchlicher Segen—auch für Lesben und Schwule?" in: *Reformierte Kirchenzeitung* (4/1996), 170-178.

Bezeichnend ist, daß zu diesen Themen bisher kaum Veröffentlichungen im deutschsprachigen Raum erschienen sind.[13] Einige unveröffentlichten Aufsätze dokumentieren immerhin den Diskussionsprozeß lesbischer Frauen in Deutschland.[14] Auch die Artikel der Netzwerkzeitschriften von Labrystheia, LuK und MuM bieten einen Spiegel der Themen, mit denen sich deutschsprachige lesbische Frauen, die an Theologie interessiert sind, seit Ende der achtziger Jahre beschäftigen.[15]

Aus diesen Arbeitsprozessen ist allerdings keine einheitliche lesbisch-feministische Theologie in Deutschland hervorgegangen. Entscheidend bei all diesen Arbeiten ist die genaue Kontextualisierung des eigenen theologischen Standpunktes und der Analyseperspektive. Der offene Forschungsprozeß wird ebenfalls als ein Grundmerkmal dieser Arbeiten und nicht als vorläufiges Charakteristikum angesehen.

Innerhalb feministisch-theologischer Arbeiten sind seit den achtziger Jahren in Deutschland insofern empfindliche Perspektivausdifferenzierungen und -verschiebungen zu verzeichnen. Dazu noch einmal ein Zitat einer lesbischen Theologin:

> "Und in dem Sinne würde ich sagen, mein Gottesbild hat sich nicht verändert durch mein Coming-out, sondern die hermeneutische Frage von Text und Kontext oder von Gottesbild und wie ich über Gott rede und in welcher Situation ich das tue. Diese Korrelation hat sich verschoben. Vorher habe ich das Thema

---

13 Ausnahmen sind: Monika Barz, Herta Leistner, Herta, Ute Wild (Hg.), *Hättest du gedacht, daß wir so viele sind? Lesbische Frauen in der Kirche* (Suttgart: Kreuzverlag 1987); Rose Wecker, "Kirche und Homosexualität. Ein ungeklärtes Verhältnis" in: *Junge Kirche* (9/1994), 473-481; Eske Wollrad, "Geschlechtshierarchische Arbeitsteilung und Zwangsheterosexualität als Zentralbegriffe einer materialistisch-feministischen Theologie" in: Hans-Martin Gutmann u.a. (Hg.), *Er stößt die Gewaltigen vom Thron* (Göttingen 1987), 51-67; dies., "Konstruktionen von Zwangsheterosexualität in feministischen Theologien. Eine lesbisch-feministische Re-Vision" in: Göttinger Frauenforschungsprojekt zur Geschichte der Theologinnen (Hg.), *Querdenken* (Pfaffenweiler: Centaurusverlag [2]1992), 47-63. Siehe außerdem Anm.1.

14 Mir liegen zwei Seminararbeiten vor: 1. Zu Dimensionen lesbisch-feministischer Ethik; 2. Zur Krankenhausseelsorge aus lesbisch-feministischer Sicht. Darüberhinaus existiert eine Arbeit zum Zweiten Theologischen Examen über Gefängnisseelsorge aus lesbisch-feministischer Perspektive, die mir ebenfalls vorliegt.

15 Zur Zeit wird von einigen lesbischen Frauen an einem Sammelband gearbeitet, das noch 1997 im Gütersloher Verlagshaus erscheinen soll. Die Herausgeberinnen sind Monika Barz und Geertje Bolle. Hier werden verschiedene biographische und inhaltliche Themen deutschsprachiger lesbischer Frauen im kirchlichen Kontext der neunziger Jahre vorgestellt.

der Lebensformen sozusagen eher in dem Spannungsfeld Kirche-für-andere-sein gesehen. Also in dem Sinne, daß wenn meine schwulen Freunde ausgegrenzt werden, wir für die was tun müssen. Und ich hab nicht bedacht, daß zur Situationsanalyse auch ich mich in den Kontext der Zwangsheterosexualität hereinstellen muß. Daß ich mich damals als heterosexuell lebende und dann später als lesbische Frau fragen muß, was bedeutet diese Tradition für mich? Was bedeutet die Rede von Gott oder von Jesus für mich? Insofern hat sich das verschoben. Da fang ich an nachzudenken. Aber ich habe jetzt nicht auf einmal das Bedürfnis, die matriarchalen Göttinnen ausbuddeln zu müssen oder am besten noch welche, die irgendwie eine lesbische Lebensweise hatten oder so, das ist nicht mein Interesse. Also ich suche nicht in Religion oder in Religiosität das Abbild meiner Lebensform, ja? Klar, Jesus war nunmal ein Mann, und er hatte in einem kulturellen Zusammenhang gelebt, der mir sehr fern ist oder uns allen. Und durch diesen Fremden und diesen Gott als der ganz andere, kann im Grunde auch erst diese kritische Bewegung stattfinden. Würde ich eine Göttin anbeten, die irgendwie jetzt mal hart gesagt, genauso leben würde wie ich selbst, da würde ja nichts passieren, da bliebe doch alles, wie es ist." (Anna B., 30 Jahre)

Theologische Fragen werden von lesbischen Frauen seit ihren Zusammenschlüssen in Gruppen, Netzwerken und Tagungszusammenhänge also immer expliziter aus ihrer Perspektive formuliert. Formal übernehmen sie dabei die Postulate feministisch-theologischer Frauengruppen.

Dadurch, daß sie bei der Kontextualisierung ihrer Arbeiten ihren Erfahrungshintergrund als lesbische Frauen benennen, verschiebt sich allerdings die Ausgangsperspektive und Blickrichtung der Arbeiten. Außerdem ziehen sie bei der Analyse gesellschaftlicher Gegebenheiten heterosexistische Gewaltstrukturen mit in ihre Untersuchungen ein. Diese Erweiterung des Analyserahmens ist ebenfalls neu.

Die inhaltlichen Ergebnisse und Schwerpunkte der Arbeiten lesbischer Frauen sind aufgrund verschiedener Ausgangsperspektiven und Themenstellungen sehr unterschiedlich. So haben die US-amerikanischen lesbischen Theologinnen wie Carter Heyward,[16] Mary Hunt[17] und Beverley Harrison[18] beispielsweise in den achtziger Jahren Ansätze für eine Theologie der Beziehung erarbeitet. Sie entwickelten das Beziehungsdrei-

16 Carter Heyward, *Und sie rührte sein Kleid an. Eine feministische Theologie der Beziehung* (Stuttgart: Kreuzverlag 1986); dies., *Touching our Strength. The Erotic as Power and the Love of God* (San Francisco: Harper & Row 1989).

17 Mary E. Hunt, *Fierce Tenderness. A Feminist Theology of Friendship* (New York: Crossroad 1990).

18 Beverley W. Harrison, *Die neue Ethik der Frauen. Kraftvolle Beziehungen statt bloßem Gehorsam* (Stuttgart: Kreuzverlag 1991).

eck zwischen Gott und Mensch, zwischen zwei Menschen und allgemein zwischen Menschen anhand des Interpretaments der wechselseitigen Liebesbeziehung zwischen zwei Frauen. Die entscheidenden Aspekte dieser Theologie sind für sie Gegenseitigkeit, Hierarchielosigkeit, Sinnlichkeit und Sexualität, Ganzheitlichkeit von Körper und Geist, Respekt und Liebe. Das Interpretament der Frauenliebe wurde somit erstmals offensiv als mögliche Form dargestellt, zwischenmenschliche Beziehungen und die Beziehungen von Menschen zu Gott angemessen zu versprachlichen.

Die Zeit des ängstlichen Verschweigens lesbischer Lebensformen wurde also schließlich auch im theologischen und kirchlichen Umfeld abgelöst von einem immer offensiveren Umgang lesbischer Frauen mit Erfahrungen, Themen und Fähigkeiten, die sich aus ihren erschwerten Auseinandersetzungen mit tabuisierten Formen des Beziehungslebens, der Frauenliebe und Sexualität unter Frauen ergaben. So forscht die US-amerikanische lesbische Neutestamentlerin Bernadette Brooten beispielsweise über homoerotische Beziehungen von Frauen zur Zeit des Urchristentums.[19] Die beiden lesbischen Pädagoginnen Monika Barz und Herta Leistner forcieren seit 1985 die kirchliche Erwachsenenbildungsarbeit mit lesbischen Frauen an der Evangelischen Akademie in Bad Boll und der Heimvolkshochschule in Loccum[20] und seit 1994 im Frauenstudien- und -bildungszentrum in Gelnhausen. In den Niederlanden gründete sich in den achtziger Jahren eine Arbeitsgruppe »Potten en Theologie« (Lesben und Theologie), die biblisch-hermeneutisch aus lesbischer Perspektive arbeitet und dazu ein spannendes Buch veröffentlicht hat.[21] Für sie ist es entscheidend, nicht nur sogenannte Frauentexte in der Bibel zu bearbeiten, sondern jeden Text vor dem Hintergrund der eigenen Er-

19 Vgl. Bernadette Brooten, "Darum lieferte sie Gott entehrenden Leidenschaften aus. Die weibliche Homoerotik bei Paulus" in: Monika Barz, Herta Leistner, Ute Wild (Hg), *Hättest Du gedacht, daß wir so viele sind? Lesbische Frauen in der Kirche* (Stuttgart: Kreuzverlag1987), 113-138; dies., *Love Between Women. Early Christian Responses to Female Homoeroticism* (Chicago, London: University of Chicago Press 1996).

20 Siehe dazu die leider nicht veröffentlichte Dissertation zum Thema Lesben in der kirchlichen Erwachsenenbildung: Monika Barz und Herta Leistner, Aus der Nichtexistenz auftauchen... Der Beitrag von Tagungsarbeit zum Identitätsbildungsprozeß lesbischer Frauen in der Kirche (unveröffentlichtes MS zur Erlangung des Grades einer Doktorin der Philosophie, Hannover 1993).

21 Vgl. Foka Brouwer und Hermine Pool (Hg.), Zo Wordt het Woord Verkeerd Gehoord. Opstellen von Potten over Theologie en Kerk (Hardinxveld/NL 1990)

fahrungen als lesbische Frauen am Rande der Kirchen und der theologischen Diskurse neu zu lesen. Sie bedienen sich dafür einer aus der Literaturwissenschaft stammenden hermeneutischen Methode von Maaike Meijer.[22] Die Kombination aus Respekt vor dem Text und dem Blick für den Kontext der Leserin ist dabei entscheidender Ausgangspunkt ihrer Arbeit. Die Niederländerinnen bezeichnen ihre Hermeneutik als eine Art des *Querlesens* biblischer Texte. Nicht zu vergessen bleibt die inhaltliche und kirchenpolitische Arbeit der Netzwerke lesbischer Frauen im Umfeld der christlichen Kirchen in Deutschland, die die ideologische "Heiligsprechung" der Ehe und den damit einhergehenden Heterosexismus in Theologie und Kirchenpraxis kritisieren. Diese Arbeit ist in lesbischen Zusammenhängen entstanden. Feministisch-theologische Arbeitsgruppen haben sich dem Thema der lesbischen Existenz und dem Thema der Lebensformen insgesamt kaum gestellt oder fangen erst langsam damit an. Hier ist inhaltlich ein entscheidender Unterschied zwischen lesbisch-feministischen und feministisch-theologischen Ansätzen zu verzeichnen.

Auch das Thema der Personalpolitik im Hinblick auf das Pfarramt ist in diesem Zusammenhang wichtig:[23] Die theologisch legitimierte und kirchenpolitisch umgesetzte Privilegierung heterosexueller Lebensweisen, insbesondere der Ehe, ist an allen Orten sichtbar. Offen lesbisch und schwul lebende PfarrerInnen und kirchliche MitarbeiterInnen haben vielerorts mit Kündigungen und Verleumdungen zu rechnen. Noch nicht eingestellte Lesben und Schwule riskieren bleibende Nichteinstellung. Kirchenrechtlichen Schutz für lesbische und schwule MitarbeiterInnen gibt es nicht. Uneinheitliche personalpolitische Verfahren innerhalb der Landeskirchen verunsichern darüberhinaus viele. Die Kritik an dieser diffusen Personalpolitik, in der Lesben und Schule keinerlei garantierte Rechte haben, ist kompliziert und emotional aufreibend, da sie unter anderem auch die Frage eines öffentlichen Coming-outs in der Kirche nach sich ziehen. Solidarität und Unterstützung von anderen ist demgegenüber

22 Vgl. Maaike Meijer, De Lust tot Lezen. Nederlandse Dichteressen en het Literaire Systeem (Amsterdam, Van Gennep 1988).

23 Ich beziehe mich ausschließlich auf die Personalpolitik der evangelischen Landeskirchen im deutschen Kontext, da ich über die Situation in anderen europäischen Kirchen zu wenig Fakten vorliegen habe. Auch die Personalpolitik der katholischen Kirche müßte gesondert betrachtet werden. Feststeht allerdings, daß sie gegenüber offen lesbisch und schwul lebenden Mitarbeiterinnen und Mitarbeitern noch rigider vorgeht als die evangelischen Kirchen.

noch gering. Lesbische Theologinnen machten darauf aufmerksam, daß selbst ihre heterosexuell lebenden feministischen Kolleginnen bei der Vergabe von Vikariatsstellen oder beim Wechsel in eine andere Landeskirche plötzlich den Ehemann oder den Verlobten als wichtiges Argument für den Verbleib in einer Stadt oder den Wechsel in eine andere anführen. Die heterosexuell angeordneten Spielregeln im Kampf um Vikariatsplätze, Landeskirchenwechsel und Pfarrstellen werden demnach von den meisten feministischen Theologinnen mitgetragen. Übrig bleiben diejenigen, die aus diesen heterosexuellen Vorgaben herausfallen: Alleinstehende und Geschiedene aus der Eheschablone, Lesben und Schwule aus sämtlichen vorgesehenen Mustern. Wichtig wäre dagegen, daß alle erkennen, daß es in der Lebensformpolitik der christlichen Kirchen um Machterhalt und Besitzstandssicherung geht, wovon nicht nur Lesben und Schwule betroffen sind. Hier sind breite Koalitionen notwendig.

Schließlich wird nach meiner Erfahrung selbst bei der Bereitschaft, über unterschiedliche Lebensformen zu diskutieren, eine Asymmetrie deutlich: Heterosexuelle reden oft über das »Problem« von Lesben und Schwulen, ohne das Thema als gesellschaftliches Problem wahrzunehmen und ihre eigene Lebensform in den Diskussionen auf ihre Selbstverständlichkeit hin kritisch zu hinterfragen. Das Problem wird dadurch allein bei Lesben und Schwulen verortet. Statt dessen müßten aber alle Beteiligten über Zusammenlebensformen und ihre kirchlichen und theologischen Bewertungen nachdenken. Nur so können heterosexistische Normen und ihre Funktionsweisen durchschaut und ihre Reproduktionssstrukturen verändert werden.

Zusammenfassend läßt sich festhalten, daß der theologische Niederschlag der stärkeren Abgrenzung lesbischer Frauen in folgenden Aspekten abzulesen ist:

- Einbezug der Kategorie der Zwangsheterosexualität in die Analyse von theologischen Ansätzen und kirchenpolitischen Handlungsweisen;
- Kritik an den Kategorien von Weiblichkeit, Mütterlichkeit, Fruchtbarkeit und Ganzheitlichkeit als angebliche Grundaspekte feministischer Gottesbilder und feministischer Anthropologien;
- Kritik an theologisch konstruierten und legitimierten Setzungen von "Normalität" und Abweichung;
- Revision biblischer Exegese und Hermeneutik: "Querlesen" biblischer Texte im Spannungsfeld von Text und Kontext, bei dem auch die Erfahrungen lesbischer Frauen einbezogen werden;

- Entwicklung von Aspekten einer Theologie der Beziehung;
- Kirchenpolitisches Engagement gegen die Diskriminierung lesbischer und schwuler MitarbeiterInnen in den Kirchen;
- Forderungen von Partnerschaftssegnungen für lesbische und schwule Paare;
- Einbezug der Erfahrungen von Lesben und Schwulen in Predigt und Liturgie;
- Kritik an der Objektivierung von Lesben und Schwulen als "pastorale Seelsorgefälle". Statt dessen Forderung einer begleitenden Seelsorge, die Selbstfindungsprozesse von Lesben und Schwulen unterstützt.

3 Die Differenzierungen der neunziger Jahre: Schubladen-Verwirrungen

Die Mitte der achtziger Jahre läßt sich aus den angegebenen Gründen als Aufbruchzeit der lesbischen Frauen im Umfeld Kirche beschreiben. Ende der achtziger, Anfang der neunziger folgt die Zeit, in der lesbische Frauen und ihre theologischen und gesellschaftspolitischen Analysen, Inhalte und Forderungen offensiver sichtbar und hörbar werden. Die neunziger Jahre sind aber auch die Jahre der Ausdifferenzierungen unter den lesbischen Frauen.

Genauso wie die Frauenbewegung der siebziger Jahre brauchten lesbische Frauen in den achtziger Jahren die Vergewisserung, daß es viele Lesben in und außerhalb der Kirchen gibt. Auch hier überwog die Verständigung über die Gemeinsamkeiten die Sensibilität für vorhandene Differenzen. Gemeinsam begannen sich lesbische Frauen als Opfer zwangsheterosexueller Strukturen in Kirche und Gesellschaft wahr- und ernstzunehmen. Sie fühlten sich von vielen heterosexuellen Feministinnen genauso ignoriert und benachteiligt wie von Nichtfeministinnen und Männern. Sie waren vielerorts enttäuscht über fehlende Solidarität im Krisenfall und die stets weitergetragene Verlängerung alter Tabuisierungsmechanismen und Verschweigemuster. Viele lesbische Frauen erwarteten daher Solidarität und Gemeinschaft nur noch von anderen Lesben, die genau wie sie unter offenen und subtilen Diskriminierungen zu leiden hatten. Separatistische Strömungen unter den lesbischen Frauen wurden stärker.[24] Viele suchten sich Gleichgesinnte, arbeiteten nur noch mit Lesben

24 Vertreterinnen sind beispielsweise Mary Daly und Sara Hoagland.

zusammen und lehnten eine Auseinandersetzung mit Anderslebenden mit dem Hinweis auf die Sinnlosigkeit solcher Unternehmungen ab. Eine lesbische Monokultur drohte die Unterschiedlichkeit unter lesbischen Frauen in einem hinsichtlich Lebensform und Alltagswirklichkeit pluralen Umfeld zu vereinheitlichen und zu vereinnahmen.

Gegen diese Vereinheitlichungstendenzen regt sich allerdings seit einigen Jahren vehementer Protest. Afrodeutsche Lesben, lesbische Migrantinnen, lesbische Jüdinnen beispielsweise haben sich auf den einmal jährlich stattfindenden Berliner Lesbenwochen und auch auf den Lesbenfrühlingstreffen, die ebenfalls einmal im Jahr in einer deutschen Stadt organisiert werden, heftig gegen die Vereinnahmungen weißer christlicher Lesben gewehrt. Sie kritisieren mit Nachdruck die Einheitsformel WIR Lesben, genauso wie lesbische Frauen in den siebziger und achtziger Jahren in der Frauenbewegung die Einheitsformel WIR Frauen als vereinnahmend kritisiert und abgelehnt haben. Das Problem von Rassismus unter Lesben und die Frage nach den unterschiedlichen Privilegien je nach Herkunft, Bildungsweg und Erwerbstätigkeit kamen mit Nachdruck zur Sprache. Auch behinderte und alte Lesben kritisieren den hohen Normdruck unter Lesben und weisen darauf hin, wie brutal die Schablonen der IDEAL-Lesbe an Orten lesbischer Subkultur zum Teil konstruiert sind: jung, schön, sportlich und politisch korrekt muß lesbe sein. Sonst ist sie gar keine »richtige« Lesbe.

So läßt sich zusammenfassen, daß die neunziger Jahre die Jahre der Kritik an essentiellen Beschwörungsformeln sind. Aufgrund der gemachten Erfahrungen stehen die Differenzen im Vordergrund, nicht mehr die Gemeinsamkeiten. Nur die Zusammenschau des Geflechts aller Unrechtsstrukturen wie Rassismus, Klassismus und Heterosexismus, deren Benennung und komplexe Bekämpfung können Veränderungen bringen.[25]

Um diese Strukturen zu verändern, ist es genauso notwendig, die Bewertungskategorien hinsichtlich der IDEAL-Lesbe abzubauen, wie die unkritische Stilisierung von Klischeeschwulen und Heterosexuellen mit dem Ziel der Abgrenzung von ihnen. Dies gilt selbstverständlich im gleichen Maß auch im Hinblick auf die Vorurteilsproduktionen der Hetero-

---

[25] Vgl. Ika Hügel u.a. (Hg.), *Entfernte Verbindungen. Rassismus, Antisemitismus, Klassenunterdrückung* (Berlin: Orlanda Frauenverlag 1993). Siehe zu dieser Debatte auch Ulrike Janz, "Die weiße Lesbenbewegung und das Thema Rassismus/ Antisemitismus" in: *Ihrsinn* (1992/6), *Landplagen*, 28-32.

sexuellen gegenüber Lesben und Schwulen. Ohne die nötigen Differenzierungen und Dekonstruktionen der Klischeebilder werden stets nur die herrschenden Ideologiediskurse über Wesen und Bestimmung der Frau und ihre angebliche Normalbiographie neu formuliert.

Die zwangsheterosexuelle Normalität braucht die Homosexualität als Abweichung von der Norm als konstitutives Moment ihrer Selbstdarstellung und Reproduktion. Lesben und Schwule, die sich in dieser dualistischen Konstruktion additiv neben heterosexuelle Lebensformen anordnen, tragen also die Grundstruktur dieser bipolar und heterosexistisch angeordneten Gesellschaft aktiv mit.[26] Sie liefern lediglich die notwendigen Ausnahmen von der Regel, statt das Regelsystem insgesamt in Frage zu stellen.

Differenzsensibilität ist notwendig in den Neunzigern!

Nach meiner Überzeugung sind in dieser Situation feministisch-theologisch arbeitende Frauen dazu aufgerufen, ihren Forschungskontext explizit zu reflektieren und in ihre Arbeiten einzubeziehen. Darüber hinaus müßten gerade *wegen* aller beschriebenen Unterschiede Koalitionen und Aktionsbündnisse geschlossen werden. Diese sollen Unterschiede nicht verwischen oder vereinnahmen, sondern die Arbeit auf der Grundlage der verschiedenen Erfahrungen, Analyseperspektiven und inhaltlichen Kenntnisse zu gestalten. So können Strategien aufgezeigt und konkrete Schritte gegangen werden, um die oben genannten vielschichtig verwobenen Normalitätskonstruktionen aufzubrechen und entsprechende Denk- und Verhaltensweisen in Theologie, Kirche und Gesellschaft zu verändern.

---

26 Vgl. dazu Kerstin Söderblom, "We're queer—we're here!—Get used to it! *Queer* im Kontext einer feministischen Befreiungstheologie" in: Schlangenbrut 54, *Schwestern und Geliebte. Lesbisch-feministische Identitäten* (August 1996), 19-23.

Abstracts

This article discusses the process of differentiation between varoius feminist and lesbian feminist theological approaches from the 1970s into the 1990s. On the basis of interviews with lesbians working in the churches and in theology, Kerstin Söderblom considers the changes in the themes and controversies which have exercised (West)German feminist theologians in this period, and the reasons which for those changes. She highlights the broadening of perspective which follows when the experiences of lesbians are taken into account in questions of hermeneutics, definition of context, church politics, and the wider utopian vision, and gives examples of possible consequences for the praxis.

Cet article étudie le processus de différenciation entre plusieurs approches théologiques, féministes et lesbiennes des années 70 aux années 90. Sur base d'interviews de lesbiennes travaillant dans l'Eglise et dans le domaine de la théologie, Kerstin Söderblom examine les changements survenus dans la thématique et dans les controverses qui ont préoccupé les théologiennes féministes d'Allemagne de l'Ouest durant cette période, ainsi que les causes de ces changements. Elle met l'accent sur l'élargissement du champ de vision qui résulte de la prise en compte des expériences des femmes lesbiennes en matière d'herméneutique, de définition des contextes, de politique ecclésiale, sans oublier l'élargissement de la vision utopique; ceci s'accompagne d'exemples relatifs aux conséquences qui pourraient servir dans la pratique.

Dr. Kerstin SÖDERBLOM (geboren 1963) Studium der Evangelischen Theologie und Diplompädagogik, Mitarbeiterin am Frauenforschungsprojekt zur Geschichte der Theologinnen in Göttingen, Dissertation zum Thema "Die Bedeutung christlicher Religion in Lebensgeschichten lesbischer Frauen in Deutschland," zur Zeit Vikarin in Frankfurt/Main.

I Bibliographie - Bibliography - Bibliographie*

I.1 Exegese (Erstes Testament, Neues Testament, nicht kanonisierte jüdische und frühchristliche Schriften) und Hermeneutik

Clark Wire, Antoinette, **The Corinthian Women Prophets: A Reconstruction through Paul's Rhetoric** (Minneapolis: Fortress 1995)

Dannemann, Irene, **Aus dem Rahmen fallen. Frauen im Markusevangelium. Eine feministische Re-Vision** (Berlin: Alektor 1996)

Femmes (Des) aussi faisaient route avec lui. Perspectives féministes sur la Bible (Montréal: Médiaspaul 1995)

Jost, Renate, **Frauen, Männer und die Himmelskönigin** (Chr. Kaiser Gütersloher Verlagshaus 1995, ISBN: 3-579-00098-5

Maier, Christl, **Die "fremde Frau" in Proverbien 1-9** (Göttingen: Vandenhoeck & Ruprecht 1995), ISBN: 3-525-53779-4

Mayer-Schärtel, Bärbel, **Das Frauenbild des Josephus** (Stuttgart: Kohlhammer), ISBN: 3-17-013913-4

Ricci, Carla, **Mary Magdalene and Many Others, Women Who Followed Jesus** (Minneapolis: Fortress 1994)

Schroer, Silvia, **Die Weisheit hat ihr Haus gebaut** (Mainz: Grünewald 1996), ISBN: 3-7867-1951-9

Schüngel-Straumann, Helen, **Denn Gott bin ich, und kein Mann** (Mainz:Grünewald1996), ISBN: 3-7867-1904-7

Seifert, Brigitte, **Metaphorisches Reden von Gott im Hoseabuch** (Göttingen: Vandenhoeck & Ruprecht 1996), ISBN: 3-525-53830-8

Selvidge, Marla J., **Notorious Voices: Feminist Biblical Interpretation, 1500-1920** (London: SCM 1996)

Siebert-Hommes, Jopie, **Let the Daughters Live! The Literary Architecture of Exodus 1 and 2 as a Key for Interpretation** (Leiden: Brill 1997)

Sölle, Dorothee / Kirchberger, Joe H. / Haag, Herbert (eds), **Great Women of the Bible in Art and Literature** (Grand Rapids: Eerdmans 1996)

Wind, Renate, **Maria—aus Nazareth, aus Bethanien, aus Magdala** (Chr. Kaiser Gütersloher Verlagshaus 1996), ISBN: 3-579-5145-8

---

* Zu Büchern mit * siehe unter "Rezensionen"—Books marked * are reviewed below—Pour les livres avec * voire sous "Critiques".

I.2 Kirchen- und Religionsgeschichte

Allen, Sister Prudence, **The Concept of Woman: The Aristotelian Revolution, 750 B.C.-A.D. 1250**, (Grand Rapids: Eerdmans 1996)

Amat, Jacqueline, **Passion de Perpétue et de Félicité** (Paris: Cerf)

ISBN: 2-204-05386-4

van Baest, Marieke, **Peotry of Hadewych: Daring God Talk** (Kampen: Kok Pharos 1997), ISBN: 90-390-0058-1

Boxler, Madeleine, **«ich bin ein predigerin und appostlorin» Die deutschen Maria Magdalena-Legenden des Mittelalters (1300–1550) Untersuchungen und Texte** (Frankfurt/M.: Peter Lang 1996)

ISBN: 3-906756-48-3

Brooten, Bernadette, **Love Between Women: Early Christian Responses to Female Homoeroticism** (Chicago: University of Chicago Press 1996)

Cloke, Gillian, **This Female Man of God: Women and Spiritual Power in the Patristic Age AD 350-450** (London: Routledge 1995)

Darling, Pamela W., New Wine: **The Story of Women Transforming Leadership & Power in the Episcopal** Church (London: SPCK 1995)

Susanna Elm, **'Virgins of God': The Making of Asceticism in Late Antiquity** (Oxford: Clarendon Press 1994) ISBN: 0-19-814920-4

Feichtinger, Barbara, **Apostolae Apostolarum: Frauenaskese als Befreiung und Zwang bei Hieronymus** (Frankfurt/M.: Peter Lang 1995) ISBN: 3-631-47683-3

Gill, Sean, **Women and the Church of England from the Eighteenth Century to the Present** (London: SPCK 1994)

Jackson, Eleanor (ed. with an introduction, transl. by John Shepherd), **The Question of Woman: The Collected Writings of Charlotte von Kirschbaum**, (Grand Rapids: Eerdmans 1996)

Jensen, Anne (Hg.), **Thekla Die Apostolin. Ein apokrypher Text neu entdeckt** (Freiburg: Herder 1996)

Jensen, Anne, **God´s Self-confident Daughters: Early Christianity and the Liberation of Women** (Kampen: Kok Pharos 1997), ISBN: 90-390-0272-X

Meurling, Birgitta, **Sarons liljor?: en etnologisk studie av prästfruars könkonstituering** (Stockholm: Carlsson 1996) (Lilies in Saron? An ethonological study of the gender constitution process of clergymen´s wives)

Power, Kim, **Veiled Desire: Augustine's Writings on Women** (London: DLT 1995)

Rapley, Elizabeth, **Les Dévotes. Les femmes et l'Eglise en France au XVIIème siécle** (Québec: Bellarmin 1995)

Roper, Lyndal, **Oedipus and the Devil: Witchcraft, sexuality and religion in early modern Europe** (London/New York: Routledge 1995) ISBN: 0-415-10581-1

Roux, Jaqueline, **Sous l'étendard de Jeanne. Les Fédérations diocésaines de jeunes filles. 1904–1945** (Paris: Cerf 1995)

Sawyer, Deborah F., **Women and Religion in the First Christian Centuries** (London/New York: Routledge 1996)

Sevegrand, Martine **Les enfants du bon Dieu. Les catholiques français et la procréation au XXème siécle** (Paris: Albin Michel 1995)

Teresa de los Andes—Correspondance. La «petite Thérèse» du Chili 1900–1920 (Paris: Cerf 1995)

Torjesen, Karen Jo, **When Women were Priests: Women's Leadership in the Church and the Scandal of their Subordination in the Rise of Christianity** (San Francisco: Harper Collins 1995)

Trevett, Christine, **Montanism: Gender, Authority and the New Prophecy** (Cambridge: Cambridge University Press 1996)

I.3 Systematische und Praktische Theologie, Spiritualität, Ökumene und Interreligiöser Dialog

Baker-Fletcher, Karen / Baker-Fletcher, Garth (Kasimu), **My Sister, My Brother: Womanist and Exodus God-Talk**, (Louisville: Westminster John Knox 1996)

Baroni, Lise et al., **Voix de femmes, voies de passages.Pratiques pastorales et enjeux ecclésiaux** (Montréal: Paulines 1995)

Bartholomeusz, Tessa, **Women Under the Bo Tree: Buddhist Nuns in Sri Lanka** (Cambridge: Cambridge University Press 1994)

Bender, Christiane / Graßl, Hans / Motzkau, Heidrun / Schumacher, Jan (Hg.), **Machen Frauen Kirche?** (Mainz: Grünewald 1996), ISBN: 3-7867-1961-6

Bons-Storm, Riet / Ackermann, Denise (eds), **Practical Theology in Feminist Perspective** (Kampen: Kok Pharos 1997),ISBN: 90-390-0282-7

Bons-Storm, Riet, **The Incredible Woman: Listening to Women´s Silences in Pastoral Care and Counseling** (Kampen: Kok Pharos 1997), ISBN: 90-390-0292-4

Brock, Rita Nakashima / Brooks Thistlethwaite, Susan, **Casting Stones, Prostitution and Liberation in Asia and the United States** (Minneapolis: Fortress, 1996)

Byrne, Lavinia (ed.), **The Hidden Voice: Christian Women and Social Change** (London: SPCK 1995)

Carr, Anne / van Leeuwen, Stewart (ed)., **Religion, Feminism, and the Family**, (Louisville: Westminster John Knox 1996)

Cooper-White, Pamela, **The Cry of Tamar: Violence against Women and the Church's Response**, (Minneapolis: Fortress 1995)

Deane-Drummond, Celia, **A Handbook in Theology and Ecology** (London: SCM 1996)

Demel, Sabine, **Abtreibung zwischen Straffreiheit und Exkommunikation** (Stuttgart: Kohlhammer, 1995), ISBN: 3-17-013909-6

Dumont, Micheline, **Les religieuses sont-elles féministes?** (Québec: Bellarmin 1995)

Edgardh Beckmann, Ninna, **Sofia—den vishet vi förunnar** (Uppsala: Svensk Kyrkans forskningsråd 1996) (Sophia: The Wisdom we proclaim, Swedish, 4 page summary in English)

L'Église et les Femmes. Bibliographie signalétique de la langue française (Lyon: Centre Femmes et Christianisme 1995)

Eriksson, Anne-Louise, **The Meaning of Gender in Theology. Problems and Possibilities** (Uppsala: 1995), ISBN 91-554-3655-2

Esser, Annette / Roll, Susan, u.a.: **Revisioning our Sources: Women's Spirituality in European Perspectives** (Kampen: Kok Pharos 1997)

Fischer, Irmtraud, **Gottesstreiterinnen** (Stuttgart: Kohlhammer, 1995), ISBN: 3-17-013508-2

*Frank Parsons, Susan, **Feminism and Christian Ethics** (Cambridge: Cambridge University Press 1996)

Götz von Olenhusen, Irmtraud, u.a., **Frauen unter dem Patriarchat der Kirchen** (Stuttgart: Kohlhammer 1995), ISBN: 3-17-013906-1

*Günter, Andrea (Hg.), **Feministische Theologie und postmodernes Denken,** (Stuttgart: Kohlhammer), ISBN: 3-17-014008-6

Günter, Andrea / Wagener, Ulrike (eds), **What does it mean today to be a (feminist) theologian?**, (ESWTR Yearbook 4, Kampen: Kok Pharos 1996)

Hampson, Daphne, **After Christianity** (London: SCM 1996)

Hampson, Daphne (ed.), **Swallowing a Fishbone: Feminist Theologians Debate Christianity** (London: SPCK 1996)

Hopkins, Julie, **Naar enn feministische Christologi. Jezus van Nazareth, Europese vrouwen en de crisis in de Christologie** (Kampen: Kok Pharos 1997) ISBN: 90-242-7965-8

Hopkins, Julie, **Verso una cristologia feminista Gesù di Nazareth, le donne europee e la crisi cristologica** (Brescia: Editrice Queriniana 1996) ISBN: 88-399-0743-2

Isasi-Diaz, Ada María, **Mujerista Theology: Theology for the 21st Century** (Louisville: Westminster John Knox 1996)

Isherwood, Lisa / McEwan, Dorothea (eds), **An A-Z of Feminist Theology** (Sheffield: Sheffield Academic Press 1996)

Isherwood, Lisa / McEwan, Dorothea, **Introducing Feminist Theology** (Sheffield: Sheffield Academic Press 1996)

Jäger-Sommer, Johanna (red.), **God opniew gedacht. Veranwoord-delijkkheid voor de schepping in feministisch perspectief. Theologische essays voor Catharina Halkes** (Baarn: Ten Have 1995) ISBN: 90-259-461-3

Jansen, Grace, **Power and Gender in Christian Mysticism** (Cambridge: Cambridge University Press 1995)

Junus, Petra, **Den levande Gudinnan-kvinnoidentitet och religiositet som förrändringsprocess** (Nora: Nya Doxa 1995), ISBN: 91-88248-78-X ((The Living Goddess. Women´s identity and religiosity as a process of change, Swedish 7 pages summary in English)

Hewitt, Marsha Aileen, **Critical Theory of Religion: A Feminist Analysis** (Minneapolis: Fortress 1994)

Kessler, Hildrun, **Bibliodrama und Leiblichkeit** (Stuttgart: Kohlhammer 1996) ISBN: 3-17-013714-X

Lindén, C and Milles, U., **Feministik bruksanvisning: essäer** (Stockholm: Norstedts 1995) (A Femminist Manual: Essays, Swedish)

Löffler, Irene, **Unsere Spiritualität entdecken und feiern** (Mainz: Grünewald 1996), ISBN: 3-7867-1938-1

Maitland, Sara, **Angel and Me** (London: Mowbray 1995)

Mananzan, Mary John / Oduyoye, Mercy / Tamez, Elsa / Clarkson, J.Shannon / Grey, Mary / Russell, Letty (eds), **Women Resisting Violence, The Struggle for Life** (Louisville: Westminster John Knox 1996)

Martin, Francis, **The Feminist Question: Feminist Theology in the Light of Christian Tradition** (Grand Rapids: Eerdmans 1996)

McKenzie, Vashti M., **Not Without a Struggle: Leadership Development for African American Women in Ministry** (Louisville: Westminster John Knox 1996)

McClintock Fulkerson, Mary, **Changing the Subject: Women's Discourses and Feminist Theology** (Minneapolis: Fortress 1994)

Meyer-Wilmes, Hedwig, **Zwischen lila und lavendel. Schritte feministischer Theologie**, (Regensburg: Pustet 1996) (erscheint im Oktober 1997 englisch u. niederländisch)

Moody, Linda A., **Women Encounter God** (Louisville: Westminster John Knox 1996)

Page, Ruth, **God and the Web of Creation** (London: SCM 1996)

Patrick, Anne E., **Liberating Conscience: Feminist Explorations in Catholic Moral Theology** (London: SCM 1996)

Pithan, Annabelle (Hg.), **Religionspädagoginnen des 20. Jahrhunderts** (Göttingen: Vandenhoek& Ruprecht 1997) ISBN: 3-525-61175-7

Pohl-Patalong, Uta, **Seelsorge zwischen Individuum und Gesell-schaft.Elemente zu einer Neukonzeption der Seelsorgetheorie** (Stuttgart: Kohlhammer 1996) ISBN: 3-17-014414-6

Praetorius, Ina **Towards a Feminist Ethics** (Kampen: Kok Pharos 1997), ISBN: 90-390-0422-6

Pryce, Mark, **Finding a Voice: Men, Women and the Community of the Church** (London : SCM 1996)

Radford Ruether, Rosemary (ed.), **Women Healing Earth: Third World Women on Ecology, Feminism and Religion** (London: SCM 1996)

Ramshaw, Gail, **God beyond Gender: Feminist Christian God-Language** (Minneapolis: Fortress 1994) ((religion and gender roles, skandinavian languages, summaries in English)

Religion och Bibel LV: Religionen och könsrollerna (Uppsala: Nathan Söderblom-sällskapets årsbok: 1996)

Russel, Letty M. / Clarkson, J. Shannon (eds), **Dictionary of Feminist Theologies** (Louisville: Westminster John Knox 1996)

Sands, Kathleen M., **Escape from Paradise: Evil and Tragedy in Feminist Theology** (Minneapolis: Fortress 1994)

Sanders, Cheryl J., **Living the Intersection: Womanism and Afrocentrism in Theology** (Minneapolis: Fortress 1994)

Schüssler-Fiorenza, Elisabeth (ed.), **The Power of Naming, A Concilium Reader in Feminist Theology** (London: SCM and Louisville: Westminster John Knox 1996)

*Sjørup, Lene, **Oneness: A Theology of Women's Religious Experiences** (Kok Pharos Publishing House, Kampen, Niederlande 1996)

*Sowle Cahill, Lisa, **Sex Gender, and Christian Ethics** (Cambridge: Cambridge University Press 1996)

Sundqvist, Olof / Svalastog, Anna Lydia (eds), **Myter och mytteorier. Religionshistoriska diskussioner of teoretiska ansatser** (Uppsala: Religionshistoriska forskningsrapporter från Uppsala 1996) (Myths and theories of myth. Discussion within history of religions and theoretical approaches, Scandinavian languages, summaries in English)

Stevenson Moessner, Jeanne (ed.), **Through the Eyes of Women: Insights for Pastoral Care** (Minneapolis: Fortress 1996)

Stuart, Elizabeth, **Just Good Friends: Towards a Lesbian and Gay Theology of Relationships** (London: Mowbray, 1995)

Stuart, Elizabeth: **Spitting at Dragons: Towards a Feminist Theology of Sainthood** (London, Mowbray 1996)

Stuart, Elizabeth / Thatcher, Adrian (eds) **Christian Perspectives on Sexuality and Gender** (Grand Rapids: Eerdmans 1996)

Troch, Lieve, **Verzet is het geheim van de vreugde. Fundamental-theologische thema's in enn feministische discussie** (Zoetermee: Boekencentrum 1996) ISBN: 90-239-1558-5

Veillette, Denise (ed.), **Femmes et religions** (Québec: Presse de l'Université Laval et Corporation Canadienne des Sciences Religieuses 1995)

van Wolde, Ellen, **Stories of the Beginning: Genesis 1-11 and Other Creation Stories** (London: SCM 1996) ISBN: 0-334-2637-7

Ward, Hannah / Wild, Jennifer / Morley, Janet (eds), **Celebrating Women,** (London: SPCK ^{2}1995) ISBN: 0-281-04836-3

II. REZENSIONEN - BOOK REVIEWS - CRITIQUE DE LIVRES

Lisa Sowle Cahill: ***Sex, Gender and Christian Ethics*** **(New Studies in Christian Ethics 9, Cambridge: Cambridge University Press 1996)**

Die katholische Ethikerin Lisa Sowle Cahill aus Boston, Vorsitzende der Society of Christian Ethics, hat nach mehreren früheren Büchern zur christlichen Sexualethik ein engagiertes und couragiertes Buch zum Verhältnis von Geschlechterdifferenz in biologischer (sex) und kultureller (gender) Hinsicht und christlicher Ethik vorgelegt.

Im ersten Teil ihres Buches entwickelt sie eine philosophische Grundlegung ihrer im zweiten Teil erfolgenden materialen Überlegungen zu "sex" und "gender". Von einer adäquaten Ethik des Geschlechts in der Gegenwart erwartet Cahill, daß sie: 1. auf konkrete Probleme des täglichen Lebens bezogen werden kann; 2. die kulturell und biologisch gegebene Geschlechterdifferenz genügend berücksichtigt und sie auf größere Gleichheit der Geschlechter hin transzendiert; und 3. gleichwohl nicht auf universale Prinzipien verzichtet. Einen Weg, dessen Verfolgung aussichtsreich wäre, kann sie statt in prozeduralistischen und abstrakt universalen der Kantischen Tradition verpflichteten Ethikansätzen in substanziell begründeter Ethik erkennen, wie sie Aristoteles und Thomas von Aquin und innerhalb der feministischen Diskussion die Aristotelikerin Martha C. Nussbaum ausgearbeitet haben. Eine solche Ethik setzt bei konkreten Erfahrungen an und geht dann induktiv vor, indem sie stets im Bewußtsein der Revisionsbedürftigkeit substanzielle Aussagen zu machen versucht. Sie zielt auf menschliches Gedeihen und Wohlergehen (flourishing).

Wenn feministische Ethik eine Änderung der Verhältnisse anders als durch Macht herbeiführen will, bedarf sie, so Cahill, des begründenden Rückgriffs auf Universalien der menschlichen Existenz, die sie vor allem in Gemeinsamkeiten des basalen körperlichen menschlichen Lebens festmacht sowie in Gemeinsamkeiten zwischen Frauen und Männern. Den Körper betrachtet Cahill als Ausgangspunkt zu führender interkultureller Dialoge über die menschlichen Bedürfnisse und Güter sowie über die praktisch einzuschlagenden Wege. Körpererfahrungen seien kulturell zwar in Einzelheiten differenziert, wiesen aber in wesentlichen Elementen wie z.B. der Elternschaft, des Alterns und auch der ihrer Auffassung nach geschlechtsdifferenziert zu reflektierenden Heterosexualität Gemeinsamkeiten auf. Sie ermöglichten eine kulturübergreifende Kommunikation und böten ein wichtiges Fundament für eine im Diskurs zu erarbeitende universale Ethik zu "sex", "gender" und Familie.

Zwischen Menschen aus verschiedenen Kulturen macht Cahill moralische Übereinstimmungen aus, die offenbar durch die in soziale Beziehungen eingebettete Körperlichkeit allgemein einsichtig und naheliegend erscheinen, so z.B. das Bestreben von Eltern, das Wohl ihrer Kinder zu fördern. Sie postuliert, daß eine angemessene und kulturübergreifende Sexualethik von der Gleichheit der Geschlechter bestimmt sein müsse, bezogen auf die sexuelle Vereinigung auf die Werte der Reproduktion, des Vergnügens (pleasure) und der Intimität. Unabhängig von unterschiedlichen Formen des Zusammenleben der Geschlechter, der Sexualität und des Familienlebens in verschiedenen Kulturen sollte sie sich insgesamt an diesen Werten orientieren.

Im zweiten Teil ihres Buches analysiert Cahill in geschichtlichen Rückblicken, wie sich eine christlich-katholische Ethik von sex und gender seit dem Neuen Testament entwickelt hat, die trotz unterdrückerischer und frauenfeindlicher Tendenzen Frauen zugute kommen konnte. Sie zeigt auf, daß für die christliche Familienvorstellung in kritischer Abgrenzung von der griechisch-römischen Familie die Gleichrangigkeit beider Eheleute konstitutiv war. Die Sakramentalität der Ehe, die ihre Unauflöslichkeit begründet, habe nicht zuletzt dem Schutz von Frauen und Kindern gedient. Die kirchliche Kritik an der Empfängnisverhütung lasse eine Leichtfertigkeit heterosexueller Sexualität nicht zu, sondern fordere gerade von Männern, mit ihrer (verschiedengeschlechtlichen) Sexualität verantwortlich und im Bewußtsein der Möglichkeit der Zeugung menschlichen Lebens umzugehen. Während die moderne Sexualethik auf sexuelle Freiheit und individuelle Erfüllung ausgerichtet sei, ermangele es ihr an einer Betrachtung der sozialen Faktoren von Sexualität sowie an einem konstruktiven Umgang mit Elternschaft und Familie. Zeugung, Schwangerschaft und die Begleitung von Kindern auf dem Weg zum Erwachsenwerden seien moralische hoch zu schätzende und gesellschaftlich unerläßliche "gute Werke" für die Allgemeinheit. Neben Wahlfreiheit und persönlicher Erfüllung solle sich eine tragfähige Sexualethik daher an gegenseitiger Verpflichtung (commitment), an Sozialität und am Gemeinwohl orientieren. Auf dieser Linie empfiehlt Cahill einen kritischen und die Kosten der Frauen berücksichtigenden Umgang mit modernen Reproduktionstechniken. Trotz aller Probleme zieht sie die Adoption von Kindern den Strapazen der Reproduktionstechnologie vor, die Frauen häufig jahrelang in Kauf nehmen, obwohl sie in der Anwendung und Ideologie dieser Technologie nachweislich zum Objekt degradiert werden.

Obwohl Cahills Ethik auf heterosexuelle Beziehungen konzentriert ist, analysiert sie kritisch die paulinische Abwehr gleichgeschlechtlicher Sexualität.

Sie kommt zu dem Ergebnis, daß gegenwärtig die Einsetzung von Homosexuellen in kirchliche Ämter der neutestamentlichen Kritik an sozialen Exklusionen durchaus entspreche. Einer gleichzeitigen Wertschätzung von Familie und heterosexueller Sexualität müsse dies nicht im Weg stehen.

Der Herausgeber der auf Gegenwartsprobleme und den interdisziplinären Dialog der Theologie bezogenen New Studies in Christian Ethics, Robin Gill merkt im Vorwort des Buches an, nur eine Katholikin könne wohl gegenwärtig solch eine die katholische Tradition konstruktiv beerbende Ethik von Sex, Gender und Familie schreiben. Spontan leuchtet mir das ein. Die Lektüre erstaunt eine Protestantin wie mich, wie Dokumente der katholischen Tradition, die im Protestantismus als repressiv und freiheitseinschränkend wahrgenommen werden, in feministisch-theologischer Perspektive als Quellen entdeckt werden können, die neben aller kritikwürdigen Geschlechtsasymmetrie die Gleichheit von Frauen stützen und die Verantwortlichkeit für Kinder auf beide Elternteile übertragen. Die von Cahill nicht problematisierte Kompatibilität einer schwach essentialistisch begründeten philosophischen Ethik und einer neutestamentlich orientierten christologisch begründeten Sexualethik provoziert die Protestantin zur kritischen Frage, ob hier Differenzen nicht stärker zu gewichten wären.

Skepsis erweckt in mir die Hoffnung Cahills, ob, wie sie es mit Nußbaum behauptet, tatsächlich humane körperliche Universalien wie das Älterwerden und geschlechtlich differenzierte Universalien wie die Fruchtbarkeit der Frauen und der Männer oder (über Nußbaum hinaus) die Möglichkeit des Vater- und Mutterseins die Grundlage für eine gemeinsame universale Moral bilden können. Sie müßten ja Interpretationen und Bewertungen finden, die von potentiell allen geteilt werden könnten und tatsächlich geteilt würden. Andererseits bleibt nach dem Ende eines metaphysisch oder rational begründeten Universalismus keine andere Chance, als auf der Suche nach einem adäquaten Universalismus die eigenen universalistischen Ansprüche möglichst einsichtig für andere darzulegen und sich in Auseinandersetzung um die beste und möglichst allen einleuchtende Form des Universalismus zu begeben.

Cahill verdient Bewunderung für ihren Mut, die aktuellen Themen der Sexualethik auf eine kritische biblisch und historisch reflektierte Weise zu behandeln und zugleich feministischen Anliegen zu entsprechen. Im Bewußtsein der Differenz zu vielen feministischen Entwürfen der vergangenen Jahrzehnte ist sie klar und pointiert in ihren Thesen. Ihrem Buch ist zu wünschen, daß es auch im deutschsprachigen Raum breit diskutiert wird.

Helga Kuhlmann, Hamburg

Andrea Günter (Hrsg.): ***Feministische Theologie und postmodernes Denken. Zur theologischen Relevanz der Geschlechterdifferenz*** **(Kohlhammer: Stuttgart/Berlin/ Köln 1996)**

"Postmoderne"—eins der herausragenden Schlagwörter der letzten Jahre, ein Begriff, der für die einen mit dem "Ende der großen Erzählungen" die Befreiung von restriktiven, normativen Konzepten verspricht und gleichzeitig den anderen als Paradigma befürchteter Beliebigkeit, allgemeiner Kriterien- und Orientierungslosigkeit gilt. Feministische Befreiungstheologie hat bisher im Verein etwa mit feministischen Sozialwissenschaftlerinnen eher auf die Gefahren aufmerksam gemacht. Umso mehr weckt ein Buch Interesse, das verspricht, postmodernes Denken als positives Potential in feministisch-theologische Reflexion einzubringen. Wie die Herausgeberin in ihrer Einführung deutlich macht, will der Sammelband den anti-essentialistischen Impetus postmodernen Denkens für feministische Theologie fruchtbar machen. Welche Möglichkeiten bieten sich somit, "Frau", "Weiblichkeit" und "Gott" jenseits traditioneller Wesenszuschreibungen zu denken? Neben Postmoderne bildet dabei "Geschlechterdifferenz" den zweiten Leitbegriff des Nachdenkens, wodurch sich das Buch im feministischen Diskurs verortet: Verbunden mit den Namen Luce Irigarays sowie der italienischen Denkerinnen der Gruppe Diotima und des Mailänder Frauenbuchladens, bezeichnet der Begriff der sexuellen Differenz nicht etwa eine Position der Bejahung und Aufwertung sog. "weiblicher Werte". Vielmehr ist die Differenz nach dem Denken der italienischen Feministinnen so radikal zu verstehen, daß "Frau" aus der dichotomen Opposition zu "Mann" befreit werden muß (so Andrea Günter in dem Beitrag "Der Ort Gottes", S. 53f). Was eine Frau ist, kann nicht durch Abgrenzung von Mannsein definiert werden, sondern bestimmt sich im Miteinander der Frauen.

Die "Differenz" kann leider einige Begriffsverwirrung stiften, wie in Claudia Rehbergers Beitrag "Differenz und Gleichheit der Geschlechter in der Theologie des 20. Jahrhunderts" deutlich wird. Wenn sie gegenüber der feministischen Hinwendung zur 'Differenz' kritisch anmerkt "Im kirchlichen Bereich und aus theologischen Verlautbarungen ist uns eine Rede von der Differenz der Geschlechter wohl vertraut (41)," so bezeichnet sie mit dem Begriff hier die traditionelle Geschlechterdichotomie, was nicht dem Differenzbegriff der Italienerinnen entspricht. Metatheoretisch stellt sich hier die Frage, warum feministisches Denken immer wieder zwischen den Ansätzen Gleichheit oder Differenz schwankt. Wie Anne Claire Mulder in ihrer Auseinandersetzung mit den feministischen Ansätzen von Simone de Beauvoir und Rosemary Radford Ruether einerseits sowie Luce Irigaray andererseits ("Überlegungen zur 'imago dei': Minimalisierung oder Maximalisierung der Differenz zwischen den Geschlechtern") zeigt, beruht die feministische Vorliebe für Gleichheit oder Differenz auf einer je korrespondierenden Wahrnehmung der patriarchalen Unterdrückungsstrukturen. Hier erweist sich jedoch die Stärke des italienischen Ansatzes: Richtet sich seine Kritik primär gegen die androzentrische "Logik des Einen", und damit gegen die Auslöschung der ursprünglichen Differenz, so ist die traditionelle Betonung der Unterschiede von Mann und Frau etwa in der theologischen Anthropologie, auf die Claudia Rehberger zu Recht hinweist, im Denken der Geschlechterdifferenz keineswegs übersehen: Sie wird hier als sekundäre Differenzierung, und damit als männliche Projektion entlarvt.

Beim Denken der Geschlechterdifferenz geht es um philosophische Arbeit an der Sprache und damit an der Struktur, die sie zum Verständnis der Wirklichkeit zur Verfügung stellt. Weist diese dekonstruktive Arbeit an der "symbolischen Ordnung" das Denken der Geschlechterdifferenz als postmodernes Projekt aus, so ist diese Zuordnung andererseits auch infragezustellen. Stellt das Denken der Geschlechterdifferenz doch der postmodernen Ent-essentialisierung eine Re-essentialisierung der sexuellen Differenz entgegen und postuliert—wie es Andrea Günter in ihrem Beitrag "Die Frau als Subjekt in Kirche und Gesellschaft" tut—"Das Subjekt Frau (103)" als transzendenten Bezugspunkt für das Subjektsein der einzelnen Frauen. Neben den schon genannten Aufsätzen wird der Geschlechterdifferenz auch in einem Beitrag von Veronika Schlör nachgegangen: Sie unternimmt eine Grundlegung der Ethik von der Ästhetik her, mit Hilfe der ästhetischen Konzepte von "Mimesis" und dem "Erhabenen".

Natürlich kommt kein Buch über postmodernes Denken an einer Diskussion des Subjektbegriffs vorbei. Neben dem schon genannten Beitrag von Andrea Günter findet sich der äußerst interessante Artikel von Susanne Hennecke "'Nur ein Gott kann uns retten (?)'—die theologischen Implikationen poststrukturalistischer Subjektauffassung bei Luce Irigaray und Donna Haraway." Sie findet in diesen beiden unterschiedlichen Ansätzen—ebenso überraschend wie plausibel vorgestellt—die kontroversen Positionen von Ludwig Feuerbach und Karl Barth wieder. Susanne Sandherr setzt sich in ihrem Beitrag sehr differenziert mit der "Verweiblichung des Subjekts" bei Emanuel Lévinas auseinander, angesichts der gegenwärtigen intensiven Lévinas-Rezeption in Deutschland ein wichtiger Beitrag.

Das Buch wird abgeschlossen durch zwei "Text-Lektüren". Berthe van Soest analysiert "Die Rolle der Frauen bei der Enthauptung von Johannes dem Täufer" in Mk 6,16-28. Mit Hilfe dekonstruktivistischer Leseweisen Derridas erhellt sie, wie in den bisher vorherrschenden Lesarten des biblischen Textes das Bild der Herodias als böser Frau und Hauptschuldiger am Tod des Johannes konstruiert worden ist. Dieser Zusammenhang hat in letzter Zeit auch an anderer Stelle feministisches Interesse gefunden: Mit einem ähnlichen Ansatz und u.a. zum gleichen Text arbeitet die sehr empfehlenswerte Untersuchung von Irene Dannemann, Aus dem Rahmen fallen. Frauen im Markusevangelium. Eine feministische Re-Vision, Berlin 1996. Hier zeigt sich eine Neuorientierung der feministischen Exegese, insofern mit der Wendung weg von den identitätsstiftenden positiven Frauengestalten hin zu den negativen Figuren eine Hinwendung zu den literarischen Strategien des Textes einhergeht. Der letzte Beitrag des Sammelbandes von Dorothee Sandherr-Klemp beschäftigt sich mit "Christine Lavants Lyrik auf der Suche nach einem Ort weiblicher Fruchtbarkeit zwischen Klage und Anklage". Gegenüber der in Alltagswelt und Literaturwissenschaft üblichen Abwertung der Klage von Frauen als "unkontrollierter Ausbruch von Emotionalität und Irrationalität (147)" will die Autorin deren "transzendierende Kraft" vernehmbar machen, um weibliche Subjektivität zu stärken.

Der Sammelband besticht durch seine Vielfältigkeit, die durch die Arbeit mit theologischen, literaturwissenschaftlichen, philosophischen und psychoanalytischen Ansätzen und Methoden zustandekommt. Ein Buch, das für das notwendigerweise disziplinenübergreifende feministische Gespräch entscheidende Anstöße bereithält. *Ulrike Wagener, Münster*

Maaike Meijer: *In tekst gevat. Inleiding tot een kritiek van representatie* (Amsterdam: Amsterdam University Press 1996)

Contrary to what her title, "Set in Text: Towards a Critique of Representation," might suggest, Meijer offers examples of a feminist critique of a number of Dutch and English-language novels, poems, and advertising images: the term *representation* implies not only texts but images. She argues that representations do not simply reflect what is in the hearts and minds of people and of cultures but also confirm and invigorate fundamental notions known as *topoi*. In her analysis, the author focuses on representations of gender and ethnicity. Using binary oppositions and stereotypes, these are seen as topoi of hierarchy and difference which should be exposed as they tend to perpetuate conditions of inequality and injustice. Meijer uses various fairly generally accepted approaches: classical interpretation of poetry, structuralistic analysis, narratology, intertextuality, deconstructionism, discourse analysis, and film theory.

The nine chapters of this book are to some extent self-contained. I will refer to three will to illustrate Meijer's method. Chapter Two, on Intertextuality, deals with the recycling of existing texts, some of them well-known and authoritative, into new ones. Meijer shows how this can generate new meanings, that, in her examples, convey a specifically negative view of sexuality. Readers who are familiar with the original text or its genre tend to tolerate sexual allusions that would be less acceptable, even suspicious, in other contexts. For instance, in one modern version of the fairy tale of the Little Red Riding Hood the wolf has become a rapist. By way of contrast, Chapter Three, on Intertextuality and Sex, discusses some deliberately antithetic rewriting. One of them is Adrienne Rich's *Snapshots of a Daughter in Law*, based on texts by Alfred Cortot, Horatius, Cicero, and Baudelaire; another is Christa Wolf's novel *Kassandra*, based on the classical story of the Trojan prophetess. These authors represent the female characters from the original texts by transforming their object-roles into subject-roles. Thus, their works react against well-established and influential patriarchal texts by creating a new and different reality. Chapter Nine, 'The Black Subject', presents an in-depth analysis of M. Székely-Lulofs' novel *Koelie* (1932). Set in the former Dutch East Indies (now Indonesia), *Koelie* shows how indigenous contract-labourers were exploited and often beaten up by the Dutch. A critical novel when taken at face-value, Meijer demonstrates it to be of a colonial spirit. Its textual strategies distinguish, very subtly at times, between European and indigenous, opposing 'us' and 'them', culture and nature, etc. The other chapters deal with a structural analysis of the portrayal of sexual behaviour on a billboard, imbedded misogyny, cultural studies, Susanne Keppeler's *The Pornography of Representation*, and deconstruction of whiteness.

Meijer's analyses are lucid, precise, and very convincing. Showing how topoi on gender and ethnicity are embedded in specific texts and images, her method also promises fruitful results in wider areas and on other topoi. Similar analyses can be and have been applied to biblical texts, for instance in the gender-specific readings of the Old Testament by the late Fokkelien van Dijk-Hemmes, whose work was partly based on insights from narratology and intertextuality. Furthermore, theological discourse promises to be a rich field of research, for as an intentionally persuasive *representation* of reality, it probably also contains embedded gender and other stereotypes. Finally, tying in with work by Mieke Bal on Rembrandt, Meijer's approach might give important new impulses to Christian iconography.

Anneke de Vries, Kampen

Susan Frank Parsons: *Feminism and Christian Ethics* (New Studies in Christian Ethics 8, Cambridge: Cambridge University Press 1996)

Die amerikanische Ethikerin Susan Frank Parsons breitet in ihrem Buch wie sie selbst erklart, vor Leserinnen und Leser die reflexiven Früchte einer Reise aus, die sie selbst in den letzten Jahren unternommen hat und die sie zu verschiedenen feministischen Ansätzen geführt hat. An drei großen Modellen feministischer Theorie stellt sie Muster des Denkens dar sowie die Kritik daran, am liberalen Modell der Gleichheit, am sozialkonstruktivistischen Modell und am naturalistischen Modell feministischer Theorie. Die drei Stationen markieren zugleich eine innere argumentative Entwicklung, die die feministische Diskussion in den letzten drei Jahrzehnten durchgemacht hat. Vom Gleichheitsfeminismus zu seiner sozialkonstruktivistischen In-Fragestellung zum Differenzfeminismus sind nicht nur einzelne Theoretikerinnen, wie z.B. Rosemary Radford Ruether oder Simone de Beauvoir fortgeschritten, sondern auch die allgemeine Diskussion.

Alle drei Teile beginnen mit Erinnerungen an die Mütter des Feminismus aus dem 19. Jahrhundert, ein erneuter Hinweis darauf, daß sich die Forderungen, die Kritik und die Visionen der Frauen von damals noch immer nicht erledigt sind und die feministisch engagierten Frauen der zwanzigsten Jahrhundert zwar nicht in den Details, doch aber in Grundzügen die Wege noch einmal beschreiten mußten, für die schon vor 150 Jahren Frauen kämpften und die ihnen als notwendig und als gangbar erschienen. Jeder der drei Teile ist noch einmal in zwei untergliedert, zunächst erfolgt die Darstellung des jeweiligen Modells, anschließend seine innerfeministische Kritik. Damit bietet die Autorin einen Überblick über viele verschiedene Ansätze und bringt darüber hinaus eine systematische Ordnung in die breite feministische Diskussion. Ihren Ansatz kennzeichnet, daß sie in allen drei Paradigmen nicht-christliche und christliche feministische Ansätze behandelt. Die Differenzen zwischen den drei Modellen des Feminismus und der jeweiligen immanenten Kritik erscheinen also bedeutender als die Differenzen zwischen philosophischen und christlichen Ansätzen. Parsons zeigt, daß sich parallele Diskussionen und Weiterentwicklungen sowohl in der philosophischen wie in der christlichen feministischen Moraldebatte abgespielt haben. Die Trennung zwischen nicht-christlicher bzw. nicht-religiöser feministischer Ethik und christlicher feministischer Ethik hält sie ebenso wie die Ursprungsfrage, wer von wem gelernt habe, für müßig und nicht weiterführend.

Im Anschluß an die Darstellung der drei Paradigmen feministischer Theorie des Liberalismus, des sozialen Konstruktivismus und des Naturalismus und ihrer innerfeministischen Kritik beteiligt Parsons im zweiten Teil des Buches die vorgestellten Ansätze an der Bearbeitung von drei Aufgaben, die sie in der feministischen philsophischen und theologischen Diskussion anstehen sieht: die Suche nach einem angemessenen Universalismus, nach erlösender Gemeinschaft und nach einem neuen Humanismus. Im angemessenen Universalismus will Parsons Frauen sichtbar machen, das Alltägliche und Körperliche im Leben schätzen, Gerechtigkeitskonzeptionen entwickeln, die Differenzen berücksichtigen und die auf die menschliche Ganzheit ausgerichtet sind, sowie neues Interesse an theologischen Affirmationen von menschlichem Wohlergehen und Gedeihen entwickeln. In der erlösenden Gemeinschaft kann erkannt werden, daß wir füreinander und für die Erde bestimmt sind. Politische Freiheitskämpfe allerdings reichen nicht aus, um das Leiden an zerbrochenen Beziehungen zu heilen, dies konzedieren selbst nicht-religiöse Feministinnen. Auf diese Erkenntnis beziehen sich christliche Feministinnen, wenn sie darauf aufmerksam machen, daß in christlicher Perspektive Gott als Grund aller von Beziehung stetig am Wachsen und Aufbau von gerechten und ganzheitlichen Beziehungen arbeitet. Den neuen Humanismus sieht Parsons in der Idee der Heiligkeit von Personen begründet, die jeder einzelnen ihr Geheimnis und ihre Würde zugesteht. Diesem Humanismus entspricht eine Zuwendung zum kulturellen und politischen Leben, der von der Verheißung auf ein noch nicht realisiertes Glück lebt, der aber der verwandelnden Gnade möglichst großen Raum schaffen will.

In allen Punkten des zweiten Teils denkt Parsons Autorinnen und Ansätze zusammen. Sie sammelt die Schätze auf, die sie findet, nimmt auch gegenseitige Kritik aneinander wahr, aber grenzt sich gegenüber keinem Argument und gegenüber keinem Ansatz ab. Auch die internen Abgrenzungen begreift sie nicht als Aufforderung, nun zu klären, ob die eine oder die andere feministische Position recht hat. Das hat zur Folge, daß wie die Differenzen zwischen den drei verschiedenen Konzeptionen auch die Differenzen zwischen nicht-religiös bzw. nicht-christlich argumentierenden und religiös bzw. christlich argumentierenden Ansätzen keine Unterbrechung im Gang der Argumentation markieren, sondern im Fluß hinter- und nebeneinander gestellt werden.

Bei genauerem Hinsehen allerdings macht sich eine spezifische und geistesgeschichtlich bekannte Reihenfolge bemerkbar, die wiederkehrt, nämlich von den nicht-religiösen Autorinnen zu den religiös und christlich argumentierenden. Damit ist kein Triumphalismus verbunden, keine explizite Wertung, es ginge bergauf. Man könnte die Folge damit erklären, daß Parsons immer näher zur eigenen theologischen Perspektive kommt, ohne daß damit andere als schwächer gelten. Auch die systematische Ordnung und der Schluß des Buches (und indirekt in der Erläuterung ihrer Widmung des Buches an ihre Mutter) mögen der Leserin Hinweise auf Parsons Sympathie geben, die sie aber allenfalls indirekt einbringt, für eine im französischen Differenzfeminismus und besonders bei Luce Irigaray etablierte Wiederentdeckung der Nähe der Frauen und des Weiblichen zum Göttlichen.

In Parsons Zurückhaltung gegenüber einer Bewertung und Präferenz sehe ich die Stärke, daß sie die dargestellten Positionen von ihren Potentialen her in den Blick nimmt, und zugleich die Schwäche, mögliche Schwachstellen, Widersprüche, Dissonanzen zu glätten, weich zu machen und den vielleicht schwierigen und schmerzhaften, aber klärenden Streit zu umgehen. Diese Haltung unterscheidet sich wohltuend vom zumindest in der deutschen Wissenschaftswelt recht verbreiteten "Vorführen" von Argumentationen anderer, um sie dann abzuschießen. Gleichzeitig bleiben manche drängende Fragen besonders hinsichtlich des letzten naturalistischen Paradigmas offen, das Parsons aufgrund der gewählten Reihenfolge doch zumindest in der Form des—als Kritik des naturalistischen Ansatzes dargestellten—französischen Differenzfeminismus indirekt als das derzeit tragfähigste nahelegt.

Ein kleiner Denkschritt könnte m.E. einige dieser Fragen beantworten, nämlich die Empfehlung, ihr Buch als Spirale zu lesen. Dann müßte sich der Differenzfeminismus auf einer höheren Ebene erneut der Kritik des Gleichheitsfeminismus stellen, die Denkbewegung erneut beginnen. Die noch nicht eingelöste liberale Vision gleichen Rechts und gleicher Würde von Differentem, die noch immer notwendige Religions- und Ideologiekritik der Zielvorstellungen und Visionen sowie die Wahrnehmung und Achtung des Anderen der Anderen kämen vielleicht deutlicher als drei bleibend aktuelle Impulse zur Bearbeitung der anstehenden Probleme und Fragen in den Blick. *Helga Kuhlmann, Hamburg*

Susan K. Roll: *Towards the Origins of Christmas* (Kok Pharos: Kampen 1995)

This book embodies the research done by Susan K. Roll for her doctoral thesis at the Catholic University of Louvain (Leuven), Belgium, for which she received the congratulations of the jury. With said jury one gladly applauds the vast amount of carefully classified documentation gathered here, which recalls and completes what past scholarship has had to say about how the Christmas feast came to be and which also reveals the limits of scholarly knowledge. The historical survey is carried out in three core chapters, respectively entitled "The Christian Calendar and the Date of Christ's Birth", "The Invincible Sun and the Feast of Christ's Birth", and "The Spread of Christmas in view of its Rhetorical

Function". These chapters research the two major hypotheses for the origin of the feast: the "calculation" hypothesis and the "history of religions" hypothesis. They conclude with the recognition that further evidence is needed to secure certainty about the historical roots of Christmas. The core chapters are set in a pastoral framework which creates links with contemporary Christianity, touching on a variety of human issues that continue to contribute to the promotion of Christmas as it is celebrated today.

It is obvious from the above that this is a book for the specialist. As a non-specialist, I would have appreciated a more approachable book. Perhaps some kind of digestive process is necessary between thesis and book: the numbered sections might be united in a smoother way under the chapter headings; the six bibliographical lists might be gathered into one. As a literary person, I have further problems with the style of the writing. Sentences are sometimes ponderous, involved, unsatisfactorily structured. Surprisingly, the highly academic tone drops here and there, especially in the last chapter, to an almost chatty level. But perhaps these grumbles are beside the point.

Mary Phil Korsak, Brussels

Lene Sjørup: *Oneness: A Theology of Women's Religious Experience* (Kok Pharos: Kampen 1997)

This is the revised English translation of Lene Sjørup's Danish dissertation published in 1992. Her research method was to begin by collating, comparing and analysing ten in-depth case studies of women's religious experience with personal stories collected at the Alister Hardy Religious Research Unit in Oxford. These 3,000 accounts have never been examined on the basis of gender analysis. By beginning with women's experience and constructing interpretative hypotheses and finally an epistemology of the self, nature, relationships and the holy based upon the results, Sjørup literally turns traditional male approaches to the phenomenology of mysticism inside out. The results are fascinating.

Contemporary western women are tentatively developing a new personal knowledge of the divine based upon tacit bodily awareness, emotion and feeling. The language connected to these experiences appears paradoxical and non-logical in the light of western linear, sceptical rationalism. However, transformation of the self with/in God and embodied exploration beyond the subject-object split is a revelatory reality for many women. Their knowledge of the beyond/depth constitutes a fundamental challenge to the social sciences, New Physics and systematic theology. For Sjørup it is the herald of a new (post)-Christian female consciousness of oneness in its many faceted dimensions.

The writer's qualitative in-depth interviews were conducted with four American and six Danish women. The choice is significant: interviewees such as Charlene Spretnak, Carol Christ and Danish film directors, writers, artists and dramatists are highly articulate, creative and critical contemporary women. Sjørup claims such "excellent observers" are "used to creating, seeing and expressing new knowledge"(p.15). Such a cognitive minority can be regarded either as the vanguard of a new movement or as elitist. Sjørup faces this problem in her first chapter where she discusses the surprising (to her) incidence of visions of Jesus in the accounts collected in the English comparative records. Clearly, religious symbolism and theology is culturally and contextually bound. However, Sjørup claims that "oneness, where the limits between outer and inner realities are dissolved and disappear seems well known" to all the women (p. 26). This sense of wholeness and melting, where immanence and transcendence coalesce is, according to her, the test of a genuine religious-mystical experience. Mystical experience is universal yet its interpretation and expression, however revelatory, is personal.

In the following four chapters, Lene Sjørup recounts and discusses the descriptions of unitive experiences she has collected under the broad categories of nature, corporal, social and aesthetic mysticism. I found it impossible to read these personal accounts as a detached observer. One is confronted by the extraordinary peak experiences of women who in paradoxical and metaphorical language speak of their inspiring encounters with the numinous One who is simultaneously both all-embracing and Other. Sjørup however has studied these accounts for ten years using gender analysis and object relation theory, and she has come to some interesting conclusions. The most important is that women have significantly more mystical experiences than men, in particular with regard to a sense of oneness with nature, and in sexuality and childbirth. Sjørup claims that the cause is biological/psychological; women can relive their primal connectedness to their mothers by merging through the body with their physical environments. The self of a woman retains a transsubjective quality which men lose in the double change of identification from baby to boy and from boy to man (p. 79).

In my opinion female transubjectivity is a mixed blessing. A sense of fluid ego boundaries can easily lead to either a sense of nothingness or over-identification with the Other, both classic female problems. It is not surprising that Sjørup discovers that the context which triggers the highest incidence of women's mystical experience is depression/despair. Carol Christ claims that 'the dark night of the soul' is a more typical state for women because "women as marginalised in patriarchal society never had what male mystics fought to give up: status, power, ego" (Christ, 1980, p.18). However from the psycho-analytic perspective of the French feminist thinkers of difference such as Julia Kriteva, depression is an inevitable human condition caused by the fundamental separation from the mother. Spirituality can be understood as the unquenchable desire to return to this paradise condition. If transubjectivity has a negative dimension it is for Sjørup nevertheless a price worth paying because she is convinced that the mystical experiences of women constitute a new revolutionary epistemology. In chapter 7 she discusses this "new logic" of non-linear, embodied knowledge of the holy. She writes, "This is a lively, multifaceted epistemology..... that is contextual or holistic, not dualist; spiral, not linear; inclusive and spiritual, not hierarchichal; ethical, not instrumental; process, not product orientated" (p. 133).

In the final chapters Sjørup attempts to reconstruct a theology based upon her findings. Using archetypal images of God drawn from five periods of western culture she offers a poetic paradigm of the holy. This brave attempt is inevitably speculative, drawing together the multi-faceted religious experience of women into a mosaic of symbols, Sjørup offers a first step towards a post-Christian religious discourse.

This empirical research is a fundamental resource for feminist theologians claiming to reflect upon women's religious experience. The methodology and conclusions inevitably raise many questions however. The most obvious is the classical objection to natural theology; if religious experience is purely subjective and ineffable, how can we formulate criteria for evaluating ethics, rituals and theology? Further, do all women experience peak mystical experiences? Whilst I too believe that grace and revelation are available to everybody, historical experience demonstrates that a discipline of attentive openness is required to be able to recognise, surrender into and integrate such transformative disclosures. This discipline, traditionally nurtured through prayer, fasting, silence and meditation is undervalued in our hyperactive western societies. Nevertheless, Sjørup believes that women are entering a new phase of religious consciousness. I hope that her optimism proves prophetic.

Julie Hopkins, Amsterdam

Corinna FRIEDL und Dagmar ALTHAUSEN

Die Erste Europäische Frauensynode und der synodale Prozeß: Befreien, Wachsen und gegenseitiges Ermächtigen von Frauen

Voller Ungeduld warteten die eigens zur Frauensynode nach Gmunden, Österreich angereisten Journalistinnen am Ende auf das "Ergebnis" in Form eines Abschlußpapieres. Sie mußten ihren meist männlichen Redaktionsleitern beweisen, daß sich die weite Reise tatsächlich gelohnt hatte, um vor Ort von dieser eigentümlich anmutenden Veranstaltung zu berichten. Ohne ein Schlußdokument hätten ihre ArbeitgeberInnen und damit auch die durch die Presse informierte Welt diese Versammlung von über eintausend europäischen Frauen als gescheitert angesehen.

Der Ruach sei Dank: Die Teilnehmerinnen der Ersten Europäischen Frauensynode verabschiedeten am letzten Tag, dem Synodentag, eine Abschlußresolution und retteten damit sowohl ihre journalistisch arbeitenden Schwestern als auch die Frauensynode selbst vor dem Anschein einer Niederlage.

Das "Ergebnis" der Synode ist aber das basisdemokratisch abgestimmte Abschlußdokument mit Verlautbarungen zu den großen Themen Politik, Ökonomie, Spiritualität und Identität nicht. Die Resolution ist allenfalls ein schwacher Abglanz der vielen Vorgänge von Austausch und Entscheidungen, Vernetzungen und Begegnungen, die zwischen den aus eigenen Stücken gekommenen, nicht-delegierten und hochmotivierten Frauen aus 46 europäischen und außereuropäischen Ländern stattgefunden haben.[1] Der gesamte Vorgang—angefangen von der Idee einer Euro-

---

[1] In der Einladung zur Synode hieß es: "Jede Teilnehmerin repräsentiert sich selbst, mit ihren Erfahrungen und aus ihrem gesellschaftlichen Hintergrund. Daher verzichtet die Europäische Frauensynode auf das Delegiertenprinzip." Spenden sowie die Solidarbeiträge reicherer Teilnehmerinnen hatten ärmeren Frauen das Kommen ermöglicht; die ökonomische Ungleicheit zwischen und innerhalb der Länder Europas sollte nicht als Ausschlußmechanismus fungieren und an die Stelle der Delegierung treten. Allerdings kamen von den 1000 Teilnehmerinnen nur 120 aus Süd- und Osteuropa, und über 700 allein aus Österreich, Deutschland, den

päischen Frauensynode vor mehr als 10 Jahren über die langjährige Konzeption bis hin zur eigentlichen Durchführung und der Abschlußresolution—kann als "synodaler Prozeß" bezeichnet werden. Um verschiedene Aspekte dieses noch nicht abgeschlossenen synodalen Prozesses soll es im folgenden gehen.

Die Strukturfrage: ein (nicht nur) deutsches Problem

Das internationale Vorbereitungskomitee zur Frauensynode war eine zufällig zusammengesetzte Gruppe von Frauen aus zuletzt 15 verschiedenen Ländern[2] mit sehr unterschiedlichen Vorstellungen solch einer Synode, und jede mit ihrem eigenen Hintergrund: manche bereits gewohnt, sich auf internationalem ökumenischen Parkett zu bewegen, andere ohne jegliche Erfahrung auf diesem Gebiet, manche als Vertreterinnen von Frauengruppen oder -organisationen ihres Landes, andere als engagierte Einzelfrauen.

So verschieden die Frauen der Vorbereitungsgruppe, so unterschiedlich war ihr Verständnis von Feministischer Theologie. Schon bei der Vorbereitung wurde deutlich, daß Feministische Theologie in Osteuropa entweder ein Fremdwort oder häufiger noch ein Wort der Abschreckung war.[3] Wahrscheinlich hätten die westeuropäischen Frauen eine rein westeuropäische Veranstaltung als feministisch-theologisch ausgeschrieben. Letztlich mußte dies aber offen bleiben, da für das gesamteuropäische Treffen dieser Terminus bewußt nicht gewählt wurde. Ein zweiter umstrittener Begriff hat sich dagegen durchgesetzt: der der "Frauensynode". Die Verwendung des Wortes "Synode" für eine Versammlung nichtdelegierter Frauen war einerseits eine Provokation für die bestehenden Kirchen. Andererseits entspricht die ursprünglich demokratische Bedeutung—das "gemeinsame auf dem Weg sein" von Gleichgesinnten—im Kern der Intention der Frauensynode.

Niederlanden und der Schweiz. Vgl. Pressemeldung von Anne-Kathrin Koppetsch am 28.7.1996.

2 Deutschland, England, Frankreich, Kroatien, Litauen, Niederlande, Österreich, Polen, Rumänien, Schottland, Schweden, Schweiz, Spanien, Tschechien und Ungarn.

3 Anne-Kathrin Koppetsch stellt das Problem in ihrer Pressemeldung vom 28.7.1996 folgendermaßen dar: "'Eine Pastorin hatte mich gewarnt. Ich würde hier nur Frauen treffen, die Männeranzüge tragen und Zigaretten rauchen', erzählt Judit, eine junge Ungarin. ..."

Seit 1992 bzw. 1994 arbeiten wir im internationalen Vorbereitungskomitee mit. Um arbeitsfähig zu werden mußte die Gruppe einen langen und komplizierten Weg gehen. Jede Frau wurde an dem Vorbereitungsprozeß mit gleichem Recht beteiligt. Schon im Vorbereitungsprozeß ging diese Bewegung von der Basis aus und wurde keine Veranstaltung großer internationaler Organisationen. Frauen hatten sich aus ganz unterschiedlichen Gründen ermächtigt und wagten es, solch eine Frauensynode zu organisieren, auch ohne Geld und Macht.

In Deutschland ging der europäischen Frauensynode 1994 die Erste Deutsche Frauensynode voraus.[4] Dort fand sich eine Gruppe zusammen, die sich für das schwierige Unterfangen, die Europäische Frauensynode in Deutschland bekannt zu machen, engagieren wollte. Bemerkenswerterweise bestand sie zuerst vorwiegend aus ostdeutschen Frauen. Aus ihrer persönlichen Betroffenheit heraus und durch die Deutsche Frauensynode ermutigt und gewachsen, waren sie bereit, sich für dieses Projekt einzusetzten. Obwohl Deutschland im europäischen Vergleich ein reiches Land ist, gestaltete sich die Arbeit für die Europäische Frauensynode gerade hier besonders schwierig. Zum Teil hat das mit der unübersichtlichen und starren deutschen Vereinsstruktur zu tun. Für unser Empfinden wurde aber am Beispiel der Synodenbewegung sowohl die Kluft als auch ein Prozeß der Annäherung zwischen konfessionellen Frauenverbänden und feministisch-theologischen Initiativgruppen deutlich.[5]

Vor allem aus den feministischen Netzwerken kamen in Deutschland die Impulse, Ideen und Initiativen für eine Frauensynode, erst auf nationaler, dann auf internationaler Ebene. Auf der anderen Seite mußten wir bald feststellen, daß die Frauensynodenbewegung von den christlichen Frauenverbänden nicht unterstützt wird. Zum einen wurde in der Frauensynode ein Konkurrentin gesehen: "Eine neue Frauenbewegung, und als solche sehe ich die 'Frauensynode', wird immer ihr Verhältnis zu Bestehendem (das auch um seinen Bestand—auch finanziell—sorgen muß) klären müssen. Diese Klärung ist im Falle der Frauensynode wohl

---

4 Vgl. *Frauen und Macht. Dokumention der Ersten Deutschen Frauensynode,* (Frankfurt/ Main Spener-Verlag 1994) vgl. auch Anm. 21.

5 Vgl. Leonore Siegele-Wenschkewitz, *Die Rezeption und Diskussion der Genus-Kategorie in der theologischen Wissenschaft,* 61-111, bes. 69ff. In: Hadumod Bußmann, Renate Hof (Hg.), *Genus. Zur Geschlechterdifferenz in den Kulturwissenschaften* (Stuttgart: Kröner 1994). Die im folgenden dargestellte Tendenz einer Annäherung stimmt mit Siegele-Wenschkewitz Beobachtungen überein.

noch nicht befriedigend erfolgt, wird aber angestrebt", schrieb am 27.8.1994 die damalige Vorsitzende der Evangelischen Frauenhilfe in Deutschland, Gudrun Althausen, zur Erläuterung, warum sie nicht eine Schirmfrau der Ersten Europäischen Frauensynode werden konnte. Zum anderen hatte durch den Namen Frauen-'Synode' eine eindeutige Positionierung stattgefunden, die es etablierten kirchlichen Frauenverbänden und -organisationen unmöglich machte, diese Bewegung offiziell zu unterstützen, obwohl viele einzelne Frauen, die in diesen Strukturen arbeiteten, sich an der Vorbereitung und Durchführung der Frauensynode beteiligten.

In ihrer Antwort auf die Frage, ob sie Schirmfrau der Ersten Europäischen Frauensynode werden wolle, schrieb Sigrid Häfner, Frauenreferentin der EKD:

> mein zentraler Auftrag (ist), Repräsentanz und Interessen von Frauen **innerhalb** der Institution zu stärken und zu fördern, d.h. Frauen Räume und Freiräume in den Strukturen der verfaßten Kirche zu sichern und auszubauen. Dieser Auftrag verträgt sich nicht mit einer institutionellen Unterstützung von Gegen- oder Parallelstrukturen, wie sie durch "Frauensynoden" intendiert oder suggeriert werden.[6]

Wir erhielten also in Deutschland weder ideelle noch wesentliche finanzielle Unterstützung von Kirchen, Verbänden und Organisationen. Die Vorbereitungsarbeit zur Ersten Europäischen Frauensynode wurde in Deutschland vor allem von Basisgruppen, d.h. von kleinen Initiativen und Netzwerken, Gemeinden und Einzelpersonen finanziell unterstützt. Im Laufe der Zeit konnten Berührungsängste zwischen der Frauensynodenbewegung und den Frauenverbänden teilweise abgebaut werden. Es hat aber über die Jahre eine Verständigung und Annäherung stattgefunden, bis dahin, daß die jetzige Vorsitzende der Evangelischen Frauenhilfe, Brunhilde Raiser, vom Vorstand offiziell beauftragt wurde, sich an der Vorbereitung einer Zweiten Deutschen Frauensynode zu beteiligen.

Ähnliche Fragen tauchten auch im Blick auf das Verhältnis der Frauensynode zum Ökumenischen Forum christlicher Frauen in Europa (ÖFCFE) auf. In diesem Verhältnis spiegelten sich die Probleme, denen wir in Deutschland begegneten, auf europäischer Ebene wieder. So kristallisierte sich immer mehr heraus, daß die Frauensynode eine Bewegung vieler einzelner, feministisch-theologisch interessierter Frauen und nicht der Verbände ist. Die Chancen, die darin stecken, wurden uns im Laufe

---

6 Brief vom 18. Juli 1994.

der Vorbereitung immer mehr bewußt: Durch die offene Struktur wurde besser gewährleistet, daß sich auch Frauen ohne Rang und Namen auf der Europäischen Frauensynode artikulieren können und die diskutierten Themen wirklich Themen der Frauen vor Ort sind. Vor allem für ostdeutsche und osteuropäische Frauen war das eine Befreiung.[7]

Synodenbewegung und feministische Wissenschaft

Zwischen der internationalen Vorbereitungsgruppe und Zusammenschlüssen aus dem Bereich der feministisch-theologischen Forschung gab es weniger Berührungsängste als mit den großen Frauenverbänden und -organisationen. Dabei nahm die Europäische Gesellschaft für theologische Forschung von Frauen (ESWTR) eine besondere Rolle ein. Als Vereinigung, die ihre Wurzeln feministischen Theologinnen verdankt, die im Ökumenischen Rat der Kirchen (ÖRK) zusammenarbeiteten,[8] verschrieb die ESWTR sich bei ihrer Gründung ausdrücklich dem interdisziplinären, interkonfessionellen, interreligiösen und internationalen Dialog.[9] In der personellen Präsenz von Frauen aus der ESWTR auf der Synode wie auch in der Tatsache, daß drei der vier Hauptreferentinnen der Synode Mitglieder der ESWTR sind, zeigt sich das gut funktionierendes Informationsnetz und die Relevanz der internationalen feministisch-theologischen Arbeit der ESWTR.

Ablauf der Frauensynode und inhaltliche Streiflichter

Die Hauptreferate wurden von feministischen Wissenschaftlerinnen zu den Themen Politik, Ökonomie, Spiritualität, Identität gehalten. Sie prägten die Arbeit in Workshops, Austauschgruppen und der allabendlichen Plenumsdiskussion. Die Abschlußresolution summiert zentrale, von den Teilnehmerinnen im Verlauf der Synode eingebrachten und am letzten

7 Während der Frauensynode wurden den Osteuropäerinnen die bestehenden Differenzen zwischen ihren Ländern deutlicher und bewußter. Die spontane Einrichtung eines osteuropäischen Begegnungsraumes zeigte, daß sie die Auseinandersetzung in Angriff nehmen wollen. Außerdem entwickelte sich die Idee einer eigenen osteuropäischen Frauensynode.

8 So die Gründungsinitiatorinnen Fokkelien Van Dijk, Catharina Halkes, Elisabeth Moltmann-Wendel und Luise Schottroff.

9 So der Gründungsaufruf vom 27.10.1985, (vgl. Leonore Siegele-Wenschkewitz, 1994, 86 Anm. 9).

Synodentag abgestimmten Themen und Forderungen. Die ausgesprochen enge Verknüpfung zwischen Hauptreferaten und Abschlußresolution zeigt, daß der Anspruch feministischer Wissenschaft, im gemeinsamen Dialog und im Bemühen um die Anliegen europäischer Frauen auf der Schwelle zum 21. Jahrhundert zu stehen und sich den Fragen der Frauenbewegung zu verpflichten, eingelöst wurde.

Es ist ausgeschlossen, den vielen auf der Ersten Europäischen Frauensynode präsenten Themen, Ideen und Ergebnissen hier gerecht zu werden. Alleine in den angekündigten und spontan entstandenen über 100 Workshops wurde eine Vielzahl von Anliegen diskutiert und Beschlüsse gefaßt. Ebenso haben während der Synode Treffen für neu zu gründende oder bereits bestehende Netzwerke und nationale Zusammenkünfte stattgefunden.[10] Hier sollen lediglich einige zentrale Gedanken aus zwei Hauptreferaten[11] und aus einem Workshop dargestellt werden, die während der Synode eine Rolle gespielt haben und auch in der Abschlußresolution wiederkehren.

Die in der Schweiz lebende deutsche Sozialethikerin Ina Praetorius leitete den Tag zum Thema "Ökonomie" ein.[12] Die in ihrem Beitrag "Ökonomie denken: jenseits der androzentrischen Ordnung" dargestellten Überlegungen sind Frucht eines langjährigen Austausches zwischen feministisch arbeitender Wissenschaftlerinnen unterschiedlicher Disziplinen.[13] Sie kritisiert ein gängiges Verständnis von Wirtschaft, das Wirtschaft mit Geld und Erwerbsarbeit gleichsetzt und damit zu einem abgetrennten Bereich macht, zu dem einige Menschen Zugang haben und andere nicht.[14] Diesem Verständnis stellt Praetorius die "Weiberwirt-

---

[10] Begründet würden bsp. ein europäisches Liturgie-Netzwerk, eine Vernetzung lesbischer Frauen und Gruppen und das Netzwerk WOW (Women's Ordination World Wide).

[11] Die vier Hauptreferate sind veröffentlicht in: *epd-Dokumentation* 33/96.

[12] An ihrer Stelle sollte Regine Hildebrandt als Nicht-Theologin, Politikerin und Vertreterin auch osteuropäischer Anliegen sprechen, die jedoch kurzfristig absagen mußte. Für den geplanten Beitrag Regine Hildebrandts, die die Synode auch im Vorfeld besonders unterstützt hatte, siehe "Was geschieht mit unserem Geld? Wir fordern gerechte Verteilung?" in: *epd-Dokumentation* 33/96, S. 41-43.

[13] Vgl. Heidi Bernhard Filli et al, *Weiberwirtschaft. Frauen - Ökonomie - Ethik* (Luzern: Exodus 1994), Vorwort.

[14] Ina Praetorius zeigt, daß dieses Denkmuster auch in Äußerungen von Frauen zum Thema Ökonomie zentral ist. So weist sie dieses Verständnis von Wirtschaft im

schaft" gegenüber, ein ursprünglich negative Begriff der neu gefüllt wird. Frauen verstehen sich demnach nicht mehr als am Rande der Wirtschaft stehend sondern als selbst Wirtschaft treibend:

> Wirtschaft umfaßt alle Maßnahmen weltweit zur Deckung der Bedürfnisse der Menschen (von Geburt an), als Beschaffung, Verteilung und Verbrauch von Mitteln zum Leben. Wirtschaft beginnt mit der Herstellung von Menschen: mit Gebähren, Nähren, Erziehen, damit, daß das Überleben der Menschen, die geboren worden sind, sichergestellt wird.[15]

Mithilfe der "Weiberwirtschaft" sollen Frauen sich zunächst denkerisch und sprachlich ins Zentrum stellen. Sie sollen ihr Handeln als echtes wirtschaftliches Handeln verstehen, ja als Kulturleistung und als Basis des Wirtschaftsgeschehens. Ina Praetorius übt auch Kritik an wirtschaftlichen Bemühungen, die allein das persönliche Wohlergehen im Blick haben. Das Modell der Weiberwirtschaft habe nicht nur die eigene Person sondern auch die Gemeinschaft im Blick, sei dies die Weltgemeinschaft, die kommunale Gemeinde oder die Familie. Sie ziele immer auch auf "das gute Leben aller".[16]

Mit diesem Beitrag traf Ina Praetorius einen Nerv vieler Synodenteilnehmerinnen. Die Umbrüche, die die Einführung eines neuen Wirtschaftssystems in den Ländern des Ostblocks bedeuten und die Härte der neoliberalen Marktwirtschaft, die immer mehr soziale Errungenschaften als Ballast abstreift, wirken sich zuerst und besonders auf die Frauen aus. Ihr Modell der Weiberwirtschaft bietet Ansätze für Alternativen zur bestehenden ökonomischen Logik der Wirtschaft. Wenn etliche der inhaltlichen Aussagen auch nicht eigentlich neu waren, war der Vortrag doch für viele Frauen ein erster und wichtiger Anstoß für die Auseinandersetzung mit dem bisher viel zu wenig beachteten Thema „Frauen und Ökonomie".

Die schwedische Pfarrerin Anna-Karin Hammar hielt das Hauptreferat zum Tagesthema "Spiritualität".[17] Plastisch skizziert sie darin

---

Abschlußpapier der Weltfrauenkonferenz in Peking nach (ebd., 113f); vgl. Bericht der Vierten Weltfrauenkonferenz (Peking, 4.-15. Sept. 1995) und deutsche Übersetzung des Dokuments A/Conf. 177/20 vom 17.10.95, Punkte 150ff).

15 *epd-Dokumentation* 33/96, S.15.

16 ebd.

17 1985 hatte Anne Kathrin Hammar als Mitarbeiterin des ÖRK (Women's Desk), die Durchführung einer Frauensynode angeregt und ist somit eine der frühen Initiatorinnen der Synodenbewegung in Europa. Die Erste Deutsche Frauensynode vom 22.–24.4.1994 bezog sich ausdrücklich auf die vom ÖRK für 1988-1998

Frauen in Europa auf dem Weg zwischen zwei Arten des Daseins: Zum einen als Unterstützerinnen eines gewaltvollen und ausschließenden Europas und zum anderen auf dem Weg zu Prophetinnen, die entgegen diesen Unterdrückungen das Leben auf allen möglichen Ebenen verteidigen. Wir alle sind eingeladen, so Hammar, auf einer lebenslangen Reise das Leben zu erfahren und zu verteidigen. Um Kraft zu schöpfen für diese prophetische Arbeit, stehen uns viele verschiedenen Quellen zur Verfügung. Eine dieser Quellen ist eine neue Mystik, geboren aus der Solidarität des gemeinsamen Kampfes.[18] Als eine weitere Quelle, die Kraft zu prophetischem Handeln und zum Ausleben solche Gemeinschaft von Frauen gibt, nennt Hammar das gemeinsame Mahl am Küchentisch als Sakrament des täglichen Lebens.

Hammar sprach den Frauen aus der Seele, die sich bei den liturgischen Handlungen ihrer Kirchen aus verschiedenen Gründen nicht angesprochen und deshalb heimatlos fühlen. Insbesondere für orthodoxe und römisch-katholische Teilnehmerinnen war die Ermächtigung von Frauen zur Feier der heiligen Kommunion am Küchentisch ein wichtiger befreiender Gedanke. Die Forderung des Zugangs von Frauen zu allen kirchlichen Ämtern und der Austausch über Handlungsstrategien hat einen wesentlichen Teil der Synode bestimmt. Andere Frauen stimmten dagegen mit der im Vortrag dargestellten Form der Spiritualität des alltäglichen Lebens und mit der in der Resolution erkennbaren Schöpfungstheologie nicht überein. Für sie hatten diese Formulierungen entweder einen zu mystischen Gehalt oder den Anklang an eine natürliche Theologie, die Gotteserfahrung einseitig in der Natur ansiedelt. Das Thema Spiritualität wurde so kontrovers diskutiert wie kaum ein anderes. Hatte der Austausch zu politischen und ökonomischen Themen die gemeinsamen Probleme und den bestehenden Handlungsbedarf der europäischen Frauen herausgestellt, so reizte die Diskussion um Spiritualität zur Unterstreichung der Unterschiede. Allerdings wurden während der Synode die unterschiedlichsten liturgischen Handlungen miteinander gefeiert; die Unterschiede wurden wahrgenommen, toleriert und durchaus geschätzt. Die Abstimmung einer gemeinsamen Resolution bereitete dagegen große Probleme.

---

ausgerufenen Dekade der "Solidarität der Kirchen mit den Frauen" und fand genau zur Halbzeit der Dekade statt. Ebenso ist die Zweite Deutsche Frauensynode derzeit für das Ende der Dekade (1998) geplant.

18 Vgl. *epd-Dokumentation* 33/96, S.25.

Der Gedanke der solidarischen Teilhabe kommt in zahlreichen Äußerungen zum Ausdruck. Der Austausch über die eigenen Probleme und die Anliegen anderer kann als eine Grundmotivation für die Durchführung der gesamten Frauensynode gesehen werden. Ein Beispiel dafür, wie sich solche Solidarität zwischen Frauen in der Praxis auswirken kann, ist eine Erklärung, die zum Thema Spiritualität in das Evening House eingebracht wurde. Sie ist aus einem Workshop hervorgegangen, den Flois Knolle-Hicks, Musikpädagogin, Kirchenmusikerin und Mitglied der Initiative von Schwarzen Deutschen, zum Thema Sexismus und Rassismus geleitet hat:

> Wir wollen, daß unsere weißen Schwestern sich dieser Probleme (des Rassismus in einem muli-kulturellen und multi-ethnischen Europa) bewußt werden und die institutionellen Formen des Rassismus reflektieren und untersuchen. Diese Formen des Rassismus unterdrücken nicht nur schwarze Frauen, sondern führen auch dazu, daß weiße Frauen ein Teil des Problems sind, anstatt ein Teil des Prozesses des "UN-LERNENS" zu sein, der beiden, schwarzer und weißer Befreiung, dient. Dieser Prozeß des "UN-LERNENS"—oder neu Lernens—ist sicherlich ein Weg des gemeinsamen Austausches und Wachsens. Vielleicht können wir eine Atmosphäre des Vertrauens schaffen, die uns verbindet, so daß andere uns nicht auseinanderreißen können.[19]

Der Rassismus war ein Thema der Synode, das schon im Vorfeld intensiv diskutiert, mit dem aber wenig zufriedenstellend umgegangen wurde. Nicht nur die Tatsache, daß der internationalen Vorbereitungsgruppe keine scharzen Frauen angehörten, ist dafür ein Zeichen. Die Erklärung aus der Arbeitsgruppe von Flois Knolle-Hicks und die Diskussionen in anderen Gruppen während der Synode zeigen, daß die Auseinandersetzung mit Rassismus im Gange ist und einer Fortsetzung bedarf.

Die Erste Europäische Frauensynode war noch vorwiegend eine Veranstaltung von und für weiße, heterosexuelle und westeuropäische Frauen. Vieles aber wurde angestoßen, aufgebrochen und in Gang gesetzt. Vor allem drei Bereiche haben zu wenig Beachtung gefunden und werden uns in Zukunft weiterhin beschäftigen: Die Auseinandersetzung mit dem Thema Rassismus, der Umgang mit Homo- und Bisexualität in Gesellschaft und Kirche, und die Frage der Partizipation ost- und süd- und nordeuropäischer Frauen an der Entscheidung heute anstehender Fragen.

---

19 Zitiert nach einer Kopie des schriftlich eingereichten Workshopergebnisses (Nr. 228 und 322); Übersetzung aus dem Englischen C.F.

In dem Vorwort zur Dokumentation schreibt die Präsidentin der Europäischen Frauensynode, Wies Stael-Merkx: "Die Synode in Gmunden kann erst dann als Erfolg bezeichnet werden, wenn Frauen den Prozeß auf ihre je eigene Weise in den verschiedenen Ländern weitertragen; wenn die Themen weiter vertieft, Probleme besprochen und Netzwerke gegründet werden"[20]. In diesem Sinne hoffen wir, daß der synodale Prozeß weitergeht und sind überzeugt, daß die Zweite Europäische Frauensynode ein ebenso reizvolles und doch ein anderes Gesicht haben wird, als die Erste.[21]

Dagmar Althausen geb. 1959 in Berlin (Ost), lebt als evangelische Pfarrerin in Cottbus. Aktivitäten im Ökumenischen Jugendbeirat in Europa und im Arbeitskreis Feministische Theologie der DDR. 1992–1996 Mitglied des internatinalen Vorbereitungskomitees der Europäischen Frauensynode.

Corinna Friedl geb. 1966 in Frankfurt/Main, Promotion zu einem ersttestamentlichen Thema. Arbeit in feministisch-theologischen Initiativen (u.a. Koordinierungsgruppe Feministische Theologie) und in praktischen Bereichen (Krankenhausseelsorge, Religiopnsunterricht). Seit 1994 Mitglied des internationalen Vorbereitungskomitees der Europäischen Frauensynode.

---

20 Vgl. die zur Zeit der Abfassung diese Artikels noch unveröffentlichte deutschsprachige Dokumentation der Ersten Europäischen Frauensynode (s.u).

21 Weitere Auskünfte sowie die Bestellung der Dokumentation auf Deutsch, Englisch oder Niederländisch für je ca. 25 DM unter: International Women's Synod Office, Postbus 19, NL-3970 AA Driebergen, Niederlande.

EUROPEAN SOCIETY OF WOMEN IN THEOLOGICAL RESEARCH

EUROPÄISCHE GESELLSCHAFT FÜR THEOLOGISCHE FORSCHUNG VON FRAUEN

L'ASSOCIATION EUROPÉENNE DES FEMMES POUR LA RECHERCHE THÉOLOGIQUE

President - Präsident - Président:
Prof.Dr. Helen Schüngel-Straumann,
Universität Gesamthochschule Kassel, Germany

Vice-President - Vizepräsidentin - Vice-Président:
Dr. Lene Sjørup, University of Copenhagen, Denmark

Secretary - Sekretärin - Secrétaire:
Dr. Julie Hopkins, Amsterdam, The Netherlands

Vice-Secretary - Vizesekretärin - Vice-Secrétaire:
Annette Esser, Köln, Germany

Treasurer - Schatzmeisterin - Trésorière:
Dr. Regula Strobel, Fribourg, Switzerland

Vice-Treasurer - Vizeschatzmeisterin - Vice-Trésorière:
Dr. Maaike de Haardt, Tilburg, The Netherlands

Revisor - Revisorin - Reviseur:
Dr. Charlotte Methuen, Heidelberg, Germany

Contact for Bulletin of the ESWTR:
Dr. Julie Hopkins, The Netherlands